Studies in the Religious Life of Ancient and Medieval India

D. C. SIRCAR

Carmichael Professor and Head of the Department of Ancient Indian History and Culture,
University of Calcutta.

MOTILAL BANARSIDASS
DELHI .. PATNA :: VARANASI

First Edition : 2013

MOTILAL BANARSIDASS
Head Office : BUNGALOW ROAD, JAWAHARNAGAR, DELHI-7
Branches : 1. CHOWK, VARANASI (U.P.)
2. ASHOK RAJPATH (OPP. PATNA COLLEGE), PATNA (BIHAR)

Printed in India
BY SHANTI LAL JAIN, AT SHRI JAINENDRA PRESS, BUNGALOW ROAD, JAWAHAR NAGAR, DELHI-7, AND PUBLISHED BY SUNDARLAL JAIN, FOR MOTILAL BANARSIDASS, BUNGALOW ROAD, JAWAHARNAGAR, DELHI-7.

PREFACE

The present volume is the fifth of the series of my *Studies*, its predecessors being those in Geography (1960 and 1971), Society and Administration (Vol. I—*Society*, 1967), Indian Coins (1968) and Political and Administrative Systems (in the press). It contains most of my papers on the Religious Life of Ancient and Medieval India, which appeared in various publications during the past three decades and a half. I am extremely thankful to the authorities of the said publications.

The plan of the present volume is the same as followed in its predecessors, more than one paper having often been clubbed together for the facility of presentation. In one case, however, the matter for a dissertation has been distributed among three Chapters (I-III). Thus more than forty papers and notes have been offered in 17 Chapters and 3 Appendices. The papers have all been suitably edited, some of them being considerably modified in the course of revision. There are of course a few omissions. A note on the Sectarian Difference among the Early Vaiṣṇavas appearing in the *Bhāratīya Vidyā*, Bombay, Vol. VIII, Nos. 9-10, September-October, 1946, pp. 109 ff., has been left out because its gist has been included in Chapter III. The paper on Ardhanārī-Gaṇapati (*Journal of Ancient Indian History*, Calcutta, Vol. IV, pp. 181-86) could not be included in this volume as it had not been completed in time.

The sources of the various Chapters of the volume are indicated below.

Chapter I—*The Cultural Heritage of India*, Vol. IV, ed. H.D. Bhattacharya, R.K.M. Inst. Cult., Calcutta, 1956, pp. 108 ff. (cf. *History and Culture of the Indian People*, Vol. II—*The Age of Imperial Unity*, ed. R. C. Majumdar, Bombay, 1951, pp. 431 ff.); *Quarterly Journal of the Mythic Society*, Bangalore, Vol. XXV, No. 4, April, 1935, pp. 301-02; *Bhakti Cult and Ancient Indian Geography*, ed. D. C. Sircar, Calcutta, 1970, 36ff.

Chapter II—*The Cultural Heritage of India, op. cit.*, pp. 114 ff. (cf. *The Age of Imp. Unity, op. cit.*, pp. 434ff.).

Chapter III—*The Cultural Heritage of India, op. cit.*, pp. 131 ff. (cf. *History and Culture of the Indian People*, Vol. III—*The Classical Age*, ed. Majumdar, 1954, pp. 414 ff.).

Chapter IV—*Indian Studies Past and Present*, Calcutta, Vol. VIII, No. 3, April-June, 1967, pp. 269 ff. (cf. *Indo-Asian Culture*, Vol. II, New Delhi, No. 2, October, 1963, pp. 120 ff.); *Journal of Oriental Research*, Madras, Vol. XVII, Part IV, June, 1948, pp. 209 ff.; *Epigraphia Indica*, Delhi, Vol. XXXIII, 1959-1960, pp. 181 ff.; *ibid.*, Vol. XXXV, 1963-1964, pp. 171 ff.

Chapter V—*Epigraphia Indica*, Vol. XXXI, 1955-1956, pp. 67 ff.; *ibid.*, Vol. XXX, 1953-1954, pp. 85 ff.; *Quarterly Journal of the Mythic Society*, Bangalore, Culture and Heritage Number, 1956, pp. 221 ff. (cf. *Proceedings of the Indian History Congress*, Waltair, 1953, pp. 39 ff.); *Our Heritage* Calcutta, Vol. VIII, 1960, pp. 69 ff.; *Maharaja Ranjit Singh Centenary Volume*, Cawnpore, 1940, pp. 101 ff.

Chapter VI—*The Śakti Cult and Tārā*, ed. D.C. Sircar, Calcutta, 1967, pp. 86 ff., pp. 128 ff.; *Journal of the Kalinga Historical Research Society*, Bolangir, Vol. I, No. 1, June, 1946, pp. 87-88.

Chapter VII—*Epigraphia Indica*, Vol. XXX, 1953-1954, pp. 59 ff.; *ibid.*, Vol. XXXV, 1963-1964, pp. 44ff.

Chapter VIII—*Epigraphia Indica*, Vol. XXX, 1953-1954, pp. 210ff.; *ibid.*, Vol. XXXII, 1957-1958, pp. 55 ff.

Chapter IX—*Epigraphia Indica*, Vol. XXX, 1953-1954, pp. 237 ff.; *Journal of the Bihar Research Society*, Patna Vol. XXXIX, Parts 1-2, 1953, pp. 41 ff. (cf. *Proceedings of the Indian History Congress*, Gwalior, 1952, pp. 58 ff.).

Chapter X—*Epigraphia Indica*, Vol. XXX, 1953-1954, pp. 46 ff.; *Calcutta Review*, Calcutta, June, 1938, pp. 320 ff.

Chapter XI—*The Successors of the Sātavāhanas in the Lower Deccan* by D. C. Sircar, Calcutta, 1939, pp. 50 ff. (cf. *Journal of the Royal Asiatic Society*, London, 1934, pp. 729 ff.); *ibid.*, pp. 343ff.; cf. *Indian Culture*, Calcutta, Vol. I, 1934, pp. 311 ff.; *ibid.*, Vol. II, 1936, pp. 789 ff; *ibid.*, Vol. IV, 1937, pp, 272-73; *Prof. P. Sundaram Pillai Commemoration Volume*, Madras, 1957, pp. 93ff.; *Indian Historical Quarterly*, Calcutta, Vol. XXI, No. 2, June, 1945, pp. 143ff.

Chapter XII—*Bhāratīya Vidyā*, Bombay, Vol. XIII, 1952, pp. 55 ff.; *Journal of the Royal Asiatic Society of Bengal*, Letters, Vol. XV, No. 2, 1949, pp. 101 ff.; *Indian Historical Quarterly*, Vol. XXIX, No. 3, September, 1953, pp. 302-03; *Epigraphia Indica*, Vol. XXXIII, 1959-1960, pp. 271 ff.

Chapter XIII—*Calcutta Police Journal*, Vol. III, Nos. 1-2, January-June, 1955, pp. 766; *Epigraphia Indica*, Vol. XXX, 1953-54, pp. 42 ff.

Chapter XIV—*Foreigners in Ancient India and Lakṣmī and Sarasvati in Art and Literature*, ed. D.C. Sircar, Calcutta, 1970, pp. 25-34.

Chapter XV—*Dr. P. B. Desai Felicitation Volume, Dharwar*, 1971, pp. 151-62.

Chapter XVI—Read at the Inter-University Seminar held at the Centre of Advanced Study in AIHC, Calcutta University, February, 1971.

Chapter XVII—Cf. *Journal of Ancient Indian History*, Vol. IV, (1970-71), 1971, pp. 304-05.

Appendix I—Read at the All-India Oriental Conference, Jadavpur Session, October, 1969.

Appendix II—Cf. *Journal of Ancient Indian History*, Vol. III (1969-70), 1970, pp. 290-91; *ibid.*, Vol. IV (1970-71), 1971, pp. 308-09.

Appendix III—*Satkari Mookerji Felicitation Volume*, Varanasi, 1969, pp. 42 ff.

I crave the indulgence of sympathetic readers for the mistakes and blemishes that may have crept into the book in spite of my sincere efforts to make it useful to the students.

For the index of the volume, I am indebted to Dr. Sm. K. Saha, Dr. Sm. J. Maitra and others.

Department of Ancient Indian History and Culture,
Calcutta University, 51/2,
Hazra Road, Calcutta-19.

D. C. SIRCAR

July 15, 1971.

CONTENTS

Chapter I

VEDIC VIṢṆU AND THE BHAKTI CULT

I

The age covered by the composition of the Ṛgvedic hymns, not to speak of the various works of the entire Vedic literature, is considerably wide—between c. 1400 and 1000 B.C. according to some writers. It can be shown that, possibly owing to the wide prevalence of the union of Aryan males with Nonaryan females, the speech as well as the social and religious life of the Aryan people began to be modified very early on the Indian soil. Attention may be drawn in this connection to the borrowing of the cerebral consonantal sounds from Nonaryan speech, to the gradual amalgamation of the Ṛgvedic god Rudra and the pre-Aryan Father-god Śiva-Paśupati, and to the germ of theism, a Nonaryan institution later completely absorbed in Indian (i.e. mixed Aryo-aboriginal) religious life, possibly to be traced in the reference in the *Ṛgveda*[1] itself to the *Sūris* (meaning 'sectarian devotees of the god Viṣṇu' according to later works) as a class favoured by Viṣṇu.[2]

Viṣṇu is represented as one of the great gods even in some sections of the *Ṛgveda*; but he was not regarded as the greatest god in early Vedic times. The *Ṛgveda*[3] conceives Viṣṇu as one of the manifestations of the sun.[4] He is called *śipiviṣṭa*, i.e.

1. I. 22. 20.
2. Cf. Sircar, *The Śākta Pīṭhas*, pp. 100ff; see below.
3. I. 155-56.
4. Viṣṇu is described as setting in motion, like a revolving wheel, his 90 steeds (days) with their four names (seasons), which apparently refers to the solar year of 360 days. According to some writers, the word means 'a bird'. Macdonell (*Vedic Mythology*, p. 39) interprets the name as 'the active one' representing solar motion (from the root *viṣ.*). In a paper on the Name of the God Viṣṇu and the Kṛṣṇa Legend (translated from French in *QJMS*, Vol. XXV, pp. 39-48), Jean Przyluski tried to prove that the Prakrit variants *Viṭha*, *Viṭhū* and *Veṭha* as well as Sanskrit *Viṣṇu* are all of Nonaryan origin. Separating 'the suffixal vowel *-a*, *-ū*' from the Prakrit variants, he found the Austro-Asiatic radicals *viṭh* and *veṭh* which in his

'clothed with rays of light' ('bald' according to some writers) and his greatness is said to be inconceivable.[5] Viṣṇu is described as enveloping the earth on all sides with his *mayūkhas*, i.e. rays of light. He is believed by scholars to represent the sun in its daily and yearly courses. According to a legend in the *Śatapatha Brāhmaṇa*,[6] Viṣṇu's head was, by a trick of the gods, severed from his body and became *āditya*, i.e., the sun.[7] The later conception of him as *udyat-koṭi-divākar-ābha* and *savitṛ-maṇḍala-madhyavartin*[8] as well as his association with the *cakra* or disc resembling the disc of the sun and with the bird Garuḍa, adapted from the Ṛgvedic conception of the sun as a winged celestial bird, also point to his solar character. In many passages of the *Ṛgveda*, Viṣṇu is mentioned along with the Ādityas, while later works represent him as one of them.

The three strides of Viṣṇu, which no doubt formed the background of the Purāṇic legend of Vāmana (an epithet of Viṣṇu in the *Śatapatha Brāhmaṇa*)[9] and Bali, as well as his highest place, are quite famous in the *Ṛgveda*.[10] Viṣṇu, the unconquerable preserver, strode the three steps over this universe, thereby maintaining fixed ordinances (*dharmāṇi*). He is said to have three spaces associated with the three steps. Two of these spaces are called earthly, while the 'highest' of them is described as known to himself and visible only to the *Sūris* 'like an eye fixed in the sky'.[11] This *parama pada* of Viṣṇu, where

opinion are the same as *viḍ* in *Drāviḍa*, Sanskritised form of *Tamiḻ*. He further thought that *Viṣṇu* was originally pronounced as *Viṣṭnu*. Przyluski's philological speculation regarding the origin of the name Viṣṇu is, however, fanastic, because in several Neo-Indo-Aryan dialects Sanskrit *ṣṇ* is modified to *ṣṭ* from which *ṭṭh*, etc., can be easily derived. Cf. Bengali *Kṛṣṇa*=*Keṣṭa* or *Kriṣṭa*, *tṛṣṇā*=*teṣṭā*, *Vaiṣṇava*=*Boṣṭom*, etc.

5. VII. 99. 1; 100. 5-6.

6. XIV. 1. 1.

7. The word *āditya* is derived from the name of the female divinity Aditi, the personification of the boundless sky. *Āditya* indicates the sun as well as a group of divinities associated with the sun and the sky.

8. *Śabdakalpadruma*, s. v. *Viṣṇu*; Bhattacharya, *Purohitadarpaṇa* p. 53.

9. I.2. 5. 5.

10. I. 22. 18, etc.

11. I. 22. 20.

there was a well of honey[11a] is said to be a land (*pāthas* or *vāstu*) beyond ordinary mortal ken which 'man apprehends not, nor can the soaring winged birds pursue'[12] and in which 'gods rejoice'[13] and 'god-seeking men delight.'[14] The Ṛgvedic poets pray[15] that people may go to this blessed abode of Viṣṇu, 'where he himself dwells, inscrutable', to enjoy felicity. Hopkins[16] thinks that the later popularity of the god lies in the importance of his *parama pada* which is said to have been the home of departed spirits.[17] In later times, *Viṣṇu-pada* became a synonym of the sky, and the abode of Viṣṇu became the goal of the spiritual aspirations of the devotees of that god and several places (usually on the top of hills) came to be styled Viṣṇupada.

According to Aurṇavābha, as indicated by Durgācārya in his commentary on Yāska's *Nirukta*,[18] the three steps of Viṣṇu are the three periods of the sun's course, i.e., his rise, culmination, and setting.[19] But some scholars point out that this interpretation is not in keeping with the 'highest' place of Viṣṇu.[20] Another ancient commentator, named Śākapūṇi,[21] believed that the three *padas* refer to the threefold manifestation of light in the three divisions of the universe, viz. fire on earth, lightning in the atmosphere, and the sun in the sky. According to the *Śatapatha Brāhmaṇa*[22] also, the three places of Viṣṇu are the earth, air and sky. Viṣṇu's three imperishable steps or places, mentioned in the *Ṛgveda*, were endowed in later times with a spiritual meaning. The Besnagar inscription[23]

11a. I. 154. 5.
12. I. 155. 5.
13. VIII. 29. 7.
14. I. 154. 5.
15. I. 154. 6.
16. *Religions of India*, p. 56.
17. I. 154. 5-6.
18. XII. 19.
19. Cf. *Samārohaṇe Viṣṇu-pade Gaya-śiras=iti Aurṇavābhaḥ. Samārohaṇa, Viṣṇu-pada*, and *Gaya-śiras* have been explained as accession, meridian sky, and the hill of setting respectively. This tradition seems to have had something to do with the recognition of the Viṣṇupada hill at Gayā as a holy place (Sircar, *Stud. Geog. Anc. Med. Ind.*, p. 229). It should be noticed that the word *pada* is of ambiguous import, meaning 'foot', 'step', 'station', etc.
20. Cf. Macdonell, *Vedic Mythology*, p. 38; Kieth, *Religion and Philosophy of the Veda and the Upaniṣads*, Vol. I, p. 108.
21. Cf. Macdonell, *Vedic Mythology, loc. cit.*
22. I. 9. 3. 9.
23. Sircar, *Select Inscriptions*, Vol. I, pp. 90f.

of the close of the second century B.C. interprets the 'immortal' *padas* as denoting 'self-control, renunciation, and vigilance which lead one to heaven', apparently pointing to the dwelling of Viṣṇu as the God of gods.

The *Ṛgveda*[25] also regards Viṣṇu as a youth who is no longer a child, and as a leader in battle who is said to have defeated Śambara. In the capacity of a warrior, Viṣṇu is often associated with Indra and the two gods are supposed to be masters of the world.[25] Viṣṇu is described as the worthy friend of Indra and is said to have walked the three strides with Indra's energy.[26] Indra is sometimes represented as deserted by all the gods excepting Viṣṇu whom he asked to exert his greatest prowess in the slaying of Vṛtra.[27] According to a legend in the *Aitareya Brāhmaṇa*,[28] Varuṇa, Bṛhaspati and Viṣṇu successively helped Indra in turning out the *Asuras*. The Vedic legends no doubt contributed largely to the development of the Viṣṇu mythology in later times. Barnett[29] suggests that, according to lay imagination, a transfusion took place of some of the live blood of Indra, the most truly popular god of action among the Ṛgvedic deities, into the veins of Viṣṇu, as a result of the close relation between the two gods in early Vedic conception.

A passage of the *Ṛgveda*[30] calls Viṣṇu the germ (*garbha*) of *ṛta* which may mean sacrifice or moral order. According to the *Śatapatha Brāhmaṇa*,[31] 'Viṣṇu truly is the sacrifice; by striding, he obtained for the gods that all-pervading power which now belongs to them.' The equation of Viṣṇu with the spirit of sacrifice[32] was possibly suggested by the fact that both were considered to be helping or strengthening Indra and other gods. In later literature, Viṣṇu is essentially connected with sacrifice and is endowed with such names as Yajña, Yajñāvayava, Yajñeśvara, Yajñapuruṣa, Yajñabhavana, Yajña-

24. I. 155. 6.
25. VI. 69; VII. 99.
26. I. 22. 19; VIII. 12. 27.
27. IV. 18. 11.
28. III. 50.
29. *Hindu Gods and Heroes*, p. 41.
30. I. 156. 3.
31. I. 9.3.9.
32. Barnett, *op. cit.*, pp. 39 ff.

varāha, Yajñakṛt, Yajñatrātṛ, Yajñabhoktṛ, Yajñakratu, Yajñavāhana, Yajñavīrya, etc. According to the *Aitareya Brāhmaṇa*,[33] he averts the evil consequences of the defects in sacrifice, while Varuṇa protects the fruits of its successful performance. This work regards Agni and Viṣṇu as the two *dīkṣāpālas* or guardians of initiation.

The *Śatapatha Brāhmaṇa*[34] contains a legend which, with some variations, recurs in the *Taittirīya Āraṇyaka*[35] and *Pañcaviṁśa Brāhmaṇa*.[36] According to this legend, there was a contention among the gods as to which of them was the greatest. It was proposed that he who by his deeds reached the end of sacrifice should attain to the highest place among them. In this contest, Viṣṇu was victorious and hence it was said, 'Viṣṇu is the most excellent of the gods.' That Viṣṇu had already become the greatest god in the later Vedic period, at least with a section of the people, is also indicated by the *Aitareya Brāhmaṇa*[37] which calls him the *parama* (highest) and Agni the *avama* (lowest) among the gods, unless we understand by these two terms a 'heavenly' and an 'earthly' god respectively. But the same work also regards Viṣṇu as the *dvārapa* or door-keeper of the gods.[38] This is no doubt an uncomplimentary epithet, although the idea is probably that Viṣṇu regulated entrance into the heavenly world.

In the *Maitrī Upaniṣad*,[39] food that sustains the universe is called Bhagavat Viṣṇu, while, in the *Kaṭha Upaniṣad*,[40] the progress of human soul is compared to a journey, the goal of which is said to be Viṣṇu's *parama pada*, the abode of eternal bliss.[41] This shows that Viṣṇu was often regarded as the greatest god in later Vedic times. According to the *Āpastamba*, *Hiraṇyakeśin* and *Pāraskara Gṛhyasūtras*, the bridegroom is required to say to the bride at the time of taking the seven steps, 'May Viṣṇu be with you !' This is a development of

33. III. 38; I. 4.
34. XIV. I. I.
35. V. I.
36. VII. 5. 6.
37. I. I.
38. I. 30.
39. VI. 13.
40. III. 9.
41. Cf. *RV*, I. 22. 20.

the Ṛgvedic idea of the god as the protector of embryos and promoter of conception.[42]

Viṣṇu's association with cows is probably indicated by the epithet *gopa*, meaning 'protector of cows' or 'herdsman', found in the *Ṛgveda*.[43] The same work[44] also describes the highest place of Viṣṇu as the dwelling of 'many-horned swiftly-moving cows'. The *Baudhāyana Dharmasūtra*[45] calls him *govinda* (cow-keeper or chief herdsman) and *dāmodara*, 'one with the cord round one's belly', i. e. a herdsman. This last name is usually believed to be derived from wheat-sheaf; but herdsmen, in some parts of India, are known to tie a rope round their waist, from which coils of rope hang.[46] In later times, spiritual interpretations were offered for both the names.[47]

In the *Ṛgveda*, Viṣṇu is sometimes[48] compared to an animal causing depredations (*kucara*),[49] and is represented as stealing cooked mess.[50] In later Vedic literature, he is often found to have recourse to cunning devices to help Indra and other friends and to defeat the *Asuras*. These legends, some of which may be of Nonaryan origin, were no doubt responsible for some aspects of the Viṣṇu mythology in the epic and Purāṇic literature.

II

The Indian religious life is characterised by the existence of a number of theistic religions, the votaries of a particular divinity worshipping him as the Supreme God. Thus Viṣṇu is greater than any other deity to the Vaiṣṇavas, and Śiva is the greatest god to the Śaivas. The personal approach of the votaries of a theistic order to the deity worshipped is distin-

42. Cf. VII. 36. 9; X. 184. 1.
43. I. 22. 18; X. 19. 4.
44. I. 154. 6.
45. II. 5. 24.
46. Cf. D. C. Sen, *Vaṅgasāhityaparicaya*, Vol. I, p. 721—*Kathokṣane Sahadeva goālā-veśete, Go-puccha-lomer daḍi veḍiyā kaṭite.*
47. Cf. *Mbh.*, V. 70. 8.
48. I. 154. 2.
49. Sāyaṇa and others interpret *kucara* often as meaning 'pervading all the quarters.'
50. I. 61. 7; VIII. 77. 10.

guished by an intense devotion and a sense of absolute surrender to the god, the technical name for which is *bhakti* explained as 'exceptional attachment to God' (*par=ānuraktir=Īśvare*). This may be regarded as an un-Aryan concept gradually adopted by the mixed Aryo-Nonaryan population of the country, because the religious life of the Ṛgvedic Aryans is known to have been dominated by the sacrificial cult having a different basis and approach.

While dealing above[51] with the origin of the sectarian religion called Vaiṣṇavism, we have pointed out that its germ is traceable even in the *Ṛgveda*, since, of the three *padas* of Viṣṇu whereby the god maintained the *dharmas* or fixed ordinances, the highest is described in the said work as known to himself and visible only to the *Sūris*[52] who must, therefore, have been persons or spirits favoured by the god Viṣṇu and remind us of the name *Sūri* applied to the sectarian devotees of Viṣṇu in later works like the *Pādma Tantra*.[53] We have also drawn attention, at the same time, to the Ṛgvedic poets' prayer that the people may go after death to the blessed abode of Viṣṇu, which was his highest station beyond ordinary mortal ken and in which god-seeking men delight, as well as to the later Vaiṣṇava conception of Viṣṇu's abode as the goal of the spiritual aspiration of the devotees.

The adoption of an un-Aryan religious approach by the people, in whom Aryan and Nonaryan blood became mixed up in the several centuries (c. 1400-1000 B.C.) covered by the composition of the Ṛgvedic hymns,[54] is not at all unexpected.[55] But J. N. Banerjea has expressed doubts about the plausibility

51. Cf. also *The Age of Imperial Unity*, ed. Majumdar, p. 431 and note.

52. *RV*, I. 22. 20—*tad=Viṣṇoḥ paramaṁ padaṁ sadā paśyanti Sūrayaḥ| div=īva cakṣur=ātatam ||*

53. *JRAS*, 1911, p. 935—*Sūriḥ Suhṛd=Bhāgavataḥ Sātvataḥ Pañcakālavit | Ekāntikas=Tanmayaś=ca Pañcarātrika ity=api ||* The name *Tanmaya* is the same as Tamil *Āḻvār* (literally, 'one who is in deep meditation on the attributes of the Supreme Being'), the name applied to a well-known class of Vaiṣṇava saints of the South. *Suhṛt* may have been the name of a group that worshipped the god as the Friend and emphasised the mode of worship called *Sakhya* (cf. R. G. Bhandarkar, *Vaiṣṇavism, Śaivism and Minor Religious Systems*, p. 57).

54. Cf. *CHI*, Vol. I, p. 697 · c. 1200-800 B.C.

55. Sircar, *The Śākta Pīṭhas*, pp. 100-01.

of our views in his *Paurāṇic and Tantric Religion* recently published by the Calcutta University. This led us to reconsider our position and we are inclined to draw the attention of scholars to a few more traces of sectarianism in ancient Indian literature and in our antiquities.

In the first place, we would like to quote three stanzas of the *Ṛgveda*, which appear to have some bearing on the problem.

1. *Yaḥ pūrvyāya vedhase navīyase*
samujjānaye Viṣṇave dadāśati |
yo jātam=asya mahato mahi bravat
sedu śravobhir=yujyaṁ cid=abhyasat || (I. 156.2)

"He who presents [offerings] to Viṣṇu, the ancient, the creator, the recent, the self-born; he who celebrates the great birth of that mighty one; he verily, possessed of abundance, attains [the station] that is to be sought [by all]" (Wilson).

2. *tamu stotāraṁ pūrvyaṁ yathāvida*
ṛtasya garbhaṁ januṣā pipartana |
asya jānanto nāma cid=vivaktana
mahas=te Viṣṇo sumatiṁ bhajāmahe || (I. 156. 3)

"Hymnors, propitiate, of your own accord, that ancient Viṣṇu, since you know him as the germ of sacrifice; cognizant of his greatness, celebrate his name; may we, Viṣṇu, enjoy thy favour" (Wilson).

3. *pra tat=te adya Śipiviṣṭa-nām=ā-*
ryaḥ śaṁsāmi vayanāsi vidvān |
taṁ tvā gṛṇāmi tavasam=atavyān
kṣayantam=asya rajasaḥ parāke || (VII. 100. 5)

"Resplendent Viṣṇu, I, the master of the offering, knowing the objects that are to be known, glorify today thy name: I, who am feeble, praise thee who art powerful, dwelling in a remote region of this world" (Wilson).

The word *bravat* used in connection with Viṣṇu's birth in the first of the three stanzas, which Wilson translates as 'celebrates', has been explained by Sāyaṇa as *brūyāt, saṁkīrtayet*. Likewise the word *vivaktana*, used in the second stanza in relation to Viṣṇu's name and translated by Wilson in the same way, has been interpreted by Sāyaṇa as *vadata, saṅkīrtayata*. Thus the first of the three stanzas refers to the recitation or singing of the birth of Viṣṇu, while the second speaks of the recitation or singing of his name by the people who knew him. The third stanza alludes to the praising of Viṣṇu's name. It seems that we have here a reference to the recitation or singing of Viṣṇu's birth-story and his name. This would suggest that a mythology around the birth of Viṣṇu was already developing and this may be the root of the later growth of the birth-story of Vāsudeva-Kṛṣṇa identified with Viṣṇu. The recitation or singing of Viṣṇu's name likewise reminds us of the importance later attached by the Vaiṣṇavas to the *nāma-japa* or *nāma-saṅkīrtana* of the god worshipped by them.[56] It is well known that later works often offer lists of the *śata-nāma* or *sahasra-nāma* of the god Viṣṇu-Kṛṣṇa.[57] That such lists of the hundred or thousand names of certain deities were compiled even as early as the days of the later Saṁhitās (c. 1000-800 B.C.) is proved by the *Śatarudriya* section of the *Yajurveda*[58] and the expression *sahasra-nāman* occurring in the *Atharvaveda*.[59] It therefore seems to us that the passages of the *Ṛgveda* quoted above, if they are read together, suggest the existence of some sort of sectarian worship of Viṣṇu at least at a particular stage of its development.

Similar is the case with the god Rudra, later identified with Śiva. We have referred above to the *Śatarudriya* section of the *Yajurveda*, which contains one hundred names of Rudra. This shows beyond doubt that considerable importance was attached to the recitation or singing of the names of Rudra apparently by a section of his devotees. Rudra is described as *Mahādeva* and *Mahān Deva*, i.e. the Great God, in the *Yajurveda*[60] and *Śatapatha Brāhmaṇa*[61] respectively, while the *Keśi-sūkta* of the *Ṛgveda*[62] refers to the devotees of the said god as *Keśin* (people having long or matted hair), who were half-naked, wearing short garments of brown colour soiled with

56. Cf. the texts cited by the *Śabdakalpadruma*, s. v. *saṅkīrtana*; see also Bhandarkar, *op. cit.*, p. 57.

57. See Monier-William's *Sans.-Eng. Dict.*, s. v. *Viṣṇu* (*Viṣṇu-śata-nāma-stotra* and *Viṣṇu-sahasra-nāma*).

58. *TS*, IV. 5. 1; VS, 16.

59. See Monier-Williams, *op. cit.*, s. v. *sahasra.*

60. *VS*, 39.8

61. 6. 1. 37.

62. X. 136.

dust and frenzied by the performance of austerities. This description reminds us of that of the sectarian Pāśupata devotees of Rudra-Śiva as found in later works and suggests that these were the people who recited or sang the *Śatarudriya* incorporated in the *Yajurveda*. The reference in the said *sūkta* of the *Ṛgveda* to the *Keśi-muni* drinking a cup of poison with Rudra may have the germ of the later conception of Śiva as Nīlakaṇṭha.[63]

It may be mentioned in this connection that Śiva as the name of a people occurs in the *Ṛgveda*,[64] and, according to some scholars, it means 'having Śiva as their chief god.'[65] Patañjali's *Mahābhāṣya*[66] mentions Śivapura, 'the city of the Śivas', which has been identified with modern Shorkot in the Jhang District of West Pakistan.[67] Alexander's historians mention the same people as Sibae who lived in the said area and are reported to have dressed themselves with the skins of wild beasts and had clubs for their weapon.[68] It has been pointed out that the above description of the people reminds one of that of the god Śiva and his disciples found in later works.[69]

Clearer traces of the cult of Rudra as some sort of a sectarian god have been noticed in the *Śvetāśvatara Upaniṣad* which describes the god in such passages as the following—

> *tam=īśvarāṇāṁ paramaṁ Maheśvaraṁ*
> *taṁ devatānāṁ paramaṁ ca daivatam* (VI. 7);
> *yo Brahmāṇaṁ vidadhāti pūrvaṁ*
> *yo vai vedāṁś=ca prahiṇoti tasmai* (VI. 18).

The first of the two passages represents Rudra as the Maheśvara (Great God) among the gods (*īśvaras*) and as the Supreme Deity among the divinities, while the second passage mentions him as one who created the god Brahman and pre-

63. Cf. J. N. Banerjea, *op. cit.*, pp. 72-73.
64. VII. 18. 7; cf. *Ved. Ind.*, Vol. II, s. v. *Śiva*.
65. Dandekar, *Some Aspects of the History of Hinduism*, p. 5.
66. On Pāṇini, IV. 2. 2.
67. Raychaudhuri, *PHAI*, 1938, p. 204.
68. *Loc. cit.*; Banerjea, *Paur. Tant. Rel.*, p. 71.
69. Banerjea, *loc. cit.*

sented the Vedas to the latter. Thus, in the days of the *Śvetāśvatara Upaniṣad*, Rudra was regarded by a class of his votaries as the greatest god who was the creator of other gods like Brahman. This approach is of course remarkably similar to that of a sectarian devotee.

Reference should also be made in this context to two well-known seals from Mohenjo-daro representing a god in the *yoga* posture with a kneeling human figure, with hands uplifted in prayer, on either side of him. This ascetic god has been identified with the well-known Paśupati-yogin represented on another Mohenjo-daro seal and regarded by most scholars as Proto-Śiva.[70] The kneeling human figures may suggest the existence of a kind of sectarian devotees of the prototype of Rudra-Śiva as early as the days of the Indus Valley civilization.

In the same context, attention may be drawn to the existence of tutelary deities during the age covered by the composition of the Ṛgvedic hymns. It is well known that the Āprī hymns[71] refer to the goddess Bhāratī, regarded as the personified divine protective power of the Bharata people who lived on the Sarasvatī, conceived as a river-goddess. In the said hymns, Bhāratī is associated with Sarasvatī, while, in later mythology, the former is usually identical with the latter. Whatever that might be, there is little doubt that the goddess Bhāratī was at first exclusively worshipped by the Bharatas, that is to say that Bhāratī was something like the tutelary deity of the Bharata people. Needless to say that the conception of a tutelary deity is analogous to that of a sectarian divinity. The name Bhāratī reminds us of those of Kauśikī and Kātyāyanī which some scholars associate with the fact that the two aspects of the Mother-goddess were originally worshipped by the sages of the Kauśika and Kātya clans.[72]

When all the points raised above are taken into consideration together, it appears that sectarianism of some sort was the characteristic of the religious life of India even before the advent of the Aryans some of whom had gradually adopted it before the latest hymns of the *Ṛgveda* were composed.

70. See *ibid.*, pp. 64-65.

71. *RV*, I. 22. 10; 142. 9; 188. 8; II. 1. 11; 3. 8; III. 4. 8; etc.

72. Banerjea, *op. cit.*, p. 119.

III

The Vedic Aryans tried to please Viṣṇu and other gods by means of sacrifice; but this sacrificial religion was fundamentally different from the later religion characterized by *bhakti* (devotion of the faithful to God) and *prasāda* (God's grace to the faithful). We have reason to believe that the conception of devotion and grace was borrowed from the Nonaryan religious thought. According to Śāṇḍilya, as we have seen, *bhakti* is *parā=ānuraktir=Īśvare*, 'supreme attachment to God.' Some resemblance to *bhakti* is noticeable in the Ṛgvedic hymns addressed to Varuṇa (with whom Viṣṇu was associated as a benefactor of the sacrificer in later Vedic literature), but not in those addressed to Viṣṇu. In the Vedic texts, Viṣṇu is associated more with sacrifice than with devotion and grace. Bhandarkar[73] thinks that the origin of the *bhakti* doctrine may be traced to the Upaniṣadic idea of *upāsanā* or fervent meditation, which magnifies what is meditated upon and represents it in a glorious form in order to excite admiration and love. He also draws our attention to the *Bṛhadāraṇyaka Upaniṣad*[74] which conceives the internal *Ātman* (soul) as dearer than the son, wealth and everything else. But, as we have seen above, *bhakti* seems to be a much older belief of the Nonaryans adopted by the composite Indian society at a later date.

Some scholars find an early reference to the *bhakti* doctrine in the rule in the *Aṣṭādhyāyī*[75] of Pāṇini (fifth century B.C.) for the formation of the words *Vāsudevaka* and *Arjunaka* in the senses of 'a person whose object of *bhakti* is Vāsudeva' and 'a person whose object of *bhakti* is Arjuna' respectively. As Vāsudeva seems to have been held in esteem by the people of Mathurā in the days of Megasthenes in the fourth century B.C. and was undoubtedly regarded as the highest god in the days of the *Gītā* (third century B.C.) and the Besnagar inscription (second century B.C.), Raychaudhuri[76] may be right in his contention that the word *bhakti*, in regard to Vāsudeva,

73. *Vaiṣṇavism, Śaivism and Minor Religious Systems*, p. 28.
74. I. 4. 8.
75. IV. 3. 98.
76. *Materials for the Study of the Early History of the Vaiṣṇava Sect*, 2nd ed., pp. 30 f.

is used in the above *sūtra* by Pāṇini in the sense of religious adoration. But the word is also used in the *Aṣṭādhyāyī* with reference to cakes, and the possibility of the meaning 'fondness' is not altogether precluded. The reference to two groups of persons as *Vāsudeva-bhakta* and *Kaṁsa-bhakta* in Patañjali's *Mahābhāṣya*[77] also is not quite clear. We do not know if Vāsudeva's deification by his own people at Mathurā was recognized, at such an early date, in Gandhāra where Pāṇini flourished. More important is therefore the *Śvetāśvatara Upaniṣad*[78] (a work nearly of the same age as the *Aṣṭādhyāyī*) which teaches *parā bhakti* (supreme devotion to God). That the idea of religious adoration for a leader of thought was not unknown in the days of Aśoka (c.272-232 B.C.) is indicated by the Rummindei pillar inscription,[79] according to which the Buddhist king went in person to, and offered worship at, the birth-place of Śākyamuni Buddha, styled the *Bhagavat* (the holiest or most worshipful one).[80] Reference may also be made in this connection to the installation of the Buddha's relics for worship, referred to in early Buddhist literature as well as in records belonging to the time of Aśoka and king Menander (close of the 2nd century B.C.),[81] to the implication of *bhakti*, in the reference to religious adoration, in the stanzas of the *Therīgāthā*, and to the representation of some cult-deities of the Brāhmaṇical pantheon on the pre-Christian coins of India.

The elaborate and mechanical system of sacrifice offered to the gods by the Vedic Aryans did not satisfy the religious aspiration of all sections of the people, especially after they had intermarried with the pre-Aryan population and became familiar with the religious and philosophical beliefs of the latter. This led to religious speculations of a different type, and

77. Patañjali was a contemporary of Puṣyamitra Śuṅga (c. 185-149 B.C.); but the *Mahābhāṣya* appears to contain interpolations of about the beginning of the Christian era. Cf. *Indian Historical Quarterly*, Vol. XV, pp. 633 ff.

78. Cf. V. 14. This Upaniṣad inculcating devotion to Śiva, originally a Nonaryan god, points to the Nonaryan contribution to the development of the *Bhakti* doctrine.

79. *Select Inscriptions*, Vol. I, p. 70.

80. Cf. *Journal of the Royal Asiatic Society of Bengal*, Vol. XIV, pp. 7-8.

81. *Ibid.*, pp. 102ff; *Select Inscriptions*, Vol. I, 1965 ed., p. 517.

thinkers like the author of the *Muṇḍaka Upaniṣad*[82] began to question the value and efficacy of sacrifice. The philosophical speculations of this age gave rise, among others, to religious sects like those of Vardhamāna of the Jñātṛkas, Siddhārtha of the Śākyas, and Vāsudeva of the Vṛṣṇis (all three favouring the doctrine of *ahiṁsā*) as well as to the philosophical ideas clothed in the words of the Upaniṣads.[83] We have to note that, even though the Jñātṛkas, Śākyas, and Vṛṣṇis all claimed the status of the Kṣatriya, the first and second clans were possibly Aryanized Mongoloids, like their kinsmen the Licchavis, while the third, if not originally Nonaryan, at least absorbed enough Nonaryan blood.[84] At the beginning, the following of

82. Cf. I. 2. 7.

83. A comparative study of the Upaniṣadic philosophy and the religious and philosophical ideas of the Polynesians has led some writers to think that the common conceptions were of Austric origin. The history of creation is described in different parts of the Polynesian world in hymns that echo the Ṛgvedic hymn of creation. E. S. Craighill, who has studied the Polynesian religion, says : 'The ancient esoteric teaching in cosmology postulated the pre-existence of a self-created world-soul which evolved the world and the universe out of itself and called manifest existences out of nothingness by the power of the Word. Many of the creational accounts make no mention of this Being; the evolutionary process by which the universe evolved from nothingness is stated merely as a succession of stages, the first of which is characterized as Void or Night. But other records describing the course of evolution in terms similar to these definitely attribute it to a Supreme Being as the cause of the emergence of tangible and visible reality out of or in the empty and lightless Void in which this Being existed alone.' Cf. *Bhārata Kaumudi*, Vol. I, pp. 204ff. The word *tābuva* in the *Atharvaveda* (V.1B. 3.10) is believed to be an old form of the well-known *tabu* (taboo) of the Polynesians. There are also other coincidences.

84. The tradition of the Ikṣvāku origin of the Śākyas proves nothing as the Nonaryans often claimed to have belonged to the maternal grandfather's family and as the Aryan origin of the Ikṣvākus themselves is as yet unproved. The Licchavis and Mauryas appear to have been two other Himalayan tribes of Mongolian origin claiming the status of the Kṣatriya. Some of these tribes are known to have been regarded by the orthodox Brāhmaṇas as Śūdra, Vṛṣala, or degraded Kṣatriya and were often classed with the Nonaryan peoples and foreigners. Cf. the case of the Dravidian Śātavāhanas (Andhras) who claimed the status of the Brāhmaṇa (probably as a result of matrimonial relations with a Brāhmaṇa family), but were called Vṛṣala in the Purāṇas. The Greek and Scythian foreigners were sometimes regarded as clean Śūdras, but sometimes as degraded Kṣatriyas (cf. Sircar, *Stud. Soc. Adm. Anc. Med. Ind.*, Vol. I, pp. 48-49).

Vardhanāna, Siddhārtha and Vāsudeva (religious leaders of whose type are known to have flourished in India in all ages in numbers) was meagre; but their systems gradually became prominent. The later success of Vāsudevism was principally due to the identification of Vāsudeva with the Vedic god Viṣṇu, with an ancient defied sage named Nārāyaṇa, with a number of tribal deities, as well as with *Parabrahman* (the Supreme Spirit or All-Soul), conceived by the Upaniṣads.[85]

85. Originally the Yādavas were looked down upon because of their Nonaryan association, though later the Yādava clan came to be regarded as aristocratic like the solar and lunar houses. This was the result of the identification of Vāsudeva with the Supreme God. See Sircar, *Stud. Soc. Adm. Anc. Med. Ind.*, Vol. I, p. 46.

Chapter II

VĀSUDEVA-KṚṢṆA AND NĀRĀYAṆA IN EARLY VAIṢṆAVISM

I

In the epics and the Purāṇas, the ruling clan of Mathurā is called Yadu or Yādava, which was divided into numerous septs. Vṛṣṇi and Andhaka were the sons of the Yādava prince Sātvata. The names Sātvata and Vṛṣṇi are therefore both used often to indicate the same family in ancient Indian literature, as the names Raghu and Ikṣvāku are applied to the solar dynasty, and Bharata, Kuru and Puru to the lunar. The Vṛṣṇi sept of the Yādava people was famous in later Vedic times as is proved by its mention in the *Taittirīya Saṁhitā*[1] and *Brāhmaṇa*,[2] the *Śatapatha Brāhmaṇa*,[3] and the *Jaiminīya Upaniṣad Brāhmaṇa*.[4] The Vṛṣṇis and the Andhakas are mentioned in Pāṇini's *Aṣṭādhyāyī*.[5] The *Kauṭilīya Arthaśāstra*[6] refers to the *saṅgha* or republican corporation of the Vṛṣṇi people. A coin assigned to the Vṛṣṇirājanya-gaṇa (republic of the Vṛṣṇi Kṣatriyas) and to the first century B.C., bearing a *cakra* on the reverse and a pillar surmounted by an animal (believed to be half-lion and half-elephant, but may be really a crude representation of Garuḍa) on the obverse, was discovered probably in the North Punjab.[7] The Sātvats, mentioned in the *Śatapatha* and *Aitareya Brāhmaṇas*, are apparently the same as the Sātvatas of the epic and Purāṇic literature. Yadu, possibly a Nonaryan clan, is mentioned in the *Ṛgveda* occasionally with Turvaśa.[8] In later literature, Yadu and

1. III. 11. 9. 3.
2. III. 10. 9. 15.
3. III. 1. 1. 4.
4. I. 6. 1.
5. IV. 1. 114.
6. Shamasastry's trans., p. 12.
7. See Allan, *Catalogue of Indian Coins* (*Ancient India*), pp. clv ff.; Banerjea, *Development of Hindu Iconography*, p. 145 and note 1. The coin was really issued by the *Vṛṣṇi-rāja* Jñāgaṇa (Sircar, *Studies in Indian Coins*, p. 357, No. IV/19).
8. *Ved. Ind.*, s. v.

Turvasu are two of the four disobedient sons of Yayāti, who were cursed by their father and became the progenitors of the Yādavas, Yavanas, Bhojas and Mlecchas respectively. We have to note in this connection the irreverent attitude of the Vṛṣṇis towards the Brāhmaṇas, which is attested by a number of authorities, and the fact that the most distinguished Vṛṣṇi hero was dark-complexioned (*atasī-kusuma-śyāma*). Thus, even if the Yādava-Sātvata-Vṛṣṇi people were not actually of Nonaryan origin, at least they must have absorbed a good deal of Nonaryan blood.

The *Bhagavad-Gītā*, which seems to contain the earliest dogmatic exposition of the religion characterized by *bhakti* that may be called Vaiṣṇavism, represents Vāsudeva, otherwise called Kṛṣṇa and identified with the god Viṣṇu as well as with the Supreme Spirit (but not yet with Nārāyaṇa), as a scion of the Vṛṣṇi (i.e. the Yādava-Sātvata-Vṛṣṇi) family. The *Mahābhāṣya* and the *Kāśikā* give the forms *vāsudeva*, *bāladeva* and *āniruddha*, as derivatives of Vṛṣṇi names, meaning the sons of Vāsudeva, Baladeva and Aniruddha respectively.[1] The names of the five Vṛṣṇi heroes, referred to in the Morā (near Mathurā) inscription of the first century A.D., are given in the *Vāyu Purāṇa* as Saṅkarṣaṇa (son of Vasudeva by Rohiṇī), Vāsudeva (son of Vasudeva by Devakī), Pradyumna (son of Vāsudeva by Rukmiṇī), Sāmba (son of Vāsudeva by Jāmbavatī of Nonaryan origin), and Aniruddha (son of Pradyumna), all of whom are known to have been apotheosized and worshipped.[2] The *Mahābhāṣya* also speaks of the *Vāsudeva-vargya* or *Vāsudeva-vargin* to signify a follower of Vāsudeva. Curtius says that an image of Herakles (i. e. Vāsudeva-Kṛṣṇa) was being carried in front of the Paurava army, as it advanced against the Greeks led by Alexander the Great.[3] The *Mahābhārata* (which sometime mentions Vāsudeva as the *Saṅghamukhya* or Elder of the Republican Confederacy of the Vṛṣṇi, Andhaka and other associate peoples)[4] and the Purāṇas usually identify Vāsudeva-Kṛṣṇa of the Sātvata (i.e. Yādava-Sātvata-Vṛṣṇi) clan with the highest god, and represent him as the founder of the religion characterized

1. Under Pāṇini, IV. 1. 114.
2. Cf. *Proceedings of the Indian History Congress*, 1944., pp. 82ff.
3. See Majumdar, *The Classical Accounts of India*, p. 119.
4. XII. 81. 25.

by *bhakti* and called the Bhāgavata, Sātvata, or Vaiṣṇava Dharma. In the *Bhāgavata Purāṇa*, the highest Brahman is stated to have been called *Bhagavat* and *Vāsudeva* by the Sātvata people, while the *Mahābhārata* states, apparently in reference to the *Gītā*, that the Sātvata or Bhāgavata Dharma was taught first by Vāsudeva-Kṛṣṇa to Arjuna.[1] It has to be noted that the word *sātvata* has been used together with *sūri* and *bhāgavata* in the sense of a devotee of Vāsudeva-Viṣṇu in a canonical work of the Vaiṣṇavas.[2] The *Gītā*[3] speaks of the Bhāgavata religion as *yoga*. The Tusam (Hissar District, Punjab) inscription,[4] of about the fourth century A.D., also mentions a *bhagavad-bhakta* (i.e. Bhāgavata) as *Ārya-Sātvata-yog-ācārya*, 'teacher of the noble Sātvata *yoga*'.

Megasthenes (fourth century B.C.), the Greek envoy at the Maurya court, speaks of the Sourasenoi (Śūrasena people), whose country contained the two cities Methora (Mathurā) and Kleisobora (probably, Kṛṣṇapura), and was watered by the great river Jobares (Yamunā), as holding Herakles (apparently the Greek substitute of Vāsudeva-Kṛṣṇa) in special veneration.[5] The Śūrasenas were a branch of the Yādava-Sātvata-Vṛṣṇi people. This is indicated by the fact that the *Ghaṭa Jātaka*[6] speaks of the ruling clan of Mathurā in the North—as distinguished from Mathurā (Madurai) in the South in the Pāṇḍya country,—of which Vāsudeva-Kṛṣṇa was a member, as having perished owing to the irreverent conduct of its members towards the Brāhmaṇa Kṛṣṇa-Dvaipāyana (Vyāsa), while the *Kauṭilīya Arthaśāstra*[7] refers to the destruction of the republican corporation of the Vṛṣṇi people as a result of their attempt against Dvaipāyana (i.e. Vyāsa). The epic and Purāṇic traditions that associate the Yādavas, especially Vāsudeva-Kṛṣṇa, with Mathurā and its neighbourhood have already been referred to above. The worship

1. *Bhāgavata*, IX. 9. 50; *Mbh.*, XII. 348. 6-8.

2. Cf. *Sūris=Suhṛd-Bhāgavatas=Sātvataḥ Pañcakālavit*, etc. quoted above from the *Pādma Tantra*, one of the 108 Vaiṣṇava Tantras or Saṁhitās (cf. *Journ. Roy. As. Soc.*, 1911, p. 935).

3. IV. 1.
4. *Corp. Ins. Ind.*, Vol. III, p. 270.
5. Majumdar, *The Classical Accounts of India*, pp. 221-22.
6. Cowell's trans., Vol. IV, pp. 55 f.
7. I. 6.

of Vāsudeva in that locality is further proved by a Mathurā inscription[1] of the time of the Śaka Satrap Śoḍāsa (first quarter of the first century A.D.). This inscription records the erection of a gateway, a terrace, and a *devakula* at the *mahāsthāna* of Vāsudeva.

The Buddhist canonical work *Aṅguttara Nikāya*[2] mentions a number of religious sects such as Ājīvika, Nirgrantha (Jaina), Muṇḍaśrāvaka, Jaṭilaka, Parivrājaka, Magaṇḍika, Traidaṇḍika, Aviruddhaka, Gautamaka (Buddhist) and Devadharmika; but it does not speak of Vāsudevaka or Bhāgavata. The inscriptions of Aśoka, which mention the Śramaṇas, Brāhmaṇas, Ājīvikas, and Nirgranthas,[3] do not speak of the followers of Vāsudeva. However, in a passage occurring in the Buddhist canonical commentaries (first century B.C.) called the *Mahāniddesa* and the *Cullaniddesa*,[4] mention is made of the Ājīvika, Nirgrantha, Jaṭila, Parivrājaka and Avaruddhaka side by side with the worshippers of the elephant, horse, cow, dog, crow, Vāsudeva, Baladeva (Saṅkarṣaṇa), Pūrṇabhadra, Maṇibhadra, Agni (Fire), the *Nāgas*, *Suparṇas*, *Yakṣas*, *Asuras*, *Gandharvas*, *Mahārājas* (the four *Lokapālas*),[5] Candra, Sūrya, Indra, Brahman, *Deva* and *Dik*. The Bhāgavata sect worshipping Vāsudeva may not have been so prominent outside the Mathurā region (especially in the eastern part of India) about the third century B. C. The religion probably originated with the Yādava-Sātvata-Vṛṣṇi people of the said area and spread to Western India and the Northern Deccan with the migration of Yādava tribes to those regions. Vāsudeva appears to have been deified and worshipped by his own people as early as the age of Pāṇini or even earlier; but he may or may not have been regarded as the Supreme God. We have to note that the identification of

1. *Journ. Bihar Res. Soc.*, Vol. XXXIX, Parts 1-2, pp. 45-48.
2. P.T.S. ed., Vol. III, pp. 276ff.
3. Sircar, *Inscriptions of Aśoka*, 2nd ed., pp. 77-78.
4. Cf. R. G. Bhandarkar, *Vaiṣṇavism, Śaivism and Minor Religious Systems*, p. 3.
5. This is the generally accepted meaning and accords best with the context. Divinity was claimed by kings as, for instance, by Samudragupta (see *infra*). Reference may also be made to the Kuṣāṇa title *devaputra* and the representation, on coins, of one early Kuṣāṇa monarch as flying above the clouds and as having flames springing from the shoulder.

Vāsudeva with the highest God is not recognised in the earlier sections of the *Mahābhārata*. A well-known scene of the Sabhāparvan[1] proves that Vāsudeva-Kṛṣṇa's claim to divine honours was sometimes openly denied. Sometimes Vāsudeva is described as a pious hypocrite. Even the *Gītā*[2] represents Vāsudeva-Kṛṣṇa as lamenting that the person of great soul who says 'Vāsudeva is All' is rare and that people scorn him when he dwells in human form. It is only some late passages of the *Mahābhārata* that represent him as a friend of the Brāhmaṇas and the origin of the Vedas, and also as perfectly identical with Viṣṇu.[3] The *Mahābhāṣya* refers to the antagonism between the *Kaṁsa-bhaktas* who were *kāla-mukha* (dark-faced) and the *Vāsudeva-bhaktas* who were *rakta-mukha* (red-faced),[4] although the reference may be to a dramatic representation of the slaying of Kaṁsa.

The Besnagar (Vidisa District, Madhya Pradesh) inscription of the last quarter of the second century B.C. refers to the setting up of a *Garuḍa-dhvaja* (column surmounted by the figure of Garuḍa, the emblem or *vāhana* of Viṣṇu) at Vidiśā in honour of Vāsudeva, the *Deva-deva* (the greatest God), by his Yavana (Greek) devotee Heliodoros of Takṣaśilā in Gandhāra, who called himself a Bhāgavata, i. e., a worshipper of the *Bhagavat* (Vāsudeva-Viṣṇu). Another inscription from Besnagar refers to the erection of a Garuḍa column for a temple of the *Bhagavat*. The Ghosundi (Chitorgarh District, Rajasthan) inscription[5] of the first century B.C. records the construction of a *pūjā-śilā-prākāra* (stone enclosure for a place of worship, or an enclosure for the sacred stone called *śālagrāma*, the symbol of Viṣṇu as the *liṅga* is of Śiva), styled Nārāyaṇa-vāṭaka (or °*vāṭikā*), by a *Bhāgavata* who had performed the Aśvamedha sacrifice in honour of Saṅkarṣaṇa and Vāsudeva. They are both called here *Bhagavat* as well as *anihata* (unconquered or respected) and *sarveśvara* (supreme lord). The Nanaghat (Maharashtra State) inscription[6] of

1. Ch. 42.
2. VII. 19, 24; IX. 11; XVIII. 57.
3. XII. 47. 94—*Namo Brahmaṇyadevāya go-Brāhmaṇa-hitāya ca | jagaddhitāya Kṛṣṇāya Govindāya namo namaḥ ||*
4. Cf. *Ind. Ant.*, 1874, p. 15; *JRAS*, 1911, p. 1008.
5. *Select Inscriptions*, Vol. I, pp. 91 f.
6. *Ibid.*, pp. 186 ff.

about the same age, belonging to the queen of a Śātavāhana performer of Vedic sacrifices including the Aśvamedha, begins with an adoration to the gods Dharma, Indra, Saṅkarṣaṇa and Vāsudeva, the moon and the sun, and the four *Lokapālas*, viz. Yama (differentiated from Dharma), Varuṇa, Kubera and Vāsava (differentiated from Indra). The epigraphs cited above support what we already know from literary sources as regards Vāsudeva's association with Garuḍa and therefore with Viṣṇu, with the Vṛṣṇi hero Saṅkarṣaṇa and with Nārāyaṇa, considerably before the birth of Christ. He is not called Kṛṣṇa in the early Indian inscriptions ; but the use of Kṛṣṇa, as another name of Vāsudeva, in works like the *Mahābhārata*, especially in the *Gītā* belonging to its early stratum, Patañjali's *Mahābhāṣya*, and the *Ghaṭa Jātaka* is probably pre-Christian. The spread of the Bhāgavata religion outside the Mathurā region and Vāsudeva's own clan (i. e. the Yādava-Sātvata-Vṛṣṇis), especially amongst the performers of Vedic sacrifices, has therefore the support of epigraphic evidence. But some people did not regard Vāsudeva, as late as the first century B.C., as the greatest of all gods, but only as an equal of deities like Dharma, Indra and others. Even in the second century A.D., the Śātavāhana king Gautamīputra Śātakarṇi is described as an equal of Rāma (Balarāma), Keśava (Kṛṣṇa), Arjuna and Bhīmasena, referring to Keśava as a hero merely.[1] But the Chinna (Krishna District, Andhra Pradesh) inscription of Yajña-Śātakarṇi (last quarter of the second century) begins with an adoration to Vāsudeva alone and indicates the progress of Bhagavatism in the South.

There is no iconic representation of the god Viṣṇu-Vāsudeva assignable to a date very much earlier than the beginning of the Christian era.[2] A four-armed figure of the deity with *cakra* in the upper left hand is found on the coins of a Pañcāla king named Viṣṇumitra in evident allusion to the name of the issuer. A similar representation of the four-armed Viṣṇu, with *śaṅkha*, *cakra*, *gadā* and an indefinite

1. *Select Inscriptions*, *op. cit.*, p. 198.

2. One of the earliest Vaiṣṇava images so far discovered in India is that of an attendant of Viṣṇu (having his appearance and attributes), now worshipped as Caturbhuji Bhagavān at Burhikhār near Malhar in the Bilaspur District of Madhya Pradesh. See below.

object in the hands, is found on a Kuṣāṇa seal-matrix[1] attributed by Cunningham to Huviṣka. The Kuṣāṇa king is represented here as facing the deity in a reverential attitude with his hands in the *añjali* pose. Possibly he became, for some time, a worshipper of Vāsudeva. Some of Huviṣka's coins[2] bear the figure of the four-armed god named Ooshna in Greek characters (probably Viṣṇu and not Śiva as usually believed). The fact that Huviṣka's successor assumed the name Vāsudeva also indicates the Bhāgavata leanings of the later Kuṣāṇas who had an important gubernatorial centre at Mathurā.

Patañjali[3] seems to make a distinction between Vāsudeva the *tatrabhavat* (i. e. the most worshipful Vāsudeva) and the Kṣatriya Vāsudeva. The canonical Bhāgavata work *Pādma Tantra*[4] similarly makes a distinction between the two Vāsudevas. It is said in a *Mahābhārata*[5] story that, besides Kṛṣṇa of the Yādava-Sātvata-Vṛṣṇi family, there was another claimant for the status of Vāsudeva in Pauṇḍraka-Vāsudeva, i.e. Vāsudeva, ruler of the Pauṇḍraka people, probably of North Bengal. Pauṇḍraka-Vāsudeva may have been really the leader of a rival religious sect.

The age of Vāsudeva-Kṛṣṇa cannot be determined with certainty. The evidence of the *Chāndogya Upaniṣad* would suggest a date in the sixth or seventh century B.C., to which the work is usually attributed. The story of his association with the legend of the Kuru-Pāṇḍava war, the authenticity, date and original form of which are uncertain, appears to be less reliable, although some scholars are inclined to accept tenth or ninth century B.C. as the date of the event.[6] Jain tradition[7] makes the Kṣatriya prince Vāsudeva-Kṛṣṇa a contemporary of the legendary twenty-second Tīrthaṅkara Ariṣṭanemi who preceded Pārśvanātha, predecessor of Mahāvīra (6th-5th century B.C.), and may support the date suggested by the *Chāndogya Upaniṣad*.

1. Banerjea, *Development of Hindu Iconography*, pp. 143-44.
2. Cf. *Select Inscriptions*, *op. cit.*, pp. 155-56, note 5.
3. Under Pāṇini, IV. 3. 98-99.
4. *JRAS*, 1911, p. 936; Raychaudhuri, *op. cit.*, p. 35.
5. I. 186. 12; II. 14. 20; etc.
6. Cf. *Journ. Roy. As. Soc. Beng.*, Letters, Vol. XVI, p. 77. Cf. *The Bhārata War and Purāṇic Genealogies*, ed. Sircar, pp. 18ff.
7. *Uttarādhyāyanasūtra*, XXII.

II

There is reference in the *Śatapatha Brāhmaṇa*[1] to the *puruṣa* (a word used often in the sense of the Supreme Spirit) named Nārāyaṇa who is stated to have thrice offered sacrifice at the instance of Prajāpati. Nārāyaṇa is, however, not identified here with Viṣṇu or any of the Ādityas. Elsewhere, the same work[2] mentions Puruṣa-Nārāyaṇa as the performer of a *pañcarātra-sattra* (sacrifice continued for five days), who obtained, as a result, superiority over all beings and 'became all-beings'. Some scholars trace the name Pañcarātra or Pañcarātrika applied to the Bhāgavatas (or to one of their important branches) to this five-day *sattra* attributed to Nārāyaṇa. The earliest evidence in favour of the identification of Nārāyaṇa with Viṣṇu is probably to be traced in the *Baudhāyana Dharmasūtra*[3] (about the fifth century B.C.). The *Taittirīya Āraṇyaka*[4] contains the passage : *Nārāyaṇāya vidmahe Vāsudevāya dhīmahi / tan=no Viṣṇuḥ pracodayāt* // in which Nārāyaṇa, Vāsudeva and Viṣṇu are regarded as one and the same deity. Here Nārāyaṇa is also called Hari and 'the eternal Deity, the Supreme, and Lord'. But this part of the *Taittirīya Āraṇyaka* is a later addition, and appears to be considerably later than the *Baudhāyana Dharmasūtra*. Several passages of the *Mahābhārata* support the identification of Vāsudeva, Viṣṇu and Nārāyaṇa as found in the above passage.

According to certain passages of the *Mahābhārata*, Nārāyaṇa was an ancient *ṛṣi* who was the son of Dharma and was associated with another *ṛṣi* called Nara.[5] They both went from the world of men to the world of Brahman and, being worshipped by the gods and the *Gandharvas*, existed only for the destruction of the demons. Indra was helped by Nara and Nārāyaṇa in his struggle with the *Asuras*. In a passage which was apparently retouched by a Śaiva, Nārāyaṇa, son of Dharma, is stated to have practised austerities in the Himalayas (the exact place is sometimes specified as Badarī) and thus become Brahman (the All-Soul); he is said to have

1. XII. 3. 4.
2. XIII. 6. 1.
3. II.5.24; Raychaudhuri, *op. cit.*, p. 111.
4. X. 11.
5. Cf. Bhandarkar, *op. cit.*, pp. 42-46.

become invincible by propitiating Śiva. According to one story, the sage Nara, equal to Nārāyaṇa himself, was born from Nārāyaṇa's austerities. Nara is identified with Arjuna and Nārāyaṇa with Vāsudeva-Kṛṣṇa.[1] The late *Nārāyaṇīya* section of the Śānti-parvan states how Nārāyaṇa, the Eternal and Universal Soul, was born as the son of Dharma in the quadruple form of Nara, Nārāyaṇa, Hari and Kṛṣṇa. It also speaks of the white people of the White Island (Śveta-dvīpa), on the northern shores of the Milk Ocean, engrossed in the worship of Nārāyaṇa, a thousand-rayed deity, who, in consequence of his sun-like brightness, could not be seen by persons not devoting themselves exclusively to him. According to some scholars, the Nārāyaṇīya section of the *Mahābhārata* suggests a journey really undertaken by some Indian Vaiṣṇavas to the Christian countries, and points to an attempt, in the Indian eclectic fashion, to include Christ among the incarnations of the Supreme Spirit Nārāyaṇa. Others, however, take the story to be a mere flight of imagination. Raychaudhuri[2] seems to be right in emphasizing Nārāyaṇa's solar associations and in comparing Nārāyaṇa in the Śveta-dvīpa of the White Islanders with the Ṛgvedic Viṣṇu in his highest station observed only by the *Sūris*. According to Bhandarkar,[3] Nārāyaṇa has a cosmic character and is not an historical or mythological individual. He takes the word Nārāyaṇa in the sense of the resting place or goal of *nāra*, i. e. the multitude of *naras* (men). But it seems more reasonable to think that Nārāyaṇa (cf. Kāṇvāyana, Kātyāyana, etc.) was an ancient leader of thought, born in the family of another sage called Nara and that both of them probably advocated solar worship that ultimately led to the identification, especially of the former, with the solar deity Viṣṇu. It is difficult to determine whether the family of Nārāyaṇa had anything to do with the Yādavas. It is, however, not impossible that the followers of Nārāyaṇa

1. There is some evidence in favour of the deification of Arjuna and the existence of a sect that worshipped him. It is possible that the conception of Nara as a companion of Nārāyaṇa was based on the interpretation of the word *puruṣa* in the expression Puruṣa-Nārāyaṇa in the sense of *nara*, as well as on the tradition regarding the association of Arjuna with Vāsudeva-Kṛṣṇa.

2. *Op. cit.*, pp. 135, 157.

3. *Op. cit.*, pp. 42-43.

were originally called Pañcarātrika and were later merged into the worshippers of Vāsudeva-Kṛṣṇa. It is also possible to think that the Sātvatas originally worshipped Nārāyaṇa.

We have referred to the Nārāyaṇa-vāṭaka mentioned in the Ghosundi inscription (first century B.C.). A fourth century record from the Guntur District speaks of a *devakula* of *Bhagavat* Nārāyaṇa.[1]

III

The *Mahābhārata* and the Purāṇas usually explain the name Vāsudeva as 'the son of Vasudeva', although sometimes philosophical interpretations are also offered.[2] Bhandarkar[3] draws our attention to the commentaries on the *Aṣṭādhyāyī* and the *Ghaṭa Jātaka* and suggests that Vāsudeva is not a patronymic, but the proper name of the person whose name Kṛṣṇa shows that he belonged to the Kārṣṇāyaṇa-gotra. In his opinion, the Brāhmaṇical *gotra* called Kārṣṇāyaṇa sprang from an ancient sage named Kṛṣṇa with whom Vāsudeva of a Kṣatriya family of the Kārṣṇāyaṇa-gotra was identified at a later date. Although Kṛṣṇa may be a *gotra* name as suggested by the commentator on the *Ghaṭa Jātaka*, later traditions, according to which a son of Vasudeva was called Kṛṣṇa owing to the darkness of his complexion (cf. the names of Kṛṣṇa-Dvaipāyana and Kṛṣṇā-Draupadī), appear to be more reasonable. Patronymics like Vāsudeva as well as metronymics like Gautamīputra (as in the Vākāṭaka family) were often used in ancient India exactly as proper names. Other names like Janārdana, Keśava, etc., later applied to Vāsudeva-Kṛṣṇa, were derived in some cases from his identification with Viṣṇu[4] and Nārāyaṇa, and in others, probably, also from his equation with certain local and tribal gods.

The *Chāndogya Upaniṣad*,[5] supposed to be a pre-Buddhistic work, mentions the sage Kṛṣṇa-Devakīputra (i. e. Kṛṣṇa, son

1. Cf. *Select Inscriptions*, Vol. I, pp. 443 ff.
2. Cf. *Mbh.*, V. 70. 3; XII. 341. 41.
3. *Op. cit.*, pp. 10f.
4. The name or epithet Vāmana is applied to Viṣṇu in the *Śatapatha Brāhmaṇa* (I. 2. 5. 5) and to Kṛṣṇa in the *Mahābhārata* (XII. 43. 12).
5. III. 17. 6.

of Devakī) who was a disciple of the *ṛṣi* Ghora of the Āṅgirasa family. Kṛṣṇa is not called Vāsudeva in this work, probably because the patronymic and metronymic of a person were not generally used together. His identification with Kṛṣṇa who lived on the river Aṁśumatī and is mentioned in the *Ṛgveda* is doubtful; but it cannot be regarded as impossible in vew of the facts that the Aṁśumatī, which flowed through the Kuru country, may be the same as the Yamunā,[1] on the bank of which both the Kuru city Indraprastha and the Śūrasena city Mathurā stood, and that the said section of the *Ṛgveda* may belong to the latest stratum of the work. Some scholars are doubtful as regards the identity of Kṛṣṇa-Devakīputra of the *Chāndogya Upaniṣad* with Kṛṣṇa, son of Devakī by Vasudeva of the Yādava-Sātvata-Vṛṣṇi clan of the Mathurā region, as suggested by the *Mahābhārata* (especially its early stratum)[2] and the Purāṇas as well as by works like the *Ghaṭa Jātaka* and Patañjali's *Mahābhāṣya*. Vāsudeva's association with Saṁkarṣaṇa (Baladeva, son of Vasudeva by Rohiṇī) in pre-Christian epigraphs, as well as such passages of the *Mahābhāṣya* as *Saṅkarṣaṇa-dvitīyasya balaṁ Kṛṣṇasya vardhatām*, seems to support the epic and Purāṇic tradition.[3] The *Mahābhāṣya* also speaks of popular dramatical representation of the life-story of Vāsudeva-Kṛṣṇa with special reference to the *Bali-bandha* and *Kaṁsa-vadha* episodes, and actually quotes passages like *asādhur =mātule Kṛṣṇaḥ* and *jaghāna Kaṁsaṁ kila Vāsudevaḥ*, from a poem on a similar subject.[4] Kṛṣṇa's association with the Yādava-Sātvata-Vṛṣṇis of the Mathurā area seems also to be indicated by the name Kṛṣṇapura (Kleisobora), 'city of Kṛṣṇa', applied to a town in the neighbourhood of Mathurā by Megasthenes in the fourth century B. C. The story of Herakles and Pandaia, known to Megasthenes, points to the antiquity of the tradition regarding

1. The name may have association with the solar rays. In later mythology, Yamunā appears as the daughter of Vivasvat (Sūrya) and sister of Yama to whom is ascribed, from the earliest times, the same father in both Indian and Iranian traditions.

2. Cf. *Gītā*, I. 41, etc.

3. Under Pāṇini, II. 2. 23; Raychaudhuri, *op. cit.*, pp. 73, 105.

4. Cf. Raychaudhuri, *op. cit.*, p. 37.

Kṛṣṇa's connection with the Pāṇḍavas.[1] It has also to be noted that both the *Chāndogya Upaniṣad* and the *Mahābhārata* mention Kṛṣṇa's mother as Devakī which was rather an uncommon name.[2] The Āṅgirasa family, to which the Upaniṣadic Kṛṣṇa's teacher Ghora belonged, was related to the Bhojas, (*RV*, III. 53. 7) who were, like the Vṛṣṇis, a sept of the Yādava clan. In this connection, Raychaudhuri's attempt[3] to trace some of the doctrines enunciated in the *Bhagavad-Gītā*, sung by Vāsudeva-Kṛṣṇa to Arjuna, in the lessons received by Kṛṣṇa-Devakīputra from Ghora Āṅgirasa, according to the *Chāndogya Upaniṣad*, is very interesting. There is, of course, palpable difference between the character of the Upaniṣadic Kṛṣṇa and that of the epic Kṛṣṇa-Vāsudeva; but this may be due to the latter representing a later stage in the development of the Vāsudeva saga. In spite of the difference, the same person can probably be discerned in the two figures. In the *Chāndogya Upaniṣad*, Kṛṣṇa appears in a passage where *tapas*, *dāna*, *ārjava*, *ahiṁsā* and *satya-vacana* are extolled;[4] the same virtues are inculcated by the epic Kṛṣṇa in the *Gītā*[5] as well as in several other passages of the *Mahābhārata*. Just as Ghora deprecates *vidhi-yajña*, in the same way the *Gītā*[6] belittles *dravyamaya-yajña* or material sacrifice. Ghora says that all the actions of the virtuous life of a man constitute a kind of sacrifice to the deities and help him to attain to the God of gods. This seems to be essentially identical with the theory of absolute resignation (i.e. dedication of the results of all actions to God) inculcated in the *Gītā*. While the Upaniṣadic Kṛṣṇa and his teacher were worshippers of the sun, the *Gītā*,[7] attri-

1. The story of Pandaia reminds us of the facts that the Pāṇḍyas had their capital at Mathurā (Madurai) and that their name is derived by Kātyāyana, in a *vārttika*, from *Pāṇḍu*. See below. It is thus possible that the ancestors of the Pāṇḍyas migrated from the north.

2. The occurrence of the word *Acyuta* in the *Chāndogya Upaniṣad* (III. 17. 6) is rather significant, as this appears as an epithet of Kṛṣṇa in the *Mahābhārata*.

3. *Op. cit.*, pp. 57 ff.

4. See III. 17. 4.

5. Cf. *dāna*, *dama*, *yajña*, *svādhyāya*, *tapas*, *ārjava*, *ahiṁsā*, *satya*, etc., in XVI. 1-2.

6. IV. 33.

7. VIII. 9-11.

buted to Kṛṣṇa, emphasized the importance of meditation 'at the last hour' on the 'word which knowers of the Veda call Imperishable' and on 'the sun-coloured being beyond the darkness' as the best means of attaining to the Supreme Being. As both the *Chāndogya Upaniṣad* and the *Gītā* associate essentialy the same doctrines with one and the same person called Kṛṣṇa, son of Devakī, it is quite probable that they were originally learnt by Kṛṣṇa from Ghora, and were later taught by the former to his disciples.[1] But although the teaching of Ghora-Āṅgirasa to Kṛṣṇa appear to be the kernel of the *Gītā*, this work of the later followers of Vāsudevism shows considerable development of the original doctrine.

The Bhāgavata religion, propounded by Vāsudeva, which incorporated the earlier cult of Nārāyaṇa and was the source of later Vaiṣṇavism, was therefore the development of an original sun-cult. In the *Mahābhārata* (XII. 335. 19), the *Sātvata-vidhi* is stated to have been declared in old times by the sun. The *Gītā* (IV. 1) says that the Bhāgavata doctrine was first taught by the Lord to the sun, then by the sun to Manu, and ultimately by Manu to Ikṣvāku.

At a later date a pastoral character was attributed to Kṛṣṇa. In the *Harivaṁśa* (a supplement to the *Mahābhārata*) and the Purāṇas (e.g. *Viṣṇu*, *Bhāgavata*, etc.) are to be found stories about his tender babyhood and wanton childhood as well as—conspicuously in some later works—about the dalliances of his youth. The popularity of the cowherd god can be gathered from the name of the Pallava king Viṣṇugopa (fourth century A.D.) and literary evidence from the third or fourth century A.D. Hopkins[2] believes that it was not till Kṛṣṇa became a very great, if not the greatest, god and condescended to be born in low life that such tales about his youthful performances began to grow. The stories regarding the early life of the pastoral Kṛṣṇa probably developed partly out of the Vedic legends about Viṣṇu, called *gopā* and *gopāla* in the *Ṛgveda*[3] and *govinda* and *dāmodara* in the *Baudhāyana Dharmasūtra*.[4] But there appear to be other factors

1. For comments on these views of Rayhcaudhuri, see De, *IHQ*, Vol. XVIII, pp. 297 ff.
2. *Op. cit.*, p. 467.
3. *Vedic Index*, Vol. I, p. 238.
4. II. 5. 24.

that also contributed to the development of the mythology of the cowherd Kṛṣṇa. The Yamunā valley was possibly conspicuous for its cows as early as the age of the *Ṛgveda*,[1] and a Vārṣṇa (i. e. a member of the Vṛṣṇi clan) named Gobala (literally, 'one strong in the wealth of cows') is known from the *Taittirīya Saṁhitā*[2] and the *Jaiminīya Upaniṣad Brāhmaṇa*.[3] It is thus probable that the Yādava-Sātvata-Vṛṣṇi people possessed large herds of cattle as did their neighbours, the Matsyas (cf. the epic reference to Virāṭa's *gogṛhas*). Most of the stories about Kṛṣṇa's early life, especially the late tales about his questionable relation with the cowherd women,[4] appear, however, to have been principally due to his identification with certain gods worshipped by the Ābhīras and other allied peoples. It may be noted in this connection that the god Śiva was similarly brought into relation with Koch girls in some late mediaeval works (especially Tantras) of Bengal, apparently as a result of his identification with a tribal god of the Hinduized Koch people.[5]

According to Barth[6] and Hopkins,[7] Kṛṣṇa was not a human being, but a popular divinity whose identification with Viṣṇu resulted in the growth of sectarian Vaiṣṇavism. Both the scholars admit the possibility of his solar association; but the latter considers Kṛṣṇa to be the tribal god of the

1. Raychaudhuri, *op. cit.*, p. 46.
2. III. II.9.3.
3. I. 6. 1.
4. A Pabhosa inscription (*Ep. Ind.*, Vol. II, p. 482) of the seventh or eighth century refers to a maker of images of Śrī-Kṛṣṇa and the milkmaids. One of the earliest extant poetical compositions (cf. quotations in the *Mahābhāṣya* from a work on the *Kaṁsavadha* episode) on Kṛṣṇa's early life is the *Bālacarita* attributed to Bhāsa who was a predecessor of Kālidāsa (c. 400 A.D.). This work speaks of Dāmodara and Saṅkarṣaṇa as *Vṛṣṇikumāra*, of Kaṁsa, king of Mathurā, as *Śauraseni-māta*, 'one whose mother is a Śūrasena girl', and of Vasudeva as *Yādavī-māta*. It also refers to Dāmodara's foster-parents, Nanda-gopa and Yaśodā or Nanda-gopī, and to his relations with the cowherds, but not to his amorous ecstasies. A Mathurā sculpture representing Vasudeva as crossing the Yamunā with baby Kṛṣṇa in a basket has been assigned to the age of the Kuṣāṇas (*Arch. Surv. Ind.*, Annual Report, 1925-26, pp. 283-84, Plate LXIII V, Fig. c).
5. Cf. *Jour. Roy. As. Soc. Beng.*, Letters, Vol. XIV, p. 105.
6. *Religions of India*, pp. 166 ff.
7. *Op. cit.*, pp. 466 ff., 488.

Pāṇḍavas, supposed to be an aboriginal people, while the former regards him to be the *kula-devatā* or ethnic god of some powerful confederation of Rajput clans.[1] But the theory of Kṛṣṇa's solar character has been rightly dismissed by Keith[2] with the remark that 'the "dark sun" requires more explanation than it seems likely to receive'. Macnicol[3] and Keith[4] think that the conception of Kṛṣṇa who is believed to appear in the *Mahābhāṣya* in a 'vegetation masque', contending with Kaṁsa for the possession of the sun, developed out of one of the vegetation deities extensively worshipped in all parts of the world. But the evidence discussed above seems to bear testimony to the human character of Kṛṣṇa, who was gradually associated with certain popular cults and festivals. The suggestion that Kṛṣṇa is a myth is unconvincing. It reminds us of similar attempts to prove that the Buddha and Christ are imaginary figures.

IV

The method of salvation taught in the *Gītā* is that a man should live a life of actions without hankering after their results which should be dedicated to God. This is referred to as the Ekāntika Dharma in the Nārāyaṇīya section in the Śānti-parvan of the *Mahābhārata*. Chapter I of the work is introductory, while in the following five chapters the process of *Karma-yoga* (i.e. to do action without regard to results, having surrendered oneself to God), which leads to the attainment of freedom from passions, is described. In the next six chapters *Bhakti-yoga* (i.e. loving adoration of God) is delineated, while the remaining chapters sum up the discussion. Some of the teachings of the *Gītā* are paraphrased below.

By devoted performance of acts without attachment to other objects, man gets his desires uprooted, and finally attains inflexibility of will and complete serenity of soul. He obtains quiescence in Brahman (Supreme Spirit) at the time of death (II. 71-72).

1. Barth, *op. cit.*, p. 168.
2. *Journ. Roy. As. Soc.*, 1908, p. 171.
3. *Indian Theism*, pp. 37-38.
4. *Journ. Roy. As. Soc.*, 1915, p. 841.

By knowing God man is purified, has his passions destroyed, and attains to the condition of God. The highest knowledge, by means of which man sees all things in himself and in God, makes man free from all sins and destroys the polluting effect of his actions. It makes man a totally free spirit (IV. 35-38).

Both *sannyāsa* (renunciation of work when Self is realized) and *Karma-yoga* (performance of work, dedicated to God, before the dawn of Self-knowledge) lead men to the same goal (V. 2). By means of *yoga*, man obtains *jñāna* when all things are seen in the same light, and Brahman is realized (VI. 29). The best *yogin* regards all as himself in matters of happiness and misery. He becomes absorbed in God in peace (VI. 31-32).

God is the source and the resting place of the world, and there is nothing higher than He (VII. 6-7). When man takes refuge in Him, he gets rid of God's *māyā* consisting of the three *guṇas* or qualities and conditions resulting from them (VII. 14).

God is easily attained by a man who meditates on Him with concentration of mind and absolute devotion, especially at the time of death. A man who reaches God is freed from subjection to transmigration (VIII. 10, 15).

Men worshipping various deities are also worshippers of God; but they do not get freedom from rebirth (IX. 23-24). A person who resorts to God attains the highest place and obtains perfect peace (IX. 31-32).

God is the soul dwelling in the heart of man. He is the beginning, the middle and the end of all beings (X. 20). Persons with their souls centered on God enlighten one another about Him and become happy (X. 9).

The universe is only a fractional aspect of God (X.42).

A man should fix his mind on God and concentrate his will on Him; if this is not possible, he should obtain God by constant remembrance; if this also is not possible, he should perform deeds for God's sake; if even this is not possible, he should give up desire for the results of his deeds (XII. 8-11).

The virtues especially dear to God are absence of hatred, friendship for all, kindness, humility, indifference to praise and censure, etc. (XII. 13-19).

The thing to be known is *Parabrahman* that has no beginning or end, is neither existent nor non-existent; that has hands and feet, head and face, and eyes and ears everywhere, and that pervades all. The Supreme Spirit dwelling in the body is devoid of qualities and is unchangeable. It does not do any deed and is not contaminated (XIII. 12-14, 31).

The man who resorts to God by *Bhakti-yoga* becomes immortal by being free from the three qualities (*guṇa*) that cause bondage (XIV. 26); he comes to possess a serene mood in which pleasure and pain are alike, and agreeable and disagreeable things have no difference (XIV. 24).

There are two categories of beings in the world, of which one (viz. the body-mind complex) changes, but the other (viz. the soul) is unchangeable. There is also the highest Soul which is *Paramātman*, i. e. God, the support of the three worlds (XV. 16-17).

There are two classes of men, viz., good and bad. The second class includes men who do not care for God or morality and follow doctrines other than the one preached in the *Gītā* (XVI. 6ff.). Desire, anger, and greed constitute the three roads to hell and lead to spiritual death (XVI. 21).

Men may be divided into three classes, according to the three elements (*guṇa*), as good, active and ignorant. Of these three classes, the first worships gods, the second evil spirits, and the third ghosts and spectres (XVII. 2, 4). This third class performs activities leading to attenuation (or mortification) of the elements of the body wherein God dwells (XVII.6).

True renunciation is attained not by complete inactivity, but by giving up actions arising from desires and by abandoning the fruits of actions. Worship, charity and austerity lead to purity of the soul and should not therefore be given up. Duty must be done without thinking of the result (XVIII. 1, 5-6). A person should surrender himself absolutely to God who will then free him from all sins (XVIII. 66).

V

The *Vyūha* doctrine[1] is one of the principal tenets of the old Pañcarātra system, which was absorbed in the Bhāgavata

1. The *Mahābhāṣya* (on Pāṇini, VI. 3. 6) alludes to the doctrine in the passage *Janārdanas=tv=ātma-caturtha eva*.

religion, as well as of the later Śrī-Vaiṣṇava philosophy. According to this doctrine, Lord Vāsudeva in his *para* aspect is the highest object of *bhakti*. He created from himself the *vyūha* (phase of conditioned spirit) Saṅkarṣaṇa and also Prakṛti (the indiscrete primal matter of the Sāṅkhya). From the association of Saṅkarṣaṇa and Prakṛti arose the *vyūha* Pradyumna and also *manas* (*buddhi* or intelligence of the Sāṅkhya). From the combination of Pradyumna and *manas* sprang the *vyūha* Aniruddha as also *ahaṅkāra* (consciousness), and from the association of Aniruddha and *ahaṅkāra* arose the *mahābhūtas* (elements with their qualities) and the god Brahman who made out of those elements the earth and all that it contains. While Vāsudeva alone possesses the six ideal *guṇas* or qualities, viz., *jñāna*, *bala*, *vīrya*, *aiśvarya*, *śakti* and *tejas*, each one of his three emanations possesses only two of the said *guṇas* in turn.[1] This philosophical interpretation of the relation of Vāsudeva with the other deified heroes of the Vṛṣṇi clan is apparently a later development. The *Gītā*, the earliest religious text of the Bhāgavatas, does not refer to the *vyūhas*, although they are referred to in several other (presumably late) sections of the *Mahābhārata* (e.g. a section of the Bhīṣma-parvan, the Nārāyaṇīya section of the Śānti-parvan, etc.). But these references do not give a consistent account of the *vyūhas*. Bhandarkar[2] thinks that, out of the five *prakṛtis* of Vāsudeva (viz. the five elements, mind, *buddhi*, egoism and *jīva*) as mentioned in the *Gītā*, *jīva*, mind and egoism were later on personified into the *vyūhas* Saṅkarṣaṇa, Pradyumna and Aniruddha. The *vyūha* doctrine, as we have seen, may be alluded to in the *Mahābhāṣya* passage *Janārdanas=tv=ātma-caturtha eva*, quoted apparently from an unknown poem on the life of Vāsudeva-Kṛṣṇa.

The Morā (seven miles west of Mathurā) inscription of the first century A.D. speaks of *bhagavatāṁ Vṛṣṇīnāṁ pañca-vīrāṇāṁ pratimāḥ*, 'the images of the group of five divine heroes of the Vṛṣṇi family.'[3] The *Vāyu Purāṇa*[4] mentions the five

1. Schrader, *Introduction to the Pañcarātra and the Ahirbudhnya Saṁhitā*, pp. 32-35. For the sub-*vyūhas*, see *ibid*., p. 41.
2. *Op. cit*., pp. 12f.
3. *Proc. Ind. Hist. Cong*., Madras, 1944, pp. 82-90; Banerjea, *Development of Hindu Iconography*, pp. 114-15.
4. 97. 1-2.

vaṁśa-vīras of the Vṛṣṇis, and they were Saṅkarṣaṇa, Vāsudeva, Pradyumna, Sāmba and Aniruddha. There can hardly be any doubt that the Vṛṣṇi heroes were apotheosized and worshipped with the title *bhagavat* in the Mathurā region about the beginning of the Christian era, probably by people associated with the old Yādava-Sātvata-Vṛṣṇi clan. In the *Viṣṇudharmottara*, a work mentioned by Al-Bīrūnī (1030 A.D.) and probably used by Brahmagupta (628 A.D.), there are rules for the construction of images of various divinities related to the Bhāgavata cult. These include the five Vṛṣṇi heroes mentioned above. Varāhamihira's *Bṛhatsaṁhitā*[1] (sixth century) also contains details for the making of the images of Viṣṇu (Vāsudeva), Baladeva (Saṅkarṣaṇa), Sāmba and Pradyumna; but it does not mention Aniruddha. The preference of Sāmba to Aniruddha exhibited in this work may point to the fact that its author Varāhamihira belonged to the community of the sun-worshipping Maga-Brāhmaṇas (hailing originally from Persia) who appear to have held Sāmba in special esteem. Sāmba, however, soon fell in the estimation of the Bhāgavatas. This was probably because he was represented as the champion of solar worship in India and was sometimes identified with the Sun-god himself. Banerjea suggests that all the Vṛṣṇi heroes (i. e. the four *vyūhas* together with Sāmba) were independently worshipped. He is inclined to identify Sāmba with certain sculptured figures hailing from the Mathurā area. The custom of erecting *dhvajas* or votive columns in honour of different sectarian deities, especially near their temples, was popular in ancient India; and Banerjea thinks that the fragmentary capitals with the figures of Garuḍa, *Tāla* (fan-falm) and *Makara* (crocodile), found at Besnagar and Pawaya, point to the existence of the *dhvajas* and shrines respectively of the deities Vāsudeva, Saṅkarṣaṇa, and Pradyumna.[2] Certain early coins, including a few from Taxila, are supposed by the same scholar to bear the representation of columns with fan-palm capitals.[3] The earliest sculpture representing Balarāma comes from Mathurā and is now preserved in the Lucknow Museum.

1. 57. 31-40.
2. Cf. *Proc. Ind. Hist. Cong.*, *loc. cit.*
3. Banerjea, *op. cit.*, p. 144.

On stylistic grounds it has been assigned to the second century B.C., although it may actually belong to the early Kuṣāṇa age.

The *catur-vyūha* doctrine was undoubtedly an outcome of the deification of several Vṛṣṇi-vīras besides Vāsudeva. But the non-mention of Pradyumna and Aniruddha along with Saṅkarṣaṇa and Vāsudeva in the Ghosundi and Nanaghat inscriptions, both belonging to the first century B. C., appears to suggest that the independent worship of the third and fourth *vyūhas*, who are not known to have been great religious teachers, was perhaps limited to the Vṛṣṇi circle. Their apotheosis may have been influenced partly by the practice, prevalent in the Mathurā region, of the installation of images of deceased ancestors in *devakulas*, as is indicated by an inscriptions[1] of Huviṣka. Saṅkarṣaṇa, also called Baladeva, Balarāma and Rāma, however, appears to have been a more important figure and his independent worship spread over a wide area before the birth of Christ. The Ghosundi inscription, as we have seen, calls him *bhagavat* and *sarveśvara* jointly with Vāsudeva. It is also interesting to note that, both in the Ghosundi and Nanaghat records, Vāsudeva is mentioned after Saṅkarṣaṇa, apparently because he was the younger of the two brothers, and that these records do not give more prominence to Vāsudeva, as is done in the works on the *vyūha* doctrine. In the *Mahābhārata*, Saṅkarṣaṇa is represented as specially honoured by the Kuru king Duryodhana. The *Kauṭilīya Arthaśāstra*[2] speaks of a class of ascetics who had shaven heads or braided hair and adored Saṅkarṣaṇa as their *devatā*. The votaries of Baladeva are also mentioned side by side with those of Vāsudeva in the Buddhist *Niddesa* works. In the Jain *Aupapātikasūtra*,[3] mention is made not only of the votaries of Baladeva and Vāsudeva, but also of Balarāma who is referred to as one of the eight renowned Kṣatriya teachers. Independent worship of Saṅkarṣaṇa, before the birth of Christ, is belived to be suggested by his image in the Lucknow Museum referred to above. In epic and Purāṇic traditions, Saṅkarṣaṇa is sometimes represented

1. *Journ. Roy. As. Soc.*, 1924, p. 402. For some references to the images of later kings, cf. Raychaudhuri, *Pol. Hist. Anc. Ind.*, 1938, p. 432, note. Cf. the *Pratimā-nāṭaka*, Act. III, attributed to Bhāsa.
2. XIII. iii.
3. Ed. Leumann, pp. 61, 69-70.

as the incarnation of Śeṣa or Anantanāga.[1] This seems to point to his identification with some tribal god of the Nāgas. The Kālīya-nāga episode in the Kṛṣṇa saga probably suggests the victory of Bhāgavatism over the tribal cult of the Nāgas who are known to have ruled in the Mathurā area about the 3rd-4th century A.D. In these traditions, Saṅkarṣaṇa figures as a great helper in the deeds of valour of his younger step-brother Kṛṣṇa, especially in the latter's struggle with Kaṁsa. The pastoral association of Saṅkarṣaṇa may have come partly from his relations with Kṛṣṇa and partly also from his identification with some tribal god or gods. In the Bhīṣma-parvan of the *Mahābhārata* and the *Ahirbudhnya Saṁhitā*, he is represented as an exponent of the Sātvata or Pañcarātra system. The Nārāyaṇīya section of the Śānti-parvan regards Vāsudeva as identical with the *Param-ātman* (Supreme Soul) and Saṅkarṣaṇa with the *Jīv-ātman* (individual soul). In later times the devotees of Saṅkarṣaṇa appear to have merged themselves in those of Vāsudeva. The independent worship of the last two *vyūhas*, viz. Pradyumna and Aniruddha, gradually declined. Even the worship of Saṅkarṣaṇa lost its popularity owing to the increasing enthusiasm for the worship of some of the *Avatāras* of Viṣṇu since the age of the Imperial Guptas.

VI

The Ājīvikas were the followers of a great champion of fatalism named Maṣkarīputra Gośāla who flourished, like the Buddha and Mahāvīra, in the sixth century B.C. Utpala (tenth century), while commenting on Varāhamihira's *Bṛhajjātaka*, seems to include the Ājīvikas amongst the *Nārāyaṇ-āśrita* (i.e. devotees of Nārāyaṇa or Viṣṇu),[2] although this has been doubted by some scholars. In later days the Ājīvikas appear to have mostly merged into the followers of Vāsudeva.

Jainism shares the doctrine of *ahiṁsā* with Bhāgavatism and Buddhism, and is permeated with the influence of Hinduism, especially of the Kṛṣṇa cult. The Jains regard Vāsudeva and Baladeva as two of their sixty-three *śalākā-puruṣas* who

1. Śeṣa and Ananta are often distinguished in literature.
2. Cf. *Ind. Ant.*, 1912, pp. 266f., in this connection.

are believed to be directors of the course of the world. The legends of Mahāvīra's birth as known from Jain mythology, again, appear to be modelled on those of Kṛṣṇa's birth. The later conception of the twenty-four forms of Viṣṇu, on the other hand, was very probably imitated from that of the twenty-four Jain Tīrthaṅkaras. It may be noted that the Jain Tīrthaṅkara Ṛṣabha was regarded by some Bhāgavatas[1] as an *Avatāra* of Viṣṇu.

Senart and Poussin suggest[2] that the worshippers of Nārāyaṇa exerted considerable influence on the making of the Buddhist doctrine from its very inception. The theory can hardly be accepted in its entirety, because the early centres of influence of the two creeds were different. It must be admitted, however, that the importance of *ahiṁsā* is recognized by both the Bhāgavatas and the Buddhists as by the Jains. There is also an obvious resemblance between the *Dharamcakra* of the Buddhists and Viṣṇu's *Sudarśana-cakra*. The adoration of the Buddha's footprints may have been borrowed from the conception of Viṣṇu's *pada*, a term, as already shown above, of equivocal import. The full development of the *Avatāra-vāda*, on the other hand, was probably influenced by the Buddhist conception of the former Buddhas who are known to have been worshipped in their own *stūpas* as early as the age of Aśoka (third century B.C.). The absorption of a large number of Buddhists into the fold of the Vaiṣṇavas in the Gupta and post-Gupta periods seems to be suggested by the recognition of the Buddha as one of Viṣṇu's *Avatāras* before the mediaeval age.

According to some scholars, much of Bhāgavatism, including the idea of *bhakti*, was borrowed from Christianity. It has been suggested that Kṛṣṇa himself was an adaptation of Christ.[3] We should, however, remember that the origin of *bhakti* in India, the deification and worship of Vāsudeva and his identification with Kṛṣṇa are all pre-Christian conceptions. Much has been made of the resemblance between the

1. See below.

2. Cf. Macnicol, *Indian Theism*, pp. 63, 241-48.

3. Cf. Seal, *Comparative Studies in Vaishnavism and Christianity*, pp. 30 ff.; also *Asiatic Researches*, Vol. I, pp. 274 ff.; *Ind. Ant.*, 1873, pp. 285 ff.; 1874, pp. 21 ff.; etc.

stories about the child Kṛṣṇa and the child Christ. Hopkins[1] thinks that the coincidences are direct importations from Christian lands to India and points to the late date of the development of the Kṛṣṇa legends. But the fact that the *Mahābhāṣya* quotes passages from a *kāvya* on the *Kaṁsa-vadha* episode may suggest a pre-Christian origin of the Kṛṣṇa saga. Kṛṣṇa's cowherd association was widely known before the rise of the Imperial Guptas in the fourth century A.D. It has been shown, on the other hand, that the adoration of Virgin Mary is not much earlier than the fifth century. Kennedy[2] rightly points out, 'there is no Christian representation of the suckling mother before the twelfth century; [but] there is a much earlier Hindu one.' The influence of Christianity on Vaiṣṇavism cannot be proved satisfactorily with the evidence at our disposal. Bhandarkar's theory[3] that the Ābhīras were responsible for bringing Christian legends to India and introducing them into the Kṛṣṇa saga is not supported by any evidence.

1. *Op. cit.*, p. 430.
2. *Journ. Roy. As. Soc.*, 1907, p. 484.
3. *Ind. Ant.*, 1912, p. 15.

CHAPTER III

VAIṢṆAVISM IN THE GUPTA AND POST-GUPTA AGES

I

In the fourth century A.D., the Guptas established an empire comprising the major part of Northern India and extended their influence over the peninsula of the Deccan. They were devotees of Viṣṇu as is suggested by their adoption of Garuḍa as the distinguishing emblem of the family. The coins of the Gupta emperors bear the representation of their Garuḍa standard. The Allahabad pillar inscription[1] refers to the *garutmad-aṅka* (Garuḍa seal) of Samudragupta and represents him actually as the god Viṣṇu in human form. Samudragupta is described as equal to the four *Lokapālas*, viz., Kubera, Varuṇa, Indra, and Yama, and also as 'one who is a mortal only in celebrating the observances of mankind, but is otherwise a god dwelling on the earth'. This no doubt refers to the conception of a divine king similar to that found in the *Manusmṛti*.[2] But more important is another passage of the same record in which Samudragupta is represented as identical with the *Acintya-puruṣa* or Inscrutable Being, i. e. Viṣṇu, who is 'the cause of the prosperity of the pious and the destruction of the wicked.'[3] It is quite clear that this passage is an echo of a verse of the *Gītā*[4] which refers to the descent of God on the earth, in physical form, for protecting the pious and destroying the sinners.

Though Samudragupta was a Vaiṣṇava, he was apparently not a Bhāgavata. This is indicated by the fact that his successors apply the epithet *paramabhāgavata* only to themselves and not to that king.[5] Although in some cases the word *bhāga-*

1. *Select Inscriptions*, Vol. I, pp. 254 ff.
2. VII. 4-8.
3. *Select Inscriptions*, Vol. I, 2nd ed., p. 266—*sāddhv-asādh-ūdaya-pralaya-hetu-puruṣasy=ācintyasya*.
4. IV. 8.
5. Cf. *Bhāratiya Vidyā*, Vol. VIII, pp. 109-11; *Ep. Ind.*, Vol. XXVI, pp. 318 ff.

vata no doubt implies Viṣṇu-worshippers in general,[1] it was sometimes also used in the sense of a particular sect of the Vaiṣṇavas. Bāṇa (seventh century) in his *Harṣacarita*[2] mentions the Bhāgavata and the Pāñcarātrika separately in a list of different religious sects. A late commentator explains these two expressions as *Viṣṇu-bhakta* and *Vaiṣṇava-bheda* respectively. If Bāṇa and the commentator are believed to have taken *Bhāgavata* in the sense of Viṣṇu-worshippers in general and *Pāñcarātrika* as one of their sects, we have to assume the existence of sects among the Vaiṣṇavas at least from the seventh century. A study of the early history of Vaiṣṇavism makes it clear that the growth of sectarian or doctrinal difference among the early worshippers of Viṣṇu was inevitable. We have to remember that the Vaiṣṇavas effected a synthesis of different elements, among which prominent mention should be made of the worshippers of various divinities such as the Vedic Viṣṇu, the deified ancient sage Nārāyaṇa, and the deified Vṛṣṇi heroes Vāsudeva and Baladeva-Saṅkarṣaṇa. The followers of Arjuna, of the Vṛṣṇi heroes Pradyumna, Aniruddha and Sāmba, of the *Avatāras* including the Buddha before their identification with Viṣṇu, and of such tribal gods as those of the Ābhīras may be included in the above list. The fact that the early Vaiṣṇavas were a combination of different religious sects no doubt points to the existence of some sort of original sectarian difference among them. But it is impossible to determine the nature of such difference in the present state of insufficient information. In a narrow sense, Bhāgavatism may have indicated the worship of Vāsudeva as Viṣṇu, originally advocated by the Vṛṣṇi people or a section of them. Samudragupta therefore probably followed some other form of early Vaiṣṇavism like the original worshippers of the Vedic Viṣṇu and of the deified sage Nārāyaṇa who was first identified with Viṣṇu and later with Vāsudeva.

From the days of Samudragupta's son Candragupta II (376-414 A.D.), the Gupta emperors were the most influential advocates of the Bhāgavata form of Vaiṣṇavism. Their patronage seems to have been one of the causes of the great popu-

1. Cf. *Bṛhatsaṁhitā*, 60. 19.
2. Ed. Parab, pp. 236-37 (Ch. VIII).

larity of this creed all over the country from the fifth century A.D. The title *parama-bhāgavata* (in some cases *parama-vaiṣṇava* or *parama-daivata*)[1] is noticed from this time in various royal families in different parts of India. On the obverse of the *Cakravikrama* type of the coins of Candragupta II, the king is represented as receiving a gift from the god Viṣṇu.[2]

II

An important aspect of the Bhāgavata religion of the Gupta age was the popularity of the worship of the *Avatāras*, i.e. descents or incarnations of Viṣṇu. The origin of the *Avatāra* conception may be traced in the later Vedic literature. Even in the *Ṛgveda*,[3] we have reference to Viṣṇu's three steps taken for, according to some, 'the man in distress'. The conception of the Dwarf (Vāmana), Fish (Matsya), and Tortoise (Kūrma) *Avatāras*, not yet associated with that god, are found in the *Śatapatha* and other *Brāhmaṇas*. There is a story in the *Śatapatha Brāhmaṇa*,[4] which speaks of the contention between the gods and demons for a place of sacrifice. The latter are stated to have agreed to concede as much land as was equal to the size of a dwarf. Viṣṇu, the dwarf, was then made to lie down. But he grew so big as to encompass the whole earth which consequently passed on to the gods. The same Brāhmaṇa also says how, 'having assumed the form of a tortoise, Prajāpati created offspring', and 'in the form of a boar, he (Prajāpati) raised the earth from the bottom of the ocean.'[5] According to the late *Taittirīya Āraṇyaka*,[6] the earth was raised from the waters by a black boar with a hundred arms. The same work also alludes to the *Nṛsiṁha* or Man-lion. The story of the Great Deluge in the *Śatapatha Brāhmaṇa*[7] represents

1. *Parama-daivata* really means 'devoted to the gods'. See *Indian Studies Past and Present*, Vol. V, No. 1 (October-December, 1963), pp. 89ff.
2. *Journ. Num. Soc. Ind.*, Vol. X, p. 104.
3. VI. 49. 13.
4. I. 2. 5.
5. XIV. 1. 2; cf. *Taittiriya Saṁhitā*, VII. 1. 5; *Taittiriya Brāhamaṇa*, I. 1. 3.
6. X. I. 6.
7. I. 8. 18; *Vedic Index*, Vol. II, p. 130.

the fish that towed Manu's vessel into safety as a form of Prajāpati Brahman, and this is sometimes supported by epic and Purāṇic tradition. In later mythology, however, the function of the Boar, Fish, and Tortoise forms of Prajāpati Brahman is attributed to Viṣṇu, the most benevolent of the gods. In the *Gītā* and some other sections of the *Mahābhārata*, Viṣṇu is represented as an ideal divinity and an almighty saviour of mankind, as delighting in both moral goodness and ritualistic purity, and as incarnating himself from time to time in human or animal form for the maintenance of the standard of righteousness in the world.[1] The theory of *Avatāra*, however, presents only a stage of development in the *Mahābhārata*, as the earlier sections of the epic contain no list of the incarnations.

Traditions as to the number of *Avatāras* varied and their later lists, though the usual number, i.e. ten, is generally adhered to therein, very often offer different names. But the Purānic verse enumerating Matsya, Kūrma, Varāha, Narasiṁha, Vāmana, the three Rāmas, Buddha, and Kalki as the ten *Avatāras*, almost universally recognized since the mediaeval period, is found in a Māmallapuram inscription of about the eighth century A.D.[2] The *Avatāra* theory, which must have undergone several stages of evolution, appears to be based on old tales about strange animals exhibiting mysterious powers of helpfulness.[3] Some of them, however, had originally little to do with Viṣṇu. As already stated, the Buddhist conception of the former Buddhas may have influenced the development of the conception.

A passage of the late Nārāyaṇīya section of the *Mahā-*

1. The idea of the *Gītā* (IV. 7-8) that God manifests Himself in all ages for the protection of the pious, for the destruction of the wicked, and for the establishment of religious order seems to have a universal approach. The attempt appears to be to regard all religious teachers of the world as manifestations of God Himself.

2. *Mem. Arch. Surv. Ind.*, No. 26, p. 5.

3. Cf. the conception of Dakṣiṇarāya, the tiger-divinity of the Sundarbans. Stories of mysterious helpers living in the waters of certain *bils* (lakes) are still current in rural Bengal; cf. *Journ. Roy. As. Soc. Beng.*, Vol. XV, p. 106.

bhārata[1] mentions only four *Avatāras*, viz., Boar, Dwarf, Man-lion, and Man (i.e. Vāsudeva-Kṛṣṇa). Another passage of the same section[2] adds the deified heroes Rāma-Bhārgava and Rāma-Dāśarathi to the list making a total of six *Avatāras*, while in a third passage[3] a list of ten incarnations is offered, by adding, to the above six, Haṁsa, Kūrma, Matsya and Kalki (or Kalkin). The *Matsya Purāṇa*,[4] which also gives a list of ten incarnations, states that there were three divine *Avatāras*, viz., Nārāyaṇa, Narasiṁha, and Vāmana, besides seven human *Avatāras*, viz., Dattātreya, Māndhātṛ, Rāma-Jāmadagnya, Rāma-Dāśarathi, Veda-Vyāsa, Buddha, and Kalki. The above section also occurs in the *Vāyu Purāṇa*;[5] but there the name of Kṛṣṇa replaces that of the Buddha. The *Harivaṁśa*[6] quotes another list of ten incarnations which omits Matsya, Kūrma, one of the Rāmas and the Buddha to make room for Pauṣkaraka, Datta (Dattātreya), Keśava (Kṛṣṇa) and Vyāsa.[7] There are no less than four lists of the *Avatāras* in the *Bhāgavata Purāṇa*;[8] but they are different from one another. One of these lists[9] admits that the incarnations are really innumerable (cf. the *Avatāra* theory of the *Gītā*), but mentions Brahman, Varāha, Nārada, Nara and Nārāyaṇa, the philosopher Kapila, Dattātreya, Yajña, the Jain Tīrthaṅkara Ṛṣabha, the ancient king Pṛthu, Matsya, Kūrma, the physician Dhanvantari, Mohinī, Narasiṁha, Vāmana, Rāma-Jāmadagnya, Veda-Vyāsa, Rāma-Dāśarathi, Rāma Haladhara, Kṛṣṇa, the Buddha and Kalki. The *Agni Purāṇa*[10] states that the incarnations including the past and future ones

1. XII. 349. 37.
2. 339. 77-99.
3. *Loc. cit.*, 104.
4. 57. 237-48.
5. 98. 71-104.
6. I. 41. Cf. also *Brahma Purāṇa*, Ch. 213.
7. Rāma and the Buddha are represented as *Avatāras* in a Vaiṣṇava temple of about the seventh century at Sirpur in the Raipur District. The figures of Narasiṁha, Vāmana, Varāha, and Kṛṣṇa (holding the Govardhana over the cow-settlement) are found in the Daśāvatāra temple at Ellora attributed to the eighth century. Some of the *Avatāras* are also represented in the Pallava temple at Māmallapuram.
8. I. 3; II. 7; VI. 8; XI. 4.
9. I. 3.
10. Chs. 2-16; cf. *Varāha Purāṇa*, Chs. 39-48.

are really innumerable; but describes only ten *Avatāras* including the Buddha and Kalki, while the *Garuḍa Purāṇa*[1] mentions no less than nineteen *Avatāras* (called *mūrtis*), viz., Matsya, Trivikrama, Vāmana, Narasiṁha, Rāma, Varāha, Nārāyaṇa, Kapila, Datta, Hayagrīva, Makaradhvaja, Nārada, Kūrma, Dhānvantari, Śeṣa, Yajña, Vyāsa, the Buddha and Kalki. The Pañcarātra work *Ahirbudhnya Saṁhitā*,[2] which may be assigned to a date earlier than the eighth century, mentions thirtynine *vibhavas* or manifestations of the Supreme Being, which include almost all the well-known *Avatāras*, viz., Ekaśṛṅga-tanu (i.e. Matsya), Vihaṅgama (i.e. Haṁsa), Kamaṭheśvara (i.e. Kūrma), Varāha, Narasiṁha, Vāmanadeha, Paraśurāma (i.e. Rāma-Jāmadagnya), Rāma Dhanurdhara (i. e. Rāma-Dāśarathi), Ananta (i.e. Rāma Haladhara), Kalki and Kṛṣṇa. In other early Pañcarātra works like the *Viṣvaksena Saṁhitā*, the Buddha, Arjuna and others are included in the list of secondary *Avatāras*. The Buddha is mentioned as one of the ten *Avatāras* in the *Daśāvatāracarita* of Kṣemendra (c. 1050 A.D.) of Kashmir and in the *Gītagovinda* of Jayadeva (c. 1200 A.D.) of Eastern India, and also, as we have seen above, he is mentioned as an *Avatāra* in a Purāṇic verse quoted in an eighth century inscription of the Tamil country. Jayadeva eulogizes Kṛṣṇa as Viṣṇu himself and sings in praise of his ten *Avatāras*, viz., Fish, Tortoise, Boar, Man-lion, Dwarf, Rāma-Bhārgava, Rāma-Dāśarathi, Rāma Haladhara, the Buddha and Kalki. This list came to be regarded as the most authentic since the early mediaeval period, though there was still some difference of opinion in regard to the position of Kṛṣṇa. The Belāva (Dacca District, East Bengal) inscription of c. 1125 A.D., which belongs to a *paramavaiṣṇava* ruler of East Bengal, mentions Kṛṣṇa as *gopī-śata-kelikāra* and *Mahābhārata-sūtradhāra* and also as *aṁśakṛt-āvatāra*, i.e., a partial incarnation.[3] But

1. I. 202.

2. Schrader, *Introduction to the Pañcarātra and the Ahirbudhnya Saṁhitā*, p. 42. For the origin of the *Avatāras* out of the *vyūhas*, as in the *Viṣvaksena Saṁhitā* and the *Pādma Tantra*, see *ibid.*, p. 48.

3. Later Vaiṣṇava literature recognized three kinds of *Avatāras*, viz. (1) complete incarnation (*pūrṇāvatāra*), (2) incarnation of a portion of the power of a divine being called *aṁśāvatāra*, and (3) partial incarnation of

an Ajmer inscription[1] of about the same age mentions Kṛṣṇa as the eighth among the ten *Avatāras* of Viṣṇu.

The popularity of the worship of several *Avatāras* is attested by the Indian epigraphic records of the period between the fourth and the eighth century A.D. The name Matsyagupta (literally, 'protected by the Fish') occurring in an inscription[2] of 101 A.D. seems to indicate the popularity of the Fish-god before the rise of the Guptas, although he may or may not have been identified with Viṣṇu at that date.

The worship of Paraśurāma in Western India is indicated by another early record of the second century A.D.; but his being conceived as an *Avatāra* of Viṣṇu does not seem to be so early. An inscription[3] of Śaka Ṛṣabhadatta at Nasik mentions Rāmatīrtha which is known from the *Mahābhārata*[4] to have been the holy abode of Rāma-Jāmadagnya situated in the suburbs of Sūrpāraka (modern Sopara in the Thana District of Maharashtra), not far to the north of Bombay.

It is usually believed that the worship of Rāma-Dāśarathi was not popular in the Gupta age. But the idea seems to be wrong. As regards the *Avatāra* theory, it has to be remembered that the apotheosis and worship of an incarnation are earlier than his identification with Viṣṇu. Kālidāsa's *Raghuvaṁśa* (X. 44,XI.85, etc.) speaks of Rāma, son of Daśaratha, as an incarnation of Viṣṇu. The Vākāṭaka queen Prabhāvatī (fifth century), daughter of Candragupta II, was devoted to *Bhagavat* Rāmagirisvāmin (lord of the Rāmagiri, i. e., modern Ramtek near Nagpur), who appears to be identical with Rāma-Dāśarathi.[5] The worship of the Ikṣvāku king in the sixth century is indicated by Varāhamihira's *Bṛhatsaṁhitā*[6] containing rules for the construction of Rāma's

a more or less temporary character called *āveśa*. Rāma-Dāśarathi and Kṛṣṇa are often regarded as complete *Avatāras*. But there seems to have been difference of opinion on these points.

1. *Ep. Ind.*, Vol. XXIX, p. 179.
2. *Ibid.*, Vol. XXVIII, p. 43.
3. *Select Inscriptions*, Vol. I, p. 161.
4. III, 85. 42.
5. *Select Inscriptions*, Vol. I, p. 415. Cf. the *Meghadūta* (I. 12) reference to the footprints of Raghupati on the Rāmgiri and the worship of Rāma, Sītā and Lakṣmaṇa in the temples of Ramtek at the present time.
6. 58.30.

image. Saint Kulaśekhara (c. 8th century), king of Kerala in the Malabar coast, was a votary of Rāma.

The Dwarf (Vāmana) is implied by the epithets *Indr-ānuja* and *Upendra* (both meaning Indra's younger brother) applied to Viṣṇu in records like the Bihar pillar inscription[1] of the fifth century. The Junagadh inscription[2] of Skandagupta also refers to Viṣṇu 'who, for the sake of the happiness of the lord of the gods, seized back from Bali the goddess of wealth and splendour'.

The identification of Kṛṣṇa and Viṣṇu is alluded to in the name Viṣṇugopa,[3] popular among the early Pallavas from the fourth century, and in epigraphic passages mentioning the god Viṣṇu as 'a mighty bee on the water-lily which is the face of Jāmbavatī',[4] or as 'Mādhava, whose feet are graced by the attentions of Śrī (Lakṣmī) and who is born from Vasudeva'.[5] The Maukhari chief Anantavarman installed an image of Kṛṣṇa in a cave in the Pravara-giri (Barabar hills) in the fifth century.[6]

The Narasiṁha incarnation is alluded to in such epigraphs as the Alina plates.[7] But the most popular *Avatāra* appears to have been the Boar. who was widely worshipped in different parts of India in the Gupta age. The legend of this *Avatāra* of Viṣṇu seems to have been originally associated with that of the Great Deluge. A stone image of Varāha bearing an inscription[8] of the reign of king Toramāṇa (c. 500 A.D.) records the construction of a stone temple of 'Nārāyaṇa who has the form of a boar' at Eran in the Saugor District of Madhya Pradesh. A Damodarpur (North Bengal) inscription[9] of the time of Budhagupta (477-95 A.D.) speaks of the gods Śvetavarāhasvāmin and Kokāmukhasvāmin, both representing the Varāha *Avatāra*. The temples of these gods

1. *Select Inscriptions*, Vo. I, p. 316. See also the Alina plates of 766 A. D. (*Corp. Ins. Ind.*, Vol. III, p. 174).
2. *Select Inscriptions*, Vol. I, p. 300.
3. Cf. Kālidāsa's *Meghadūta*, I. 15.
4. *Corp. Ins. Ind.*, Vol. III, p. 270.
5. *Ibid.*, p. 206.
6. *Ibid.*, pp. 222 ff.
7. *Ibid.*, p. 188. See *Satkari Mookerji Vol.*, pp. 42 ff.
8. *Select Inscriptions*, Vol. I, pp. 396 f.
9. *Ibid.*, pp. 328 ff. See Sircar, *Geog. Auc. Med. Ind.*, pp. 217 ff.

stood on the Himavac-chikhara (peak of the Himalayas) apparently at Varāhachatra (Varāha-kṣetra) at the junction of the rivers Kauśikī and Kokā in Nepal.[1] In the fifth century, an inhabitant of North Bengal seems to have visited the Varāha-kṣetra or Kokāmukha-tīrtha on pilgrimage and constructed temples for the installation of two deities of the same names near Damodarpur in the Dinajpur District of North Bengal. A Kadamba record[2] from Tagare belonging to the sixth century points to the popularity of the Varāha *Avatāra* in the far south of India. The early Cālukyas of Bādāmi had the boar as their family emblem which they are said to have obtained through the grace of Nārāyaṇa. Most of the inscriptions of these monarchs and their subordinates begin with a stanza in praise of the Boar form of Viṣṇu.

There is only one reference[3] to the independent worship of the *Vyūha* or *Avatāra* Balarāma-Saṅkarṣaṇa, but none to Pradyumna and Aniruddha, in the inscriptions of the Gupta age. The *Vyūha* doctrine, however, finds a prominent place in the Pañcarātra literature, some of the Saṁhitās being composed, according to Schrader, in Kashmir between the fourth and the eighth century. The *Amarakoṣa* (c. sixth century) also refers to all the *Vyūhas*. It seems that the doctrine was not quite popular with the ordinary Viṣṇu-worshippers of the Gupta period. A modified form of the *Vyūha-vāda* can, however, be traced in the joint worship of Baladeva, Kṛṣṇa and Subhadrā or Ekānaṁśā (sometimes identified with Subhadrā, but sometimes with the Devī born as the daughter of Nanda-gopa). Varāhamihira's *Bṛhatsaṁhitā*[4] gives rules for the construction of the joint images of Baladeva and Kṛṣṇa with Ekānaṁśā standing between them. An inscription[5] of the thirteenth century from Bhubaneswar, referring to the adoration of Baladeva, Kṛṣṇa and Subhadrā, points to the popularity of their worship in mediaeval Orissa.

Some scholars believe that Bhāgavatism and Pañcarātra

1. Cf. *Ind. Hist. Quart.*, Vol. XXI, pp. 56-60.
2. *The Successors of the Sātavāhanas in the Lower Deccan*, p. 304.
3. See the Umachal inscription (5th century A. D.) from the Kamrup District, Assam, in *Ep. Ind.*, Vol. XXXI, pp. 67 ff. See below.
4. 58. 37-39.
5. *Ep. Ind.*, Vol. XIII, p. 155.

had possibly been related at the beginning, but became completely different in the Gupta period.[1] They further suggest that the *Vyūha-vāda* was exclusively associated with Pañcarātra, and that it was completely different from the *Avatāra-vāda* in its ideological basis. The first of the two suggestions cannot be proved in the present state of our knowledge. The second also seems to go against the evidence of Pañcarātra works like the *Ahirbudhnya Saṁhitā* and *Viṣvaksena Saṁhitā*, discussed above. It is clear that, while the *Vyūhavādins* were very much influenced by the *Avatāra* theory as early as the days of the early Pañcarātra Saṁhitās, Kṛṣṇa and Balarāma were recognized as *Avatāras* in the Vaiṣṇava literature from practically the same age. We have, however, to note that there are indications regarding the existence of doctrinal differences amongst the Viṣṇu-worshippers of the Gupta age, to which reference has already been made above. This difference, the nature of which cannot be determined with certainty, appears to be illustrated, as indicated above, by the *Harṣacarita* and its commentary which make a distinction between the Bhāgavatas and the Pāñcarātrikas. Even in the Gupta age, the Pañcarātrikas, who may have favoured some of the doctrines inculcated by the ancient sage Nārāyaṇa, were probably sometimes regarded as a sect of the Bhāgavatas, the term *bhāgavata* (essentially, a worshipper of Vāsudeva-Viṣṇu according to the *vidhi* or rules of the Sātvatas) being occasionally used, together with the term *vaiṣṇava*, in the sense of Viṣṇu-worshippers in general. The age of the Guptas witnessed the evolution of neo-Vaiṣṇavism from the tribal form of Bhāgavatism which was originally practised by the members of the Yādava-Sātvata-Vṛṣṇi clan.

III

Another interesting feature of Vaisnavism in the Gupta age is the conception of Lakṣmī or Śrī as the consort of Viṣṇu. This goddess is called Śrīmā Devatā in a Barhut inscription[2] of the Śuṅga age and Śrī's temple is referred to in the

1. *History of Bengal* (Dacca University), Vol. I, p. 402.

2. Barua and Sinha, *Barhut Inscriptions*, pp. 73-74. Barua distinguishes Siri and Sirimā Devatā. Prakrit *Sirimā* actually stands for Sanskrit *Śrīmatī*.

Kauṭilīya Arthaśāstra.[1] Her popularity is indicated by her appearance on early Indian coins such as the inscribed coins of Kauśāmbī and Ujjayinī, the issues of some early kings of Ayodhyā and Mathurā, and those of the Satraps of Mathurā and of Pantaleon, Agathokles, Maues, and Azilises.[2] The representation of Lakṣmī is conspicuous on the coins of the Imperial Guptas and some of their successors. Śrī-Lakṣmī is a Vedic goddess and, according to the Brāhmaṇa literature, she is full of riches, of which the gods despoil her.[3] Her conception as the wife of Viṣṇu is, however, considerably late. The Junagadh inscription of Skandagupta mentions Viṣṇu as a perpetual resort of Lakṣmī who is represented as Vāsudeva's wife in the Sarnath inscription of Prakaṭāditya. In the Aphsad inscription of Ādityasena, Dāmodara is spoken of as the slayer of demons, and the feet of Mādhava, son of Vasudeva, as graced by the attentions of Śrī. The kings of Śarabhapura and some other royal families adopted the Gaja-Lakṣmī device, found on the Barhut sculptures and some early coins, as their emblem. A Kadamba record of c. 500 A.D. begins with a stanza in adoration of the *Bhagavat* with Śrī on his breast and Brahman on the lotus sprung from his navel.[4] The Earth (*Bhū*), called Vaiṣṇavī in the *Mahābhārata* and many early epigraphic records, was conceived as a second wife of Viṣṇu whose *dhyāna* describes the god as *Indirā-Vasumatī-saṁśobhi-pārśva-dvaya.*[5] The early Cālukya emperors claiming to be *Śrī-Pṛthivī-vallabha* (lord of Śrī and Pṛthivī) apparently claimed to be incarnations of Viṣṇu.[6] Sarasvatī is

Another early representation of the goddess has been traced in a Besnagar sculpture of about the second century B. C. Cf. Banerjea, *op. cit.*, pp. 370-71.

1. II. 4.

2. Cf. Allan, *op. cit.*, pp. 131, 149, 173 ff., 252; Whitehead, *Catalogue of Coins in the Punjab Museum*, Vol. I, pp. 16, 135; Banerjea, *op. cit.*, p. 151.

3. Banerjea, *DHI*, 1956, pp. 371-72.

4. *The Successors of the Sātavāhanas*, p. 292, note 1.

5. Sircar, *Ind. Ep.*, p. 177; *Śabdakalpadruma*, s. v. *Viṣṇu*—
udyat=koṭi-divākar-ābham=aniśaṁ śaṅkhaṁ gadām paṅkajaṁ
cakraṁ bibhratam=Indirā-Vasumatī-saṁśobhi-pārśva-dvayam |
koṭīr-āṅgada-hāra-kuṇḍala-dharaṁ pītāmbaraṁ kaustubh-od-
dīptaṁ viśvadharaṁ sva-vakṣasi lasac-chrīvatsa-cihnam bhoje ||

6. Cf. *Ind. Cult.*, Vol. II, pp. 131-33.

not referred to in the inscriptions of the Gupta age as Viṣṇu's wife. Indeed it is a late conception popular only in certain parts of the country, especially in Eastern India.

The Śrī-Lakṣmī cult may have something to do with the worship of Greek goddesses, especially Pallas Athene, which was introduced in India by the Indo-Greek kings as suggested by their coins from the beginning of the second century B.C. The Sāṅkhya doctrine of Puruṣa and Prakṛti also appears to have considerably influenced the conception of Lakṣmī as the consort of Viṣṇu, as well as of the Devī as the consort of Śiva.

IV

In the Gadhwa inscription[1] of Kumāragupta I and many other records, Viṣṇu is mentioned, without reference to his name, only as the *Bhagavat*. The Eran inscription[2] of 484 A.D. describes the god Janārdana as 'the four-armed lord whose couch is the broad waters of the four oceans, who is the cause of the continuance, production, destruction, etc., of the universe, and whose ensign is Garuḍa'. A Kadamba inscription of the sixth century[3] refers to the god Hari as *jagat-pravṛtti-saṁhāra-sṛṣṭi-māyā-dhara*. The god Caṅgu-Nārāyaṇa, i.e., Nārāyaṇa on Caṅgu or Garuḍa, seems to have been in worship in a temple on the Dola-parvata in Nepal before the incision of an inscription of 464 A.D.[4] The god is described in various epigraphs as the troubler of the demons called Puṇyajana, as the supporting pillar of the three worlds (in the form of the boar), as the slayer of the demons Madhu and Mura, and as the bearer of the disc, the club, the bow of horn, the sword called Nandaka, the jewel called Kaustubha, and the garland of lotuses. The slumber of Madhusūdana during the four months of the rainy season is alluded to in the Gangdhar inscription of 423 A.D.[5] The Alina copper-plate grant (766 A.D.) appears to refer to the *Pārijātaharaṇa*

1. *Corp. Ins. Ind.*, Vol. III, p. 41.
2. *Select Inscriptions*, Vol. I, pp. 326 ff.
3. *The Successors of the Sātavāhanas*, p. 297, note 1.
4. *Select Inscriptions*, Vol. I, pp. 366 ff.
5. *Ibid.*, pp. 379 ff.

episode. The Mandasor inscription[1] of 404 A.D. probably refers to the Śakra festival as dear to Kṛṣṇa. The same record describes Vāsudeva as the lord (*vibhu*) who is *śaraṇya*, *jagad-vāsa*, *aprameya*, and *aja* (cf. *ātma-bhū* of the Jaunpur inscription of the Maukharis)[2] and as a great tree with the gods as its fruits, the heavenly damsels as its fine shoots, the celestial palaces as its many branches, and the rains as its flow of honey. In this, there seems to be an imperfect allusion to the Viśvarūpa conception of Viṣṇu, the germ of which is probably to be traced to a Ṛgvedic idea[3] and to the Upaniṣadic concept of Brahman.

The influence of Vaiṣṇava mythology is also noticed in the archaeological remains in different parts of the country. The bas-reliefs at Bādāmi, which belong to the age of the early rulers of the Cālukya family, some of whom were *paramabhāgavatas*, depict Viṣṇu lying on the serpent Ananta with Lakṣmī rubbing his feet, the Boar, Dwarf and Man-lion incarnations, and also Hari-Hara. They also depict many legends of the Kṛṣṇa saga.[4] A temple at Deogarh (Jhansi District, U.P.), probably assignable to the sixth century, has the representation of Viṣṇu reclining on Ananta-nāga, while a sculpture at Pathari in Central India, probably belonging to the sixth century, is believed to represent the new-born Kṛṣṇa lying by his mother's side. There are representations of the *Avatāras* and other deities of the Viṣṇu pantheon also in the Daśāvatāra and Kailāsanātha temples at Ellora, attributed to the eighth century, as well as in the works of art at Māmallapuram near Madras, assignable approximately to the same age. A sculpture from Paharpur (North Bengal), attributed to the sixth or seventh century, represents Kṛṣṇa and his consort (probably Rukmiṇī). Her identification with Rādhā is rendered improbable by the fact that we have no undoubted reference to Rādhā in genuine epigraphic or literary records of an early date.

Some scholars believe that the Khoh copper-plate inscription of the fifth or sixth century[5] records a grant of land

1. *Ibid.*, pp. 377 ff.
2. See *Corp. Ins. Ind.*, Vol. III, p. 229.
3. X. 90; cf. I. 155.6; VII. 100.6.
4. See R. D. Banerji, *Bas-reliefs of Badami*, pp. 24 ff.
5. *Select Inscriptions*, Vol. I, p. 370.

in favour of the *Bhagavat* and Āditya-bhaṭṭāraka, pointing to the solar association of Vaiṣṇavism. But the suggestion is unjustifiable as the language of the record seems to suggest that a person named Viṣṇunandin constructed a temple of the *Bhagavat* and obtained from the king half of a village on behalf of the god, while three merchants named Śāktināga, Kumāranāga and Skandanāga who had built a temple of the Sun-god, secured for that deity the other half of the same village. The inscription therefore does not prove that the same person worshipped both Viṣṇu and the Sun-god. That the Sun-god was not adored by the Vaiṣṇavas in the fifth century is indicated by the degradation of Sāmba, a champion of the solar cult and sometimes identified with the Sun-god, in the estimation of the Vaiṣṇavas. This seems to be also supported by verses 21-22 of the Gangdhar inscription of 423 A. D. This epigraph, however, speaks of the building of a temple, full of *ḍākinīs*, by a devotee of Viṣṇu, in honour of the divine Mothers, 'who utter loud and tremendous shouts in jov and stir up the oceans with the mighty wind rising from the magic rites of their religion (*tantra*). It evidently points to the influence of the Tantra cult on the Vaiṣṇavas of the fifth century A.D. It may be pointed out in this connection that the Maukhari chief Anantavarman installed in the same century an image of Kṛṣṇa in one of the caves in the Nagarjuni hills and also the images of Bhūtapati (Śiva) and the Devī, i.e. Durgā (or probably a joint image styled Ardhanārīśvara), in another cave in the same hill. This apparently points to an early accord between Vaiṣṇavism, on the one hand, and the worshippers of Śiva and Śakti, on the other.[1] The early Cālukyas of Bādāmi, who had Viṣṇu as their family god, similarly proclaimed their devotion to the god Kārttikeya and the Seven Mothers. In this connection we may also mention the cult of Hari-Hara (a combination of Viṣṇu and Śiva), Devī's rôle as the daughter of Kṛṣṇa's foster-father Nandagopa,[2] and the Trimūrti conception of the gods Brahman, Viṣṇu and Śiva. The attempt to identify different gods and to conciliate rival religious sects is old.[3] But, although one

1. Cf. *Journ. Roy. As. Soc. Beng.*, Letters, Vol. XIV, pp. 104 ff.
2. Cf. the *Harivaṁśa* and Bhāsa's *Bālacarita*.
3. The same attempt is noticed in the enumeration of the 108 or

god, viz., Agni, is represented as the same as Varuṇa, Mitra Indra and some other gods and goddesses, in such an early text as the *Ṛgveda*,[1] both sectarianism and attempt at conciliation were probably due mainly to Nonaryan inspiration. A gold coin of Huviṣka is believed to represent a composite image of Viṣṇu and Śiva, while a Gandhāra relief has been supposed to be the representation of a three-headed and six-armed Trimūrti.[2] These cases are, however, not entirely free from doubt. Adoration to Hari-Hara-Hiraṇyagarbha or to Hara-Nārāyaṇa Brahman are found in several early Kadamba inscriptions of the fifth and sixth centuries.[3] As already noted above, the representation of Hari-Hara is found in a cave temple of the sixth century at Bādāmi.

V

We have already referred to the adoration of Vāsudeva in the Chinna (Krishna District, Andhra Pradesh) inscription of the close of the second century A.D. and to the name of Pallava Viṣṇugopa in records dating from the fourth century. Reference has also been made to an inscription from the Guntur District, which may be assigned to the middle of the fourth century, as speaking of a temple of Nārāyaṇa.[4] The inscriptions of the Gupta age occasionally refer to temples or flagstaffs of the god Viṣṇu-Nārāyaṇa-Vāsudeva in all parts of India—in Nepal and the upper reaches of the Beas in the north, in Bengal in the east, in Kathiawad in the west, and in the trans-Krishna region in the south. In the southernmost parts of India, some of the early Pallava and early Western Gaṅga kings were devout *Bhāgavatas*. The worship of Viṣṇu was also prevalent in the kingdom of the early Kadambas; but the popular religion appears to have been Jainism in that area. Some of the early Kadamba rulers, who called themselves

1,000 names of gods and goddesses. Cf. *Journ. Roy. As. Soc. Beng.*, Letters, Vol. XIV, p. 24 and note.

1. See Macdonell, *Vedic Mythology*, p. 95.
2. Banerjea, *op. cit.*, p. 137; *Arch. Surv. Ind.*, Annual Report, 1913-14, pp. 276 ff., Plate LXXII, fig. a.
3. Cf. *The Successors of the Sātavāhanas*, pp. 278, 190.
4. *Select Inscriptions*, Vol. I, pp. 443 ff.

brahmaṇya or *parama-brahmaṇya*,[1] may have been Vaiṣṇavas. Several southern rulers claim to have been *kaliyuga-doṣ-āvasanna-dharm-oddharaṇa-nitya-sannaddha*.[2] Probably they tried to suppress heretical doctrines like Buddhism and Jainism, to revive the Brahmanical religion, and possibly also to represent themselves, like king Samudragupta of the North, as incarnations of the god Viṣṇu, emulating his doings in the Boar form. There is another indication of the influence of Vaiṣṇava Brāhmaṇism in the Far South of India. This is the importance attached to *go-brāhmaṇa* (i.e., the cow and Brāhmaṇa) in some Pallava and Kadamba records,[3] exactly as in the Vaiṣṇava records from Eran.[4] Certain later sections of the *Mahābhārata*[5] represent Viṣṇu as the benefactor of the cow and the Brāhmaṇa (*go-Brāhmaṇa-hita*). This indicates the association of the Brāhmaṇas with Viṣṇu-worship, and also the important position they attained in social estimation.

There is some evidence to show that the association of Vāsudevism with the Pāṇḍya country is old. In the fourth century B.C., the grammarian Kātyāyana[6] explains the word *Pāṇḍya* as 'one sprung from an individual of the clan of the Pāṇḍus or the king of their country'. Kātyāyana therefore associates the Pāṇḍya country with the Pāṇḍus or Pāṇḍavas whom epic traditions intimately connect with Vāsudeva. Greek tradition, attributed to Megasthenes,[7] associates the name of the Pāṇḍya country with its queen named Pandaia who is said to have been the daughter of Herakles (Vāsudeva-Kṛṣṇa). It is possible to think that there was a section of the Vṛṣṇi people among the colonizers of the Pāṇḍya country. At least this seems to be suggested by the name of its capital Madurai which is the same as Mathurā and is often specifically called the Mathurā of the South. This probably explains how the Tamil country soon became the greatest stronghold of the Bhāgavata religion and gave birth to the Āḻvārs and their compositions in Tamil on *bhakti* and the Kṛṣṇa cult. Ancient

1. Cf. *Suc. Sat.*, pp. 130, 266.
2. *Ibid.*, pp. 196, 199
3. See *ibid.*, pp. 194, 198, 269, 298.
4. *Select Inscriptions*, Vol. I, 2nd ed., pp. 336, 422.
5. XII. 47. 94.
6. On Pāṇini, IV. 1.168.
7. Majumdar, *The Classical Accounts of India*, pp. 222-23.

Tamil works prove the popularity of the worship of Kṛṣṇa and Baladeva in the Tamil land about the age of the Guptas. In the *Śilappadikāram* (sixth century A. D.) there are references to temples of the two gods at Madurai, Kāveripaṭṭinam and other cities.[1] They are described by the poet Kari-Kannan of Kāveripaṭṭinam as the dark-complexioned god bearing the wheel and the white-complexioned one having the flag of the palmyra.[2]

VI

The best evidence of the great influence exercised by the Bhāgavata religion over the Tamil country is furnished by the devotional songs of the Āḻvārs consisting the Vaiṣṇava *Prabandham* of four thousand verses in classical Tamil. The Āḻvārs sang in praise of Nārāyaṇa and Kṛṣṇa as well as the *Avatāras* Dāśarathi-Rāma, Balarāma and Vāmana. Kṛṣṇa's dalliance with the *gopīs* or cowherd girls was also well known to them. A female Āḻvār is known to have regarded herself as a *gopī* and the god (in the form of Śrī-Raṅganātha of the Śrīraṅgam temple) as her lover. The Āḻvārs knew the principal Purāṇas and revered the Vedic literature. The recitation of God's names, meditation on His different forms, and their worship in temples like those at Śrīraṅgam, Tirupati and Alagarkoil were inculcated by them. The activities of the Āḻvārs, representing the emotional side of Tamilian Vaiṣṇavism, and their successors, the Ācāryas, representing its intellectual side, must have given rise to the tradition recorded in the *Bhāgavata Purāṇa*,[3] a work referred to by Al-Bīrūnī[4] about 1030 A.D., that large numbers of the worshippers of Vāsudeva-Viṣṇu flourished in the Draviḍa or Tamil country in the Kali age when they were rare elsewhere in India.

The date of the Āḻvārs is a disputed question; but they may be roughly placed between the sixth and ninth centuries A.D. All of them appear to have flourished before the early

1. Kanakasabhai, *The Tamils Eighteen Hundred Years Ago*, pp. 13, 26.
2. *Ibid.*, pp. 68-69.
3. XI 5. 38-40
4. Sachau, *Alberuni's India*, Vol. I, p. 131.

Vaiṣṇava Ācāryəs—Nāthamuni (tenth-eleventh century) and his disciple Puṇḍarīkākṣa (eleventh century) and grandson Yāmunācārya (eleventh century). The Vaiṣṇava tradition of the Tamil country speaks of twelve Āḻvārs, viz. (1) Poygai Āḻvār or Saro-yogin, (2) Bhūtattāḻvār or Bhūta-yogin, (3) Pey Āḻvār or Mahad-yogin or Bhrānta-yogin, (4) Tirumaḻiśai Āḻvār or Bhaktisāra, (5) Nammāḻvār or Śaṭhakopa, (6) Madhurakavi, (7) Kulaśekhara, (8) Periyāḻvār or Viṣṇucitta, (9) Āṇḍāl or Godā, (10) Toṇḍaraḍippodi or Bhaktāṅghrireṇu, (11) Tiruppāṇ Āḻvār or Yogivāhana, and (12) Tirumaṅgai Āḻvar or Parakala. The first four Āḻvārs are believed to have flourished in the land of the Pallavas and the last three in that of the Coḻas. The seventh hailed from Kerala and the rest from the Pāṇḍya country. They came from different strata of the society. Only the eighth of the above list is stated to have been a Brāhmaṇa, although some regard him as a Pariah. The fifth was a Veḷḷāḷa (agriculturist) by caste and, while the seventh was a king, the twelfth came from a Kaḷḷa family, i.e., a family of robbers.

The three earliest Āḻvārs, who were supposed to be mythical in origin, are said to have composed a hundred stanzas each. They often refer to the *Avatāras* of Viṣṇu, especially Trivikrama and Kṛṣṇa, and cannot be assigned to a date earlier than the Gupta age, as has sometimes been suggested. Tirumaḻiśai, the fourth Āḻvār, is regarded by some to have been a contemporary of Pallava Mahendravarman I (c. 600-30 A.D.). The fifth Āḻvār, named Nammāḻvār or Śaṭhakopa, composed nearly one thousand and three hundred stanzas in four works, of which *Tiruvāymoḻi* ('the holy word of the mouth'), with 1102 stanzas, forms the fourth and the last part of the *Nālāyira Divya Prabandham*. Madhurakavi, the sixth Āḻvār, was a worshipper of his *guru* Nammāḻvār. The seventh Āḻvār Kuluśekhara was a king of Travancore. The *Mukundamālā*, attributed to him, quotes a verse from the *Bhāgavata Purāṇa*.[1] Bhandarkar[2] is inclined to assign him to the first half of the twelfth century; but there are no sufficient grounds for the date. Viṣṇucitta, the eighth Āḻvār, composed

1. XI. 2. 36.
2. *Op. cit.*, pp. 49 f.

numerous songs. The ninth Āḻvār, named Āṇḍāl was Viṣṇu-citta's daughter. She has 173 stanzas to her credit, which are highly mystical. Toṇḍaraḍippoḍi, the tenth Āḻvār composed two small works, and the eleventh Āḻvār named Tiruppāṇ composed only ten stanzas. The twelfth and last Āḻvār Tirumaṅgai composed 1361 verses (in six works) out of the 4000 constituting the celebrated *Nālāyira Divya Prabhandham* attributed to the Āḻvārs. There is a story that Tirumaṅgai was a contemporary of the Śaiva saint Tirujñāna Sambandhar who was himself a contemporary of the Pallava king Narasiṁhavarman I (c. 630-68 A.D.) of Kāñcī. If this tradition be true, Tirumaṅgai Āḻvār has to be assigned to the seventh century A.D., although he is placed by some scholars in the eighth century.

VII

There is evidence to show that, with the spread of Indian culture outside the limits of India, the Viṣṇu cult also spread abroad, at least from the early centuries of the Christian era. In Java, a king named Pūrṇavarman, probably belonging to the fifth century A.D., is compared to Viṣṇu in the Ci-arutön rock inscription.[1] He was deified probably as an incarnation of Viṣṇu and his footprints are known to have been worshipped.

The earliest incription of the ancient kingdom of Campā in Annam, referring to Viṣṇu together with Maheśvara, Umā, Brahman and other deities, is on the My-son stelae belonging to the fifth-sixth century.[2] Lakṣmī, Śrī or Padmā, wife of Viṣṇu, was also a well-known goddess in Campā. In a later period the kings of Campā, like some of the Indian rulers, often claimed to have been incarnations of Viṣṇu.

The earliest inscriptions referring to the the spread of Vaiṣṇavism in Cambodia (earlier Fu-nan and later Kambuja) are to be assigned to the beginning of the sixth century.[3] The Neak Ta Dambang Dek (province of Treang in South

1. *Select Inscriptions*, Vol. I, p. 468, note 4.
2. *Ibid.*, p. 474.
3. Cf. Majumdar, *Kambujadeśa*, pp. 33, 40-42.

Combodia) inscription[1] begins with an invocation to Viṣṇu and refers to Śrī as the wife of that god, while the Thup Muoi inscription of Guṇavarman records a donation to the image of Viṣṇu called Cakratīrthasvāmin, which is said to have been consecrated by Brāhmaṇas versed in the Vedas, Upavedas and Vedāṅgas as well as sages versed in the *śruti*. This record also speaks of the Bhāgavatas and refers to the cult of *bhakti* and to the theory of Karman. Although, as in India itself, the most popular god in early Cambodia, as also in other parts of Greater India, seems to have been Śiva, the composite form of Śiva and Viṣṇu, styled Śaṅkara-Nārāyaṇa, Śambhu-Viṣṇu (name applied to a *liṅga*), Hara-Acyuta, Hari-Śaṅkara, etc., was also in great favour.

1. *Select Inscriptions*, Vol. I, 1965 ed., pp. 509f.
2. *Ibid*., pp. 511 ff.

Chapter IV

PURUṢOTTAMA-JAGANNĀTHA

I

The town of Purī in the District of the same name, on the sea coast of Orissa, is celebrated throughout the world for the great temple of the god who is called Puruṣottama or Jagannātha and is identified with Viṣṇu. As a matter of fact, the name of the town is a part of the fuller name Puruṣottama-purī or Jagannātha-purī, i.e. the city of the god Puruṣottama-Jagannātha. It is sometimes also called Puruṣottama which is likewise a part of the fuller name Puruṣottama-purī or Puruṣottama-kṣetra. Purī is now considered to be the greatest of the East Indian *tīrthas* (holy places), although this status was originally enjoyed by Gaṅgāsāgara situated at the junction of the Bhāgīrathī and the Bay of Bengal. Gaṅgāsāgara gave place to Purī, as the greatest *tīrtha* about the eastern border of India, finally during the reign of the Imperial Gaṅgas of Orissa (from the 12th century onwards),[1] although the latter had already become popular a few centuries earlier, as we shall see below.

The *Mahārājas* of Purī may be regarded as the modern representatives of the imperial rulers of medieval Orissa, and it is well known that they consider themselves to be servants of the god Puruṣottama-Jagannātha, sweeping the compound of the Purī temple being one of their important duties on the occasion of the Car Festival (*Ratha-yātrā*) of the said god.[2] There is evidence to prove that the Hindu rulers holding sway over medieval Orissa considered the god Puruṣottama-Jagannātha to be the ruler of their empire and regarded their own selves as mere viceroys of the deity.

1. *Proc. IHC*, 1947, pp. 91 ff.; Sircar, *Stud. Geog. Anc. Med. Ind.*, pp. 178 ff.

2. The car festival of gods and godesses is popular in South India and was probably a Dravidian religious institution. It seems to have been introduced in the worship of Puruṣottama-Jagannātha of Purī by the Gaṅgas who had come to Orissa from the South. See *JAS*, 4th Series, Vol. VI, No. 1, 1962, p. 9.

The fiction of the real ruler of a country being placed in the position of a subordinate either to a god or to a spiritual guide (whether alive or dead) is well known to the students of Indian history and is not unknown even in the annals of other countries. The dedication of one's landed property and other belongings in favour of the family deity or of the spiritual guide of the family and its administration and enjoyment as a representative of that deity or saint is a familiar custom in all parts of India,[1] there being also a number of instances of similar dedication of an entire kingdom in favour of a god or saint in the history of India. Thus the rulers of Travancore regarded the god Padmanābhasvāmin as the king of their territories and considered themselves as the god's viceroys, while the Guhilot kings of Mewar represented themselves as the Dewāns (chief administrators) of the god Ekaliṅga who was believed to have been the real lord of their dominions. Likewise, Śivājī, the great founder of the Marāṭhā kingdom in the latter half of the 17th century, is said to have dedicated his dominions to his spiritual guide Rāmadāsa and to have administered the country in the saint's name. In the same way, the Kalacuri monarch Gāṅgeyadeva Vikramāditya (*circa* 1015-41 A. D.), also called Sāhasika (Sāhasāṅka), is known to have dedicated his empire covering the present Jabalpur region in favour of his preceptor, the Śaiva saint Vāmaśambhu or Vāmadeva, and, from that date for several centuries, his descendants are known to have regarded themselves as the viceroys of the saint.[2] The conception of the god Puruṣottama-Jagannātha of Purī as the ruler of Orissa, so far as we know, originated in the days of the Imperial Gaṅgas.

The mighty Gaṅga monarch Anantavarman Coḍagaṅga (1078-1147 A.D.) had his capital at Kaliṅganagara which is identified with modern Mukhalingam near Srikakulam (Chicacole) in Andhra Pradesh. He is known to have con-

1. Cf. *devottara* and *bhogottara* in Wilson's Glossary. For the issue of coins in the names of deities, see below, pp. 87 ff.

2. See *Ep. Ind.*, Vol. XXX, pp. 46 ff. While the dedication of Sāhasika's kingdom to the ascetic Vāmadeva is known from the commentary of Jayāṇaka's *Pṛthvīrājavijaya* (twelfth century), Gāṅgeya's descencendants continued to call themselves *Vāmadeva-pād-ānudhyāta* from the days of Karṇa (1041-71 A.D.) to the end of the dynasty, and the Malkapuram inscription of 1263 A.D. speaks of Vāmaśaṁbhu's worship by the Kalacuri kings for centuries till that date. See below.

quered the whole east coast region up to the Gangetic Delta and to have annexed the Puri-Cuttack area to the Gaṅga empire after having extirpated the rule of the Somavaṁśī kings in the said territory. The inscriptions of Coḍagaṅga's descendants state that it was he who built the great temple of the god Puruṣottama-Jagannātha on the shore of the sea as the earlier rulers of the country had neglected to do it.[1] It may be pointed out that the Somavaṁśīs, who held sway over the Puri-Cuttack region before Coḍagaṅga's conquest, were Śaivas and may not have been much enthusiastic about the deity regarded as a form of Viṣṇu. Like his ancestors who worshipped Gokarṇeśvara-Śiva on the Mahendragiri in the Gangam District, Coḍagaṅga also was a staunch Śaiva in the early years of his reign. Soon after his conquest of the Puri-Cuttack area about the beginning of the twelfth century, however, we find him inclining gradually more and more towards the worship of Viṣṇu, apparently in the form of the god Puruṣottama-Jagannātha of Purī. Coḍagaṅga calls himself both a Śaiva and a Vaiṣṇava in one of his charters dated 1112 A.D., while in his later documents, the reference to his devotion to Śiva is totally omitted and the king is represented only as a Vaiṣṇava.[2]

A tradition recorded in the *Utkala-khaṇḍa* (otherwise called *Puruṣottama-māhātmya*) section of the *Skanda Purāṇa* shows beyond doubt that Puruṣottama-Jagannātha of Purī was originally worshipped by the aboriginal Śabara inhabitants of the Nīlācala (Puri hills) and that the worship of the deity became gradually popular with the orthodox Hindus at a later date.[3] Like Mīnākṣī of Madurai in South India, Kāmākhyā near Gauhati in Assam and numerous other gods and goddesses in various parts of India, the aboriginal god of Purī was absorbed in the Brāhmaṇical pantheon in course of time and was ultimately identified with Viṣṇu. The identification of the god, originally worshipped by the Śabaras of the Purī region, with Viṣṇu was apparently well established considerably before the beginning of the twelfth century when Anantavarman Coḍagaṅga annexed the Puri-Cuttack region to his empire.

1. *Ibid.*, Vol. XXVIII, pp. 251-52, verses 27-28 which are also found in other records. See below, p. 66 note 3.
2. *Ibid.*, p. 240. See below, pp. 67-68.
3. See Chapters VII-VIII below.

The fact however that Hiuen-tsang, the Chinese pilgrim who visited Orissa in 638-39 A.D., does not speak of Puruṣottama-Jagannātha in his account of the Oḍra country[1] shows that the god was no better than a local deity of limited celebrity and importance till as late as the seventh century A.D. His position in the religious life of Eastern and Central India must have been well established in the tenth and eleventh centuries as we know from epigraphic and literary references,[2] and in the twelfth century, the conversion of Anantavarman Coḍagaṅga to Vaiṣṇavism under his influence set him on the way to all-India importance.

The sucessors of Coḍagaṅga were all worshippers of Viṣṇu in the form of Puruṣottama-Jagannātha. But it was his great-grandson Anaṅgabhīma III (*circa* 1211-38 A.D.) who was really responsible for raising the god Puruṣottama-Jagannātha to an all-India figure and the temple of Purī to its present position of pre-eminence amongst the places of pilgrimage in India. The rise of Purī must have been facilitated by the gradual obscuration of Gaṅgāsāgara due to many factors including the Muslim occupation of Bengal and consequent want of royal patronage, as also the similar obscuration of Virajā (modern Jājpur), the oldest Brāhmaṇical *tīrtha* in Orissa, which enjoyed an important position during the age of the Bhauma-Kara kings (from the ninth to the beginning of the twelfth century A.D.) who had their capital in that city or its neighbourhood. By the time of Anaṅgabhīma III, the Gaṅgas had already transferred their capital to Cuttack (Kaṭaka). This king issued his charters from Abhinava-Vārāṇasī-kaṭaka or Vārāṇasī-kaṭaka which is modern Cuttack. According to a tradition recorded in the Oriya chronicle entitled *Mādalā Pāñjī*, a king named Anaṅgabhīma who at first had

1. Watters, *On Yuan Chwang's Travels in India*, Vol. II, pp. 93-94.

2. An inscription of the tenth century A.D., from Maihar in the Satna District of Madhya Pradesh, refers to the pilgrimage of a Brāhmaṇa youth of that area to the sea-shore in the Oḍra country in order to have a *darśana* of the god Puruṣottama (*Ep. Ind.*, Vol. XXXV, p. 173). The popularity of Puruṣottama-Jagannātha of Purī in the said region about the same time is further proved by Kṛṣṇamiśra's *Prabodhacandrodaya* composed in the eighties of the eleventh century A. D. at the court of the Candella king Kīrtivarman (c. 1065-1100 A.D.). See *ibid.*, Vol. XXXIII, p. 184, note 1. See below, pp. 76 ff.

his capital at Caudavāra-kaṭaka, built a new city named Vāṇarāśī (Vārāṇasī)-kaṭaka at the site of a village called Vāra-vāṭī on the opposite bank of the Mahānadī and removed his residence there.[1] The *Mādalā Pāñjī* further says that the Gaṅga king named Anaṅgabhīma built the temple of Puruṣottama-Jagannātha at Purī. This king is no other than Anaṅgabhīma III who may have completed the Purī temple begun by his great-grandfather and is actually known from the Nagarī plates to have installed a god named Puruṣottama-Jagannātha in a new temple built by him at his capital at Vārāṇasī-kaṭaka (Cuttack).[2] The earliest records in the Puri temple are four inscriptions of the reign of Anaṅgabhīma III.[3]

According to another tradition recorded in the *Mādalā Pāñjī*, a king named Anaṅgabhīma (apparently Anaṅgabhīma III) dedicated all his possessions including the empire in favour of the god Puruṣottama-Jagannātha of Purī and began to rule as a *Rāuta* (i. e. feudatory) of the said god, and his successors did not celebrate a formal coronation at the time of their accession as they considered themselves to be mere feudatories of the god.[4] These traditions have remarkable support from a large number of Gaṅga inscriptions.

In many of the inscriptions of king Anaṅgabhīma III himself and his successors, the Gaṅga monarch is described as a *Rāuta*, *Rāutta* or *Rāvuta*, which is derived from Sanskrit *Rāja-putra* (literally 'a prince', but really a title of nobility) and was

1. See *ibid.*, Vol. XXX, p. 21 and note 7 : *e uttāre Anaṅgabhīmade-vaṅka sāna-bhāi Bhīma-parirāeṅku Bhīmanagara-daṇḍapāḷuṁ āni rajā kalee-dutī Anaṅgabhīmadeva hoile. e rajā nagara Caudvāre kaṭaka vije kari thānti. emantare eka-dinare rajāe vije kari āsi Mahānadī pāra hoi e-nadīru dakṣiṇa-tīre dekhile Ko liṇḍā-daṇḍapāṭara Vāravāṭi-grāmare Viśveśvaradevaṅkara-sanidhe sāmala-pakṣiki vaga māri vasiachi. ehā dekhi rajā vaḍa āścarya pāi śubha-yoga-dinare e-Vāravāṭi-grāmare śubha dei naara tolāi kaṭaka kari e-kaṭaka-nāma Vāṇarāśikaṭaka voli nāma dei nagara-Caudvāra-kaṭaka chāḍi āsi kaṭaka kari rahile.* The epithet *Abhinava-Yayātinagara-Viṣṇu* applied to the said king in the *Mādalā Pāñjī* suggests that he had his capital previously at 'New Yayātinagara (Yayāti-pura)', i. e. modern Jājpur.

2. *Ep. Ind.*, Vol. XXVIII, pp. 247-48.

3. *Ibid.*, Vol. XXX, pp. 97 ff.

4. *Ibid.*, p. 19 : *e nagara-Kaṭaka thāi śrī-Puruṣottama śrī-Jagannātha-devaṅku samasta sa:narpi Rāuta-paṇe thāanti. rajā 2ṅka abhiṣeka na hele. Oḍiśā-rājya-rajā śrī-Jagannātha-mahāprabhu emanta kahi abhiṣeka nohile.*

often assumed by subordinate rulers. An inscription[1] from the Liṅgarāja temple at Bhubaneswar in the Puri District speaks of the dominions of Anaṅgabhīma III as *Puruṣottama-sāmrājya*, i.e. the empire belonging to the god Puruṣottama-Jagannātha. The Kanchipuram inscription of the said Gaṅga king and the Kapilas inscription of his son Narasiṁha I (1238-64 A.D.) represent the two monarchs as obeying the orders of the god Puruṣottama.[2] Out of the four inscriptions of Anaṅga-bhīma III in the Pātāleśvara shrine within the inner compound of the Purī temple, all of them recording grants made in favour of the god Puruṣottama-Jagannātha, one gives its date in the passage *śrī-Puruṣottamasya pravardhamānavijaya-rājye Rāutta-śrīmad-Anaṅkabhīmadevasya srāhī saṁ 29* which clearly mentions the Gaṅga king as a vassal of the god of Purī.[3] Two other Liṅga-rāja temple inscriptions of Anaṅgabhīma III again describe him as the son of the god Puruṣottama-Jagannātha.[4] Another inscription of the king from the same place shows how he was mentioned even by his Śaiva subjects as a *Bhagavat* (god or Lord). This undoubtedly points to the fact that the said Gaṅga king was a saintly Vaiṣṇava highly respected by different religious communities.[5] This also reminds us of Anaṅga-bhīma's representation as a devotee of Maheśvara and a son of Rudra and of Durgā, to which reference has been made above.

We have observed above that, like Anaṅgabhīma III, his successors called themselves *Rāuta*, *Rāutta* or *Rāvuta*.[6] But

1. *Ind. Cult.*, Vol. VI, p. 73.
2. *Ep. Ind.*, Vol. XXXI, p. 97; Vol. XXXIII, p. 43.
3. *Ibid.*, Vol. XXX, pp. 201-02.
4. *Ibid.*, p. 234. That these kings were not antagonistic to the worship of Śiva and Śakti is indicated by a few inscriptions in Śiva temples, in which Anaṅgabhīma III and Narasiṁha I are represented as both Vaiṣṇava and Śaiva; cf. the epithets *Paramavaiṣṇava*, *Paramamāheśvara*, *Puruṣottama-putra*, *Rudra-putra* and *Durgā-putra* applied to the former and *Paramamāheśvara*, *Durgā-putra* and *Puruṣottama-putra* to the latter (*ibid.*, Vol. XXXIII, pp. 43, 126-27). Likewise, Kapileśvara (1435-66 A.D.), founder of the Sūryavaṁśī Gajapati dynasty of Orissa, is called *Maheśvara-putra*, *Durgā-putra* and *Puruṣottama-putra* in the Warangal inscription which describes his nephew Raghudeva as *Durgā-vara-putra* and *Jagannāthadeva (labdha*)-caraprasāda* (*ibid.*, p. 127).
5. *Ibid.*, Vol. XXX, p. 19.
6. Cf. *SII*, Vol. V, Nos. 1264 and 1294 for Narasiṁha I (1238-

most of them do not specifically mention the god Puruṣottama-Jagannātha as their overlord as Anaṅgabhīma III himself does in some of his inscriptions already referred to. An interesting exception to this is Bhānu II who was the great-great-grandson of Anaṅgabhīma III and ruled in *circa* 1305-27 A.D.[1] This fact shows that, amongst the descendants of Anaṅgabhīma III, who were all no doubt continuing to suffer the fiction created by the dedication of the Gaṅga empire to the god Puruṣottama-Jagannātha by that king, Bhānu II alone was as religiously minded as his distinguished ancestor. Indeed, Bhānu II may probably be regarded as more zealous in this respect that even Anaṅgabhīma III himself since, in several records of his time, the god alone is mentioned as the lord of the realm and the king's name is altogether omitted. Unfortunately, this fact gave rise to certain unwarranted theories regarding the interpretation of the records in question. Writers like R. D. Banerji[2] believed that during the early years of Bhānu's reign, a person named Puruṣottama usurped the Gaṅga throne for several years, while others like R. Subba Rao[3] suggested that Bhānu II was also known by the names or titles, Puruṣottama and Jagannātha. An inscription (1309 A. D.)[4] from Srikurmam is stated to have been dated in the reign of Jagannātha when Bhānu II, described in the record as Jiyyana (Oriya *Jenā* which is the same as *Rājaputra* =*Rāutta*) was governing, while according to the Purī plates,[5] Bhānu II, endowed with the subordinate title *Rāutta*, made certain grants in 1313 A.D., during the reign of Puruṣottama. Another Srikurmam inscription,[6] dated 1327 A.D., mentions Puruṣottama as the reigning king and omits

64 A.D.), and *ibid.*, Vol. VI, No. 1118, for Narasiṁha II (1278-1305 A. D.).

1. *JKHRS*, Vol. I, pp. 251 ff.

2. *History of Orissa*, Vol. I, pp. 277-79.

3. *History of Kaliṅga* (offprint), p. 192.

4. *SII*, Vol. V, No. 1214; *Ep. Ind.*, Vol. V, pp. 35-36 : *śrī-Jagannāthadeva-vijaya-rājya-saṁvatsarambulu* 3 *śrī-vīra-Bāṇudeva-jiyyanaṁgāri vehcrayamunanddu*.

The reference here is to the reign of Jagannātha and the administration of Bhānu Jenā (Prince).

5. *JAS*, Letters, Vol. XVII, pp. 19 ff. : *śrī-Puruṣottamadevasya pravardhamāna-vijaya-rājye saptame='ṅke...vīra-śrīmad-Bhānudeva-rāutta-vamā*.

6. *SII*, Vol. V, Nos. 1154-55.

the name of Bhānu II altogether. Two of the Simhachalam inscriptions[1] offer valuable evidence in this regard. Neither of these records mentions the name of Bhānu II, even though they are dated respectively in 1319 and 1314 A.D., both the dates falling in the reign of the said Gaṅga monarch (*circa* 1305-27 A.D.). It should, however, be noted that the regnal reckoning of Bhānu II has been attributed in the first of the two inscriptions to *Devādideva* Jagannātha and in the second to *Devādideva* Puruṣottama. There can be no doubt that this Puruṣottama-Jagannātha, described as *Devādideva*, i.e. 'the foremost god amongst all the gods', is no other than the deity worshipped in the Purī temple, to whom Bhānu II and other rulers of the Gaṅga family owed fictitious allegiance as a theoretical viceroy or subordinate.[2]

II

In an interesting paper entitled 'The Date of the Jagannātha Temple in Purī, Orissa' published in *JASB*, Vol. LXVII, 1898, pp. 328-31, M. M. Chakravarti quoted two verses[3] found

1. *Ibid.*, Vol. VI, Nos. 714 and 938. No. 714 of Śaka 1241=1319 A.D. gives the date as *śrī-devādideva-śrī-Jagannāthadevarala-vijaya-rājya-samvatsarambulu* 13, while No. 938 has *śrī-devādideva-śrī-Puruṣottamadevasya pravardhamāna-vijaya-rājya-saṁvatsarambulu* 9.

2. See *Indo-Asian Culture*, Vol. II, Nos. 2, October, 1953, pp. 120ff.

3. *Pādau yasya dhar=āntarikṣam=akhilaṁ nābhis=tu sarvā diśaḥ*
śrotre netra-yugaṁ rav-īndu-yugalaṁ mūrdh=āpi ca dyaur=asau ı
prāsādaṁ Puruṣottamasya nṛpatiḥ ko nāma karttuṁ kṣamas=
tasy=ety=ādya=nṛpair=upekṣitam=ayaṁ cakre='tha Gaṅg-eśvaraḥ ıı
Lakṣmī-janma-gṛhaṁ payo-nidhir=asau sambhāvitasya sthitir=
no dhāmni śvaśurasya pūjyata iti kṣīrābdhi-vāsād=dhruvam ı
nirvinnaḥ Puruṣottamaḥ pramuditas=tad-vāsa-lābhād=Ram=ā-
py=etad=bhartṛ-gṛhaṁ varaṁ pitṛ-gṛhāt prāpya pramod-ānvitā ıı

Translation : "What king can be named that could erect a temple to such a god as Purṣottama, whose feet are the earth, whose navel the entire sky, whose ears the cardinal points, whose eyes the sun and moon and whose head that heaven above ? This task which had been hitherto neglected by previous kings, was fulfilled by the Lord of the Gaṅgas (i.e. Coḍagaṅga).

"The ocean is the birth-place of Lakṣmī, so thinking, in his father-in-law's house Viṣṇu lodged with some shame, though he got full adoption.

in the copper-plate grants[1] of the successors of Anantavarman Coḍagaṅga (1078-1147 A.D.) to show that a great temple was erected in Orissa on or near the sea coast by order of that Gaṅga monarch. He concluded that the temple erected by Coḍagaṅga could be no other than that of the god Puruṣottama or Jagannātha at Purī. Chakravarti no doubt meant the *Vimāna* or sanctum and the *Jagamohana* or the first *Maṇḍapa* of the Purī temple, as its *Nāṭyaśālā* (now called *Nāṭamandira*) and *Bhoga-maṇḍapa* were erected at a much later date.[2] He further pointed to a pilgrimage to Puruṣottama (i.e. Purī, otherwise called Puruṣottama-purī, Puruṣottama-kṣetra, Jagannātha-purī, etc., as we have seen) referred to in the Govindapur (Gaya District) inscription of Śaka 1059 (1137-38 A.D.)[3] and to the god Puruṣottama existing in the vicinity of the eastern ocean mentioned in the Nagpur inscription of the Paramāras of Malwa, dated in Vikrama Saṁvat 1161 (1104-05 A.D.),[4] in connection with the *digvijaya* of Paramāra Lakṣadeva (whose known date is Vikrama Saṁvat 1151=1084-85 A.D.) and suggested that the Purī temple might have been built in 1085-90 shortly after Coḍagaṅga's conquest of that part of Orissa early in his reign before 1085 A.D. Elsewhere[5] the same scholar drew attention to the astronomical work *Bhāsvatī* which was composed in Śaka 1021 (1099-1100 A.D.), according to a commentary of the *Sūryasiddhānta*, by one Śatānanda of Puruṣottama (Purī) who is said by the commentator to have based his calculations on the meridian of his native city.

In this connection, it may be pointed out that the Gaṅgas were Śaivas being devoted to Gokarṇeśvara (Śiva) installed in a temple on the top of the Mahendragiri peak in the Ganjam District. Anantavarman Coḍagaṅga is also described as a

Thus ashamed, the god Puruṣottama was glad to get this new house; and Lakṣmī, too, gladly preferred living in her husband's new house to living in her father's house."

1. Cf. *JASB*, Vol. LXIV, 1895, p. 130; Vol. LXV, 1896, p. 240.
2. Cf. R. D. Banerji, *History of Orissa*, Vol. I, p. 251.
3. *Ep. Ind.*, Vol. II, p. 334. For *Purī* as a contraction of *Puruṣottama-purī* or *Jagannātha-purī* and *Puruṣottama* as a similar contraction of *Puruṣottama-purī* or *Puruṣottama-kṣetra*, cf. *Satyabhāmā* called both *Satyā* and *Bhāmā*.
4. *Ibid.*, p. 187.
5. *JASB*, 1903, p. 110.

parama-māheśvara (i.e. devout worshipper of Maheśvara or Śiva) in his earlier copper-plate grants;[1] but the Korni plates[2] of Śaka 1034 (1112-13 A.D.) describe him both as a *parama-māheśvara* and as a *parama-vaiṣṇava* (devout worshipper of Viṣṇu), while the Visakha-pattanam plates[3] of 1040 (1118-19 A.D.) omit *parama-māheśvara* and call him a devotee of Viṣṇu only. It is interesting to note that both these grants refer to the conquest of the Utkala country by Coḍagaṅga apparently from the Somavaṁśīs[4] whose dominions in Utkala comprised the Puri District. It is therefore probable that Coḍagaṅga's conquest of Utkala had something to do with his change of religious faith from Śaivism to Vaiṣṇavism. Another interesting fact is that, unlike the earlier grants, these later records do not copy the genealogical portion from the copper-plate inscriptions of Coḍagaṅga's grandfather Vajrahasta III Anantavarman (1038-70 A.D.),[5] but that they offer a more elaborate genealogy apparently fabricated by Coḍagaṅga's court poets. This forged genealogy is important in regard to the king's leaning towards Vaiṣṇavism as it traces the descent of his family to the god Viṣṇu.[6]

Another interesting information about the god Puruṣottama or Jagannātha at Purī seems to be supplied by the passage of the verses quoted above saying that the task of building a temple for the god Puruṣottama was neglected by the previous kings of the Purī region and that therefore Coḍagaṅga took it up and fulfilled it. This no doubt suggests that the

1. Cf. the Korni and Viṣakhapattanam plates of Śaka 1003 (1081-82 A.D.) in *JAHRS*, Vol. I, pp. 40-48; *Ind. Ant.*, Vol. XVIII, pp. 61-65. Coḍagaṅga conquered Utkala after 1081-82 A.D. and before 1112-13 A.D. The Somavaṁśīs appear to have been extirpated about the beginning of the twelfth century.

2. *JAHRS*, Vol. I, pp. 113-24.

3. *Ind. Ant.*, Vol. XVIII, pp. 165-72.

4. *IHQ*, Vol. XXII, pp. 300-07.

5. Cf. the Nadagam plates in *Ep. Ind.*, Vol. IV, pp. 188 ff.

6. It must be admitted that the Visakhapattanam plates of Śaka 1057 (1135-36 A.D.) describe Coḍagaṅga as a *parama-māheśvara* and do neither refer to his suzerainty over Utkala nor offer the fabricated genealogy (*Int. Ant.*, Vol. XVIII, pp. 472-76). But there are many other cases of the utilisation of an earlier draft of the *praśasti* even after the introduction of a later draft. See *Ep. Ind.*, Vol. XXXIII, p. 330, note 2; Vol. XXXV, p. 203.

god Puruṣottama was being worshipped at Purī before the date of Coḍagaṅga's conquest of that region, but that the Somavaṁśīs, whom the Gaṅga king ousted, being staunch devotees of the god Śiva,[1] neglected the construction of a suitable temple for Puruṣottama. As indicated above, the deity at Purī, like Veṅkateśvara-Bālājī at Tirupati, Mīnākṣī at Madurai, Vindhyavāsinī near Mirzapur, Kāmākhyā near Gauhati and numerous other gods and goddesses in different parts of India, was originally being worshipped by the aboriginal inhabitants of the locality and came gradually to be identified with a god of the recognised Brāhmaṇical pantheon.[2] But, as also pointed out above, the identification of Puruṣottama or Jagannātha of Purī with the Brāhmaṇical god Viṣṇu seems to have been fully recognised before Coḍagaṅga's occupation of the Purī region.

The celebrated Oriya chronicle called *Mādalā Pāñjī*, however, attributes the construction of the temple of Puruṣottama-Jagannātha not to Anantavarman Coḍagaṅga, but to his great-grandson Anaṅgabhīma III (1211-38 A.D.), and it is usually believed by scholars that the Purī temple and the buildings connected with the shrine 'may have been actually finished during his reign.'[3] We have seen[4] that Anaṅgabhīma III was a staunch devotee of the god Puruṣottama and considered the deity as the *de jure* lord of his dominions and himself as a mere deputy of the god. It has also been shown that his successors ruled their dominions as subordinates of the theoretical overlord Puruṣottama-Jagannātha of Purī. As Anaṅgabhīma III was the Gaṅga monarch who dedicated his kingdom to the god Puruṣottama, he must have been regarded as the most remarkable royal devotee of the deity[5] and popular tradition may have attributed to him, wrongly of course, his great-grandfather's achievement of building the temple for the god. But another fact seems to lie at the root of the confusion.

1. The Somavaṁśī kings are described as *parama-māheśvara* in their inscriptions.

2. Cf. *JRASB*, Letters, Vol. XIV, 1948, pp. 103-06.

3. Ray, *Dynastic History of Northern India*, Vol. I, p. 478.

4. See above, pp. 63 ff.; *JKHRS*, Vol. I, pp. 251-53.

5. As we have seen above, Anaṅgabhīma was a saintly Vaiṣṇava, so that even his Śaiva subjects called him a *Bhagavat*. See p. 64; *Ep. Ind.*, Vol. XXX, p. 19.

There is evidence to show that Anaṅgabhīma III installed an image of the god Puruṣottama-Jagannātha in a temple at Cuttack[1] which became the later capital of the Gaṅga kings who were ruling first from Kaliṅganagara (modern Mukhalingam in the Ganjam District), and then from Jājpur (called 'New Yayātinagara' or Yayātipura) in the Cuttack District. We know that Śivāji's patron-deity was the goddess Bhavānī at Tuljāpur near Osmanabad in the old Hyderabad State; but, since Tuljāpur was not within easy reach to him, Śivājī, when he built the fort of Pratapgarh near Javlī, set up there a new image of his patron deity.[2] The Gaṅga king Anaṅgabhīma III seems to have similarly set up an image of his patron-deity Puruṣottama-Jagannātha at his capital at Cuttack owing to his desire to live constantly near the god.

That there was a temple of Jagannātha (Puruṣottama) at Banārasī (i.e. Vārāṇasī-kaṭaka or the present Cuttack), capital of Jājnagar (i.e. the Orissan kingdom of the Gaṅgas) was long ago known from the *Tārīkh-i-Firūz Shāhī* of Shams-i-Sirāj. According to this work,[3] Sulṭān Firūz Shāh of Delhi led an expedition against the kingdom of Jājnagar (the Gaṅga kingdom) about 1360 A.D. when the kingdom was under the rule of Bhāndeo, i.e. Bhānudeva III (1352-78 A.D.), who had his headquarters at Banārasī (i.e. Vārāṇasī-kaṭaka or the present Cuttack). The Sulṭān is said to have occupied Banārasī when the king fled from the capital. In connection with this expedition, the *Tārīkh-i-Firūz Shāhī* says, "It is reported that, inside the Rāī's fort (i.e. king Bhānu's fort at Banārasī or Cuttack), there was a stone idol which the infidels called Jagannāth and to which they paid their devotions. Sulṭān Firūz in emulation of Maḥmūd-i-Subuktigīn, having rooted

1. The city is called Vārāṇasī-kaṭaka in the Gaṅga inscriptions and Banārasī in the Muslim chronicle. See Ray, *op. cit.*, pp. 491-94. As will be seen below, this city called 'New Banāras' was already the residence of the Gaṅga king during the reign of Anaṅgabhīma III. As *Puri* is a contraction of *Puruṣottama-puri* or *Jagannātha-puri*, *Kaṭaka* (Cuttack) is an abbreviation of *Vārāṇasī-kaṭaka* or *Abhinava-Vārāṇasī-kaṭaka*. For Aṭak-Banāras, named by Akbar after Kaṭak-Banāras, see *Akbarnāmā*, trans., Vol. III, pp. 520-21; *Muntakhabut Tawārikh*, trans., Vol. II, p. 301.

2. See J. N. Sarkar, *History of Aurangzeb*, Vol. IV, p. 32. Cf. Sircar, *Stud. Geog. Anc. Med. Ind.*, p. 223, for imitation gods.

3. See Elliot and Dowson, *The History of India as told by its own Historians*, Vol. III, pp. 312-15.

up the idol, carried it away to Delhi, where he subsequently had it placed in an ignominious position." Recently evidence has come to light to show that this image of Jagannātha (Puruṣottama) at Cuttack was installed by the Gaṅga king Anaṅgabhīma III.

Sometime ago, a new set of copper-plates was discovered at a place called Nagarī in the Cuttack District.[1] This interesting record belongs to the Gaṅga king Anaṅgabhīma III and gives details of a number of grants made by the king in favour of several Brāhmaṇas. We have to analyse them before discussing the light the record throws on the problem under discussion.

I. On the occasion of the Mīna-saṅkrānti on Saturday, Caitra-sudi 9, in the Śaka year 1151, king Anaṅgabhīma-rāutta-deva, while he was taking a bath in the Mahānadī between the temples of Citreśvara and Viśveśvara at Abhinava-Vārāṇasī-kaṭaka (literally, at the camp or residence of 'New Banāras'), granted twenty *vāṭis* of land at Pūraṇagrāma in the Sāilo *viṣaya* (district) to a Brāhmaṇa named Saṅkarṣaṇānandaśarman. The date of the grant corresponds to the 23rd February, 1230 A.D.

II. Next year (i.e. in Śaka 1152) on Thursday, Māgha-badi 6, while the king was taking a bath in the same river, he granted a township covering 30 *vāṭis* of land in the villages of Pūraṇagrāma and Jayanagaragrāma in the same *viṣaya* to the same Brāhmaṇa Saṅkarṣaṇāndaśarman. The date corresponds to Thursday the 26th December, 1230 A.D., which was the day of the Makara-saṅkrānti.

III. In the same year (i.e. Śaka 1152) king Anaṅgabhīma III also made the following gifts :

(a) While he was taking bath in the Mahānadī, on the occasion of a lunar eclipse on Thursday, Mārgaśīrṣa-sudi 15, he granted 18 *vāṭis* of land in the said Pūraṇagrāma to *Dīkṣita* Rudrapāṇiśarman. The date corresponds to the 21st November, 1230 A.D.

(b) On the occasion of the Makara-saṅkrānti (Thursday, the 26th December, 1230 A.D.) he granted 5 *vāṭis* of land apparently in the same village to the Brāhmaṇa Somapālaśarman.

(c) He granted, on the occasion of the installation of the

1. See *Ep. Ind.*, Vol. XXVIII, pp. 235 ff.

god Puruṣottama, 2 *vāṭis* of land, apparently in the same village, to the Brāhmaṇa Candrakaraśarman.

IV. Apparently in the same year (Śaka 1152), on the occasion of a solar eclipse on Karkaṭak-āmāvāsyā,[1] while the king was at Puruṣottama-kṣetra (i.e. Purī) on the bank of the Southern Ocean, he granted 5 *vāṭis* of land in the same Pūraṇa-grāma to Kāyaḍīśarman and some other Brāhmaṇas.

V. Apparently in the same year (Śaka 1152) when the king was standing before the god Puruṣottama at Abhinava-Vārāṇasī (New Banāras or Cuttack)[2] on the occasion of the Makar-āmāvāsyā on Sunday, he granted 4 *vāṭis* of land in Vilāsapuragrāma in the Kuddiṇḍā *viṣaya* to the Brāhmaṇa Devadharaśarman. The date corresponds to the 5th January 1231 A. D.

It will be seen from the details quoted above that they refer to a deity called Puruṣottama at Cuttack and to its installation not very long before Sunday the Makar-āmāvāsyā day in Śaka 1152, corresponding to the 5th January 1231 A.D., no doubt by king Anaṅgabhīma III (1211-38 A.D.). This Puruṣottama-Jagannātha was worshipped at Cuttack for 130 years and was desecrated by Sulṭān Firūz Shāh about 1360 A.D.

III

Some time ago, the removal of a coating of plaster from the walls of the temple of Śiva called Mārkaṇḍeśvara at the well-known city of Purī in Orissa revealed the existence of a number of inscriptions which had previously been hidden from the eye.

All the epigraphs record the installation of perpetual lamps in the temple of the god Mārkaṇḍeśvara. The earliest of these records is engraved on the right wall of the second gate and belongs to the time of the great Anantavarman Coḍagaṅga (1078-1147 A.D.) who conquered the Puri-Cuttack region from the Somavaṁśīs about the beginning of the twelfth century.[3]

1. In Śaka 1152, the Karkaṭak-āmāvāsyā fell on Thursday the 11th July, 1230 A.D. According to Svamikannu Pillai's *Indian Ephemeris*, there was a solar eclipse this year on the *Vṛṣabh-āmāvāsyā* (Tuesday the 14th May, 1230 A.D.) and not on the Karkaṭak-āmāvāsyā day. The *Vṛiṣabh-amāvāsyā* may be intended in the inscription in the place of *Karkaṭak-āmāvāsyā*.

2. The inscription has *Abhinava-Vārāṇasyāṁ bhagavataḥ śrī-Puruṣottama-devasya sannidhau*.

3. See *Ep. Ind.*, Vol. XXXIII, pp. 181ff.

The inscription of Coḍagaṅga appears to have been engraved in 1114-15 A.D. It begins with the *Siddham* symbol and the date referred to above. The first sentence in lines 1-4 apparently means to say that, in the year 37 during the reign of the illustrious Coḍagaṅgadeva, *Sādhu* Bhīmadeva, a resident of Niralo-grāma called an *Aṅgabhoga* of the god Puruṣottama, as well as Ruda (Rudra ?) and Hari (both probably of the same place) accepted some amount or coins of gold for one *chāyā-dīpa* meant to be a perpetual lamp to be burnt before the god Mārkaṇḍeśvara. The epithet *sādhu* applied to Bhīmadeva shows that he belonged to the mercantile community. Possibly Ruda and Hari were also members of the same community. The expression *aṅga-bhoga* often occurs in Telugu and Kannaḍa inscriptions in association with *raṅga-bhoga* (cf. also *aṅga-raṅga-bhoga*) and is sometimes translated as 'decorations and illuminations of a god'.[1] In the present case, the epithet *aṅga-bhoga* is applied to a village, the income from which appears to have been utilised for the *aṅga-bhoga* or decoration of the deity in question. Thus the village of Niralo seems to have been a rent-free holding in the possession of the god Puruṣottama-Jagannātha of Purī. The expression *chāyā-dīpa* means a lamp held in the hand of an image generally of the donor. The word *chāyā*, 'image', is known from other inscriptions also. A Srikurmam inscription[2] of Śaka 1275, belonging to the reign of Gaṅga Bhānu III, speaks of the dedication of the *chāyās* of the king's father Narasiṁha III and the latter's wife Gaṅgāmbikā, which were represented as holding lamps for offering light to the god in the Srikurmam temple. The responsibility of Bhīmadeva and his two colleagues was no doubt to supply oil for the lamp in lieu of the interest of the gold deposited with them.

The next sentence in line 4 states : "Now Bhīmdeva's son Nāna arranged for the discharge [of his obligation]." This shows that, probably after Bhīmadeva's death, his son Nāna refunded the deposit and thereby freed himself from the obligation of supplying oil for the perpetual lamp. That the res-

1. See *loc. cit.* Cf. Sreenivasachar, *A Corpus of Inscriptions in the Telingana Districts*, Part II, p. 201. For *bhoga*, 'a jāgir', see p. 170. See also Sircar, *Ind. Ep. Gloss.*, s. v.

2. *SII*, Vol. V, No. 1205.

ponsibility fell upon the son of Bhīmdeva alone may further suggest that Ruda and Hari were his own brothers or sons. From the above two sentences we learn that formerly an endowment had been created by depositing some amount or coins of gold with Bhīmadeva and others and that, in the 37th regnal year of the Gaṅga king Anantavarman Coḍagaṅga, Bhīmdeva's son Nāna freed himself from the responsibility. But who created the endowment that was terminated by Nāna is not mentioned in these sentences. The names of the persons responsible for the creation of the endowment are, however, possibly known from the following sentences which describe the creation of a new endowment in the place of the terminated one.

The next sentence in lines 4-6 mentions three person and refers to an image representing all the three of them. The following sentence in line 6 states that Jīvanta-śreṣṭhin accepted the gold for the lamp. This apparently means that the said three persons had originally created an endowlment for the supply of oil for a perpetual lamp held in the hands of their own images in the temple of Mārkaṇḍeśvara and that, on the termination of the old endowment, they created another endowment by depositing the same gold with another person named Jīvanta-śreṣṭhin. The condition binding Jīvanta-śreṣṭhin is found in the following sentence in lines 6-7, which states that, in respect of the said perpetual lamp, the god Mārkaṇḍeśvara would receive two hundred [measures] of oil every month. The name of the measure is not given in the record. In a similar context in the Bhubaneswar inscription of Anantavarman Coḍagaṅga, mention is made of the *karaṅka*, i.e. a small pot usually made out of coconut-shell and used in measuring oil.[1] The same *karaṅka* measure may be referred to in the present case as well. The names of the three persons who created the endowment are given as : (1) Hari, the *Pūjāhāri* of the god Mārkaṇḍeśvara (2) Vāndau (probably another *Pūjāhāri* of the same god), and (3) Vāsu, the *Pūjāhāri* of another god whose name appears to be Kohṛiṇeśvara. *Pūjāhāri* is the same as *Pūjārī* meaning 'a priest.'

Lines 7-9 at the end of the record mention the names of

1. *Ep. Ind.*, Vol. XXX, pp. 30-31.

the persons who were witnesses to the above transaction. These were (1) *Mudrāhasta* Devadhara; (2) Nīlakamuṇḍa (possibly another *Mudrāhasta*); (3) *Pasāpālaka* Śrīdhara; (4) Nārāyaṇa (possibly another *Pasāpālaka*); (5) *Sāṁmavāji* Mahādeva; (6) Devameṇḍi (possibly another *Sāṁmavāji*); and (7) *Śrikaraṇa* Hari. *Mudrāhasta* (Oriya *Mudiratha*) is now the designation of a class of servants of the god Puruṣottama-Jagannātha of Purī. Devadhara may have been a similar servant of the god Mārkaṇḍeśvara. *Pasāpālaka* may be the same official designation found in inscriptions in the forms of *Pasāyita*, *Pasāita* or *Pasāyati*.[1] *Sāṁmavāji* may be mistake for *Somayājin*. *Śrikaraṇa* is the designation of a scribe. These people appear to have been temple officials.

The inscription is interesting from several points of view. It is the only inscription of Anantavarman Coḍagaṅga so far discovered at Purī where the Gaṅga king is known to have built the great temple of Puruṣottama-Jagannātha after its annexation to the Gaṅga empire and the transference of his allegiance from Śaivism to Vaiṣṇavism in the early years of the twelfth century. It is not possible to determine when exactly and by whom the Mārkaṇḍeśvara temple was built. But it is not unlikely that this temple had been in existence when Coḍagaṅga built the temple for Puruṣottama-Jagannātha. We do not know whether the Puruṣottama-Jagannātha temple was built by Coḍagaṅga before or after the 37th year of his reign, though the absence of any reference to the achievement in any of his own records may probably suggest that the construction was undertaken in the later years of his life. We also do not know as to who was responsible for granting the village of Niralo in favour of the god Puruṣottama-Jagannātha, although it is clear that this deity was already enjoying considerable influence when the inscription under study was engraved. The suggestion is supported by the reference to *sāgara-tīra-sanniveśe Puruṣottama-śabditaṁ devāyatanam* in Kṛṣṇmiśra's *Prabodhacandrodaya* which was staged in the presence of the Candella king Kīrtivarman (c. 1065-1100 A. D.).[2]

It is difficult to say whether the suggestion is further sup-

1. Cf. *ibid.*, Vol. XXIX, p. 107 and note 3; Sircar, *Ind. Ep. Gloss.*, s. v. *Pasāyita* = *prasādita*, probably 'a Jāgīrdār'.

2. *Or. Hist. Res. Journ.*, Vol. III, pp. 1 ff. See above, p. 62, note

ported by the fact that the *Anargharāghava* of Murārimiśra (ninth or tenth century according to some, but c. 1050-1135 A.D. according to others) was staged on the occasion of the *yātrā* of the god Puruṣottama of Purī since the epithet *lavaṇ-oda-velā-van-ālī-tamāla-taru-kandala*, applied to the deity, does not refer to his worship on the sea-shore and since Viṣṇu's name Puruṣottama was not unknown elsewhere.[1] It has to be noticed that Murāri's drama gives a rapid description of well-known places like Ujjayinī, Vārāṇasī, Kailāsa, Prayāga, Tāmraparṇī on the sea, Campā in Gauḍa, Pañcavaṭī, Kuṇḍina in Mahārāṣṭra, Kāñcī in Drāviḍa and Māhiṣmatī in the Cedi-maṇḍala, but not of Puruṣottamapurī or Purī.[2]

IV

The town of Maihar is the headquarters of the former State which now forms a Tahsil of the Satna District of Madhya Pradesh. A *praśasti* is engraved on a slab of stone lying in the temple of Sāradā on the hill near the town.

The *praśasti* was noticed by J. D. Beglar, who visited Maihar (spelt by him as Mahiyār) in 1871-72, in Cunningham's *A.S.I. Reports*, Vol. VII, p. 51, in the following words: "..........to the right of the steps leading upto the chief statue (in the shrine of Devī Sāradā) is a large slab, now cracked, which contains an inscription perfectly illegible from the effects of weather.........." This description of the record with reference to the state of its preservation is not quite correct. The characters of the epigraph belong to the Early Nāgarī alphabet of the tenth century A.D. The language is Sanskrit and the record is written in verse.

The inscription begins with the *maṅgala*: *Oṁ namaḥ Sarasvatyai* which is followed by a fairly big *praśasti* in fiftyone stanzas composed in various metres. Verses 1-2 of the *praśasti* describe the goddess [Sarasvatī] as identical with Brāhmī, Kamalā and Gaurī and as installed 'on this peak [of the hill]'.

1. For the date of Murāri, see De, *Hist. Sans. Lit.*, p. 449; Kieth, *Sanskrit Drama*, p. 225; *ABORI*, Vol. XXXVIII, p. 88; etc.

2. The other references pertaining to dates earlier than the eleventh century, cited in *Or. Hist. Res. Journ.*, Vol. III, pp. 6 ff., are even more dubious.

The reference is no doubt to the hill at Maihar, on which the inscribed slab has been found. The following stanza records the author's obeisance to the goddess Sarasvatī.

Verses 24-35 of the epigraph narrate a story relating to the antecedents of the Brāhmaṇa Dāmodara. It is said that he was really the son of the goddess Sarasvatī and was living in Brahma-loka along with the preceptor of the gods (Bṛhaspati) and that once there was a Śāstric dispute between the two, in which Bṛhaspati was defeated by the young boy (verses 24-26.) Being angry at his defeat, the preceptor of the gods cursed the boy to be born on the earth (verse 27). The boy's mother Sarasvatī then appeased Bṛhaspati (verse 28) who consoled the daughter of Brahman (Sarasvatī)[1] by predicting that her young son would be born in a family of pious Brāhmaṇas and would become a great scholar (verses 29-34). The last stanza of this section (verse 35) puts the following words in Bṛhaspati's mouth: "Verily, this child will again come back to you as a result of being drowned in [the waters of] the sea after having seen Puruṣottama in the Oḍra country."[2] The reference here is to the god Puruṣottama-Jagannātha of Purī in Orissa.

Verses 35-40 describe Dāmodara's career on the earth, the first two stanzas (verses 35-36) stating that, at the time Bṛhaspati was consoling Sarasvatī in heaven, Dāmodara was born as the son of Devadhara on the earth. It is further stated that, as predicted by the preceptor of the gods, he stayed in his (i.e. his father's) house till be became sixteen years old. The following two stanzas (verses 37-38) state how then Dāmodara left his parents, friends and relations and, resolving to set out on pilgrimage, reached in due course the sea-shore where he saw the god Puruṣottama.[3] Verse 40 states that Dāmodara

1. Attention may be drawn to the representation of the goddess Sarasvatī as identical with Brāhmī, Kamalā and Gaurī and also as the daughter of the god Brahman. We know that our goddess of learning is variously represented in Purāṇic literature as the daughter or wife of Brahman (though Brahman's more well-known wife in Gāyatrī or Sāvitrī) and sometimes also as identical with Durgā, the wife of Śiva, as the wife of Viṣṇu or Manu, and as the daughter of Dakṣa. See Monier-Williams, *Sans.-Eng. Dict.*, s. v.

2. *Samudra-majjanān=nūnam=Oḍreṣu Puruṣottamam* |
dṛṣṭvā tav=āṁtike bhūyaḥ pur=āgacchaty=ayoṁ śiśuḥ ||

3. *Tatas=tu gaṇitair=eva divasair=deva-durlabhaḥ* |
prāptavān jaladhes=tīraṁ dṛṣṭaś=ca Puruṣottamaḥ ||

went back to the world of Brahman where he told the people the story about himself. As indicated by the prediction in verse 35, he must have lost his life while bathing in the waters of the Bay of Bengal near the temple of Puruṣottama-Jagannātha in Orissa. The next stanza (verse 41) says how his father became greatly mortified at the news of his son's death.

The reference to Dāmodara's pilgrimage to Purī is very interesting. As we have seen, there is evidence to show that the god Puruṣottama-Jagannātha of Purī in Orissa was a celebrated deity in the latter part of the eleventh century A.D. when Kṛṇṣamiśra wrote his *Prabodhacandrodaya* at the court of the Candella king Kīrtivarman (c. 1065-1100 A.D.). It is now clear from the present record that the god was enjoying the same celebrity as early as the middle of the tenth century and probably even some time earlier.

CHAPTER V

BALABHADRA AND OTHER DIVINITIES

I

Due to the uprooting of a very old banyan tree several years back, a huge rock bearing an inscription in very bold characters was exposed to view near the Umachal Asram on the north-eastern slope of the Kamakhya or Nilachal hill near Gauhati. This part of the hill is known as the Umachal hill. The inscription was found to be in a perfectly satisfactory state of preservation.

The inscription consists of four lines of writing and its characters belong to the Eastern variety of the 'Gupta' alphabet assignable to a period between the fourth and the sixth century A.D. On palaeographical grounds, the inscription may be assigned to a date near about that of the Barganga inscription[1] of Bhūtivarman (*circa* 518-42 A.D.), with which it has very close resemblance in respect both of palaeography and style. The language of the inscription is Sanskrit . There is a grammatical error in the passage *bhagavataḥ Balabhadrasvāmināya* in lines 3-4, the intended reading apparently being either *bhagavataḥ Balabhadrasvāminaḥ* or *bhagavate Balabhadrasvāmine*. It is clear that, for °*svāmināya*, Sanskrit °*svāmine* was the intended reading, although the word *bhagavataḥ* suggests that the scribe had originally °*svāminaḥ* in his mind.

The inscription was meant to serve the purpose of a label of an artificial cave (*guha*)[2] or cave-temple constructed by *Mahārājādhirāja* Surendravarman for *Bhagavat* Balabhadrasvāmin. The epigraph is small; but its contents have some importance in view of the fact that *Mahārājādhirāja* Surendravarman, known from this record to have held sway over the heart of the Prāgjyotiṣa or Kāmarūpa country during the age

1. *Ep. Ind.*, Vol. XXX, pp. 62 ff. and Plate.

2. The use of the word *guha* in the neuter, probably in the sense of Sanskrit *guhā*, 'cave', is of lexical interest. The word *guha*, as used in the epigraph, does not appear to be derived from Sanskrit *gṛha* under the influence of local pronounciation.

of the Imperial Guptas, is not known from any other source, while the deity *Bhagavat* Balabhadrasvāmin is not mentioned in any epigraphic records of the Gupta period so far known. The construction of artificial caves and the installation of deities therein are well known to the students of Indian history and epigraphy.[1] But the present inscription supplies the only instance of the kind for Assam. The record also appears to be the earliest so far discovered in that State.

We know that, from the middle of the fourth till the middle of the seventh century, Prāgjyotiṣa or Kāmarūpa was under the rule of kings of a family called Bhauma or Nāraka and rarely also Varman. This dynasty was founded by Puṣyavarman who seems to have flourished in *circa* 350-74 A.D. His successors were his son Samudravarman (c. 374-98 A.D.), grandson Balavarman (c. 398-422 A.D.), great-grandson Kalyāṇavarman (c. 422-46 A. D.) and great-great grandson Gaṇapativarman (c. 446-70 A.D.). Gaṇapativarman's successor was Mahendravarman (c. 470-94 A.D.) whose son Nārāyaṇavarman (c. 494-518 A.D.) and grandson Bhūtivarman or Mahābhūtavarman (c. 518-42 A.D.) were both performers of the horse-sacrifice. The Barganga inscription, which seems to be slightly later than the record under review was incised during the reign of the said Bhūtivarman. It therefore appears that the Umachal rock inscription was engraved during the reign of one of the said rulers of the Bhauma-Nāraka dynasty. It has to be remembered that the Umachal hill lies within a short distance from Gauhati where (or, in the vicinity of which) the capital of the Bhauma-Nāraka kings is believed to have been situated.[2] The question is therefore whether Surendravarman of the present record was identical with one of the above kings or he was a usurper. In the latter case, we have to determine whether he was a scion of the Bhauma-Nāraka dynasty or belonged to a different family. None of these questions can be settled satisfactorily in the present state of insufficient information. Since, however, in ancient India kings often enjoyed a number of different names, it may

1. Cf. *Corp. Ins. Ind.*, Vol. III, pp. 221 ff., 223 ff., 226 ff.

2. Cf. P. N. Bhattacharya, *Kāmarūpaśāsanāvali*, intro., pp. 8, 22; *Ep. Ind.*, Vol. XXX, p. 92.

not be unreasonable to identify Surendravarman of our inscription with one of the known rulers of the Bhauma-Nāraka dynasty, who flourished about the fifth century. Since again, in ancient India kings were sometimes mentioned by synonyms of their names, Surendravarman may be tentatively identified with Mahendravarman of the Bhauma-Nāraka dynasty, who flourished in c. 470-94 A.D. The names *Surendra* and *Mahendra* both indicate Indra, the lord of the gods.

As regards *Bhagavat* Balabhadrasvāmin, for whom king Surendravarman is stated in the record to have built an artificial cave or cave-temple, it may be argued that he was a saint held by the monarch in special esteem. It is, however, more likely that *Bhagavat* Balabhadrasvāmin of the present inscription is no other than the well-known Vaiṣṇavite deity variously called Balabhadra, Baladeva, Balarāma, Saṅkarṣaṇa, etc. He was one of the five deified heroes of the Yādava-Sātvata-Vṛṣṇi clan, the others being Vāsudeva (Kṛṣṇa), Pradyumna, Aniruddha and Sāmba. Of these, Vāsudeva, Balabhadra-Saṅkarṣaṇa, Pradyumna and Anirudha came to be worshipped as the four *Vyūhas* by the followers of the Bhāgavata or Pañcarātra form of early Vaiṣṇavism, although Balabhadra-Saṅkarṣaṇa and Vāsudeva were the more respected among the four. There is enough evidence regarding the independent worship of Balabhadra in the period before the rise of the Imperial Guptas in the fourth century A. D. The inscriptions of the Gupta age do not refer to his independent worship, although the *Vyūha* doctrine finds a prominent place in the Pañcarātra *Saṁhitās*, some of which were composed between the fourth and eighth centuries. The *Amarakoṣa*, composed during this period, speaks of all the four *Vyūhas*. A modified form of the *Vyūha* doctrine is also noticed in the joint worship of Balabhadra, Kṛṣṇa and Ekānaṁśā (or, Subhadrā), their combined image being referred to by Varāhamihira in the sixth century A.D. Gradually Balabhadra came to be regarded as one of the *Avatāras* of Viṣṇu.[1] The importance of the Umachal rock inscription therefore lies in the fact that it testifies to the indepen-

1. For the worship of Balabhadra, see above, pp. 32ff., 47; also *History and Culture of the Indian People*, Vol. II (*The Age of Imperial Unity*), pp. 447 ff.; *ibid.*, Vol. III (*The Classical Age*), p.418.

dent worship of Balabhadra in Assam about the fifth century A.D. Thus it appears that, even though the independent worship of this Vaiṣṇavite deity was no longer popular, it did not die out in the Gupta age.

II

A terracotta plaque was discovered in a village under the Teghra Police Station of the Begusarai Subdivision in the Moghyr District, Bihar. It is semi-circular in shape and has a flat obverse and raised reverse. The base of the semicircle is about $2\frac{1}{2}$ inches long while its bisector is about $1\frac{3}{4}$ inches in length. There are four or probably five lines of writing engraved on the obverse. A few letters from the right end of the inscription on the obverse have broken away.

The characters employed in the inscription on the obverse of the plaque belong to a cursive form of the Gauḍīya alphabet while those in the writing on the reverse have the standard forms of the letters of the same script. It is obvious that the two lines of writing on the reverse were impressed on the plaque when the clay was quite soft before it had dried up or had been baked in the sun. An examination of the letters of the inscription on the obverse shows that they were engraved before the plaque had been burnt in fire. It is not certain whether this record was engraved when the clay was still a little soft or it had already quite hardened as a result of baking in the sun, although an examination of the engraving appears to support the first alternative. In any case, there could not have been a long interval between the impressing of the sealing on the reverse of the plaque and the engraving of the inscription on its obverse. But there is no doubt that the record on the reverse is earlier, at least by a few hours, than the epigraph on the obverse.

The cursive Gauḍīya characters of the inscription on the obverse of the plaque resemble in some respects the letters of the modern Bengali and Maithili alphabets. On palaeographical grounds, the record may be assigned to the thirteenth or fourteenth century A.D. As indicated above, the writing on the reverse of the plaque should also have to be assigned to the same age. The language of both the records is Sanskrit.

The date, quoted in line 1 of the inscription on the obverse, reads : *Saṁ* 67 *Dhauṣa-dine* no doubt standing for *Saṁvat* 67 *Pauṣa-dine*. The record was therefore incised on a day of the solar month of Pauṣa (i.e., Dhanus) in the 67th year of some era. Considering the provenance of the plaque and the date of the epigraph suggested by its palaeography, it is possible to think that the era to which the year has to be referred is none other than the Lakṣmaṇasena-saṁvat or La-Saṁ which started in the Gaya region of South Bihar and later spread to Mithila (North Bihar). There is considerable confusion in regard to the epoch of this era, and it has been said that 'the initial year of the era, as reckoned at different times and places, varied between 1108 and 1120 A.D.'[1] But the earliest dates of the era, viz. years 51, 74, and 83, are supposed to have been counted from 1179 A.D. which is the date of king Lakṣmaṇasena's accession.[2] The date of the record under study, viz., year 67, thus may correspond to c. 1245 A.D.

Both the lines of writing, impressed on the reverse of the plaque by means of a sealing, read *Śrī-Suhmakasya*, the passage being followed by a double *daṇḍa* and a symbol. The sealing, used in imprinting the lines, therefore belonged to a person named Suhmaka. It is clear that the same sealing was employed twice. The reason for this may be that the letters of the lower line, originally impressed, did not all of them come out quite clearly.

The inscription on the obverse of the plaque consists of four or probably five lines of writing, of which the first, giving the date of the record, has been quoted and discussed above. The object of the inscription appears to be that three persons named Śādhi, Eci and Āka made a gift of a lotus at the feet of Keśavā at Nāgalḍāmaka. Keśavā appears to have been the name of a god or goddess worshipped at a place called Nāgalḍāmaka. Whether the name is a mistake for Keśava, meaning Viṣṇu, cannot be determined. It seems that Suhmaka was the chief priest of the temple of the deity in question or a royal official whose seal was believed to impart the required authenticity to the deed of gift.

1. *History of Bengal*, Vol. I (Dacca University), pp. 233-38; cf. *JBRS*, Vol. XXXVII, Parts 3-4, pp. 10-13.
2. Sircar, *Ind. Ep.*, p. 276.

The fact that the offering of a lotus in favour of a deity was regarded as important enough to be recorded in an inscription, albeit on a terracotta plaque, appears to suggest that the flower was not an ordinary one. It was probably a lotus made of gold or silver.[1] The inscription points to the custom of using clay plaques or tablets as writing material side by side with other objects such as copper plates. Terracotta plaques, which were not as durable as copper plates, but were much cheaper and more easily procurable, were probably used to record minor donations of poorer people.

III

Burhikhar is a small hamlet adjacent to the famous village of Malhar in the Bilaspur District of Madhya Pradesh. A small Brāhmī inscription was noticed sometime ago on a stone image that is being worshipped now at the village under the name of Caturbhujī Bhagavān. Unfortunately the image being covered with a thick coating of white paint which filled in much of the fairly deep incision of the inscription, the writing was found to be almost undecipherable.

I was told in 1950 that the image of the so-called Caturbhujī Bhagavān was formerly not an object of special veneration in the locality. Of late a Sādhu came to the village and his attention was attracted by the neglected image. It was this Sādhu who was responsible for raising a thatched shelter over the image and painting it with the white coating referred to above. He also instituted a sort of regular worship of the image.

The Caturbhujī Bhagavān, as the name would suggest, is a male figure with four arms. It is about two and a half feet in height; but its feet are built into the floor apparently because

1. Flowers made of gold have been discovered at such ancient sites as Salihundam (Srikakulam District, Andhra Pradesh) in the course of excavations (cf. *Indian Archaeology*, 1953-54, p. 11). For an offering of silver flowers, cf. *SII*, Vol. IV, No. 1019. The Kathmandu inscription (*Ind. Ant.*, Vol. IX, pp. 178 ff.) of Jayadeva speaks of the gift of a precious silver lotus in favour of a Śivaliṅga made by the queen-mother Vatsadevī daughter of Maukhari Bhogavarman and granddaughter of king Ādityasena of Magadha.

the lower part of the image was broken. The figure holds the *cakra* (discus) in the upper left hand and the top of a big *gadā* (mace) by the upper right, while the palms of the lower two hands are folded in the *añjali* pose. The *gadā* is a rather long flat staff and stands under the right arm of the image. He wears a *karaṇḍa-mukuṭa* (a particular kind of conical crown), usually found on the head of subordinate deities. There is a globular object below the ears probably representing *kuṇḍala* or curled hair loops. The inscription in question is engraved in one line on the flat shaft of the *gadā*. The line begins in the upper part of the *gadā* and comes downwards.

The characters of the inscription are Early Brāhmī. They resemble the alphabet of the Nanaghat cave inscriptions,[1] but may be slightly later in date. The letter *ra* is of the straight and not of the older corkscrew type. *Da* has the cursive form, occasionally found in the Nanaghat and some other early inscriptions side by side with the unmodified older form. The downward projection of the left member of *bha* is shorter than in the Nanaghat alphabet and seems to suggest a little later date. *Ya* is usually of the Indian-plough type; but, in one case, the straight upper stroke joins the lower curve not in the middle, as is usual, but above its right end. *Ya* with a slanting stroke like this is only rarely found in inscriptions and coin legends.[2] The epigraph may be palaeographically assigned to a date about the close of the first century B.C. or the beginning of the first century A.D.

The language of the inscription is Prakrit. Interesting from the orthographical point of view is the *ya-śruti* in the names *Payāvati* for *Prajāvatī* and *Bhāradāyi* for *Bhāradvājī*.

The object of the inscription was to record the fact that the image on which it is engraved was the gift of a lady named Prajāvatī and that it was caused to be made by another lady named Bhāradvājī. The relation between the two ladies has not been stated and cannot be determined. The image was no doubt installed in a Vaiṣṇava religious establishment that must have existed in the Burhikhar-Malhar region in ancient times.

1. See *Select Inscriptions*, Vol. I, Plate facing p. 186.
2. Cf. Ojha, *Prācīn Bhāratiya Lipimālā*, Plate X, 1; cf. Plate XII, ii, and Plate XIII.

The importance of the inscription lies not so much in its contents, but in the fact that its early characters prove the antiquity of the image on which it is engraved. The description of the sculpture will show that it is a Vaiṣṇava image. The lower hands in the *añjali* pose suggest that it is not Viṣṇu, but is probably a *parivāra-devatā* of that god. The discovery of the image no doubt points to the existence of a Vaiṣṇavite religious establishment in the Burhikhar-Malhar region of the Bilaspur District of Madhya Pradesh. Considering the antiquity of the image, the Vaiṣṇavite establishment, to which it belonged may be regarded as the earliest in that part of India and one of the earliest in the whole country.

IV

While writing on the history of Northern India after the downfall of the Kuṣāṇa empire,[1] we tried to draw the attention of scholars to two interesting points among others. These two are: (1) that the appearance of legends on early Indian money including the so-called tribal coinage was due to the influence of foreign coins, particularly those of the Indo-Greeks who established themselves in North-Western India about the beginning of the second century B.C., and (2) that the word *bhagavata* sometimes used in the legend of certain tribal coins in relation to a deity has often been wrongly taken to be *Bhāgavata* and as an epithet of the people who circulated the monetary issues. The second of these two suggestions relates to the interesting custom of issuing coins sometimes exclusively in the name of a god and sometimes in the names both of a god and the human issuer or issuers of the money, the former no doubt being the tutelary deity of the latter.

The Prakrit legend on two silver coins in the British Museum, which are attributed to the Audumbaras, has been read in both Kharoṣṭhī and Brāhmī as *bhagavata mahadevasa*. This has been taken to stand for Sanskrit *Bhāgavata-Mahādevasya* and translated into English as 'of Mahādeva, the worshipper

1. *The Age of Imperial Unity*, Bhāratīya Vidyā Bhavan, Bombay, 1951, pp. 159 ff.

of the Bhagavat'.[1] There is, however, little doubt that the legend really stands for Sanskrit *Bhagavato Mahādevasya*, "[This is the coin] of Lord Mahādeva." That the coins were not issued by a *Bhāgavata*, meaning 'a devotee of the god Viṣṇu,' seems to be suggested by the fact that they bear the representations of a humped bull and a trident (or trident-battle-axe) among others. While the trident is the typical weapon of Śiva, the bull here has to be regarded either as Śiva's *vāhana* or as the animal form of the god.[2] Thus the coins were issued in the name of the god Mahādeva-Śiva.

There is the word *rajarana* in Kharoṣṭhī in the exergue on the obverse of these coins, which is given in Brāhmī on the reverse as *rājarāja*. These stand for Sanskrit *Rājarājasya*, 'of the king of kings,' which refers to the god Mahādeva in the main part of the legend. We have several instances of a kingdom being dedicated to the tutelary deity by a king so that the said ruler and his successors regarded themselves as the viceroys of the deity who was considered to be the real king of the country.[3] Mention may be made in this connection of the later Eastern Gaṅgas of Orissa, the Guhilas of Mewar and the *Mahārājas* of Travancore, who respectively regarded the gods Puruṣottama-Jagannātha, Ekaliṅga and Padmanābhasvāmin as their overlord.[4] Of course it is difficult to be sure whether the Audumbaras considered the god Mahādeva to be the ruler of their country. But another class of their coins leaves no room for doubt that the said god was their tutelary deity.

The full Prakrit legends on four types of Audumbara coins have been read respectively as follows :

(1) *Mahadevasa raña Sivadasasa Odubarisa*;
(2) *Mahadevasa raña Rudradasasa Odubarisa*;

1. Allan, *Catalogue* (Anc. Ind.), pp. lxxxv, 123-24.

2. Cf. the representation of the bull with the legend *jayatu Vṛṣaḥ* on the reverse of the coins of the Hūṇa king Mihirakula who was a staunch Śaiva (Smith, *Catalogue*, p. 236; *Select Inscriptions*, p. 401, note 3).

3. See above, p. 60; *Ep. Ind.*, Vol. XXX, p. 19.

4. Likewise, the Kalacuris regarded themselves as the feudatories of the Śaiva ascetic Vāmadeva or Vāmaśambhu (*Ind. Ep.*, *op. cit.* pp. 46 ff.). Cf. also the story of Chatrapati Śivājī's dedication of his kingdom to his *guru* Rāmadāsa. For Vāmadeva, see below.

(3) *Mahadevasa raña Dharaghosasa Odubarisa*; and

(4) *Mahadevasa raña Odubarisa*.[1]

In Nos. 1-3, *Mahadeva* (*Mahādeva*) has been regarded as the regal title of the kings Śivadāsa, Rudradāsa and Dharaghoṣa, while, in No. 4, the same word has been taken to be either the personal name of an Audumbara king or the regal title as in the other cases.[2] But in all these cases, *Mahadevasa* (*Mahādevasya*) has to be separated from the rest of the legend, viz. *raña Sivadasasa Odubarisa* (*rājñaḥ Śivadāsasya Audumbareḥ*), etc. Thus the whole legend would mean, "[This is the coin] of Mahādeva [and] of king Śivadāsa of the Audumbara clan." There is no doubt that, in No. 4, a royal name like Śivadāsa, Rudradāsa and Dharaghoṣa is cut off. We have also no doubt that Mahādeva of these coins is identical with the god of this name known from the silver coins discussed above. Thus, in Nos. 1-4, the coins are represented as having been issued in the names of both the Audumbara king and his tutelary deity. That the kings were Śaivas is indicated by the appearance of the trident-battle-axe on the coins.

The legend on a type of coins attributed to the Kuṇindas has been finally read by Allan as *Bhāgavata-Catreśvara-mahātmanaḥ* which appears to have been taken to mean, "This is the coin of the exalted Catreśvara who is the devotee of the *Bhagavat*," as in the case of *Bhagavata-Mahadevasa*[3] discussed above. But the fact that the figure of the god Śiva holding a trident appears on the obverse of these coins shows that they were not issued by a *Bhāgavata* or devotee of the god Viṣṇu. The legend is thus apparently *Bhagavataḥ Catreśvara-mahātmanaḥ* meaning, "[This is the coin] of Lord Catreśvara who is the Supreme Spirit." Thus Catreśvara was the name not of a king, but of a form of the god Śiva. He was the deity in whose name the coins were issued probably by the Kuṇindas as in the case of the Mahādeva issues attributed to the Audumbaras.

On some specimens of the coins of the Yaudheyas, the

1. Allan, *op. cit.*, p. lxxxiv.

2. Cf. *ibid.*, p. lxxxiii : "As *Mahādeva* is also found as a regal title on these coins, it is possible that some of the specimens attributed to him in the Catalogue are really incomplete specimens of other rulers."

3. *Ibid.*, p. ciii; cf. pp. 167-68.

legend has been read as *Yaudheya-bhāgavata-svāmino Brahmaṇyasya*[1] which has been translated as, 'of Brahmaṇya (a name of Kārttikeya), the divine lord of the Yaudheyas'. But the intended reading of this legend is apparently either *Yaudheyānāṁ Bhagavataḥ Svāmino Brahmanyasya* or *Bhagavataḥ Svāmino Bramaṇyasya Yaudheyānām*. The first of these may be translated as either (1) "[This is the coin] of the Yaudheyas and of the Divine Lord Brahmaṇya," as in the case of the Mahādeva issues of the Audumbara kings Śivadāsa, Rudradāsa and Dharaghoṣa, or (2) "[This is the coin] of the Divine Lord Brahmaṇya who is the tutelary deity of the Yaudheyas." The alternative reading, which may really be the same as the first, can also be interpreted in the same way.

As in the case of the Mahādeva and Catreśvara coins ascribed respectively to the Audumbaras and Kuṇindas, some specimens of Yaudheya coins appear to mention the god Brahmaṇyadeva Kumāra without reference to the Yaudheyas. This legend has been read as *Bhāgavata-svāmino Brahmaṇyadevasya Kumārasya*[2] and translated as 'of Kumāra, the divine lord Brahmaṇyadeva.' But the intended reading is no doubt *Bhagavataḥ Svāmino Brahmaṇyadevasya Kumārasya*, "[This is the coin] of Lord Brahmaṇyadeva *alias* Kumāra."

There is a group of interesting coins coming from Agroha and its neighbourhood in the Hissar District of the Haryana State.[3] There are two types in this group, the first bearing the legend : *Agodakā Agāca-janapadasa* probably standing for Sanskrit *Agrodakāt Agratya-janapadasya*, "[This is the coin] of the Agratya-janapada issued from Agrodaka."[4] This reminds

1. Allan, *op. cit.*, p. cxlix. The legend read as *Bhāgavata-svāmino Brahmaṇya-Yaudheya* also belongs to the same class.

2. *Ibid.*, p. cl. *Kumarāsya* is apparently a misprint like many others in this part of the book.

3. *Ibid.*, pp. clvii ff.; L. D. Barnett in *BSOS*, Vol. X, pp. 279 ff.; P. L. Gupta in *JNSI*, Vol. IV, pp. 49ff. Gupta quotes the views of several other writers on the coins. See also *JNSI*, Vol. VIII, p. 32.

4. For *Agratya=Agāca*, cf. *āgatya=āgāca* in the Rummindei pillar inscription (*CII*, Vol. I, p. 164). Bernett speaks of the Sanskrit form as *Agratya* or *Agrattya* while Gupta and others derive *Agāca* from *Āgreya*, a people known from the *Mahābhārata*. We do not agree with the latter view, though *Agratya* and *Āgreya* both mean 'the people of Agra'. K. N. Dikshit derived it from *Agatya*, *Agastya* or *Aṅgatya* (cf. *JNSI*, Vol. V. p. 50).

us of the legend on the Śibi coins, which reads *Majhamikāya Śibi-janapadasa* (Sanskrit *Madhyamikāyāḥ Śibi-janapadasya*), "[This is the coin] of the Śibi-janapada [issued] from Madhyamikā."[1]

The form *Agāca* seems to be derived from *Agratya* through the intermediate Prakrit form *Aggacca* by simplifying the reduplication of *cca* and compensating the loss by lengthening the preceding vowel, though the simplification of *gga* to *ga* is due to the avoidance of reduplication in the Prakrit of early inscriptions and coins, i.e. *Agratya*>*Aggacca*>*Aggāca*=*Agāca*. The word *Agratya* would literally mean the inhabitants of the Agra country[2] while Agrodaka seems to have been the headquarters of the *janapada* or republican corporation of the Agratyas. This Agrodaka is no doubt the same as modern Agroha where many of the coins under study were discovered.[3]

On the second type of the Agroha coins, Barnett read the legend as : *Agācamitrapadābhiṣṭhāyinaṁ* or *Agācamitrapadābhiṣṭhayinaḥ*, in which he understood the expression *mitrapada* in the sense of 'an allied state', i.e. a state allied with the Agāca or Agratya people. But the legend does not give any satisfactory sense in that case, and it looks rather unusual. It appears to us that the intended reading of the legend is : *Agācamitra* (*Agratyamitra*)*-pād-ābhiṣṭhayinām*, "[This is the coin] of those who dwell at the feet of Agratyamitra." The name Agratyamitra would literally mean 'the friend of the Agratyas', and Agratyamitra would appear to have been a god who was the tu-

1. Cf. Allan, *op. cit.*, p. cxxiv.

2. That the name of the land was Agra seems to be supported by the name of the Agravāla (Agrawala=Sanskrit *Agrapāla*) community which hails from it. It may be that the name Agrodaka was also often indicated by its first part, viz. Agra. The geographical name Puruṣottama-purī is known to have been shortened as Puruṣottama or Purī (above, p.67, note 3).

3. The headquarters of the Agra country may have been called *Agrodaka*, 'the Agra water', owing to the existence of a big tank (cf. *JNSI*, Vol. IV, p. 54). In that case, both the country and its capital were called Agra originally, though the latter was later called Agrodaka in order to distinguish it from the former. There is also the possibility that the Agratyas lived in a small area forming a sort of city-corporation. But, even in such a case, the locality where the administrative office of the corporation was situated may have been called Agrodaka to distinguish it from the rest of Agra.

telary deity of the Agratyas of Agrodaka. Thus these coins were issued by the Agratyas not directly in the name of their tutelary deity, as in the case of some of the coins of the Audumbaras, Kuṇindas and Yaudheyas, but in the name of themselves represented as the devotees of the god Agratyamitra of Agrodaka.

V

The religion of the Hindus is not guided by the personality of a single man like Christ or Muḥammad. In fact, it has been catholic enough to acknowledge the guidance of any religious teacher. Early Indian law-givers really believed that they wrote not for the people of a particular locality, but for all the peoples they knew. Manu, e.g., includes the following peoples in a list of degraded Kṣatriyas—

Pauṇḍrakāś=c=Auḍra-Draviḍāḥ Kāmbojā Yavanāḥ Śakāḥ ।
Pāradāḥ Pahlavāś=Cīnāḥ Kirātā Daradāḥ Khasāḥ ॥[1]

These are the Pauṇḍraka (people of North Bengal), Oḍra (people of Orissa), Draviḍa (Tamil people), Kāmboja (Iranian settlers of the Kandahar region and elsewhere), Yavana (Greek), Śaka (Scythian), Pārada (Parthian), Pahlava (Persian or Sassanian), Cīna (Chinese), Kirāta (Nepalese), Darada (people of the Kishenganga Valley in Kashmir) and Khasa (a people of Kashmir or the Himalayan region). Again the Lord says in the *Gītā*—

Yadā yadā hi dharmasya glānir=bhavati Bhārata ।
abhyutthānam=adharmasya tad=ātmānaṁ sṛjāmy=aham ॥
paritrāṇāya sādhūnāṁ vināśāya ca duṣkṛtām ।
dharma-saṁsthāpan-ārthāya sambhavāmi yuge yuge ॥[2]

"Wherever there is decline of Dharma and rise of Adharma, O descendant of Bharata, there I create myself. For the relief of the pious and for the destruction of the sinners, and for the establishment of Dharma, I am born in different ages." This was said not with reference to the people we now call Hindu, but with reference to all peoples. And thus, not only the Buddha, but Christ, Muḥammad, Nānak and other great religious

1. X.44. For *c=Auḍra*, *Coḍa* is a variant reading.
2. IV. 7-8.

teachers may all be taken as *Avatāras*, the number of which is sometimes said to be *asaṅkheya* (innumerable).

All Indian religious teachers drew more or less upon the philosophical teachings of India and stood upon her traditions and customs. Like other religious teachers, the Gurus of the Sikhs could not be immune from such influence. It is not very difficult to prove that the philosophical and practical sides of Sikhism have both Hinduism as their background. Let us consider the peculiar reverence which the Sikhs exhibit to the sword. This sword-worship is not an innovation.

According to Manu—

Kurukṣetrāṁś=ca Matsyāṁś=ca Pañcālān=Śūrasenakān ।
dīrghān laghūṁś=c=aiva narān=agrāmikeṣu yodhayet ॥[1]

This verse shows that at least certain ancient Indian kings recruited their soldiers chiefly from the peoples of Kurukṣetra (the Eastern Punjab and its vicinity), Matsya (country to the west of Mathūrā), Pañcāla (Ahicchatra and Kanauj regions) and Śūrasena (Mathurā region). It is, therefore, not without a traditional background that the Sikh Gurus, eager as they were to save their community from Muslim aggression, tried to make a martial class of their followers who were generally people of the land round about the Eastern Punjab. In this connection, it is also interesting to note that the *Mahābhārata* considers sword to be 'the foremost of weapons' (*agryaḥ praharaṇānāṁ=ca khaḍgo Mādravatī-suta*)[2] and enjoins—

aseś=ca pūjā kartavyā sadā yuddha-viśāradaiḥ,[3] i.e. "the sword should always be worshipped by the people expert in fighting." The psychology of this custom may even today be noticed in the implement-worship of the Navaśākhas or Navasāyakas of Bengal. These nine middle castes of the Hindu society are the peasant, the florist, the oilman, the weaver, the confectioner, the betel-dealer, the potter, the blacksmith and the barber. On the last day of the month of Bhādra, members of these castes perform worship of the god Viśvakarman. The things actually to be worshipped in this connection are, however, the plough for the peasant, flowers and garlands for the

1. VII. 193.
2. XII. 85.
3. XII. 87.

florist, the oil-presser for the oilman, the weaving machine for the weaver, sweets for the confectioner, betel leaves for the betel-dealer, pots, etc., for the potter, the anvil and bellows for the blacksmith, and the razor, etc., for the barber.[1]

1. Cf. Risley, *People of India*, p. 235 : "The soldier worships his sword; the cultivator his plough; the money-lender his ledger; the Thags... the pickaxe with which they dug the graves of their victims; and...the operatives in the jute mills near Calcutta...the Glasgow-made engines which drive their looms."

CHAPTER VI

ŚAKTI OR THE MOTHER-GODDESS

I

The objects unearthed at the protohistoric sites of the Indus valley culture appear to point to the prevalence of the cult of the Father-god and the Mother-goddess amongst the pre-Aryan peoples of North-Western Bhāratavarṣa. Recent explorations and excavations have shown that the said protohistoric civilization spread its influence over considerable parts of Western India. It is thus possible to think that the worship of the Mother-goddess was not unknown in Western India in the protohistoric times.

The Mahiṣamardinī form of the Mother-goddess has been popular in the Rajasthan area since very early times. The earliest representation of the deity is said to be offered by certain terracotta plaques discovered at Nagar near Uniyara in the Tonk District, which are now preserved in the Amber Museum. One of these has been assigned to the first century B.C. or first century A.D.[1] Stone images of the said deity have been discovered in large numbers from all parts of Rajasthan, and the Rajputs, both the rulers and the common men, are known to have been generally devoted to the goddess and to have been worshipping her under various local names.[2]

A stanza in adoration of the same form of the Mother-goddess is found at the beginning of an inscription from the Bhramaramātā temple near Chhoti Sadri not far from the Neemuch station on the Ajmer-Khandwa railway line.[3] Another stanza of the inscription speaks of the Ardhanārīśvara conception, the right half of the form being Śiva and the left half Śakti. The epigraph records the construction and consecration of a temple of the Devī in January, 491 A.D. The

1. V. S. Srivastava, *Catalogue and Guide to the Ganga Golden Jubilee Museum*, Bikaner, 1961, p. 5.

2. *Loc. cit.* The *Mahābhārata* represents Skanda generally and Śiva and Durgā occasionally as the destroyer of Mahiṣa (Soerenson's Index, p. 458). cf. *Ind. Mus. Bul.*, January, 1969, pp. 60-61.

3. *Ep. Ind.*, Vol. XXX, pp. 120 ff.

goddess is described in the stanza referred to above as *Asura-dāraṇa-tīkṣṇa-śūlā* (holding a sharp spear piercing the *Asura*, i.e. Mahiṣ-āsura) and as *siṁh-ogra-yukta-ratham = āsthita-caṇḍa-vegā* (moving in terrific speed in a chariot drawn by a fierce lion). The second of the two epithets is interesting because, in the early representations of Mahiṣamardinī, the lion is sometimes absent and, even when present, does not usually figure as drawing a chariot carrying the goddess.[1]

It is well known that the *Bṛhatsaṁhitā* (LX. 19) by Varāhamihira, the celebrated Maga-Brāhmaṇa astronomer of the Ujjayinī school, refers to the worship of the Divine Mothers by the *Mātṛ-maṇḍala-vidaḥ* or *maṇḍala-krama-vidaḥ*. The first of the two variant readings, means 'those who know fully the circle of the Divine Mothers', while, in the other reading accepted by Utpala, the word *krama* means 'custom or rule sanctioned by tradition'. Utpala explains *maṇḍala-krama* as *pūjā-krama*, i.e. *maṇḍala-pūjā-krama* (traditional rules regarding the worship of the *maṇḍala*), and further says, *mātṛṇāṁ sva-kalpa-vihita-vidhānen = aiva*, i.e. the worship of the Divine Mothers should be performed in accordance with their individual precepts. The same meaning of *krama* is evident from the names of such works as *Oḍiyana-Tārā-krama*, 'the traditional process of worship of the goddess Tārā of Uḍḍiyāna'.[2] Instead of *Mātṛ-maṇḍala*, the expression *Mātṛ-cakra* is sometimes used. Thus Kalhaṇa's *Rājataraṅgiṇī* (V. 55) speaks of 'the temple of Bhairava who together with the *Mātṛ-cakra* (circle of the Mothers), is worshipped close to Bhūteśa'.

As regards the word *maṇḍala*, we have of course its use in expressions like *Śiva-maṇḍala-dīkṣā* and *Ārya-Tārā-maṇḍala-vidhi-nāma-sādhana*.[4] In these cases, *maṇḍala* seems to mean 'the magic circle'. But the *Mātṛ-maṇḍala*, which is also referred to in the passage *Mātṛṇāṁ loka-mātṛṇāṁ maṇḍalam* occurring in a sixth century inscription from Udaygiri (Jhansi District, U.P.) recording the construction and consecration of a temple of the

1. Banerjea, *Development of Hindu Iconography*, 2nd ed., pp. 498ff.; cf. pp. 134ff.

2. S. C. Vidyabhushan, *Bauddhastotrasaṁgraha*, Vol. I: *Sragdharā-stotra*, p. xii.

3. *Ep. Ind.*, Vol. XXXII, p. 181.

4. Cf. S. C. Vidyabhushan, *op. cit.*, p. xi.

Divine Mothers, seems to be the same as the *Mātṛ-gaṇa* or 'the group of the Divine Mothers' as mentioned in the records of the Early Kadamba kings. These rulers claimed to have been favoured by the god Ṣaḍānana or Mahāsena (i.e. Skanda Kārttikeya) and the Divine Mothers or their group, while the Early Cālukyas of Badami are stated to have been nourished by the Seven Mothers described as *Sapta-loka-mātṛ*, often interpreted as 'the Seven Mothers of mankind', though the real meaning may be 'the Mothers of the Seven Worlds'.[1] The reference in all these cases seems to be to the collective worship of the Divine Mothers regarded as seven in number and probably known as the Circle of Seven.

Although the number of the Divine Mothers is often given as eight and sometimes also as nine and sixteen, originally the goddesses appear to have been counted as seven, enumerated in certain texts as (1) Brāhmī or Brahmāṇī, (2) Māheśvarī, (3) Kaumārī, (4) Vaiṣṇavī, (5) Vārāhī, (6) Indrāṇī, Aindrī or Māhendrī and (7) Cāmuṇḍā. But the names in the different lists giving the same number of goddesses, not to speak of the bigger lists, are not exactly the same. Even in the popular list of eight deities, Yāmī, Caṇḍikā, Carcikā, Nārasiṃhī, etc., are variously introduced.[2] The Purāṇas represent the Divine Mothers as attending usually on Kārttikeya, but sometimes on Śiva. Their association with Kārttikeya, possibly determined their original number being seven, since the said god, though he is famous as Ṣaṇmātura or 'the son of Six Mothers', may be regarded as having seven mothers including the six Kṛttikās together with Pārvatī or Gaṅgā.[3]

It will be seen that, in Western India as in some other parts of the country, at least in the age of the Guptas, the Mother-

1. Cf. Sircar, *The Successors of the Sātavāhanas*, pp. 239-40.

2. See *Śabdakalpadruma*, s. v. *mātṛkā*; Monier-Wlliams, *Sans.-Eng. Dict.*, s. v. *mātṛ*; Apte, *Pract. Sans.-Eng. Dict.*, s. v. *mātṛ*. Under the *Bṛhatsaṁhitā*, LVII.56, Utpala speaks of Vāruṇī and Kauberī in the list of the Mothers.

3. Cf. Monier-Williams, *op. cit.*, s. v. *Kārttikeya*. There is a slab bearing the representation of only three Divine Mothers, viz. Brahmāṇī, Kaumārī and Vaiṣṇavī (Banerjea, *op. cit.*, p. 505). But, at the place of worship in question, there may have been other slabs bearing the figures of the other *Mātṛkās*.

goddess was worshipped in her individual aspects as well as collectively in a Circle of Seven. That there was a pronounced Tantric element in the Mother-goddess cult of the said area is clear from an Aulikara inscription of 423 A.D.[1] This epigraph records the construction and consecration of the god Viṣṇu by a person who had apparently both Śākta and Vaiṣṇava leanings.

This is an interesting feature of West Indian religious life, and another important fact is that the temple of the Mothers is described as a terrible abode full of Ḍākinīs or female ghouls (*ḍākinī-samprakīrṇa*) and the goddesses themselves are represeted as uttering loud and tremendous shouts of joy and stirring up the very oceans with the winds rising from the *tantra* or magical rites (*pramudita-ghan-ātyartha-nihrādinī* and *tantrodbhūta-prabala-pavan-odvartit-āmbhonidhī*).

The above description of the Divine Mothers and their temple in a West Indian epigraph of the fifth century A.D. is especially interesting because, in the said region, the later phases of Buddhism do not appear to have influenced Tantricism in any appreciable degree. The case is thus unlike that of East Indian areas like Bengal where Brāhmaṇical Tantricism and the later phases of Buddhism became almost inextricably mixed up particularly in the age of the Pālas who were Buddhists.

The popularity of the Mother-goddess in Western India during the post-Gupta age is indicated by a Bhilsa inscription of 878 A.D. It says how a person named Haṭiā purchased two *vīthis* (shops) and dedicated them in favour of the Mothers, i.e. the Mother-goddesses worshipped in the Bhāyillasvāmin (Sun-god) temple or in the shrines in its precincts.[2]

II

Of the many varieties of the image of the Buddhist goddess Tārā, which are emanations of the various Dhyāni-Buddhas, Khadiravanī-Tārā (i.e. the Tārā worshipped at or in Khadira

1. *Select Inscriptions*, Vol. I, pp. 284ff.

2. See *Ep. Ind.*, Vol. XXX, p. 213; also below.

vana), an emanation of Amoghasiddhi, is the commonest.[1] She is also called Śyāmā-Tārā owing to her green (dark) colour and is represented as seated or standing, as holding a *nīlotpala* in her left hand and as usually accompanied by Aśokakāntā-Mārīcī and Ekajaṭā.

The representation of a deity of the same class is found in a manuscript of the *Aṣṭasāhasrikā Prajñāpāramitā* copied in Eastern India in the year 1015 A.D., which describes the goddess as *Candradvīpe Bhagavatī Tārā*, i.e. the goddess Tārā worshipped in Candradvīpa.[2] Tārā, installed in a temple of Candradvīpa was thus one of the most celebrated Buddhist deities in Bengal during the age of the Pālas. Among the images of the same deity worshipped in other areas of the Pāla empire, one of the most important is the Hilsa (Patna District, Bihar) statue bearing the Tantric formula *Oṁ Tāre Tuttāre Ture svāhā* and an inscription of the 35th regnal year of Devapāla (c. 810-50 A.D.).[3]

In the second quarter of the seventh century A.D., the celebrated Chinese pilgrim Hiuen-tsang speaks of a Mahāyāna Buddhist establishment at Tilāḍhaka in Magadha, wherein a temple of the Buddha was flanked by those of 'To-lo'-bodhisattva and Avalokiteśvara-bodhisattva.[4] Elsewhere he mentions 'To lo'-bodhisattva as a popular object of worship installed in a brick temple at Nālandā.[5]

Watters points out that, in both the cases, 'To-lo'-bodhisattva is referred to without any indication of sex and that this Bodhisattva became 'the Holy Mother Tārā, the spiritual wife of Kuan-yin (Avalokiteśvara)'.[6] She is said to be residing at the foot of a mountain in the Southern Ocean, i.e. the Indian Ocean or the Bay of Bengal. There may be reference here to Tārā's temple in Candradvīpa, literally 'the Dwāb or island of Candra'.[7]

1. *History of Bengal*, Vol. I, ed. Majumdar, p. 472.
2. *Ibid.*, p. 422; Bhattasali, *Catalogue of Buddhist and Brahmanical Sculptures in the Dacca Museum*, p. 12. There was also Buddhardhitārā worshippped in Samataṭa.
3. *JBORS*, Vol. X, pp. 31 ff.
4. Watters, *On Yuan Chwang's Travels in India*, Vol. II, p. 105.
5. *Ibid.*, p. 171.
1. *Ibid.*, p. 107.
2. If such was the case, the hill near the Tārā temple may be regarded as a big mound like the hillocks at Chittagong.

In the 16th and 17th centuries, Candradvīpa was a small principality in the Buckergunge District, and it had its headquarters first at Kachuwā and then at Mādhavapāśā. It has been identified with the Pargana of Bāglā or Bāklā in the Sarkār of the same name known from the 'Ain-i-Akbarī.[1] Tārā of Candradvīpa was thus worshipped in the Bāklā-Candradvīpa or Kachuwā-Mādhavapāśā area of the Buckergunge District. Some scholars are inclined to identify Candradvīpa of earlier records with modern Sandvip, an island (*dvīpa*) in the Bay of Bengal between the Buckergunge and Chittagong Districts.[2] There is, however, no support in favour of this suggestion excepting the similarity of the names, the word *dvīpa* being often used to indicate the *dwāb* or land between two rivers. The same meaning is noticed in the name of Bāklā-Candradvīp which is not an island.

The antiquity of the goddess Tārā of Candradvīpa is suggested by the fact that the celebrated Buddhist grammarian Candragomin, who is said to have settled in Candradvīpa and is called *Dvaipa* (an inhabitant of the Dvīpa, i.e. Candradvīpa), wrote his *stotra* of Tārā, entitled *Ārya-Tār-āntarbali-viddhi*,[3] very probably inspired by the goddess of Candradvīpa. Candragomin is supposed by many scholars to have flourished in the Gupta age[4] in the 5th and 6th centuries, since he is believed to refer to the Gupta victory over the Hūṇas, which is to be ascribed to Skandagupta (455-67 A.D.) or to Bālāditya (sixth century).[5] As the Chinese pilgrim Hiuen-tsang noticed the prevalence of the Tārā cult in the first half of the 7th century A.D., the worship of the goddess seems to have been prevalent also in the 5th and 6th centuries, while Hirananda Sastri has tried to show that the goddess does not date further back than the 5th century A.D.[6] Tārā worshipped in a temple of Candradvīpa seems to be one of the earliest representations of the goddess. It also appears that Syāmā or the green (dark) variety is one of the earliest forms of Tārā, Syāmā as the name of the Mother-

1. Majumdar, *op. cit.*, p. 18.
2. *Ibid.*, p. 298, note 6.
3. *Ibid.*, p. 299, note 2.
4. See *ibid.*, p. 297.
5. Cf. *loc. cit.*, note 6.
6. *Ibid.*, p. 299, note 2.

goddess being still very much popular in Bengal. It is, however, difficult to say whether Khadiravana, from which Khadiravanī-Tārā received her name, was a locality situated in ancient Candradvīpa.[1]

The recently discovered Nesari plates of the Rāṣṭrakūṭa king Govinda III (794-814 A.D.) refer to the great veneration in which the goddess Tārā was held by the Pāla kings of Eastern India. The official records of the Pālas speak of their seal as the *Dharmacakra-mudrā* representing the Buddhist Wheel of Law flanked by a deer on either side, and the said seal was affixed to the top of the copper-plates on which their charters were engraved. But the Nesari plates show that the Pāla standard or banner bore the representation of *Bhagavatī* Tārā. As in the case of several other ruling families of early medieval India, the Pālas thus appear to have had two different emblems, viz. the Dharmacakra for their seal and the goddess Tārā for their standard or banner.[2]

It is stated in the Nesari plates that Govinda III defeated the contemporary rulers and snatched away their standards or banners: (1) the fish from the Pāṇḍya king, (2) the bull from the Pallava rulers, (2) the tiger from the Cola, (4) the elephant from the Gaṅga (Western Gaṅga), (5) the bow from the Kerala, (6-8) the boar from the Andhra (Eastern Cālukya), Cālukya and Maurya, (9) the board bearing the kettle-drum and serpent from the Gurjara king, (10-12) the name from the kings of Kosala, Avanti and Siṁhala, and (13) *Bhagavatī* Tārā from Dharma (Dharmapāla), the king of Vaṅgāla.

It will be seen that, excepting Dharmapāla, no other adversary of the Rāṣṭrakūṭa king has been mentioned, in the list, by name and that, excepting the kings of the Kosala, Avanti and Siṁhala countries, who had their individual names on their banners, the reference is generally to dynastic emblems on the rulers' banners or standards, which were often the same as those on the seals of the royal families in question. Tārā on Dharmapāla's standard or banner was very probably

1. It is a matter of investigation whether Khadira was grown in the Sundarbans or elsewhere in the Buckergunge District. Of course even a single Khadira tree in a wood near about the Tārā temple would have justified the name.

2. *Ep. Ind.*, Vol. XXXIV, p. 137.

the dynastic emblem of the Pālas for their standard or banner just as the *Dharmacakra* was for their seals.

That Dharmapāla alone is mentioned by name in the whole list is no doubt due to his recognition as one of the most powerful monarchs of his time, while his mention merely as the lord of Vaṅgāla, which was originally a small part of Vaṅga, in spite of his suzerainty over much wider areas including Bengal and Bihar, indicates a sneering tone in the language of the Rāṣṭrakūṭa court poet whose purpose was to belittle his patron's strongest adversary.

In the 16th century, Abu'l Fazal regards Vaṅgāla as another name of Vaṅga, the derivation of which he explains by saying that the former rulers of Vaṅga raised huge mounds or embankments called *āl,* all over the area. Since such embankments are made even today to keep off sea-water from the corn-fields in coastal Bengal including the Buckergunge District, Abu'l Fazal's derivation of *Vaṅgāla* from *Vaṅga-āl* would suggest that Vaṅgāla was originally situated in the coastal areas of South Bengal.[1] This is probably supported by the fact that, while the inscriptions of the Candra dynasty represent the early Candra king Trailokyacandra as the ruler of Candradvīpa, the Tirumalai epigraph of Rājendra-coḷa speaks of the later Candra monarch Govindacandra as the king of the Vaṅgāla country exactly as Dharmapāla has been described in the Nesari plates of Govinda III.[2] Thus Candradvīpa would appear to be essentially identical with Vaṅgāla, although the conquest of East Bengal by the Candras of Candradvīpa or Vaṅgāla led to the application of the name Vaṅgāla to the whole of that area, while the emergence of Vikramapura in Vaṅga, also called Vaṅgāla since the days of the later Candras, as the capital of the rulers of Bengal finally made Vaṅgāla, in the medieval period, the name of the entire Bengali-speaking region.[3]

With the representation of Dharmapāla in the Nesari plates as the king of Vaṅgāla, we have to compare the Tibetan tradition speaking of Dharmapāla's father Gopāla, the founder of the Pāla empire, as originally ruling in the Bhaṅgala or

1. Sircar, *Studies in the Geography of Ancient and Medieval India*, p. 132.
2. Cf. *Ep. Ind.*, Vol. XXXIV, pp. 139-40.
3. Cf. Sircar, *op. cit.*, p. 126.

Vaṅgāla country.[1] This would appear to suggest that the Pālas began their career as the rulers of Vaṅgāla otherwise called Candradvīpa. Thus, probably, the great devotion of the Pāla kings to Tārā, the celebrated goddess of Candradvīpa, whose representation they adopted as the emblem of their standard or banner, is easily explained.

It may be mentioned here that the goddess Tārā appears to have been originally worshipped by some aboriginal people (probably of Eastern India) and was adopted in both the Brāhmaṇical and Buddhist pantheons in the early centuries of the Christian era. Several goddesses, including a few Mongoloid ones, merged in Tārā in the course of time.

III

According to the *Harivaṁśa*,[2] Himavat or Himālaya, the lord of the mountains, had five children by his wife Menā or Menakā. Two of them were sons and three were daughters. The sons were Krauñcha and Maināka and the daughters Aparṇā, Ekaparṇā and Ekapāṭalā. Aparṇā, while practising a severe penance, gave up food altogether. Menā in her anxiety to dissuade her daughter cried out *u mā*, i.e. "oh [my daughter], do not [practise penance]" whence Aparṇā came to be known as Umā. Aparṇā-Umā was given in marriage to Mahādeva (Śiva), while her sisters Ekaparṇā and Ekapāṭalā were married respectively to the sages Asita-Devala and Jaigīṣavya. The *Amarakoṣa*[3] supports the tradition recorded in the *Harivaṁśa* as it enumerates Umā and Aparṇā as two of the names of Durgā, daughter of the Mountain (Himālaya) and Menā and the wife of Īśvara-Śiva. Kālidāsa also explains the word *Umā*[4] as the name of Himālaya's daughter and Śiva's wife in the same way as the *Harivaṁśa*. The poet further explains the name Aparṇā[5] by referring it to the fact that Umā, during the latest stage of her penance, did not take any food, not even

1. Majumdar, *op. cit.*, p. 184; cf. *IHQ*, Vol. XVI, pp. 227-35.
2. I. 18. 15 ff.
3. I. 36 ff.
4. *Kumārasambhava*, I. 26.
5. *Ibid.*, V. 28.

dried leaves (*parṇa*) which she had been taking earlier. The story of the *Harivaṁśa* is found in a slightly modified form in works like the *Matsya Purāṇa*[1] where the identification of Umā and Aparṇā is not maintained. It is said that the three daughters of Himālaya and Menakā were named Umā, Ekaparṇā and Aparṇā who were married respectively to Rudra (Śiva), Asita and Jaigīṣavya. The section of the *Matsya Purāṇa* in question seems, however, to be a medieval interpolation.

Indian traditions represent the great Mother Goddess (Ādyā Śakti) with a very large number of names; but it has been suggested that they are not merely names of the same goddess, but that they originally indicated different goddesses worshipped by different tribes in different parts of the country and that they were afterwards identified with the Mother Goddess. It is also believed that aboriginal elements have largely contributed not only to the conception of Śiva, but also to that of his wife. Śiva's relation with hill tribes is indicated by his name *Giriśa*, 'one who dwells on the mountain'. His wife on the other hand is intimately associated with the Himalayas and therefore with the Himalayan mountaineers. There is reason to believe that a number of deities worshipped by hill tribes are traceable in Durgā. The aboriginal tribe of the Śabaras is actually mentioned in the *Kālikā Purāṇa*[2] in connection with the ceremonial worship of that goddess. It is now usually admitted that the traditional interpretation of the name Umā is merely a fabrication and that the word is apparently the same as Dravidian *amma* meaning 'mother' used in the sense of the Mother Goddess.

The traditional interpretation of the name Aparṇā, like that of Umā, seems also to have been fabricated. As the use of leaves for covering the loins can be traced among some of the primitive tribes of India even to-day, it is very probable that the word *Aparṇā* really means 'one without leaves covering one's loins', that is to say, 'naked'. The *Bṛhatsaṁhitā*[3] refers to two branches of the well known Śabara people as Nagna-

1. 13. 7 ff.
2. 61. 17 ff.
3. XIV. 10.

Śabara (the naked Śabaras) and Parṇa-Śabara (the leaf-clad Śabaras).[1] It is interesting to note that there is a Buddhist deity called Parṇa-Śabarī, apparently named after the Parṇa-Śabaras. Very probably this goddess was originally worshipped by the above branch of the Śabara people. In representations, the deity is actually found with leaves round her loins. Aparṇā, 'the naked goddess', may likewise have been originally worshipped by a naked aboriginal tribe such as the Nagna-Śabara. It is well known that one of the celebrated names of the Indian Mother-Goddess is Digambarī, 'the naked woman'.

1. Cf. reference to *tammidala Śabara*, 'the Śabara having turmeric leaves for his garment', in Vākpati's *Gauḍavaha*, verse 338.

Chapetr VII

KUMĀRA AND VINĀYAKA IN UTTARĀPATHA

I

An inscribed stone slab was discovered from a spring-tank about three miles from Abbottabad in the Hazara District of the former North-West Frontier Province of what is now West Pakistan. It was secured for the Lahore Museum and was noticed by Daya Ram Sahni in the *Annual Report of the Superintendent, Hindu and Buddhist Monuments, Northern Circle, for the year ending* 31*st March*, 1919.[1] There are two notes on the record in the said work, one at p. 18 and the other in Appendix C(No. 2). The date of the epigraph is quoted in the latter as the year "25 or 125 of an unknown era, possibly the Gupta era," while in the former it is said, "It is dated in the year 25 on the first day of Mārgaśira. The era employed is not specified; but there seems to be no doubt that the era intended is the Gupta era. The date of the inscription would then correspond to A.D. 344." The latter quotes the name of the ruler mentioned in the inscription as *Mahārāja* Kadambeśvaradāsa; but the former says, "The name of the reigning chief was *Mahārāja* Kadambeśvara; but nothing is known of him from any other source." As regards the object of the record, Sahni says, "The purpose of the inscription is to record the making of something, the nature of which cannot be clearly made out. But as the slab bearing this record was found in a spring-tank three miles from Abbottabad, it is possible that the construction of the tank itself is meant. The author of the work was a certain person named Ṣāphara Kumāra Sthānaṁgaśūra. Both the names are curious and appear to be foreign." Unfortunately, these observations regarding the purport of the inscription contain a number of errors.[2] The record has not been noticed in D. R. Bhandarkar's *List of the Inscriptions of Northern India*.

1. Diacritical marks are wanting in this publication. We have supplied them in our quotations. It is said that West Pakistan is again going to be divided into its old provinces in the near future.

2. It will be seen that, with reference to "Ṣāphara Kumāra Sthānaṁga-

The epigraph is written in Brāhmī characters and may be assigned on palaeographical grounds to a date about the third century A.D. The palaeography of the inscription may be regarded as showing the characteristics of a period between the second and the fourth centuries and may therefore be roughly assigned to the third century A.D. although it does not appear to be earlier than the middle of that century. The characters of the present epigraph resemble those of the Shorkot (Jhang District, West Pakistan) inscription,[1] assigned to 403 A.D., but exhibit earlier traits especially in the formation of the medial vowel-marks. The most interesting fact about the palaeography of the present inscription in Brāhmī characters in that it was discovered in an area where Kharoṣṭhī was the popular script. The popularity of Kharoṣṭhī in the Peshawar-Hazara region as late at least as the third century A.D. is indicated by inscriptions and accepted by scholars.[2] The discovery of the epigraph under study has therefore some bearing on the gradual ousting of Kharoṣṭhī by Brāhmī in the area about the former North-West Frontier Province. Again the language of the Kharoṣṭhī inscriptions discovered in this region is Prakrit

śūra", Sahni speaks of one personal name as well as two personal names. This is apparently because he had in his mind *Ṣāphara-kumāra Sthānamgaśūra*, i.e. "Sthānamgaśūra, son of Ṣāphara". Unfortunately, no such passage actually occurs in the inscription.

1. *Ibid.*, Vol. XVI, pp. 15 ff. and Plate.

2. G.H. Ojha, *Prācīn Bhāratīya Lipimālā* (*The Paleography of India*), p. 37; Bühler, *Ind. Ant.*, Vol. XXXIII (Appendix), p. 18. Sten Konow assigns the latest known Kharoṣṭhī inscriptions, found in India, to the fourth or fifth century A.D. (*Corp. Ins. Ind.*, Vol. II, Part i, p. xiii). He reads the dates in some records as the years 318, 359, 384 and 399 and refers them to an old Śaka era starting from 84-83 B.C. (*ibid.*, p. xci). Cf. also the inscriptions bearing dates in the years 303 (*Ep. Ind.*, Vol. XXIV, pp. 8 ff.) and 359 (*ibid.*, Vol. XIX, pp. 203 ff.). But even if the old Scytho-Parthian era is identified with the Vikrama Saṁvat of 58 B.C. (cf. *The Age of Imperial Unity*, p. 125, note; p. 144, note; Sircar, *Indian Epigraphy*, pp. 244 ff.), the latest date in Konow's list (year 399) would correspond to 343 A.D. It is also not very easy to be definite about the era. Lüders in the *Ācārya-puṣpāñjali Volume* (D.R. Bhandarkar Volume), pp. 281 ff., refers dates in the years 270 and 292 (or 299) found in two early Brāhmī inscriptions from Mathurā to the Parthian era of 248 B.C. although the dates of the Kharoṣṭhī inscriptions cited above cannot be assigned to that era. A few Kharoṣṭhī records from Taxila have been assigned to the fifth century (Marshall, *Taxila*, Vol. I, pp. 374-76).

while the present record is couched in Sanskrit. We know that Prakrit was originally the language of Indian records, but that it was ousted by Sanskrit from the Brāhmī inscriptions of Northern India by the third century and from South Indian records about a century later. The inscription under study is interesting from this point of view also.

The inscription begins with the date *Sa* 25 *Mārgaśira-di pratha*, i.e. *Saṁvatsare pañchaviṁśe Mārgaśira-dine prathame*. Thus the record was incised on the first day of the month of Mārgaśira or Mārgaśīrṣa in the year 25 of the regnal reckoning of a ruler. The object of the inscription is given in the following passage which reads *kārito =yaṁ Kumāra-sthānam*, i.e. *kāritam =idaṁ Kumāra-sthānam*, "this *Kumāra-sthāna* has been made (i.e. constructed)." As regards the mistake *kāritaḥ* for *kāritam*, it may be pointed out that the use of nominative singular for accusative singular is sometimes noticed in the Prakrit records from the old North-West Frontier Province and has been regarded as a dialectic peculiarity of the area in question.[1] The expression *Kumāra-sthāna* appears to mean 'a temple of the god Kumāra'. The inscribed stone thus originally belonged to the structure referred to in this passage. Kumāra is regarded as another name of the god Skanda, also called Viśākha and Mahāsena. But Patañjali's *Mahābhāṣya*[2] mentions the images of the gods Śiva, Skanda and Viśākha, while certain coins of the Kuṣāṇa king Huviṣka bear representations of two gods called in the legend by the names Skando Komaro (Skanda-Kumāra) and Bizago (Viśākha) or of three gods named in the legend as Skando Komaro, Maaseno (Mahāsena), and Bizago.[3] The facts show not only that Skanda and Kumāra, Viśākha and Mahasena had been originally the names of different deities who were identified at a later date,

1. *Ep. Ind.*, Vol. XXIV, p. 9.

2. See under Pāṇini, V. 3. 99; Kielhorn's edition, Vol. II, p. 429.

3. See R.B. Whitehead, *Catalogue of Coins in the Punjab Museum, Lahore*, Vol. I, p. 207; R. G. Bhandarkar, *Vaiṣṇavism, Śaivism and Minor Religious Systems*, pp. 214-15; D. R. Bhandarkar, *Ancient Indian Numismatics*, pp. 22-23. For two early images of the god Skanda found in the ancient Gandhāra country in the present Rawalpindi-Peshawar region, see *IHQ*, Vol. XXX, pp. 81 ff. The Skanda cult was very popular with such north-western tribes as the Yaudheyas (cf. Allan, *Catalogue of the Coins of Ancient India*, pp. 270 ff.). See Sircar, *Stud. Ind. Coins*, p. 213.

but also that Kumāra was an important popular god in the dominions of the Kuṣāṇas. This is interesting in view of the fact that the Kuṣāṇa emperors are known to have had their headquarters at Peshawar, not far away from the find-spot of our inscription in the Hazara District.

The following passage, giving the name of the person responsible for the construction of the *Kumāra-sthāna* referred to above, reads: *Gaśūraṇa Maka-putreṇa Ṣāphareṇa*, i.e. *Gaśūreṇa* (or *Gaśūrāṇāṁ*) *Maka-putreṇa Ṣāphareṇa*, "by the Gaśūra Ṣāphara, son of Maka" or "by Ṣāphara who is the son of Maka and a member of the Gaśūra clan or class." Both the names, *Maka* and *Ṣāphara*, are apparently foreign. *Maka* reminds us of such non-Indian names as *Maka* (Greek *Magas*) and *Moga* or *Moa* (*Maues*) found in Indian epigraphic and numismatic records.[1] The name Ṣāphara similarly reminds us of the well-known Pahlavī name Shāhpuhre (Shāpūr) borne by three Sassanian emperors ruling respectively in 241-72, 310-70 and 383-88 A.D. The epithet Gaśūra, applied to the name of Ṣāphara, also points to his foreign origin. This word seems to be the same as Krorayina *guśura* and Kuchean Sanskrit *gauśura* standing, as H. W. Bailey has shown, for Sanskrit *kulaputra*, "a person of good family."[2] Elsewhere Bailey explains the word *gauśurya* occurring in the Derge text as "a lady or princess of the Gauśura class of nobility."[3] Thus Ṣāphara, who constructed a temple for the Indian god Kumāra,

1. The thirteenth Rock Edict of Aśoka gives the Greek name Magas as *Maka* (Shahbazgarhi and Mansehra), *Magā* (Girnar) and *Makā* (Kalsi). See Hultzsch, *Corp. Ins. Ind.*, Vol. I, p. 210. A Scythian name is given as *Moga*, *Mevaki* and *Moa* in the Indian script and *Maues* or *Mauakes* in Greek; cf. Sircar, *Select Inscriptions*, pp. 115, 120; V. A. Smith, *Catalogue of the Coins in the Indian Museum*, Vol. I, pp. 38-41; *The Age of Imperial Unity* (*The History and Culture of the Indian People*, Vol. II), ed. Majumdar, p. 120, note; etc.

2. *Trans. Phil. Soc.*, 1947, pp. 149 f.; *BSOAS*, Vol. XIII, 1949-50, p. 121. The word *guśura* occurs in the Central Asian Kharoṣṭhī document No. 702; cf. T. Burrow, *Language of the Kharoṣṭhī Documents from Chinese Turkestan*, p. 87; *A Translation of the Kharoṣṭhī Documents from Chinese Turkestan*, p. 141.

3. *BSOAS*, Vol. XIII, p. 393; cf. H. Lüders, *Zur Geschichte und Geographie Ostturkestanes*, p. 255.

seems likewise to have been a member of the Guśura or Gaśūra class of nobility.[1]

The next passage of the inscription reads: *mahārāja-Kadambeśvaradāsa-rājye*, "in the reign (or, kingdom) of *Mahārāja* Kadambeśvaradāsa". It is probable that the 25th year of this ruler has been quoted in the date at the beginning of the record. This presupposes the fact that *Mahārāja* Kadambeśvaradāsa was an independent or at least a semi-independent ruler of the Hazara region. It should, however, be noted that the Chinese writer Yu-houan, author of the *Wei-lio*, speaks of Yueh-chi or Kuṣāṇa sovereignty over the Punjab, the former North-West Frontier Province and Afghanistan about the middle of the third century A.D., while the prominent mention of the Kuṣāṇa king as the *Daivaputra-Ṣāhi-Ṣāhānuṣāhi* in a Gupta inscription of the middle of the fourth century A.D. shows that the Kuṣāṇas were still regarded as a notable power in the Uttarāpatha division of Bhāratavarṣa.[2] The relation of Kadambeśvaradāsa with the Kuṣāṇa imperial family cannot be determined without further evidence. If he actually belonged to that imperial line, the inscription under study should probably have borne a date in the Kaṇiṣka era and not in his regnal reckoning. Even if it is believed that the later members of the Kuṣāṇa dynasty discontinued the use of the Kaṇiṣka era of 78 A.D.,[3] it is not easy to regard Kadambeśvaradāsa definitely as a Kuṣāṇa of Kaṇiṣka's house as he is mentioned without the typical title *Devaputra*. Of course the king's Sanskrit name does not offer any serious obstacle as we have a Vāsudeva with such a name amongst the immediate successors of the founder of the Kuṣāṇa era (i.e. Kaṇiṣka I). Similar difficulties are also felt if it is proposed to refer the year of the date of our record to the regnal reckoning of an unknown Kuṣāṇa overlord of Kadambeśvaradāsa.[4]

1. The name of a Central Asian people is written as *Khazar*, *Gazar Ghyssr* and *Ghusar* which are supposed to have been Indianised as Gujar or Gurjara. See *Ind. Ant.*, Vol. XL, 1911, p. 30.

2. *The Age of Imperial Unity*, pp. 152-53. Uttarāpatha was also called Udīcya.

3. I do not now entertain the view that a *Mahārāja Devaputra* Kaṇiṣka started a new era in the 3rd century A.D.; cf. *ibid.*, p. 146; *Ep. Ind.*, Vol. XIX, pp. 96-97. See now *Sel. Ins.*, 2nd ed., p. 518 and note.

4. For a sketch of the history of the area about the former North-West

Sahni was inclined to refer the year 25 in our inscription to the Gupta era. But it is difficult to believe that the suzerainty of the Guptas and the use of their era ever spread over the Hazara District where the inscription was found.

The name of king Kadambeśvaradāsa literally means "the servant (i.e. devotee) of Kadambeśvara", in which Kadambeśvara is certainly the name of a deity, probably Śiva in the Liṅga form. Śiva-liṅgas with names ending in the word *īśvara* are known from all parts of India[1]. Kadamba is primarily the name of a particular tree (Nuclea Cadamba), but may also be taken to be the names of a person, family or clan. But whether the name of the deity Kadambeśvara was due to his installation by a person named Kadamba or his association with a particular Kadamba tree cannot be determined.

The inscription ends with the letters looking like *Daṭhasaka* in line 4. This seems to refer to the locality where the temple of the god Kumāra was built by Ṣāphara. In that case, we may suggest the emendation *Daṭhasake.*

II

A marble image of the god Gaṇeśa is stated to have been discovered some years ago somewhere at Gardez (famous for its fortress called Bala Hissar), about 70 miles to the south of Kabul, and was later removed to Kabul where it is being worshipped by the Hindu residents of the city at Dargah Pīr Ratan Nāth near the Pamir Cinema. At Gardez, however, the local people could not confirm the story of the discovery of the image at that place. The image under worship at Dargah Pīr Ratan Nāth measures 28 inches in height and 14 inches in breadth. There is an inscription in two lines on its base. The image has been illustrated by G. Tucci in his article entitled 'Preliminary Report on an Archaeological Survey in Swat' appearing in the *East and West*, Vol. 9, No. 4, December 1958, pp. 276-328, figure 40 (at p. 323). Tucci also quoted the epigraphic text,

Frontier Province about the third and fourth centuries, see *The Classical Age* (*The History and Culture of the Indian People*, Vol. III), pp. 50 ff.

1. Cf. *Ep. Ind.*, Vol. XXVIII, p. 182, note 4.

as read by him on the basis of a photograph of the image, in footnote 29 (at pp. 327-28) of his article. But the published transcript of the inscription is not free from errors.

The characters of the Kabul Gaṇeśa image inscription belong to the North Indian (Siddhamātṛkā) alphabet of the sixth or seventh century A.D. That it is not much later than the middle of the seventh century is clear from the use of the tripartite form of the letter *y*. The latest occurrence of this form of the said letter has been noticed in Eastern India in such early seventh century inscriptions as the Patiakella plate[1] of Śambhuyaśas, dated 602 A.D., and the Dubi plates[2] of Bhāskaravarman (c. 600-50 A.D.), while, in the Rajasthan area of Western India, it is also found rarely in the late seventh century epigraphs like the Dhulev plate[3] of Bhetti, dated in the Harṣa year 73 corresponding to 679 A.D. The number 13 has been written in the inscription with the symbols for 10 and 3. In some cases (cf. *Ṣāhi-pādaiḥ* in line 2), the letter *h* looks like *bh*. The language of our record is Sanskrit although there are a few errors of grammar and orthography in the text.

The inscription begins with a *siddham* symbol followed by a sentence, at the end of which there is a floral design indicating the completion of the writing. The sentence states that an image of Mahā-Vināyaka was installed by *Paramabhaṭṭāraka Mahārājādhirāja* Ṣāhi Khiṅgāla on the thirteenth of the bright half of the month of Jyeṣṭha in the year 8, apparently of the Ṣāhi king's reign, when the constellation was Viśākha and the *lagna* Siṁha. The last passage containing the Ṣāhi king's name has been read by Tucci as °*Khiṅgal-otyāna-ṣāhipādaiḥ*. He observes, "I am not absolutely sure about the reading *otyāna*; it could also be *oḍyāna* or *odyāna* ....A good rubbing can settle the point. If the reading is confirmed, we have here the first mention of a king of Udyāna, Uḍḍiyāna (i.e. the Swat Valley)." The name of the king is, however, *Khiṅgāla* and not *Khiṅgala*, while the vowel-mark with the letter *l* is clearly *au* and not *o* as read by Tucci. Outside this passage, the letter *n* occurs only once in *Mahā-Vināyaka*, while *t* occurs

1. *Ep. Ind.*, Vol. IX, Plate between pp. 286 and 287.
2. *Ibid.*, Vol. XXX, pp. 287 ff. and Plates.
3. *Ibid.*, Plate facing p. 4.

several times. In *n* in this case, both the left and right lower limbs are shorter than those of *t*. If this is a purposeful distinction made by the engraver, we should better read the two *akṣaras* following *lau* as *tyāta*, though the readings *nyāna*, *nyāta* and *tyāna* cannot be regarded as altogether impossible, since, as indicated above, the distinction between the letters *bh* and *h* is not carefully indicated by the engraver of the record. In any case, the readings *khyāta*, *ḍyāna* or *dyāna* are not supported by the photograph. As regards Tucci's suggestion that the king might have been a Ṣāhi ruler of Uḍyāna (*Uḍyāna-ṣāhi*), it is doubtful whether the Ṣāhis of Swat, if any Ṣāhi house ruled there, can be regarded as in occupation of the Gardez region within the dominions of the Ṣāhis of Kapiśā or Kabul since, in the period in question, the latter were probably the strongest amongst the Ṣāhi houses, although it may of course be conjectured that the image in question was carried to Gardez from the Swat Valley.

In the second quarter of the seventh century A.D., when the Chinese pilgrim Hiuen-tsang was passing through Uttarāpatha or the north-western division of Bhāratavarṣa, the emperor of Kapiśā which then dominated over ten neighbouring States and comprised Lampāka (Laghman), Nagara or Nagarahāra (Jalālābād), Gandhāra (the Peshawar region)[1] and probably also Jāguḍa (Southern Afghanistan with Ghaznī as the chief city), had a residence (i.e. a secondary capital) at Udabhāṇḍa or Udabhāṇḍapura (modern Und near Attock).[2] It appears that under pressure of the Turks and Chinese from the north and the Arabs from the south-west, the Ṣāhi kings of Kapiśā left the western provinces of their empire in the hands of viceroys and gradually made Udabhāṇḍa their main seat. This is suggested by the Arabic work *Hududul Alam* (982-83 A.D.) and Kalhaṇa's *Rājataraṅgiṇī* (c. 1150

1. The Takṣaśilā region about the Rawalpindi District had been formerly subject to Kapiśā, but was at Hiuen-tsang's time a dependency of Kashmir (Watters, *Yuan Chwang's Travels in India*, Vol. I, p. 240).

2. Ray, *DHNI*, Vol. I, pp. 60-61; Beal, *The Life of Hiuen-tsiang*, p. 192.

A.D.)[1] which mention the said city as the capital of the Ṣāhi emperors. While Hiuen-tsang mentions Udabhāṇḍa as the residence of the king of Kapiśā about the middle of the seventh century, Kalhaṇa speaks of it as the capital of the Ṣāhis since the time of Lalliya Ṣāhi (c. 875-90 A.D.).[2] He further mentions Lalliya's kingdom as lying between the lands of the Darads (i.e. Dardistan) and the Turuṣkas (Turks).[3]

The name of Ṣāhi Khiṅgāla reminds us of Khiṅkhila *alias* Narendrāditya mentioned as an ancient king of Kashmir and as a successor of Mihirakula, apparently the Hūṇa king of that name who ruled in c. 510-35 A.D., in Kalhaṇa's *Rājataraṅgiṇī*.[4] There are some copper coins with the legend *Khiṅgi*[5] (the fuller form may have been *Khiṅgila*) while another coin is known to bear the legend *Deva-Ṣāhi-Khiṅgila*.[6] It is difficult to say whether Khiṅgāla of our inscription is identical with Khiṅgila of the coins and Khiṅkhila of the Kashmir chronicle. His identification with Khiṅkhila Narendrāditya would, however, suggest that, at the time of the ruler in question, Kashmir formed a part of the Ṣāhi empire.

The names of the following Ṣāhi kings have been recently revealed by the Gilgit manuscripts: (1) Paṭoladeva-ṣāhi Vajrāditya Nandin; (2) Śrī-Devaṣāhi Surendravikramāditya Nanda (Nandin) who seems to have had a queen named Śamidevī Trailokyadevī; and (3) *Ṣāhānuṣāhi* Paṭola-ṣāhi Śrī-nava-Surendrāditya Nandideva who had a queen named Anaṅgadevī and is apparently identical with *Paramabhaṭṭāraka Mahārājādhirāja Parameśvara* Paṭola-ṣāhi Śrī-nava-Surendrāditya Nandideva claiming descent from the Bhagadatta family and mentioned in the Hatun inscription.[7] These Ṣāhis, who probably ruled about the seventh century A.D., have been supposed to have ruled over the Darad country in the upper valley of the Kishenganga. Their names, in which several names have been clubbed together, are interesting in view of

1. *Proc. IHC*, 1939, p. 670; *Rājatar.*, V. 155.
2. Sircar, *Studies in the Geography of Ancient and Medieval India*, p. 235.
3. V. 155.
4. Cf. I. 364; Stein's trans., Vol. I, verse 347, note 107.
5. Smith, *Catalogue of Coins*, pp. 265, 267.
6. Cunningham, *Later Indo-Scythians*, 1893, pp. 97, 110; Plate VII, No. 11.
7. *Ep. Ind.*, Vol. XXX, p. 229.

the double name of the king mentioned in our record. Otyāta-ṣāhi seems to be a second name of Ṣāhi Khiṅgāla and is probably not connected with the territory over which he ruled.

The image of Gaṇeśa, called Mahā-Vināyaka in the inscription, represents the deity as standing in the *ālīḍha* pose. His limbs are muscular. The trunk, which was turned to the left, is broken. The tusk, indicated on the left, is also broken. He has a close-fitting coronet on the head and a close-fitting necklace on the neck. The ears look like foliage. There were four hands, all of which are broken. The god has a snake as his *yajñ-opavīta* and his under-garment is decorated with a lion's or tiger's head and claws apparently to satisfy the prescription that Vināyaka's cloth should be the tiger's skin.[1] The image is characterised by the god's usual pot-belly (*lamb-odara*) and also the *ūrdhva-meḍhra*. It is difficult to say whether the image represents a Brāhmaṇical or a Buddhist deity.

The elephant-headed god Gaṇeśa or Vināyaka is a Non-aryan divinity adopted in the Brāhmaṇical pantheon not much earlier than the third or fourth century A.D.[2] The earliest images of the deity are supposed to be those found in the Sankisa mound (Etah District, U.P.) and Bhumara (Satna District, Madhya Pradesh), both of about the fifth century A.D., while its representation on a terracotta bas-relief from Akra (Bannu District, West Pakistan) is also assigned to the same age.[3] The discovery of the Akra bas-relief and the image bearing the inscription discussed above points to the popularity of the god in the Uttarāpatha division of Bhāratavarṣa not long after he was adopted in the Brāhmaṇical pantheon.

1. Cf. *Ind. Cult.* Vol. IX, p. 124.
2. Cf. *IHQ*, Vol. XIX, p. 14, note 7; Hopkins, *Epic Mythology*, pp. 206-07.
3. A. Getty, *Gaṇeśa*, p. 26.

Chapter VIII

BHĀYILLASVĀMIN AND BHILLAMĀLADEVA

I

Bhīlsā or Bhelsā (24° N, 76° E), standing on tne bank of the Betwa (ancient Vetravatī), is the headquarters of a District of the same name in the old Gwalior State now forming a part of the State of Madhya Pradesh.[1] Near it, on the opposite bank of the river, lies the village of Besnagar representing the ancient city of Vidiśā or Vaidiśa, capital of the Ākara or Daśārṇa *janapada*, roughly corresponding to East Malwa. As the principal city in this area, Vidiśā gave place to Bhīlsā in the early medieval period. Such facts as the issue of the Vadner plates[2] of the Kalacuri king Buddharāja in the Kalacuri year 360 (608 A.D.) from Vaidiśa and the mention of Vidiśā in Varāhamihira's *Bṛhatsaṁhitā*[3] (sixth century) and Rājaśekhara's *Kāvyamīmāṁsā*[4] (earlier part of the tenth century) show that the old city retained some of its importance even in the post-Gupta period. But soon we notice the total eclipse of Vidiśā and the rise of Bhāyillasvāmin, Bhaillasvāmin or Bhailasvāmin, of which Bhīlsā or Bhelsā is a later corruption. Bhāyila°, Bhailla° or Bhailasvāmin was originally the name of an image of the Sun-god worshipped in a great temple at the place which became gradually famous under the deity's name.

An inscription[5], noticed by F.E. Hall at Bhīlsā nearly a century ago, has the passage *Bhāyillasvāmi-nāmā ravir=avatu bhuvaḥ svāminaṁ Kṛṣṇarājam.* This shows that Bhāyillasvāmin was regarded as a representation of Ravi or the Sun-god and that the record was incised during the rule of king Kṛṣṇa. This ruler has been supposed to be the Rāṣṭrakūṭa monarch

1. For some years now Bhīlsā is being called 'Vidisha' (i.e. Vidiśā).
2. Bhandarkar's List of Inscriptions, No. 1207.
3. Chapter XVI, verse 32.
4. G.O.S. edition, p. 9.
5. See *JASB*, Vol. XXXI, 1862, p. 111; *Ep. Ind.*, Vol. XXIX, p. 21, note.

Kṛṣṇa III (*circa* 939-68 A.D.).[1] Another inscription, discovered at Bhīlsā and supposed to be written in characters of the tenth century, is stated to contain a eulogy of the said god;[2] but, as will be shown below, the earliest Bhīlsā inscription referring to the temple of Bhāillasvāmin bears a date in the second half of the ninth century. About 1030 A.D., Al-Bīrūnī mentions the city of Bhailsān (Bhāyilla° or Bhailasvāmin) and places it on the road from Mathurā to Ujjayinī and Dhārā.[3] He further says that it was 'a place most famous among the Hindus' and that 'the name of the town is identical with [that of] the idol worshipped there'. A charter of the Candella king Madanavarman, dated Vikrama 1190 (1133 A.D.), was issued from his camp near Bhailasvāmin, apparently meaning the deity who seems to be also mentioned as 'Bhāsvat on the bank of the Mālavanadī (Vetravatī)' in an earlier Candella record[5] of Vikrama 1011 (954 A.D.). An inscription[6] from Udaypur (founded by and named after Paramāra Udayāditya) in the Bhilsa District, dated Vikrama 1229 (1173 A.D.), speaks of the surrounding area as Bhāillasvāmi-mahādvādaśaka-maṇḍala (i.e. the district called Bhāillasvāmin consisting of twelve sub-divisions) which included Bhṛṅgārikā-catuḥṣaṣṭi-pathaka (i.e. sub-district called Bhṛṅgārikā consisting of sixty-four villages) governed by a *Daṇḍa* (i.e. *Daṇḍanāyaka*) probably having his headquarters at Udayapura (i.e. Udaypur, the findspot of the record). The name of the district was no doubt derived from that of its chief city which again assumed the name of the deity worshipped there.

1. An inscription (No. B 159 of 1952-53) in the Gwalior Museum, seems to lend some colour to this identification. The epigraph, assignable to a date about the tenth century on palaeographical grounds, records the death of a warrior in a battle with the Karṇāṭas who may have been no other than the Rāṣṭrakūṭas.

2. *Annual Report of the Archaeological Department*, Gwalior State, Saṁvat 1979, No. 25; Hariharnivas Dvivedi, *Gwalior Rājyake Abhilekh* (in Hindi), p. 101, No. 743.

3. Sachau, *Alberuni's India*, Part I, p. 202; cf. Elliot and Dowson, *History of India as told by its own Historians*, Vol. I, p. 59. See Sircar, *Cosm. Geog. E. Ind. Lit.*, p. 156.

4. Bhandarkar, *op. cit.*, No. 231.

5. *Ep. Ind.*, Vol. I, pp. 124ff. (cf. *Mālavanadi-tīra-sthiter=Bhāsvataḥ* in verse 45).

6. *Ind. Ant.*, Vol. XVIII, pp. 344ff.

In 1233 or 1234 A.D., Sulṭān Iltutmish of Delhi sent or led an army against Malwa and the Muḥammadans 'took the fort and city of Bhīlsā or Bhīlasān'. While describing the said expedition, Minhājuddīn's *Tabaqāt-i-Nāṣirī*[1] says that, at Bhīlsā, the Muḥammadans destroyed a temple which was one hundred and five gaz (yards) in height. The same work seems to indicate that the temple was built three hundred years earlier; this refers its construction to a date about the tenth century, although, as indicated above, we have now evidence regarding the existence of the Bhāyillasvāmin temple at Bhīlsā as early as the second half of the ninth century. However, the glory of the god Bhāyillasvāmin did not totally eclipse with the demolition or desecration of his temple in 1233-34 A.D. But it was not destined to continue for a long time. According to Badāūnī's *Muntakhab-ut-Tawārikh*,[2] in 1292 A.D., during the reign of the Khaljī Sulṭān Jalāluddīn Fīrūz of Delhi, his nephew 'Alaūddīn, governor of Karra, obtained permission 'to proceed to Bhīlsā and attacked that country and brought much booty thence to present to the Sulṭān, and the idol which was the object of worship of the Hindus he caused to be cast down in front of the gate of Badāūn to be trampled upon by the people'. Thus ended the worship of the god at the city which received his name and is still continuing to enjoy it in its colloquial form.

II

There is a stone inscription in the Gwalior Museum, which was collected from Mahalghāṭ at Bhīlsā. It was noticed in the *Annual Report of the Archaeological Department* of the former Gwalior State for Saṁvat 1970 (Inscription No. 8) as well as in H. N. Dvivedi's *Gwalior Rājyake Abhilekh* (p. 3, No. 10), published by the same Department. According to the account published in these works, the inscription is fragmentary and illegible and its purport not clear. But the major part of the inscription has now been satisfactorily made out and it has

1. Elliot and Dowson, *op. cit.*, Vol. II, p. 328; cf. Hodivala, *Studies in Indo-Muslim History*, p. 217; Raverty, *Tabaqāt-i-Nāṣirī*, trans., pp. 622-23.
2. Banking's trans., Vol. I, p. 96.

been found that it is the earliest among the known inscriptions mentioning the temple of Bhāyillasvāmin at Bhīlsā.[1] The record bears the date [Vikrama] Saṁvat 935, Vaiśākha-sudi 3. This date falls in 878 A.D.

The inscription records the grant of an *akṣayanikā* made in favour of the *āyatana* or temple of the illustrious Bhāillasvāmin. The expression *akṣayanikā* is apparently a mistake for *akṣaya-nīvikā*[2] which means 'a permanent endowment (providing a periodical income to be regularly and perpetually enjoyed by the donee)'. The donor was a merchant of the Pāravāḍa (Poravāḍa)[3] community (*jāti*). His name was Haṭiā and that of his father Cacchiā. It is stated that the grant was made by the libation of curds and water at the various *tīrthas* or bathing *ghāṭs* of the locality. This reminds us of the fact that the inscription was actually found at Mahalghāṭ at Bhīlsā. The inscribed stone seems to have been originally embedded in the stairs of the *ghāṭ* in question. We know that grants were made in ancient India by the donor by pouring water in the donee's name or, when the latter was a person present to receive the donation, in the cavity of his folded hands.[4] The mention of curds along with water in the same context in the present inscription is interesting.

The endowment consisted of the income derived from three *vīthis*. The word *vīthī* is used in Sanskrit literature in the sense of 'a market, a stall, or a shop in a market',[5] although in some parts of ancient India it was often used in the sense of a territorial unit smaller than a district.[6] That the word *vīthī* in this inscription means 'a stall or shop in a market' is suggested by certain early medieval records of the Malwa region,

1. See *Ep. Ind.*, Vol. XXX, pp. 211ff.

2. Some early medieval inscriptions of the Malwa region use the form *akṣayanīmī* or *akṣayanīmikā* (*Ep. Ind.*, Vol. I, pp. 160, 165).

3. This may be the same as the Por, Porwar or Porwal caste, often called Prāgvāṭa-vaṁśa in inscriptions. See Bhandarkar's List, No. 287 (cf. also Nos. 1523, etc.); Wilson's Glossary, s. v. *Porwāl*.

4. Cf. *The Successors of the Sātavāhanas*, p. 192. The practice is still prevalent in some parts of the country.

5. Cf. *Śiśupālavadha*, IX. 32.

6. Majumdar, *Inscriptions of Bengal*, Vol. III, p. 71; *Dacca University History of Bengal*, Vol. I, p. 23. See Sircar, *Ind. Ep. Gloss.*, s. v.

incorporated in the Siyadoni (Jhansi District, U.P.) inscription[1] (in corrupt Sanskrit). *Vīthīs* are frequently mentioned in these records as lying in *haṭṭas* or market-places and as objects belonging to persons or deities, or gifts made in favour of deities worshipped in a local temple, or standing on the boundaries of other *vīthīs*. They are sometimes stated to have stood on the *haṭṭa-rathyā* or market-road and often to have faced this or that direction. Some of the epithets (such as *ācchannā*, *avaliptā*, *kṛt-opasannā* and *uvaṭaka-sahitā*), applied to the *vīthīs*, are also used in the records in relation to houses. An *āvāsanikā* or house is stated to have been granted with all the rooms and *vīthīs* in it (*asy=ābhyantare samasta-gṛha-sametaṁ samasta-vīthī-sametam*) and in this connection it is further said : *yaḥ=ko='pi vīthīṣu pravasati sa ca goṣṭhī-bhāvitaṁ bhāṭakaṁ dadāti dāyādasya adhikāraṁ n=āsti*. The reference to *bhāṭaka* (rent) for staying at the *vīthī* makes its nature fairly clear. As will be seen from our discussion below, the word *vīthī* has been used in the Siyadoni inscription and the present record in exactly the same sense.

The first of the three *vīthīs*, the rent of which appears to have been assigned by the merchant Haṭiā as an *akṣayanīvikā*, is said to have been purchased by Haṭiā from its owner Vuvāka.

The inscription seems to say that the *vīthī* in question which fetched a monthly or annual rent of *pa* 13 or 130, i.e. 13 or 130 Pañciyaka-drammas,[2] was granted by Haṭiā as an *agrahāra* in favour of the god Nārāyaṇa (Viṣṇu) worshipped in the Bhāyillasvāmin temple apparently as a subordinate deity. The custom of installing the images of various gods and goddesses in the temple (or in shrines built in the temple precincts) of a well-known deity is not only prevalent even today, but is also evidenced by numerous epigraphs including the Siyadoni inscription referred to above. The word *agrahāra* usually means an area of land granted in favour of Brāhmaṇas

1. *Ep. Ind.*, Vol. I, pp. 173ff.

2. The word *dramma* was derived from the Greek *drachma* weighing originally 67.5 grains, although the Indo-Greeks adopted a modified standard for their silver issues many of which weigh about 37 grains. The Pañciyaka-dramma may have been a heavy copper coin like the Yaudheya *drammas* (cf. Smith's Catalogue of Coins., p. 182, coin, No. 18 b).

as a rent-free holding. But, in inscriptions, we have sometimes reference to other kinds of *agrahāras* such as the *Vaiśyāgrahāra* (i.e. land given as a rent-free holding in favour of certain Vaiśyas).[1] In the record under study, the *vīthī* in question was made what may be called a *dev-āgrahāra*.

The second of the three *vīthīs* belonged to a merchant whose name cannot be fully read. It was situated at Khahanāsithī which seems to have been the name of a market place. Its rent was *pa* 50 (i.e. 50 Pañciyaka-drammas). The third *vīthī* belonged to a person named Govinda. Its rent was *pa* 40 (i.e. 40 Pañciyaka-drammas). These two *vīthīs* were purchased by Haṭiā who granted them in favour of the Mothers (i.e. the Mother-goddesses worshipped in the Bhāyillasvāmin temple or in shrines in its precincts) for the merit of his parents. The rent of the three *vīthīs* was expected to meet the expenses of the regular offerings (*niyata-bhoga*) to the god and goddesses in question. The intention of the donor seems to have been that the *vīthīs* themselves could be utilised (*samālabhyāḥ*), probably implying their sale or mortgage, at critical junctures (*sandhi-pāte*) or emergencies.

The importance of the inscription lies in the fact that it refers to the existence of the temple of Bhāyillasvāmin at Bhīlsā as early as 878 A.D. So long we had no definite evidence regarding the worship of the said god at Bhīlsā before the tenth century. In regard to the name of the god Bhāyillasvāmin, it is possible to suggest that the deity was originally installed by and named after a person called Bhāyilla. Such a personal name is not unknown in the records of the Malwa region. An inscription[2] in the Gwalior Museum mentions one Bhāilla-bhaṭṭa, although, as the epigraph is palaeographically assignable to a date about the ninth or tenth century, it is uncertain whether the person in question was named after the Sun-god of Bhīlsā. That sometimes other representations of the god in different parts of the Malwa region were named after the famous deity of Bhīlsā is possibly suggested by a Siyadoni (Jhansi District, U.P.) epigraph[3] of Vikrama 1005 (948 A.D.), which mentions a god named Bhāillasvāmin installed in a temple of that locality by a merchant named

1. Cf. *JRAS*, 1952, p. 5.
2. No. B 169 of 1952-53.
3. *Ep. Ind.*, Vol. I, p. 177.

Vikrama; but it is also possible to think that Bhāillasvāmin of Siyadoni was named after another person called Bhāilla. Bāilla-bhaṭṭa, mentioned in a Gwalior inscription[1] as a person, after whom the god Viṣṇu established in a local temple was called Bāillabhaṭṭa-svāmin, may be a variant form of the same personal name.[1]

III

As Bhīlsā was once the famous seat of the Sun-god Bhāyilla° or Bhailasvāmin, two stone inscriptions in the local collections of antiquities are specially interesting because they contain each a eulogy of the Sun-god. There is little doubt that the inscribed stone slabs were originally embedded in the walls of the Bhāyilla° or Bhailasvāmin temple at Bhīlsā.

The first of the two epigraphs is extremely damaged. The right hand side of the stone has broken away and the writing of the lower lines is completely obliterated. Of the first six or seven lines of the inscription, a few expressions only can be satisfactorily deciphered. Each of the lines contains about thirty *akṣaras* in a space about 17″ in length. The characters are Nāgarī and the epigraph may be palaeographically assigned to a date about the eleventh century. The language of the record is Sanskrit. The inscription begins with one of the several forms of the *Siddham* symbol which is followed by the passage *Oṁ namaḥ Sūryāya*. Then follow the stanzas in praise of the Sun-god. The first half of verse 1 in line 1 begins with the expression *Udayagiri* and seems to end with the word *vihāya*. The second half of the stanza begins with *ambara-cūḍāma*, the following letters of the line (line 1) being broken away and lost. Line 2 begins with the expression *anitā*° possibly introducing the first or third foot of a different verse. The mention of Udayagiri and *ambara-cūḍāmaṇi* in verse 1 suggests that the stanza speaks of the Sun-god. About the beginning of line 4 we have the word *jayati*, while about the end of line 6 we can read *mohahara-dīpaka namas=te*. As the latter passage undoubtedly refers to the Sun-god and occurs

1. For the same name and its variants, see also *ibid.*, p. 168; Bhandarkar's List, Nos. 287, 1537; Cunningham's *Reports*, Vol. III, p. 43; etc.

in a stanza far removed from the beginning of the inscription, it seems that the whole record was a *praśasti* of the deity in question.

The other inscription is more interesting. In the *Quinquennial Administration Report* of the Archaeological Department of the old Gwalior State, for Saṁvats 1998-2002 (years 1942-46), pp. 1-2, it has been described as follows: ".... a loose fragment picked up in ruins is written in old Nāgarī script assignable to the 12th century A.D. on palaeographical grounds. This is broken at the top and left side. It seems to have been a *praśasti* recording the merits of a distinguished personage, perhaps a king or a minister, who is compared to the Sun, but whom, unlike the Sun, Rāhu could not hold in his grips. As the inscription is badly mutilated, its object cannot be made out. The *praśasti* was composed by *Mahākavi-cakravarti* Śrī-Dvittapa (?) at the instance of *Daṇḍanāyaka* Śrī-Candra."[1] Elsewhere in the same work, while repeating the same views, it is said that the record 'does not convey any sense nor any purport can be extracted from it'.[2] Unfortunately most of these statements are wrong. In the first place, the major part of the writing on the stone, mutilated though it is, can be satisfactorily deciphered. Secondly, the theme of the record is not the *praśasti* of a king or minister, but the *stuti* of the Sun-god. Thirdly, the name of the author of the eulogy is not Dvittapa, but Chittapa who is fortunately well known from several sources. It may be pointed out in this connection that Dvivedi's *Gwalior Rājyake Abhilekh* (also a publication of the Archaeological Department of the former Gwalior State or Madhya Bharat), referred to above, contains a similar misleading note on the same inscription.[3] Dvivedi quotes the poet's name quite confidently as Dvitraya which is, however, even more erroneous.

The piece of stone bearing the inscription is fairly big in size. The writing occupies only its upper part and covers an area about 38" in length and about 11.5" in height. The top and left sides of the inscribed stone have broken away.

1. See *op. cit.*, p. 25.
2. *Ibid.*, p. 69, No. 2.
3. See *op. cit.*, p. 92, No. 666.

The number of *akṣaras* lost at the beginning of the lines is about four in some cases, but slightly more in others. Thus line 4 of the extant part of the record originally contained seventy *akṣaras* (without counting the five cases of the use of the single or double *daṇḍa*) of which only four are now lost. There are traces altogether of twelve lines of writing in the inscription; but the last line is less than half the other lines in length. Of the first line, only traces of the lower part of a few *akṣaras* at the end can be seen. It is impossible to determine whether one or more lines of writing are lost above this, although for the sake of convenience it may be regarded as line 1 of the original record. Many of the *akṣaras* in line 2 are also either completely or partially broken away. Even in the extant part of the epigraph some letters here and there are more or less rubbed out.

The characters of the inscription are Nāgarī and may be assigned to a date about the eleventh century. Two floral designs in line 11 and the ornamental lengthening of the head of medial *e* and that of the tail of medial *i* or *e* in some cases are interesting to note. Medial *e* has been written both as a *pṛṣṭha-mātrā* as in Gauḍī and as a *śiro-mātrā* as in modern Nāgarī. The language of the record is Sanskrit. With the exception of a few passages at the end in lines 11-12, the whole record is written in verse. The metre of all the stanzas is *Anuṣṭubh*. The record bears no date; but, as will be shown below, there is reason to assign it to a date in the eleventh century.

The inscription under discussion originally contained at least twenty-three stanzas in the *Anuṣṭubh* metre. They are all addressed to the Sun-god and the last of them speaks of the composition as a *stuti* (eulogy). Out of these, the text of ten stanzas (verses 6, 8-9, 11, 13, 15, 17-18, 20, 22) only have been fully deciphered, although there is some doubt about the reading of a few letters in one of them (verse 17). Of the remaining thirteen stanzas, two (verses 1-2 in line 1) are completely lost, while the other eleven (verse 3-5, 7, 10, 12, 14, 16, 19, 21, 33) are partially preserved. The meaning of some of the damaged verses is not clear.

Verse 5 refers to the sage Agastya who is famous in the solar mythology of India not only as the son of Mitra (the Sun-god) and Varuṇa, but also as one who prevented Vindhya (the Vindhyan range) from his attempt to obstruct the sun's passage in the sky. Verse 6 says how the Sun-god's youngest brother (i.e. Viṣṇu the youngest of the twelve Ādityas including the Sun-god, according to some accounts)[1] cut off the head of Rāhu, although the demon's life was spared as a result of his entreaty. Verse 8 represents the sun's rays as the source of the splendour of such objects as the jewel on the hood of Śeṣa-nāga, the pearls in the bed of the sea and the stars in the sky. The next stanza (verse 9) says that the sun's rays, when they come into contact with the moon, the horizon and the clouds, become respectively the moonlight, the twilight and the rainbow. In regard to the idea that the moonlight is nothing but the sun's rays reflected on the moon, it may be pointed out that it was fairly popular with ancient Indian writers.[2] The ancient Indian conception about this is made quite clear by Mallinātha in his commentary on the *Raghuvaṁśa*, III. 22 : *atra Varāha-saṁhitā-vacanaṁ 'Śalilamaye śaśini raver=dīdhitayo mūrcchitās=tamo naiśaṁ kṣapayanti darpaṇ-odara-nihitā iva mandirasy=āntar'=iti; yathā darpaṇ-odara-nihitā ravi-dīdhitayas=tad-gatam=andhakāraṁ nāśayanti tathā svataḥ salila-maye candre tāḥ pratiphalitā naiśam tamo ghnant=īty=arthaḥ.* The other idea, reflected in the verse in question, that the rainbow is produced by the sun's rays falling on the dripping clouds is also very interesting. Although it is supported by modern scientific observation, it does not appear to have been quite popular with ancient Indian writers.

Verse 11 illustrates the maxim—*premṇo hi kuṭilā gatiḥ* (love's way is tortuous) by pointing out how Svarbhānu (i.e. Rāhu) prefers the moon to the sun in spite of the latter having his own name (Bhānu) and how the sun hides himself from

1. See *Mahābhārata*, I. 123. 66-67; XIII. 150. 14-15; *Harivaṁśa*, I. 9. 48; *Bhāgavata Purāṇa*, VI. 6. 39; etc.

2. Cf. *Raghuvaṁśa*, III. 22; Hayungthal plate (lines 24-25) of king Harjaravarman of Assam (*Kāmarūpaśāsanāvalī*, p. 51) ; etc. P.C. Sengupta pointed out to me that the same idea can be traced in ancient Indian astronomical works such as Varāhamihira quoted in Pṛthūdaka's commentary on Brahmagupta's *Khaṇḍakhādyaka* (Chapter VIII), the *Sūryasiddhānta* quoted in the commentary of Utpala (966 A.D.) on Varāhamihira's *Bṛhatsaṁhitā*, etc.

the lotus [at night] in spite of the latter's attachment for him. Verses 18 and 20 are remarkable for their pleasant idea and sweet expression and are really worthy of a great poet. Verse 23 refers to the conclusion of the eulogy. Then follow references in prose to the author of the said eulogy, the person who was responsible for tracing the inscription on the stone and the devotee of the Sun-god who got the stone inscribed and apparently embedded it in a wall of the temple of the deity at Bhīlsā. The eulogy is stated to have been the composition of *Mahākavicakravartin Paṇḍita* śrī-Chittapa. The name of the *lekhaka* who traced the writing on the stone with a view to facilitating the work of the engraver cannot unfortunately be made out. The person who got the eulogy written and the stone inscribed for embeddeding it in a wall of the Sun-god's temple was *Daṇḍanāyaka* śrī-Candra. We have seen above how a *Daṇḍa* (*Daṇḍanāyaka*) was probably in charge of a subdivision of the Bhāyillasvāmin (Bhīlsā) district according to an inscription of 1173 A.D. Candra of the inscription under study appears to have been a similar Subdivisional Officer of the Bhīlsā region. He was apparently a devotee of the Sun-god of Bhīlsā and got a eulogy of the deity composed by the poet Chittapa who may have been an inhabitant of the same area.

The importance of the inscription lies in the mention of the poet Chittapa, who enjoyed the title *Mahākavicakravartin*, as the author of the *khaṇḍakāvya* in praise of the Sun-god, quoted in the record.

A number of stanzas of a poet Chittapa are found in the Sanskrit anthologies and some other works. But no complete work of the poet has so far been discovered. The *pratīkas* of all the stanzas attributed to Chittapa have been quoted in alphabetical order by F. W. Thomas in the excellent introduction of his *Kavīndravacanasamuccaya*.[1] Six stanzas of Chittapa are quoted in the *Sarasvatīkaṇṭhābharaṇa* of the Paramāra king Bhoja (*circa* 1000-55 A.D.), one in the *Kavīndravacanasamuccaya* compiled before the end of the twelfth century, and forty-nine

1. The name of the work is really *Subhāṣitaratnakoṣa* (by Vidyākara). It and its translation have been recently published in the Harvard Oriental Series. The work was composed in the Jagaddala monastery in North Bengal about 1100 A.D.

in the *Saduktikarṇāmṛta* compiled by Śrīdharadāsa at the court of king Lakṣmaṇasena in 1205-06 A.D. Poet Chittapa therefore could not have flourished much later than the middle of the eleventh century. A stanza in the *Saduktikarṇāmṛta* (III. 36) suggests that Chittapa was a contemporary and probably a court poet of king Bhoja who has been identified with the Paramāra king of that name.

IV

Two copper-plate grants of the time of the Rāṣṭrakūṭa emperors of Mānyakheṭa (Mālkheḍ in the Gulbarga District, Mysore) were discovered at Chinchani in the Dahanu Taluk of the Thana District, Maharashtra. One of them was issued by a Tājika (Arab) ruler who was the viceroy of Sanjan under Indra III, while the other is a private record belonging to the reign of Kṛṣṇa III.

The second inscription is written on a single plate measuring about 17.5″ in length, 8.8″ in breadth and .1″ in thickness. It weighs about 130 tolas. There is no seal fixed with the plate which is engraved only on one side. There are 50 lines of writing. The language is Sanskrit and the document is written in prose and verse. The inscription bears no date. Since, however, it refers itself to the reign of the Rāṣṭrakūṭa king Kṛṣṇa III (939-67 A.D.), it may be assigned roughly to the middle of the tenth century A.D.

The record begins with the *praṇava* which is followed in lines 1-35 by 19 verses. Verse 1 is in adoration of the Mother-goddess. The next stanza (verse 2) introduces the Yadu or Yādava dynasty, to which the Rāṣṭrakūṭa kings are stated to have belonged. Verse 3 speaks of the following rulers of the family : (1) Dantidurga (c. 742-56 A.D.); (2) his successor Kṛṣṇarāja (Kṛṣṇa I, c. 756-75 A.D.); (3) Govindarāja (Govinda II, c. 775-80 A.D.), successor of Kṛṣṇarāja; (4) Nirupama (Dhruva, c. 780-94 A.D.); (5) Jagattuṅga (Govinda III, c. 794-814 A.D.); (6) Amoghavarṣa (i.e. Amoghavarṣa I, c. 814-78 A.D.), and (7) Amoghavarṣa's son Akālavarṣa (Kṛṣṇa II, 878-915 A.D.) The next stanza (verse 4) refers to Indrarāja (Indra III, c. 915-28 A.D.), while verse 5 speaks of Amoghavarṣa (i.e. Amoghavarṣa c. II, 928-29 A.D.)

who succeeded Indrarāja. Verse 6 mentions Govindarāja (Govinda IV, c. 929-34 A.D.), surnamed Suvarṇavarṣa, and verse 7 Amoghavarṣa (i.e. Amoghavarṣa III, c. 934-39 A.D.). The following four stanzas (verses 8-11) describe the reigning king Kṛṣṇarāja (Kṛṣṇa III, 939-67 A.D.), son of Amoghavarṣa. It will be seen that all the rulers of the Imperial Rāṣṭrakūṭa dynasty from Dantidurga to Kṛṣṇa III are mentioned in correct order, although the relationship between the successor and his predecessor has not been indicated in all the cases. It is interesting to note that the reign of Amoghavarṣa II has been recognised in the record.[1]

About the reigning monarch Kṛṣṇa III, verse 10 says that he conquered certain enemies even when he was a crown-prince, while verse 11 enumerates the following as bowing down to his feet: the Pāṇḍyas, Oḍras, Siṁhalas, Coḷas and Pārasīkas, the Andhra king, the Draviḍas, Varvaras and Tajjikas, and the Vaṁkīṇas, Hūṇas, Khasas, Gūrjaras and Mālavīyas. The success of Kṛṣṇa III against the Pāṇḍyas, Siṁhalas, Coḷas and Gūrjaras (i.e. the Gurjara-Prātīhāras of Kanauj)[2] is referred to in some of his records.[3] The name Draviḍa seems to have been applied to the Pallavas. A Pallava king named Aṇṇiga is known to have been subdued by him.[4] The Mālavīyas were probably the Paramāras who owed allegiance to him.[5] The Tajjikas (i.e. Tājikas) were the Arabs, some of whom were serving under the Rāṣṭrakūṭa kings, while the Pārasīkas or Persians appear to be the Parsees who had settled at places like Sanjan in the western coast-land forming a part of the Rāṣṭrakūṭa empire.[6] The

1. Cf. *Bomb. Gaz.*, Vol. I, Part II, p. 416, note 5. The fact that Amoghavarṣa II obtained the throne is also recognised in some other records of Kṛṣṇa III (cf. *Ep. Ind.*, Vol. IV, p. 283, verses 18-19).

2. The suggestion that the Gurjara contemorary of Kṛṣṇa III was the Caulukya king Mūlarāja (cf. *Bomb. Gaz.*, Vol. I, Part II, pp. 283, 420) seems to be wrong as the territories of the Caulukyas were outside Gurjaratrā in the age in question (cf. below, p. 131, note 4).

3. Cf. verses 30, 31 and 35 of the Karhad plates (*Ep. Ind.*, Vol. IV, pp. 278ff). See also Altekar, *The Rāṣṭrakūṭas and their Times*, pp. 115 ff.

4. *Ep. Ind.*, Vol. IV, p. 289 (verse 29).

5. Cf. the Harsola plates (*Ep. Ind.*, Vol. XIX, pp. 236ff.).

6. See Smith, *E. Hist. Ind.*, 1924, p. 444.

king's relations with the remaining peoples mentioned in the verse are not known from any other source.

Verses 12-14 speak of the god Bhillamāladeva, also called Madhusūdana (i.e. Viṣṇu), worshipped at the unspecified place whence the character was issued. The deity is stated to have been installed by the descendants of the merchants of Bhillamāla which is the modern Bhinmāl in the Jodhpur region of Rajasthan. Verses 15-19 state that, at the same place, there was another *maṭhikā*, i.e. 'monastery or temple', which had been constructed by Kautuka and at the gate of which the goddess called Bhagavatī had been installed for worship. It is clear that the god Bhillamāladeva *alias* Madhusūdana was installed in the temple standing near another made by Kautuka for the Mother-goddess. There is little doubt that Kautuka's *maṭhikā* enshrining Bhagavatī was the religious institution built by Annaiya (Annamaiya), Kautuka and Revaṇa at Saṁyāna and that the goddess is no other than Bhagavatī Daśamī installed in it, both mentioned in the grant of the time of Indra III. Verse 19 of the record under study refers to the *Anagha-parṣad* (called *Mahāparṣad* in line 35) in connection with the goddess and this is apparently the *Ārya-deśīya-mahāparṣad* or *Pañca-Gauḍīya-mahāparṣad* of Saṁyāna mentioned in the other epigraph.

The following section in prose in lines 35ff. records a *vyavasthā* which means 'a legal decision in a dispute' in the present context. It is very interesting to note that, in this case, the decision emanates from a deity and his attendants and not from any judicial or administrative authority. In this respect, the inscription under study offers a peculiar instance.

It is stated that a *vyavasthā* based on an order was offered to the *maṭhikā* (i.e. the monastery or temple of the goddess) and the *svādhyāyikas* or scholars belonging to the *Mahāparṣad* attached to it, by the god Bhillamāladeva and his *vārikas*. The word *vārika* is known to have been used in the sense of 'an official' and, in the present context, it no doubt means a priest or Pāṇḍā of the temple of Bhillamāladeva at Saṁyāna.[1] Apparently the decision of the temple authorities was passed

1. *Ep. Ind.*, Vol. XXX, pp. 171-72; cf. Vol. XXXI, p. 164, note 1

as the order of the god; but whether any device was adopted to convince the people that it was really the will of the god is uncertain. The terms of the *vyavasthā*, which follow, were that the *maṭhikā* of the goddess should pay forty *drammas* to the god Bhillamāladeva and his *vārikas* as *śrotaka* for a small piece of land that belonged to the god, but had been enclosed within the northern compound wall of the *maṭhikā*. The word *śrotaka*.[1] is not found in Sanskrit lexicons, but was apparently a kind of rent, since the periodical nature of its payment is indicated by the stipulation that the amount was to be paid on each occasion of *dīp-otsava-bhaṅga*, i.e. the end of the festival of lights, obviously in the *maṭhikā* of the goddess. The *dīp-otsava* seems to be no other than the *dīpāvalī*, a festival with illuminations held on the new moon of Āśvina or Kārttika in honour of the goddess Pārvatī. The *dramma* was a coin of copper or silver.[2] The inscription seems to specify the payment in coins minted by a trader named *Śreṣṭhin* Gambhuvaka. It appears that this tradesman of Saṁyāna enjoyed a license for minting coins on behalf of the ruling authority.[3]

It is further stated that, now that the *vyavasthā* was offered (cf. *adhunā*), if any devotee of the god (i.e. Bhillamāladeva), whether he is a Brāhmaṇa or a merchant, commits suicide or creates any other trouble with a view to increasing the amount of the *śrotaka* or to the removal of the wall of the *maṭhikā* enclosing the piece of land belonging to Bhillamāladeva, he should be looked upon as a dog or a donkey or a Cāṇḍāla even if he is dead. If a merchant was involved in such a case, his whole property should have to be confiscated by the government. On the other hand, in case the *śrotaka* was not duly paid to the *vārikas* of the god Bhillamāladeva, if any one out of the persons belonging to the *Mahāparṣad* attached to the *maṭhikā*, who kept the door of the *maṭhikā* open to the public, or of outsiders who conducted worship of the goddess, committed suicide, he would also share a similar fate even if he was dead. It is stated that this *vyavasthā*, based on the *sthiti* or decree, was a permanent one and had to be

1. For *śrotaka*, see *Ep. Ind.*, Vol. XXXII, p. 36. For the meaning of *bhaṅga*, see Apte, *Pract. Sans.-Eng. Dict.*, s. v. *nidrā-bhaṅga*, *yātrā-bhaṅga*.
2. Cf. *Ep. Ind.*, Vol. XXX, p. 213 and note 2.
3. Cf. *JNSI*, Vol. VII, pp. 79ff.

observed by both the parties of the dispute, viz. the devotees of the god Bhillamāladeva and those of the goddess worshipped in the *maṭhikā*. To the above is added the statement that anybody who would appropriate the piece of land in his attempt to avoid the payment of the *śrotaka* should be endowed with all the greater and minor sins.

It is clear from the words of the inscription that a small piece of land belonging to the temple of the god Bhillamāladeva, which seems to have been situated in the vicinity of the *maṭhikā* of the goddess, was lying within the compound wall of the latter and was in wrongful possession of the devotees of the goddess. It is also clear that, while the devotees of the god were trying to recover the land by all means including the offer of hunger-strike, the other party attached to the goddess was trying to obstruct the release of the plot equally obstinately in the same way. The decision to ease this state of tension by fixing an amount of annual rent for the piece of land, payable by the party in the possession of it, was therefore a good one. The respectful mention of the goddess in the present record exhibits a spirit of compromise which is commendable.

The above section of the record is followed in lines 46-47 by a sentence meaning to say that the giver of the decision, viz. the god Bhillamāladeva along with his *vārikas*, expressed his desire in the words of the document as written by the scribe. The following sentence saying that the god favoured the document with his assent is a well known formula with which the royal donors put their signature to a charter originally written on a perishable material and later incised on copper plates. This section is in the style of the charters issued by the contemporary rulers of the area in question.[1]

The charter ends with a stanza (verse 20) followed by a short benedictory passage. The verse mentions the person who was responsible for writing the document with the consent of both the parties, viz. the devotees of the god and those of the goddess. This writer was a *Kāyastha* named Śambhu-

1. Similar statements are found, e.g., in the grants of the Śilāhāras of the Northern Konkan, see *Ind. Ant.*, Vol. V, p. 279 (Plate III, lines 10-11); *Ep. Ind.*, Vol. III, p. 275, lines 82-84; etc.

deva who was the son of Ambaipa (Ambaiya ?) and grandson of Joggapaiya.

The place where the temples of the god and the goddess were situated is not mentioned in the record. But, as we have seen, they must have stood at Saṁyāna within the dominions of the Rāṣṭrakūṭa king Kṛṣṇa III. Saṁyāna is modern Sanjan in the Thana District of Maharashtra. Among the geographical names mentioned in the inscription, Bhillamāla, as already pointed out, is modern Bhinmāl about 100 miles to the south-west of Jodhpur in Rajasthan. It is interesting to note that there was a well-organised settlement of merchants of Bhinmāl origin at Sanjan and that they had installed a Vaiṣṇavite deity of their own and named it after their home town. A large number of peoples of various countries are mentioned in the description of Kṛṣṇa III. Most of these tracts are well known. The Pāṇḍyas lived in the Madurai-Ramanathapuram-Tirunelveli region, the Oḍras in modern Orissa and the Siṁhalas in Ceylon. The original territory of the Coḷas was in the Tanjavur-Tiruchirappalli area and of the Pārasīkas in Persia. The name Andhra was apparently used to indicate the kingdom of the contemporary Eastern Cālukya king of Veṅgī, while the name Draviḍa was probably applied to Toṇḍamaṇḍalam, the territory of the Pallavas in older times. The Varvaras probably occupied a part of the Lower Indus valley. The Tajjikas or Tājikas were the people of Arabia and Vaṅkīna may be the same as Vokkāṇa mentioned in Varāhamihira's *Bṛhatsaṁhitā* (XIV. 20) and identified with modern Wakhan in Central Asia.[1] The Hūṇas[2] appear to have lived in the Punjab and the Khasas[3] in Kashmir and Nepal. The Pratīhāras of the Gurjara stock ruled over wide areas of North India; but, even as late as the first half of the eleventh century, Al-Bīrūnī speaks of the Jodhpur-Alwar-Bharatpur region of Rajasthan as Gujarāt, i.e. Gurjaratrā or the home of the Gurjaras.[4]

1. Cf. *Ind. Cult.*, Vol. VIII, p. 55.

2. Cf. Pargiter, *The Mārkaṇḍeya Purāṇa*, p. 379, note; *Ind. Cult.*, *op. cit.*, p. 59.

3. See Pargiter, *op. cit.*, p. 346, note; Stein, *Rājataraṅgiṇī*, trans., Vol. I, pp. 47-48 (note on I.317); Vol. II, p. 430.

4. Cf. *JNSI*, Vol. VIII, pp. 135ff. The Daulatpura plate (*Ep. Ind.*,

Mālava, the land of the Mālavīyas, seems to have included in this age Hiuen-tsang's Mo-la-p'o in the Mahī valley in Gujarāt.[1] The same *mahāparṣad* being called both Āryadeśīya and Pañcagauḍīya would identify the Āryadeśa or Āryāvarta with Pañca-Gauḍa.

Vol. V, pp. 211ff.; cf. Bhandarkar's List, No. 28) of 843 A.D. includes the Jodhpur region in Gurjaratrā. In the seventh century A.D., the Chinese pilgrim Hiuen-tsang mentions Pi-lo-mo-lo (i.e. Bhillamāla or Bhinmāl) as the capital of Ku-che-lo (i.e. Gurjara).

1. See *Bhār. Vid.*, Vol. XXV, pp. 1ff.; Sircar, *Stud. Geog. Anc. Med. Ind.*, 2nd ed., pp. 205ff.

Chapter IX

THE NĀGAS AND YAKṢAS

I

I had an occasion to examine the impressions of two inscriptions relating to the worship of the Nāgas or serpents in ancient and medieval India. The first of these records is engraved on the pedestal of a Nāga image now preserved in the Lucknow Museum. The second epigraph is incised on a stone slab which was discovered at Biharsharif (Patna District, Bihar) or in its neighbourhood, but is now exhibited in the Patna Museum.

The Nāgas enjoy a prominent place in ancient Indian legends and folklore. There are literary references to numerous Nāgas, the most famous among them being Śeṣa or Ananta, Vāsuki, Takṣaka, Dhṛtarāṣṭra, Elāpatra or Airāvata, Karkoṭa or Karkoṭaka, Kauravya, Śaṅkha, Maṇi and others. The cult of the Nāgas, allied to that of another class of semi-divine beings called Yakṣa, was widely prevalent in ancient India.[1] The worship of snake-deities is popular in different parts of India even to this day.[2] In ancient times, there were many great centres of the Nāga cult in Northern India. The chronicles of Kashmir speak of the worship of several Nāgas in that land, the most important among them being Nīla who had his abode in the waters of the Vitastā and was regarded as the guardian deity of Kashmir.[3] An illustrious royal house

1. See James Fergusson, *Tree and Serpent Worship*, 1873; J. Ph. Vogel, *The Indian Serpent Lore*, 1926; N.K. Bhattasali, *Iconography of Buddhist and Brahmanical Sculptures in the Dacca Museum*, pp. 212ff.; K. K. Gupta in *Proc. IHC*, 1939, pp. 223-29 (The Nāgas and the Nāga Cult in Ancient Indian History); etc. An inscription at Gurzala and another at Macherla, both in Andhra Pradesh, invoke the presence of the eight Nāgas, viz., Śeṣa, Vāsuki, Takṣaka, Karkoṭa, Abja, Mahāmbuja, Śaṅkhadhara and Kulika, to decide the auspicious or inauspicious nature of the grants recorded in the epigraphs. See *A.R.S. Ind. Ep.*, 1910, p. 107.

2. Cf. Vogel, *op. cit.*, pp. 247ff.; Bhattasali, *loc. cit.*; Whitehead, *The Village Gods of South India*, 1916; V. N. Mandlik, *JBRAS*, Vol. IX, pp. 188-89 (Serpent Worship in Western India); etc.

3. See Vogel, *op. cit.*, pp. 220ff.; Kalhaṇa's *Rājataraṅgiṇī*, I. 28, 182, etc.

of ancient Kashmir, represented by the celebrated Muktāpīḍa Lalitāditya (eighth century), claimed descent from the Nāga Karkoṭaka who is also famous in the *Mahābhārata* episode of Nala, king of the Niṣadhas probably living near the Pāriyātra (the Western Vindhyas and the Aravalli range).[1] The Nāga kings Elāpatra and Cakravāka are mentioned in certain old Brāhmī inscriptions[2] from Barhut and were probably worshipped in pre-Christian times in the region in question. In Buddhist literature, Elāpatra is mentioned as the Nāga of Takṣaśilā (in Gandhāra),[3] where the great serpent-sacrifice of the Kuru king Janamejaya is sometimes supposed to have taken place.[4] Numerous ancient Nāga images have been discovered at Mathurā and in its neighbourhood. An inscription[5] of the year 26 of the Kaṇiṣka era, corresponding to 104 A.D., records the installation of a Śilā-paṭṭa by some persons, described as 'the sons of the actors of Mathurā, who are being praised as the Cāndaka brothers', at the *sthāna* of *Bhagavat* Dadhikarṇa, lord of the Nāgas. The existence of a temple of Dadhikarṇa-nāga at Mathurā during the age of the Kuṣāṇas is also indicated by another inscription[6] on a pillar base originally belonging to the Huviṣka monastery of that place. It states that the object was the gift of Devila who was 'a servant of the shrine of Dadhikarṇa'. Another Mathurā inscription[7] on a Nāga image, dated in the year 8 of Kaṇiṣka's reign (78-101 A.D.), records the consecration of a tank and a garden dedicated to *Bhagavat* Bhūmi-nāga. A Nāga image, discovered at Chhargaon (five miles to the south of Mathurā), bears an inscription stating that the Nāga was installed by two persons in their own tank. The epigraph ends with the *maṅgala*: "May the *Bhagavat* Nāga be pleased!" But no name is applied to the Nāga in this case. This reminds us of the custom of erecting a Nāga-kāṣṭha (i.e. a pole with its top fashioned in the shape of a serpent), at the centre

1. Vogel, *op. cit.*, pp. 214-15; *IHQ*, Vol. XXI, p. 311.
2. Barua and Sinha, *Barhut Inscriptions*, pp. 71-72.
3. Vogel, *op. cit.*, pp. 106f., 208ff., 216.
4. *Ibid.*, p. 205.
5. *A. R. Arch. Surv. Ind.*, 1908-09, p. 159.
6. *Ind. Ant.*, Vol. XXXIII, pp. 102f., No. 13.
7. *Ep. Ind.*, Vol. XVII, p. 11.

of a tank at the time of its consecration, which is prevalent in some parts of India even to this day.[1]

The popularity of the Nāga cult in the Mathurā region is also indicated by the *Harivaṁśa* episode of the famous Kāliya-nāga who lived in the waters of the Yamunā[2] as well as by the well-known conception of Balarāma as the incarnation of Ananta-nāga. The episode of Akrūra in the world of serpents, as given in the *Harivaṁśa* and referred to in the *Bhāgavata Purāṇa*, is also interesting to note in this connection. Akrūra is stated to have reached the abode of the snakes in the Nether World by diving down in the waters of the Yamunā. There he found the Nāga Ananta or Śeśa worshipped by the other Nāgas.[3] The description of the Nāga deity here is strikingly reminiscent of the iconography of Balarāma as indicated by Varāhamihira's *Bṛhatsaṁhitā*[4] and also known from sculptures.[5]

A great centre of Nāga cult in the eastern part of Northern India was Rājagṛha (modern Rājgir in the Patna District, Bihar), the ancient capital of Magadha, and its neighbour-

1. Bhattasali, *op. cit*, p. 216.

2. Cf. Vogel, *op. cit.*, pp. 87ff.

3. *Ibid.*, p. 92: "Now Akrūra dived down in the pool of the Yamuṇā, and in the Nether Region (*rasātala*) he beheld the world of snakes. In the middle thereof, he saw the thousand-headed lord of the serpents who carried a plough in one hard and whose frame was supported by a mace. His lofty banner was a golden fan palm. He was of white complexion and was wrapped in a dark-coloured garment. He wore a single ear-ring and, being intoxicated, he slept. He was seated at his ease on the shining seat formed by the mass of his coils. Long-armed was he; his breast was covered by a wreath of golden lotus flowers and his limbs were anointed with red sandal. He was worshipped by the chiefs among the Nāgas headed by Vāsuki. The two Nāgas, Kambala and Aśvatara, holding chowries, were fanning the deity who was seated on the seat of justice. The other snakes, Karkoṭaka foremost, attended him and laved their monarch by means of golden jars. Seated in his lap was Viṣṇu, dark like a thunder cloud, and wearing a yellow garment, his breast adorned with the *śrīvatsa*." In Buddhist tradition, Kambala and Aśvatara are sometimes called the Nāgas of the Gaṅgā See Vogel, *op. cit.*, p. 118.

4. Cf. LVIII, 36: "Baladeva must be made having a plough in his right hand, with eyes lively from drink, and wearing a single ear-ring. His complexion is fair like a conch-shell, the moon or lotus-fibre."

5. Cf. *The Age of Imperial Unity* (*The History and Culture of the Indian People*, Vol. II), ed. Majumdar, p. 452.

hood. A tradition recorded by Hiuen-tsang[1] seems to suggest that a Nāga named Nālanda was the guardian deity of the city of Nālandā (modern Bargaon in the Patna District), not far away from Rājgir. According to the *Mahābhārata*,[2] there were temples of the Nāga gods, Svastika-nāga and Maṇi-nāga, at Rājagṛha which was also the abode of the Nāgas, Arbuda and Śakravāpin. Ancient Nāga images have been discovered at Rājgir and the area around it, and the Maṇiyār Maṭh at Rājgir has been supposed to represent an old *Maṇināga-maṭha*.[3] A sculpture, discovered in the ruins of Maṇiyār Maṭh, is known to bear the representation of two male Nāga figures with a diminutive female figure between them, and these three figures have tentatively been identified respectively with Maṇināga, Svastika-nāga and Sumāgadhā, supposed, on the basis of a damaged inscription on the sculpture itself, to have been the sister of the Nāga brothers, Maṇi and Svastika.[4] In connection with the suggestion regarding the female snake-deity Sumāgadhā, it is interesting to note that the worship of the Nāginīs does not appear to have been popular in other parts of India in ancient times. Although Nāginīs figure in some of the epic and Purāṇic episodes, the Nāgas are always more prominent in ancient Indian literature. We have many lists in early works enumerating the names of numerous Nāgas;[5] but there is hardly any list of the

1. Watters, *On Yuan Chwang's Travels in India*, Vol. II, p. 165.

2. Cf. Vaṅgavāsī edition, II. 21. 9: *Arbudaḥ Śakravāpī ca pannagau śatru-tāpanau | Svastikasy:=ālayaś:=c:=ātra Maṇināgasya c:=ottamaḥ* || The place of Maṇināga is also located near Rājagṛha elsewhere in the same work (III. 84. 104-108).

3. Cf. *A.R. Arch. Surv. Ind.*, 1905-06, pp. 103ff.; Vogel, *op. cit.*, pp. 218-9; Ghosh, *A Guide to Rajgir*, p. 16; etc. The existence of a Maṇināga-maṭha in Orissa is known from the Kanas plates (*Ep. Ind.*, Vol. XXVIII, pp. 328ff.). Maṇināga was probably sometimes identified with the popular Yakṣa deity Maṇibhadra or Māṇibhadra who was regarded as the guardian of caravans (*JBRS*, Vol. XXXIX, Parts 1-2, pp. 41ff.). For the name Maṇibhadra and the god's association with the safety of a merchant's journey in Jain tradition, see also Dhanapāla's *Bhavissattakahā* (tenth century) in *Journ. Or. Inst.*, Vol. II, pp. 352, 354.

4. *JNSI*, Vol. XII, p. 181.

5. Cf. *Mahābhārata*, I. 35. 65 and 229; V. 102; *Harivaṁśa*, I. iii. 31 and 196; *Matsya Purāṇa*, 6; *Padma Purāṇa*, Sṛṣṭikhaṇḍa, 6; etc.; Vogel, *op. cit.*, pp. 190ff.

names of Nāginīs. Curiously enough, a Nāginī cult is known to have developed in Eastern India. Elsewhere[1] we have seen how the snake-goddess worshipped in various parts of Bengal and Bihar in the medieval period under such names as *Bhaṭṭinī* Maṭṭuvā contributed to the growth of the cult of Manasā whose worship is now popular in Eastern India. The continuity of Nāga worship at Rājgir down to quite recent times is indicated by an inscription[2] of Vikrama 1837 (1781 A.D.), recording the setting up of the footprints of Śālibhadra-nāga.

II

In Bengal and its neighbourhood, people are sometimes found to worship the Vāstu-sarpa, which is a serpent that lives in a particular house for a long time and is believed to do no harm to the inmates, as a household deity. We have also evidence to show that some ancient Indian ruling families had a snake-god as their tutelary deity.

Kings Dyutivarman and Viṣṇuvarman, who ruled the Parvatākara-rājya with their capital at the city of Brahmapura, issued two copper-plate grants discovered at Taleśvara in the Almora District, U.P.[3] King Agnivarman, father of Dyuti and grandfather of Viṣṇu, who flourished about the sixth century A.D., is described as a devotee of the god Vīraṇeśvara-svāmin, in favour of whose temple the Taleśvara charters were issued. The said god is stated to have been an incarnation of the snake-god Ananta and had the form of the lord of the snakes (*Ananta-mūrti* and *Bhujagarāja-rūpa*). Vīraṇeśvara is described in Dyutivarman's record as *sakala-jagan-mūl-orvī-cakra-mahābhāra-vahana-guṇa-vamana-phaṇa-sahasra*, "one whose thousand hoods were the base of the world, carrying the great load of the circle of the earth and spreading good qualities."[4] The other epigraph describes the god as "one observing concentration capable of supporting the earth; who reddens the surface of the lower region by the rays of the collection of the jewels growing about the array of the expanded hoods, large

1. *Ep. Ind.*, Vol. XXVIII, pp. 138-39.
2. Vogel, *op. cit.*, p. 219.
3. *Ep. Ind.*, Vol. XIII, pp. 109ff.
4. *Ibid.*, p. 117.

and wide as the surface of the earth; the excellence of whose power is without beginning, unknowable, unthinkable, wonderful, elevated and extensive; who causes the apportioning of existence and destruction of the whole world."[1]

The purpose of Dyutivarman's grant is stated to have been the continuance of *bali*, *caru* and *satra* in the temple; the bathing of the god with curds, milk and clarified butter; the worship of the god with perfumes, incense, lamps and flowers; sweeping and cleansing the temple compound and ploughing the temple lands; and repairing dilapidated, broken and fallen parts of the temple of *Bhagavat* Vīraṇeśvarasvāmin described as worthy of the honour of the gods and demons and the whole world.

III

The Nāga image inscription in the Lucknow Museum, referred to above, shows that the representation in question is of none other than the great Takṣaka-nāga.

One of the most famous of the Nāgas in ancient Indian literature is Takṣaka.[2] He seems to be mentioned in the *Atharvaveda*[3] and *Sāṅkhāyana Gṛhyasūtra*[4] as Tākṣaka Vaiśāleya. The *Kauśikasūtra*[5] and the *Viṣṇusmṛti*[6] prescribe food offering, for the protection of the house, to various deities including Takṣaka and Upatakṣaka. Takṣaka is the chief Nāga hero in the *Mahābhārata* stories about the Kuru kings, Parikṣit and his son Janamejaya. He killed Parikṣit and escaped death with great difficulty in the well-known serpent sacrifice of Janamejaya.[7] Takṣaka also figures prominently in the episode of the burning of the Khāṇḍava forest (lying near Kurukṣetra, i.e. about the modern Eastern Punjab), which was

1. *Ibid.*, p. 120—*sakala-bhuvana-bhava-bhaṅga-vibhāga-kāriṇo...anādy-āvedy-ācinty-ātyadbhut-odbhūta-prabhūta-prabhāv-ātiśayasya kṣamātala-vikaṭa-sphaṭa-paṭala-nikaṭa-prarūḍha-maṇi-gaṇa-kiraṇ-āruṇita-pātālatalasya dharaṇi-dharaṇa-yogya-dhāraṇā-dhāriṇo.........*
2. Vogel, *op. cit.* pp. 203ff.
3. VII. 10.
4. IV. 18. 1.
5. LXXIV. 8.
6. LXVII. 5.
7. Vogel, *op. cit.*, pp., 66ff., 69ff.

his abode.[1] This story of the *Mahābhārata* states how the Fire-god consumed the forest with the help of the Kuru hero Arjuna and his friend, Yādava Kṛṣṇa, during Takṣaka's absence in Kurukṣetra and how Takṣaka's son, Aśvasena, escaped from the burning forest with the greatest difficulty. There are several references in the *Rāmāyaṇa*[2] to Rāvaṇa's victory over the Nāga king Vāsuki and his conquest of the Nāga capital Bhogavatī, in connection with which the king of Laṅkā is stated to have carried away Takṣaka-nāga's wife.

Considering the importance of Takṣaka in the Indian serpent lore, his worship seems to have been widespread in ancient India. The prevalence of the Takṣaka cult in Kashmir is referred to in the *Mahābhārata*[3] as well as in Kalhaṇa's *Rājataraṅgiṇī*[4] and Bilhaṇa's *Vikramāṅkadevacarita.*[5] Unfortunately, very little is known as regards the worship of Takṣaka in other parts of Northern India. As to the survival of the Takṣaka cult in modern times, we may only refer to his shrine near Navali or Naoli in the old Indore State (now in Madhya Pradesh). Here the snake deity is worshipped under the name Takṣakeśvara or Tākhājī whose image represents the Nāga as standing with a sevenfold hood, the coils being visible on both sides. He has two arms possibly holding a cup and a fruit in his hands. The deity is accompanied by a male and a female attendant, the former holding a serpent in his right hand.[6] Unfortunately, in the absence of any inscription on the sculpture, it is impossible to determine whether the image was identified with Takṣaka-nāga even in earlier times.

Under the circumstances, the only early image of Takṣaka so far discovered in India and definitely known as such, seems to be that now housed in the Lucknow Museum with the Exhibit No. G-72.[7] The sculpture is stated to have been

1. *Ibid.*, pp. 62, 77ff.
2. III. 32. 13-14; VI. 7. 3 and 7; VII. 23. 4-5.
3. III. 80. 970.
4. I. 222.
5. XVIII. 170.
6. See Tod, *Annals and Antiquities of Rajasthan*, Vol. II, p. 718; *Prog. Rep. A.S.I.*, *W.C.*, 1919-20, p. 88, Plate XIII; Vogel, *op. cit.*, pp. 206f.
7. An inscription (*A.R. Ep.*, 1953-54, No. B 48) of about the 8th century in the Nāgeśvara temple at Narnuru (Kurnool District, Andhra Pradesh)

purchased for the Museum in 1925 from B.C. Bhattacharya of Durgakund, Banaras. But its exact findspot is unknown.

The pedestal of this Nāga image bears an inscription in one line only, which was apparently meant to serve the purpose of a label. The characters belong to the Siddhamātṛkā alphabet and may be assigned to the eighth century A.D. on grounds of palaeography. The orthography of the record exhibits the influence of local pronunciation.

The inscription begins with the *siddham* symbol and ends with a double *daṇḍa*. In between the *siddham* symbol and the double *daṇḍa*, there are only six *akṣaras* which read: *śrī-Takhaka-nāga*, the intended reading no doubt being *śrī-Takṣaka-nāgaḥ*, 'the illustrious Nāga Takṣaka'. Nothing is said in the inscription regarding the person by whom and the purpose for which the image was set up. But there is little doubt that it was installed in a temple for worship.

IV

The inscribed stone slab in the Patna Museum, referred to above, bears the exhibit No. 10601 and looks like the broken piece of a door jamb. The slab measure 4′ 9″ by 1′ 5″, and contains four lines of inscription on one side only. It was presented to the Patna Museum in January 1943 by the Sub-Divisional Officer of Biharsharif in whose quarters it had been lying for some time uncared for. Nothing is known as regards its discovery and original findspot. But it appears that it was found at Biharsharif itself or in its neighbourhood.

The inscription was noticed by A. Banerji-Sastri in a very short note entitled "Evolution of Māgadhī Script", published in *JBORS*, Vol. XXVIII, 1942, pp. 440-41. Unfortunately, he read and interpreted only the last line of the record and that also not quite correctly. He also failed to understand the real nature of the document. Thus he says, "The inscription is of the usual votive donation type. The last line runs—*likhitaṁ sūtrakāreṇa Kāmadevena karmmiṇā Śāke* 1322 *Nṛpa-Vikramārke Saṁ* 1458....Śaka 1322 = 1322 + 78 = 1400 A.D.: Saṁ 1458—58 = 1400 A.D. Thus the inscription is written in the Māghadhī script, dated 1400 A.D."

refers to a deity called Takṣakeśvara-bhaṭāra. But the name seems to have been applied to the Śiva-liṅga worshipped in the temple in question.

There are several mistakes in the above reading and interpretation of the last line of the inscription, quoted above. What Banerji-Sastri has read as *sūtrakāreṇa*, *Śāke* 1322 and *Saṁ* 1458 are actually *svarṇṇakāreṇa*, *Śāke* 1317 and *Saṁ* 1452 respectively. The date of the inscription is therefore not 1400 A.D. but 1395 A.D. Moreover it does not speak of any donation, but records the construction of a temple for a Nāga deity. The script of the inscription is again not Māgadhī, but early Bengali resembling the modern Bengali alphabet very closely. This script may also be called Gauḍī,[1] although this name may more-properly be applied to an earlier stage of the characters on the way of their development.

The four lines of writing in the inscription cover a space about 27.5 inches by 3.5 inches. The preservation of the writing is not satisfactory. The usual symbol expected at the beginning of the record and twelve *akṣaras* that followed it in line 1 are almost completely lost owing to the peeling off of a layer of the stone. The same defect has also obscured some letters here and there in other parts of the inscription. But fortunately the purport of all the lines of the inscription is quite clear.

The characters closely resemble those employed in other records of the fourteenth and fifteenth centuries, written in the Gauḍīya script prevalent in Bengal and the neighbouring regions including parts of Bihar, such as the stone inscription[2] (from the Patna District) of Vikrama Saṁvat 1553 (1496 A.D.). They exhibit characteristics slightly earlier than the letters of the Barakar (Burdwan District, West Bengal) inscriptions[3] of Śaka 1382 (1460 A.D.) or 1383 (1461 A.D.) and Śaka 1468 (1546 A.D.). It may be noticed that the *anusvāra* is written in both the Nāgarī (cf. *varāṁ* in line 3) and the Bengali (cf. *saṁ* in line 4) fashions; the figure 2 in line 4 resembles its form occasionally found in the Mehar plate of Śaka 1156 (1234 A.D.).[4] The language of the inscription is

1. See *IHQ*, Vol. XXVIII, pp. 130-31.

2. *JRASB*, Letters, Vol. XIV, pp. 114-16 and Plate. The early Bengali script was prevalent in Bihar in the medieval period. Originally the same alphabet was used in the whole of Eastern India.

3. *Ibid.*, Vol. II, pp. 21ff. and Plates.

4. *Ep. Ind.*, Vol. XXVII, pp. 182ff. (cf. e.g., 2 in '20' in line 32).

Sanskrit ; but it cannot be regarded as quite elegant and chaste. The inscription bears the date in Śaka 1317 and Vikrama 1452, in figures, at the end. At the beginning of line 3, the Vikrama year is quoted in words as *yugm-eśāsya-kṛt-aik-ābde*. The words *yugma*, *iśāsya*, *kṛta* and *eka* mean respectively 2, 5, 4 and 1 and, according to the well-known principle *aṅkānāṁ vāmato gatiḥ*, give the year 1452. The lost letters at the beginning of line 1 appear to have similarly indicated the Śaka year 1317 in words. The said lost letters are followed by the passage *c=Āśvine māsi śukle vāre Śukre daśamyām* indicating the date : Āśvina-sudi 10, Friday. The same day is further referred to in the passage *nṛpa-guros=tithau* occurring in line 3 along with the year of the Vikrama era given in words. The expression *nṛpa-guru* has apparently been used to signify 'the foremost of kings' as in the *Raghuvaṁśa.*[1] The date Āśvina-sudi 10 is here called 'the royal *tithi*' because it is the celebrated Vijayā-da'amī day which was the time prescribed for Indian monarchs to set out on *dig-vijaya.*[2] Thus the date mentioned in the inscription is the Vijayādaśamī *tithi* on Friday, Vikrama 1458=Śaka 1317. It regularly corresponds to Friday, September 24, 1395 A.D.

With the exception of the concluding passage giving the years of the Vikrama and Śaka eras, the whole inscription is written in verse. There are altogether three stanzas, the first in the Sragdharā metre and the remaining two in Anuṣṭubh. The first verse says that (in the Śaka year 1317, given in words) on Āśvina-sudi 10, Friday, several persons named Akrūra, Śrīleśa, Pati and Kuśala erected (*ropitā*) the *kīrti* of the celebrated Nāga called Kauśika, endowed with the hood-jewel, who grants whatever is prayed for and removes all obstacles [in the way of his devotees]. As in many other cases,[3] the word *kīrti* here seems to indicate a shrine meant for the Nāga deity Kauśika who may have been already in worship in the locality where Akrūra and others lived. Verse 2 says that in the Vikrama year 1452 (given in words), on 'the royal *tithi*' (i.e. the Vijayā-daśamī), a person named Deśānanda (apparently an architect or a mason) constructed

1. See II. 68.
2. Cf. *Sabdakalpadruma*, s. v. *Durgā*.
3. Cf. *JRASB*, Letters, Vol. XIV, p. 115.

(*akāri*) the beautiful *kīrti* (i.e. the temple of the Nāga deity Kauśika). The last word of this stanza goes with the following verse (verse 3) which says that a Kāyastha named Preteśvara who was a good teacher (*sad-upādhyāya*), composed the verses (contained in the inscription) and that the inscription was *likhita* (literally, 'written', but apparently meaning 'engraved') by a goldsmith named Kāmadeva. The word *Kāyastha* apparently refers to the caste of the author of the verses, who was probably the teacher of a village school. Considering the fact that it was only the Brāhmaṇas who usually learnt Sanskrit in medieval India, this Kāyastha's knowledge of the sacred language (although not very deep) is quite interesting.[1] Another interesting fact is that a goldsmith was engaged to engrave the record on stone.

The worship of Kauśika-nāga at Biharsharif or in its vicinity is of great interest in view of the fact that the *Mahābhārata* associates the same Nāga with Rājagṛha, i.e. modern Rājgir which is not far away. We have referred above to a verse occurring in Chapter 21 of the Sabhā-parvan, which mentions Rājagṛha as the abode of the Nāgas, Arbuda and Śakravāpin, and the place where the temples of the Nāgas, Svastika and Maṇi stood. The verse that immediately follows the above reads:

aparihāryā meghānāṁ Māgadhā Manunā kṛtāḥ |
Kauśiko Maṇimāṁś =c =aiva cakrāte c =āpy =anugraham ||

"The Magadha country has been so made by Manu that the clouds cannot keep away from it. Kauśika and Maṇimat also have shown it their favour." This seems to suggest that the Nāgas, Kauśika and Maṇimat, were worshipped at Rājagṛha as givers of rains, although that particular characteristic of Kauśika is not mentioned in our inscription. Ancient Indian literature speaks of various powers of the Nāgas including that of causing rains.[2] It is interesting to note that Buddhist tradition also associates the scarcity of water at Rājagṛha on account of drought, on one occasion during the reign of Bimbisāra, with the absence on exile of two Nāgarājas

1. For some good poems composed by Kāyastha authors, see *Ep. Ind.*, Vol. XXXII, pp. 341, 345; Vol. XXXIII, pp. 33, 38, 66.

2. See Vogel, *op. cit.*, pp. 4, 19, 184f., 207, 220, 233, 244, 282ff.

named Girika and Vidyujjvāla (probably elsewhere called Nanda and Upananda).[1]

V

A stone inscription was edited by Daya Ram Sahni in the *Epigraphia Indica*, Vol. XVIII, pp. 158-59, with Plate. About the stone bearing the inscription, Sahni says, "The epigraph is incised on a stone slab measuring 2′ 10″ high, 1′ wide and 2″ in thickness. The stone was fixed in the parapet of a well in the village of Masharfa situated about a mile and a half to the north-west of the stone pillar at Kosam. The inscription is engraved on the front face of the slab and consists of fourteen lines. Each line consists of five to seven *akṣaras* except the last line which probably contained only three characters, now mostly defaced. For the rest, the epigraph is in an excellent state of preservation."

The characters employed in the inscription resemble those in the Mathurā inscription of the time of Śoḍāsa (first quarter of the first century A.D.),[2] but are slightly earlier than the latter. The epigraph may thus be assigned, on palaeographical grounds, to a date in the latter part of the first century B.C. The language of the inscription under review is Prakrit with a little influence of Sanskrit.

Sahni says, "The inscription begins with a salutation to a certain *Bhagavat* whose name unfortunately is not given and ends with the wish that 'the deity may be pleased'. Here too unfortunately the name of the deity is not given or, if it was, it has been destroyed in the last line of the inscription. We are thus left to guess the identity of this god. I am inclined to think that it was the Yakṣa Maṇibhadra, the favourite deity of the grandfather of the donor." Unfortunately, it is not possible to agree entirely with Sahni's contentions quoted above.

The first three lines of the inscription read *namo bhagavato sathavāhasa Mānibhadasa*, 'Adoration to Lord Māṇibhadra, the leader of caravans', and the epigraph clearly ends with the sentence *piyataṁ* [*bhagavā*], 'May the Lord be pleased'. The

1. *Ibid.*, p. 118.
2. *JBRS*, Vol. XXXIX, Parts 1-2, 1953, pp. 5ff.

deity is called simply 'the Lord' in the concluding sentence, as his name is already mentioned as the Lord Māṇibhadra in the *maṅgala* at the beginning of the record. Sahni imagined a fullstop after *bhagavato* in line 1, which he wrongly read as *bhagavate*. He regarded the expressions *sathavāhasa Mānibhadasa* as epithets of the following name of the donor's grandfather. The expression *mānibhada* was taken by him to denote 'a votary of Maṇibhadra'. It should, however, be pointed out that Māṇibhadra is just another well-known form of the name of Yakṣa Maṇibhadra. This form of the name is not only found in the Padmāvatī Maṇibhadra statue inscription,[1] quoted by Sahni himself,[2] but is also recognised by Monier-Williams in his *Sanskrit-English Dictionary* (s. v. *māṇi*) on the authority of the *Sāmavidhāna Brāhmaṇa* and the *Mahābhārata*. The Vaṅgavāsī edition of the *Mahābhārata* (II. 10. 15), while giving the names of the Yakṣas in Kubera's palace, says :

Māṇibhadro='tha Dhanadaḥ Śvetabhadraś=ca guhyakaḥ |
Kaśerako Gaṇḍakaṇḍuḥ Pradyotaś=ca Mahābalaḥ ||

Although therefore there was in ancient India a class of people (called *Maṇibhaddavattikā* in the Pali work *Mahāniddesa* and *Maṇibhaddā* in the *Milindapañha*)[3] who worshipped the Yakṣa Maṇibhadra, there is no necessity of taking the expression *mānibhada* occurring in the Masharfa inscription in the sense of a votary of Maṇibhadra, in view of the fact that Maṇibhadra and Māṇibhadra are but different forms of the name of the same Yakṣa.

The word *sathavāha*=Sanskrit *sārthavāha* meaning 'the leader or conductor of a caravan', 'a merchant', 'a trader', used in the inscription as an epithet of the Yakṣa Māṇibhadra seems to have induced Sahni to take the expressions *sathavāhasa Mānibhadasa* as epithets of the donor's grandfather. That, however, the Yakṣa Maṇibhadra or Māṇibhadra was regarded in ancient India as the deity especially worshipped by travellers and caravans is definitely established by the *Mahābhārata*.[4] In the section in question, the *Mahābhārata*

1. *ASR, A.R.*, 1915-16, Part II, p. 106.
2. *Op. cit.*, p. 159, note 1.
3. Cf. Malalasekera, *Dict. Pali Proper Names*, Vol. II, p. 426.
4. Vaṅgavāsī ed., III. 65. 22.

describes the great plight of a caravan of merchants attacked by a herd of wild elephants in a forest. When those of the caravan that escaped unhurt gathered together, the first question they asked one another was :

> *[te='brūvan sahitāḥ sarve] kasy=edaṁ karmaṇaḥ phalam /*
> *nūnaṁ na pūjito='smābhir=Maṇibhadro mahāyasāḥ //*

The first thing that occurred to the merchants was that the calamity was probably due to their negligence in worshipping the god Maṇibhadra. This shows beyond doubt that Maṇibhadra was regarded as the protector of the caravans, while our inscription makes it clear that he was also conceived as a leader of caravans.[1] As most of the facts relating to the mythology and cult of the Yakṣa Maṇibhadra are now lost, the information supplied by the inscription is extremely interesting. Another interesting fact regarding the inadequately preserved Maṇibhadra mythology is that the Yakṣa was very probably identical with the deity called Maṇināga (sometimes believed to have been a son of the *Nāga-mātā* Kadru) whose *tīrtha* at the ancient city of Rājagṛha is mentioned in the *Mahābhārata*[2] and whose *maṭha* or temple somewhere in Orissa is referred to in the two Kanas plates of the sixth and seventh centuries A.D.[3]

The inscription records the construction of a *vedikā* apparently in honour of the god Maṇibhadra or Māṇibhadra on behalf of a householder called Gotīputa, i.e. Gauptīputra. Gotīputa or Gauptīputra is essentially a metronymic meaning 'the son born of a girl of the Gupta clan', although it is used here as if it were a personal name. There are other instances of a metronymic being similiarly stereotyped as a personal name.[4]

The *vedikā* was caused to be made by Gauptīputra in a locality called Aśikā. Whether this was the ancient name of

1. It is also possible to think that here the word *sārthavāha* is used in the modified sense of the protector of caravans. With reference to this characteristic of Maṇibhadra, the deity may be compared to the South Indian god Vaḷitunai-nāyaṇār (Sanskrit *Mārgasahayeśvara*) who was worshipped by merchants for the safe transport of their commodities.

2. *Op. cit.*, III. 84. 106ff.

3. *Ep. Ind.*, Vol. XXVIII, pp. 328ff.

4. One interesting case is that of Vākāṭaka Gautamīputra (literally, 'the son born of a girl of the Gautama-gotra or clan'), who was a son of Pravarasena I.

modern Masharfa (the findspot of the inscription) near Kosam (ancient Kauśāmbī) about 35 miles from Allahabad cannot be determined in the present state of our knowledge. Monier-Williams' *Sanskrit-English Dictionary* recognises Aśika or Asika as the name of a people on the authority on Varāhamihira's *Bṛhatsaṁhitā*, although the name seems to be based on a variant reading of a passage in the work in question. It is not easy to say whether these Aśikas were actually inhabitants of Aśikā mentioned in the present record. But it is really difficult to agree with Sahni who says, "*Aśikā* =*āśikā* corresponding to the Sanskrit *āśmikā*, the *taddhita* form of *aśman*," and translates the passage *Aśikāyaṁ kāritā vedikā* as "This railing of stone was caused to be made."

The inscription may be translated as follows :

"Adoration to the Lord Māṇibhadra, the leader (protector) of caravans. [There was] a householder named Kuśapāla who was born of Seliyā (Śailikā) [and] was the son of Vāri, the householder who was born of Ejāvati. By his son Gauptīputra, the householder, was caused to be made a railed platform (or covered balcony in the courtyard of the temple of Māṇibhadra) at Aśikā. May the Lord (i.e. Māṇibhadra) be pleased."

CHAPTER X

VĀMADEVA AND VIŚVEŚVARA

I

V.V. Mirashi has published the Saugor inscription of Śaṅkaragaṇa in the *Epigraphia Indica*, Vol. XXVII, pp. 163ff. According to his reading, *Paramabhaṭṭāraka Mahārājādhirāja Parameśvara* Śaṅkaragaṇa, during whose reign the inscription was incised, has been described in the record as *paramabhaṭṭāraka-mahārājādhirāja-parameśvara-śrī-Vāmarājadeva-pād-ānudhyāta*, although what has been read as *Vāmarāja* appears to us from the published facsimile to be *Vāvarāja*.[1] The inscription has been assigned on paleographical grounds to the middle of the eighth century. In view of this date of the record, kings Vāmarāja and Śaṅkaragaṇa, who would appear to have belonged to the Kalacuri family, have been regarded, without any reason whatever, as ancestors of the Kalacuri emperors of Tripurī. Similarly, without any convincing argument, Vāmarāja has been placed a few generations earlier than Śaṅkaragaṇa, roughly about the second half of the seventh century. It is well known that the Kalacuris of Tripurī, from the time of Karṇa (1041-71 A.D.), described themselves in

1. Hiralal read the name as *Vāgharāja*. But the disputed *akṣara* is not *gha*, and apparently also not *ma* as suggested by Mirashi who thinks that the loop of *ma*. not to be found on the facsimile, is still visible on the stone. It will be seen from the facsimile of the inscription that the upper and lower left strokes of *ma* join its loop in an acute angle, whereas the back of the letter in question is fully rounded exactly as in the preceding *ra*. Indeed much has been made on the slender basis of the reading of the letter as *ma*, which appears to be merely conjectural. For other references to the word *Vāva* or *Bāva* in inscriptions, see *pramabhaṭṭāraka-śrī-Bāva-pād-ānudhyāta* in the Lohata plate (*IHQ*, Vol. XXV, p. 288) and *paramabhaṭṭāraka-mahārājādhirāja- parameśvara-śrī-Bāva-pād-ānudhyāta* in the Maitraka records (*Corp. Ins. Ind.*, Vol. III, p. 186, note). The use of the word has to be compared with that of *Bappa* in epigraphic passages like *mahārāja-Bappa-svāmin* (*Sel. Ins.*, p. 438), *paramabhaṭṭāraka-mahārājadhirāja-Parameśvara-śrī-Bappa-pād-ānudhyāta* and *Bappa-bhaṭṭāraka-mahārāja-śrī-pād-ānudhyāta* (*Corp. Ins. Ind.*, *loc. cit*). N. Lakshminarayan Rao who carefully examined the letter agrees with us that the reading of the name is not *Vāmarāja*. He thinks that it may be *Vāparāja* or *Voparāja*.

their official charters as *paramabhaṭṭāraka-mahārājādhirāja-parameśvara-paramamāheśvara-śrī-Vāmadeva-pād-ānudhyāta*.[1] Mirashi thinks that Vāmadeva mentioned in the records of the Kalacuris of Tripurī is no other than the king of the Saugor inscription of the eighth century, whose name is Vāmarāja according to his reading.

Mirashi further refers to the Malkapuram inscription of Śaka 1183 (1261-62 A.D.) which speaks of the Śaiva pontiff Vāmaśambhu as the third in spiritual descent from Sadbhāvaśambhu who founded the Golakī-maṭha in the Ḍāhala or Cedi country (Jabalpur region) with the help received from the Kalacuri king Yuvarāja (either Yuvarāja I who reigned about the middle of the tenth century or his grandson Yuvarāja II who flourished about the end of the same century as he is known to have been defeated by Paramāra Muñja, 974-96 A.D.) and incidentally says that 'even now' the Kalacuri kings are honoured for worshipping Vāmaśambhu's feet. He further refers to my paper in the *Indian Historical Quarterly*, Vol. XV, 1938, pp. 96 ff., and says, "Dr. D.C. Sircar has recently suggested that this Vāmaśambhu was the spiritual preceptor of the Kalacuri king Karṇa and flourished in the middle of the eleventh century A.D. The description in the Malkapuram inscription that even then (i.e. in the middle of the thirteenth century A.D.) the feet of Vāmaśambhu were worshipped by Kalacuri kings squares with the fact that the expression *Vāmadeva-pād-ānudhyāta* occurs in almost all records of the Kalacuris of Tripurī from Karṇa downwards." But he next sets forth certain "reasons" for which he is "inclined to look with suspicion on the statements in the Malkapuram inscription about the early pontiffs of the Golakī-maṭha." These "reasons" are, however, extremely unlikely to satisfy all students of history. As for instance, Mirashi points out the absence of epigraphic evidence to prove the existence of Kalacuri rulers at Tripurī about the time when the Malkapuram inscription was engraved. But the possibility of the scions of the Imperial Kalacuri house of Tripurī ruling over parts of Ḍāhala in the thirteenth century at least as minor chiefs can hardly be ruled out. A writer on the history of the Kalacuris says at the end of his

1. Ray, *DHNI*, Vol. II, p. 815. For fuller lists of the Kalacuri rulers of Chattisgarh (Ratanpur and Raipur branches), see Hiralal, *Inscriptions in the C. P. and Berar*, 1932, pp. 205-07.

account of the Tummāna Kalacuris who represented a branch of the Tripurī house : "It is certain that the Muslims never succeeded in establishing their power in the Chhatisgarh Division and there is evidence to show that the Kalacuris continued to figure as chiefs of Chhattisgarh right up to the 18th century. The Khalari stone inscription of the Kalacuri king Haribrahmadeva (son of Rāmadeva and grandson of Siṁhaṇa) is dated in 1415 A.D. while the Arang plates of the Haihaya king Amarasiṁhadeva is dated as late as 1735 A.D."[1] The absence of Vāmadeva's name in the records of the Kalacuris of Chhattisgarh scarcely proves that the Śaiva saint was not held in veneration by the Kalacuris of the thirteenth century. This may merely show that their esteem for Vāmadeva was not as remarkable as in the case of the Kalacuri monarchs of Tripurī.[2] Mirashi's doubt regarding the authenticity of the statement in the Malkapuram inscription on the basis of such weak "reasons" can therefore hardly be taken quite seriously.

Vāmadeva, referred to in the records of Kalacuri Karṇa and his successors, is endowed with imperial titles just like the kings who are said to have been his *pād-ānudhyāta*. Mirashi says, "the use of imperial titles in connection with him would be difficult to explain, for we have not till now come across a single instance of the assumption of such titles by spiritual teachers." Of course, the epithet *Paramabhaṭṭāraka* applied to the Śaiva priest Vimalaśambhu or °śiva in the Mamdapur inscription of Śaka 1127 noticed in the *Corpus Inscriptionum Indicarum*, Vol. III, 1888, p. 17, note 3, has been passed over in silence together with some of our observations published from time to time. It was pointed out by us that the Śaiva saint Vāmadeva (Vāmaśambhu) was represented as an emperor because the Kalacuri kings, Karṇa and his successors, regarded their dominions as belonging to the saint and themselves as the latter's deputies just as the Guhilots of Chitor and the kings of Travancore considered themselves viceroys respectively of the gods Ekaliṅga and Padmānabhasvāmin. The tradition regarding the dedication of the Marāṭhā empire by

1. See *Ep. Ind.*, Vol. II, pp. 5, 309, etc.

2. Cf. the case of the Gaṅga devotees of Purusottama-Jagannātha (above, pp. 64-65).

Śivājī in favour of his *guru* Rāmadāsa was also referred to. It was further pointed out with quotations from a number of epigraphic records that the god Jagannātha or Puruṣottama of Purī is mentioned as the overlord of the reigning Gaṅga monarch in several later Gaṅga inscriptions.[1] Now it seems that Mirashi may be satisfied if he finds inscriptions in which a Śaiva saint is unmistakably endowed with regal or imperial epithets. Fortunately, we have come across several such records.

Among the epigraphic records on Mt. Abu (Sirohi District, Rajasthan), the Achalgadh (Mount Abu) inscription of the Devḍā Cāhamāna Tejaḥsiṁha of Candrāvatī was noticed in the *Archaeological Survey of Western India*, No. 2, Appendix, p. xv, No. 58; *Progress Report of the Archaeological Survey of India, Western Circle*, 1906-07, p. 28; and Bhandarkar's List of Inscriptions of Northern India, No. 689. The inscription gives the following information regarding its findspot and contents : "In the vicinity and in front of the Acaleśvara temple are standing some ancient temples, mostly Vaiṣṇava, the exterior of which is profusely sculptured with erotic figures. At the back is a step-well, which, as the inscription attached to it tells us, was constructed by Mokala and others in *Saṁvat* 1387 *varṣe Māgha-sudi* 3 *Bhārgava-dine* when Sarveśvara Mahāmunīndra was the high priest of the Acaleśvara-mahā-maṭha and king Tejaḥsiṁha was reigning at Candrāvatī." The date of the inscription corresponds to Friday, January 11, 1331 A.D.

The most important persons mentioned in the record are three : (1) *Paramabhaṭṭāraka-paramamāheśvara Rāja-śrī*-Sarveśvara-mahāmunīndra of the Acaleśvara-mahāmaṭha on the Arbuda-mahāśaila (i.e. Mount Abu), described in lines 4-7; (2) *Samastarājāvalīsamalaṁkṛta-Paramamāheśvara Rāja-śrī*-Tejaḥsiṁha of the Candrāvatī-bhūmaṇḍala, described in lines 7-9; and (3) Gohilotra Mokala (described in lines 9-12

1. See 'Gaṅga Bhānudeva II and Puruṣottama-Jagannātha' in *JKHRS*, Vol I, June, 1946, pp. 251-53. According to the Oriya chronicle *Mādalā Pāñjī*, Anaṅgabhīma III dedicated his kingdom in favour of the god Puruṣottama-Jagannātha and for that reason the said Gaṅga king and his successors became *Rāutas* (feudatories) of the deity (cf. *Orissa Historical Research Journal*, Vol. I, No. I, pp. 48-51; *Ep. Ind.*, Vol. XXX, p. 19). See also above, pp. 59ff.

and mentioned in line 13) who belonged to the family of Vapaka, i.e., Bappa, and was either himself a *Rājan* or was the son of *Rāja-śrī*-Bathā. Mokala was no doubt a subordinate of Tejaḥsiṁha ; but whether the latter has to be regarded as a subordinate of Sarveśvara is not made quite clear in the inscription although that is probable as Sarveśvara is mentioned before Tejaḥsiṁha and as the epithet *Parama-bhaṭṭāraka* is applied only to the former. What is, however, very interesting to note is that Sarveśvara, who was apparently the pontiff of the Śaiva establishment which is called Acaleśvara-mahāmaṭha and is still today situated within the bounds of Achalgadh on Mount Abu, has not only been called *Paramabhaṭṭāraka* and *Rājan*, but his *vijaya-rājya* is also referred to. It seems that the Śaiva saint Sarveśvara was the spiritual guide of Tejaḥsiṁha, the latter considering himself the deputy of the former in ruling his dominions. Whatever may be the value of this suggestion, Mirashi can hardly object to the Śaiva saint Vāmadeva (Vāmaśaṁbhu), like Sarveśvara of the Achalgadh inscription, being endowed with regal titles in the inscriptions of the Kalacuri kings.

With the above record mentioning the *vijaya-rājya* of a Śaiva ascetic may be compared a Jain inscription in the Gwalior Museum (originally from Bahādurpur).[1] This epigraph, dated Vikrama 1573, Āṣāḍha-badi 4, records the construction of an Ādinātha-caitya at Bhudravyapura (Bahādurpur) by the Śrīmālasaṅgha and the installation of an image therein by *Ācārya* Puṇyaratna-sūri during the *vijaya-rājya* of Jinahaṁsa-sūri of the Kharatara-gaccha. N. Lakshminarayan Rao kindly drew my attention to two Nolamba-Pallava records having a greater bearing on the question. The first[2] of those inscriptions, which has been assigned to a date about 870 A.D., mentions a Śaiva pontiff named Bhramaraśiv-ācārya as *samadhigatapañcamahāśabda-paramabhaṭṭāraka-mahārājādhirāja-parameśvara*. The other inscription,[3] dated Śaka 858 (936 A.D.), assigns the same titles to another Śaiva pontiff named Varuṇaśiva-bhaṭṭāra.

That *Paramabhaṭṭāraka Mahārājādhirāja Parameśvara* Vāmadeva of the inscriptions of Karṇa and his successors was not

1. *Ep. Ind.*, Vol. XXX, p. 49.
2. *Ep. Carn.*, Vol. X, p. 376 (Srinivaspur Taluk, No. 27); trans., p. 276.
3. *SII*, Vol. IX, Part I, p. 12, No. 24.

a king but a saint was also suggested by us on the strength of a verse of the *Pṛthvīrājavijaya* (attributed to Jayāṇaka) which is only known from Joṇarāja's commentary on that work.[1]

Verse 16 of Canto VII of the above poem[2] refers to the marriage of Someśvara, father of the hero Cāhamana Pṛthvīrāja III, while the former was at the court of Caulukya Kumārapāla (*c.* 1141-73 A.D.), with the daughter of the Tripurī-purandara, i.e., the [Kalacuri] king of Tripurī. The commentary of Joṇarāja says that Someśvara married Karpūradevī, daughter of Tejala.[3] Just to introduce the illustrious family to which the hero's mother belonged, the poet, as do the authors of the Kalacuri epigraphs, begins with the mythical account of Candra (the moon), his son Budha and the latter's descendant Kārtavīrya Arjuna surnamed Kalicuri,[4] after whom the family is said to have been known as Kalicuri (i.e., Kalacuri). The author then gives an account of the exploits of a very great Kalacuri king of Tripurī, named Sāhasika (verse 95-112 and possibly also the lost verses up to the end of Canto VII), who was a predecessor of the maternal grandfather of his hero. Who was this Sāhasika, predeccessor of the Kalacuri king Tejala who ruled at Tripurī about the middle of the twelfth century ?

In this connection, a verse, the text of which is lost but the commentary with the exception of the commencing letters is preserved, appears to be very interesting. This commentary runs : *māṇavayās=sa* (very probably *kṣīyamāṇa-vayās=sa* as suggested by Ojha and Guleri) *Sāhasikas=tapasvine Vāmadeva-nāmne nija-rājalakṣmīṁ guru-dakṣiṇāyai dattvā sarvāṁ bhūmiṁ jetuṁ prasthitavān.* Thus the Kalacuri king Sāhasika of Tripurī is stated to have offered his kingdom as *guru-dakṣiṇā* to his *guru*, the ascetic Vāmadeva, and went out on a *digvijaya.* It is very probable that the Kalacuri king Sāhasika of Tripurī men-

1. See *IHQ*, Vol. XVIII, 1942, pp. 80-81.

2. Edited by Gaurishankar H. Ojha and Chandradhar Sharma Guleri, Ajmer, 1941, p. 182.

3. H. B. Sarda in his account of the work (*JRAS*, 1913, p. 277) gives the name of Karpūradevī's father as Acalarāja.

4. The author attempted a fantastic explanation of *Kalicuri* which (together with the variants *Kaṭaccuri, Kalatsuri*, etc.) is, however, stated to be in reality an adaptation of the Turkish title *Kulchur*.

tioned in the *Pṛthvīrājavijaya* is no other than Gāṅgeyadeva (*c*. 1015-41 A.D.) who was a great conqueror and established the imperial dignity of the Kalacuri family of Ḍāhala on a firm basis. Gāṅgeya assumed the title Vikramāditya after a famous hero of Indian tradition and folklore, whose other name was Sāhasāṅka. The name Sāhasika, applied to the Kalacuri king in the *Pṛthvīrājavijaya*, seems to be another form of Sāhasāṅka = Vikramaditya.[1]

This reference to the ascetic Vāmadeva as the *guru* of a Kalacuri king who dedicated his kingdom in the former's favour is supported by the mention of Vāmadeva, for the first time, in the earliest record of Gāṅgeya's son Karṇa (*c*. 1041-71 A.D.) as the latter's overlord and also by the evidence of the Malkapuram inscription showing that the Kalacuri kings worshipped the Śaiva saint Vāmaśambhu for about two centuries before the middle of the thirteenth century. This goes against Mirashi's conjecture that Vāmadeva of the passage *Vāmadeva-pād-ānudhyāta* in the Kalacuri records has to be identified with a Kalacuri king of the seventh century whose name has been read by him as *Vāmarāja*, although it has appeared to others as *Vāgharāja*, *Vāvarāja*, *Vāparāja* or *Voparāja*. As Someśvara's marriage took place when he was staying at the court of Kumārapāla (*c*. 1141-73 A.D.) and as his son Pṛthvīrāja III was born some time before the death of Vigraharāja IV (*c*. 1153-64 A.D.), it seems possible that the Tripurīpurandara Tejala was no other than Gayākarṇa (*c*. 1125-55 A.D.), great-grandson of Gāṅgeyadeva Vikramāditya-Sāhasika (Sāhasāṅka).

If the Kalacuri kingdom was formally dedicated by Gāṅgeya about the end of his career to his *guru* Vāmadeva (Vāmaśambhu), it is easy to explain why that king's son as well as the latter's successors claimed to have been viceroys of Vāmadeva just as in the case of the deputies of other theoretical overlords like the gods Jagannātha-Puruṣottama, Ekaliṅga and Padmanābha. But what explanation can we

1. See *JUPHS*, Vols. XXIV-XXV, 1951-52, p. 232. The characteristic epithet *Sāhasika* is very often found in the description of Vikramāditya; cf. *Ind. Cult.*, Vol. VI, p. 194; *Vikrama Volume*, ed. R. K. Mookerji, 1948, pp. 637 ff.

reasonably offer for the continuous mention of a seventh century ancestor in the records of his descendants from the middle of the eleventh century ? Is not the unjustifiability of Mirashi's suggestion that Vāmarāja was mentioned as being meditated on by all his descendants from the end of the seventh century quite clearly demonstrated by the total omission of the name of this alleged illustrious ancestor of the Kalacuri emperors from the elaborate genealogy of the early members of the family found in such records as the Bilhari inscription[1] of Yuvarāja II and the Varanasi plates[2] of Karṇa ? If he was so important an ancestor as to be meditated on by all the Kalacuri emperors from Karṇa downwards, i.e., from the eleventh century onwards (as indicated by inscriptions, but from the seventh century as claimed by Mirashi), how is his omission from the genealogy to be explained ? In our opinion, there is no answer to the question except surmises which cannot be seriously considered.

There is much in Mirashi's paper which is imaginary as well as inaccurate. He says that "after the defeat of Buddharāja by Pulakeśin II, they (i.e., the Kalacuris) seem to have remained for sometime in obscurity......the Kalacuris seems to have turned their attention to the north where there was no great king to check their advance after the death of Harṣa in A.D. 647. Vāmadeva seems to be the founder of this northern Kalacuri power. He overran Bundelkhand and Vaghelkhand and established himself at Kālañjara."[3] Now, in the first place, what we know from inscriptions shows that Kalacuri Buddharāja was defeated by Cālukya Maṅgaleśa and not by Pulakeśin II.[4] Secondly, the Abhona plates[5]

1. See Bhandarkar's List, No. 1577.

2. *Ibid.*, No. 1223. As regards the absence of the passage *Vāmadeva-pād-ānudhyāta* in Kalacuri records of a date earlier than the beginning of Karṇa's rule, pointed out by us, Mirashi says that the expression "generally occurs in the copper-plate grants". He also says, "In the absence of the grants of earlier kings, it is not safe to assume that Vāmadeva was forgotten in the meanwhile." But the occurrence of the passage in question in the Sarnath stone inscription of Karṇa (*ASI, A.R.*, 1906-07, pp. 100 f.) and the Lalpahad rock inscription of Narasiṁha (*Ind. Ant.*, Vol. XVIII, pp. 211ff.) clearly shows that the contention cannot be maintained.

3. *Op. cit.*, p. 167.

4. See *Ind. Ant.*, Vol. XIX, p. 7; *Ep. Ind.*, Vol. VI, pp. 1 ff.; *Bomb. Gaz.*, Vol. I, Part II, pp. 347-48.

5. Bhandarkar's List, No. 1206.

(Kalacuri year 347 = 595 A.D.) of Śaṅkaragaṇa and Vadner[1] (Kalacuri year 360 = 608 A.D.) plates of Buddharāja, which were issued respectively from Ujjayinī and Vaidiśa (i.e., Vidiśā) show that they had established themselves in both West and East Malwa long before Harṣa (606-47 A.D.) was free from his struggles in U.P. It is therefore natural to think that king Śaṅkaragaṇa of the Saugor inscription, who was ruling over the country about East Malwa more than a century later, was a descendant of Buddharāja. Mirashi's Vāmadeva can hardly be described as the founder of Kalacuri power in that area. Thirdly, the conjecture that it was Vāmadeva who conquered Bundelkhand and Vaghelkhand and especially Kālañjara is a mere flight of fancy. There is again nothing in the present state of our knowledge to suggest that the kings mentioned in the Saugor inscription were direct ancestors of the Kalacuris of Tripurī, although that may not be altogether impossible.

II

The Malkapuram stone-pillar inscription[2] is dated in Śaka 1183 (1261-62 A.D.) and belongs to the time of the Kākatīya queen Rudradevī (Rudrāmbā or Rudramma) who was the daughter of the celebrated Kākatīya king Gaṇapati (1199-1261 A.D.) and ruled over the Andhra country from 1261 to 1296 A.D. The record is written partly in Sanskrit and partly in Telugu, and gives a very interesting account of a Śaiva monastery of the Ḍāhala-maṇḍala (about the Jabalpur District, Madhya Pradesh), situated between the Bhāgīrathī and the Narmadā. The name of the monastery was śrī-Golakī-maṭha and its founder was a Śaiva Pontiff named Sadbhāvaśambhu who is said to have belonged to the [spiritual] lineage of Durvāsas. The date of Sadbhāvaśambhu is determined by the fact that he is reported to have received as *bhikṣā* (free gift) three lacs of *grāmas*[3] from the Kalacuri

1. *Ibid.*, No. 1207.
2. *Journ. Andhra Hist. Res. Soc.* Vol. IV, pp. 152ff.; *Kākatīyasaṁcika*, Rajahmundry, 1935, Inscription No. 31.
3. The word *grāma*, 'village', may have been used in the present context in a modified sense or, probably, the number is inflated. Cf. Sircar, *Stud. Geog. Anc. Med. Ind.*, pp. 198ff.

king Yuvarājadeva, either Yuvarāja I or II both of whom ruled in the tenth century A. D. The Pontiff Sadbhāvaśambhu was succeeded by Somaśambhu, author of the *Somaśambhupaddhati*, a work on Śaiva *āgama*. Somaśambhu's successor Vāmaśambhu was apparently the *guru* of the Kalacuri king Gāṅgeva (c.1015-41 A.D.),[1] and had thousands of *śiṣyas* and *praśiṣyas*. Then, after some years, came Śaktiśambhu and his disciple Kīrtiśambhu. After them, flourished Vimalaśiva who was honoured by the Kalacuri kings. Vimalaśiva's disciple was Dharmaśambhu (also called Dharmaśiva). The Bengali Śaiv-ācārya Viśveśvara was also a disciple of Vimalaśiva.

Viśveśvara has been called Viśveśvaraśambhu or Viśvesvaraśiva, and also Viśveśvara-deśika (the Pontiff Viśveśvara) and Viśveśvara-śivācārya. He is described as a native of Pūrvagrāma in the Rāḍha division of Gauḍa. Elsewhere in the same record reference is made to his donation to the inhabitants of the village of Pūrvagrāma stated to have been situated in Dakṣiṇa-Rādha in Gauḍa. Sometimes the Pontiff is simply called Gauḍa-cūḍāmaṇi, 'the head-jewel of Gauḍa'.

Viśveśvara was famous for his knowledge in the Śaiva *siddhānta*, *āgama* or *rahasya*. Sometimes he is described as a master in all the sciences (*vidyā*). It is said that people were very pleased to have a look at this preceptor of king Gaṇapati, seated in the *vidyā-maṇḍapa* (college) with his matted hair trembling, his face smiling and his ear-ornaments made of *muktā* striking the upper part of his shoulder.

The fame of this Bengali Śaiv-ācārya spread far and wide, and some of the most influential monarchs of the time came to be his disciples. The kings of the Coḷa and Mālava countries became his *śiṣyas*, and he was the *dīkṣā-guru* of the Kalacuri king and of Kākatīya Gaṇapati, king of the Andhra country. It is difficult to determine which of the Coḷa, Mālava and Kalacuri kings were Viśveśvara's disciples. The Coḷa kings Rājarāja III (1216-46 A.D.) and Rājendra III (1246-67 A.D.) appear to have been his contemporaries. The ruler of Mālava referred to in the record may have been any one of the Paramāra kings, Devapāla (*c.* 1218-36 A.D.), Jaitugideva (*c.* 1239-43 A.D.) and Jayavarman II (*c.* 1256-60

1. See above, pp. 153-54.

A.D.). We know little about the Kalacuris of Ḍāhala from the end of the twelfth century, though they may have continued to rule as small chiefs. The mention of the Kalacuri king among the disciples of Viśveśvara is interesting in view of the fact that the Malkapuram inscription mentions his spiritual ancestor Vāmaśambhu as being worshipped by the Kalacuris as late as the time when the record was issued.[1]

It is said that Kākatīya Gaṇapati orally ordered the grant of a village called Mandara in favour of his *guru* Viśveśvara. This village was situated in Kandravāṭi in the *viṣaya* (district) of Velivāḍa, to the south of the great river Kṛṣṇaveṇī, i.e. the Kṛṣṇā. After Gaṇapati's death, his daughter Rudrāmbā, following the order of her father, granted the village together with another village called Velaṁgapūḍi and with the islets (*laṅkā*) formed in the bed of the river Kṛṣṇā. The grant was made with the eightfold proprietary rights. In specifying the boundaries correctly, all the eight directions were represented, and they were described in the *Andhrabhāṣā*, i.e., the Telugu language, so as to make them intelligible to all people of the locality.

Viśveśvara established a monastery and a perpetual resthouse evidently within the area of the above two villages. The monastery was named after him as śrī-Viśveśvara-golakī, and the rest-house was endowed with an *agrahāra* for the enjoyment of all people. He became the *Ācārya* of this monastery and enjoyed one hundred *niṣka* coins (per month or year) as *Ācārya-bhoga*.

The record also gives an interesting account of the donations made by Viśveśvara. There were sixty Drāviḍa Brāhmaṇas who appear to have been merchants. Each of these 60 Brāhmaṇas received from Viśveśvara residence and titles, and also each two *Puṭṭikās* of land (measured by the rod known as Penumbāka), a *Puṭṭikā* being about 8 acres. The villages called Mandara and Velaṁgapūḍi, given to the Pontiff by Gaṇapati and Rudrāmbā, were divided into three shares, the first of which was dedicated to the god Pinākin, i.e., Śiva. The second share was awarded to the students of the college already referred to and also to the monastery of the Śuddha-

1. See above, p. 149.

Śaivas. The third share was granted in favour of three different institutions which were a *Prasūti-śālā*, an *Ārogya-śālā* and a *Vipra-satra*. The reference to a *Prasūti-śālā*, i.e., maternity or lying-in hospital, in a record of the thirteenth century is very interesting. *Ārogya-śālā* is a hospital. It may be interesting in this connection to recall that, according to the second Rock Edict of Aśoka (*c.* 272-232 B.C.), the Maurya king claims to have established hospitals of two kinds, for men and for animals, not only all over his own kingdom, but also in the Tamil states of the Far South, in Ceylon and in the countries of the Greek kings of Syria, North Africa and Greece.[1] The word *Vipra-satra* means a rest-house established for the use of Brāhamaṇas, though it is stated that there was arrangement for feeding, at all times, without any obstruction, all people from Brāhmaṇa to Caṇḍāla, who came and asked for food.

We have already noticed the references to a college and to the students of that college. There were three Professors who taught the *Ṛk*, *Yajus* and *Sāma Vedas*. There were also five teachers who lectured on *Pada*, *Vākya*, *Pramāṇa*, *Sāhitya* and *Āgama*. A *Vaidya* and a *Kāyastha* also appear to have belonged to the college. Each of these ten persons received from Viśveśvara two *Puṭṭikās* of land. The words *vaidya* and *kāyastha* here appear to mean a physician and a scribe, and not members of the Vaidya and Kāyastha communities. Ten nautch girls pertaining to Viśveśvaradeva (probably the Śiva-liṅga worshipped at Viśveśvara-golakī and named after the Pontiff) and eight *maddala* (Bengali *mādal*) players, including two bridlers, received 1½ *Puṭṭikās* each. Seventy-three other persons were given each a *Puṭṭikā* and also $\frac{1}{16}$ *Nivartana* of land in addition to the above. They were the following—an inhabitant of Kaśmira; fourteen songstresses; six *karaṭa* players; two cooks who were Brāhmaṇas; four servants; six Brāhmaṇas belonging to the monastery and the rest-house, ten matted-haired persons from the Coḍa country, who were protectors of the villages and were known as Vīrabhadras owing to their duties such as *bīdaccheda* (?), *kukṣiccheda* and *śiraścheda*; twenty Bhaṭas (Pāiks) and Vīramuṣṭis (constables);

1. See Sircar, *Inscriptions of Aśoka*, 1967, p. 25; cf. p. 17.

ten *Kārus*, *Nāpitas* and *Śilpins*, and *Sthapatis* who worked in gold, copper, stone, bamboo and iron.

At the time of Viśveśvara, there seems to have been a settlement of his co-villagers in the Andhra country. He is said to have given three hundred Puṭṭikās of land to a number of Sāmavedin Brāhmaṇas of the Śrīvatsa-gotra, who were natives of Pūrvagrāma in Dakṣiṇa-Rāḍha in Gauḍa. These Brāhmaṇas appear to have kept written accounts of the income and expenditure of the estate (?) and possibly received 150 Puṭṭikās as *vṛtti* for doing this work. It is also stated that, in case they would die without issue, their wives, if they would take up their work (?), would enjoy the lands.

Viśveśvara established a stone-monastery in a town called Kāḷīśvara, and made an *agrahāra* of a village called Ponnagrāma. He established another monastery and a Śiva-liṅga named after him in the town called Mandrakūṭa (Mantrakūṭa in the Karimnagar District). Two villages called Māne and Palyuṭlu were granted to two rest-houses pertaining to the god established there. A Śiva-liṅga named after him was also established in the town of Candravalli. In the locality called Nandapada, Viśveśvara made a town and named it after himself. This town was granted for the enjoyment of the local god. He established a third Śiva-liṅga, named after himself, at the village of Kommūr and gave thirty *khāris* of land and five *khāris* of low land in favour of the Śiva-liṅga. At Śrīśaila (in the Kurnool District, Andhra Pradesh) he established the Śānyelīśvarapurī which appears to have been a monastery containing sixteen cells. Viśveśvara's disciple Gaṇapati, the Kākatīya king, made a gift of the village called Kaṇḍrakoṭa in the Pallināḍa *viṣaya* to his *guru* as *ācārya-dakṣiṇā*, possibly in favour of a certain rest-house of the locality.

Viśveśvara seems to have established a fourth Śiva-liṅga and to have given for its enjoyment the jungly part of a village called Dudyāla and another village called Pūnūru. A fifth Śiva-liṅga was established by the great Pontiff at North Somaśilā, and the village of Aitaprollāmāna was granted in its favour.

III

The account of the hospital and maternity home in the Malkapuram inscription reminds us of similar organisations in some other religious institutions of medieval India. Buddhist universities like the one at Nalanda maintained hospitals for the treatment of their employees and the students studying in the colleges attached to them. Mention may be made in this connection of Valabhī, Vārāṇasī and Vikramaśilā. The royal grants in favour of Buddhist monasteries often mention *glāna-pratyaya-bhaiṣajya* as one of the items for which the income could be utilised.[1] The hospitals attached to the religious institutions probably catered also to the need of the local people.

Among medieval epigraphs of South India reference may be made to the Tirumukkudal (Chingleput District) inscription of Vīrarājendra-coḷa (1063-70 A.D.) and the Srirangam inscription of Garuḍavāhana-bhaṭṭa (15th century A.D.).[2] The Tirumukkudal inscription, engraved on the east wall of the first *prākāra* of the Veṅkaṭeśa Perumāl (Viṣṇu) temple, records the provision made for the maintenance of a Vedic college, a hostel and a hospital and for meeting the expenses relating to the services in the temple. Sick students of the hostel as well as the temple servants were treated in the hospital. It had fifteen beds for in-patients and was under the supervision of a physician who was assisted by a surgeon, nurses and maid servants, persons for collecting herbs and helping in the preparation of medicines. He received 90 *kalam* of paddy and 80 *kāsu* annually in addition to the land granted to him for prescribing medicine for the patients, the servants of the temple and the teachers and students of the college.

There was also a surgeon attached to the hospital. He received 30 *kalam* of paddy while two persons who collected medicinal herbs and firewood and attended to the preparation of medicines received 60 *kalam* of paddy and 2 *kāsu*. There were two nurses who received 30 *kalam* of paddy and 1 *kāsu*. They attended on the patients and administered medicines. A barber was paid 15 *kalam* of paddy no doubt for his professional duties as well as for performing minor operations.

1. See, e.g., *Sel. Ins.*, 1965, p. 341 (Gunaighar plate).
2. See *Ep. Ind.*, Vol. XXI, pp. 220ff.; Vol. XXIV, pp. 90ff.

There was provision of 2½ *kāsu* for burning lamps at night and for storing the medicines. The sick ration was 1 *nāli* of rice per head.

The medicines stored in the hospital were—(1) Brāhmya-rasāyana, (2) Vāsā-harītakī, (3) Gomūtra-harītakī, (4) Daśamūla-harītakī, (5) Bhallātaka-harītakī, (6) Gaṇḍīra, (7) Balākeraṇḍa-taila, (8) Pañcāka-taila, (9) Lasunādyeraṇḍa-taila, (10) Uttamakarṇādi-taila, (11) Bilvādi-ghṛta, (12) Maṇḍūkara-vaṭikā, (13) Dravatti, (14) Vimala, (15) Sunetri, (16) Tāmrādi, (17) Vajrakalpa, (18) Kalyāṇaka-lavaṇa, (19) Purāṇa-ghṛta, etc. The medicines were prepared from herbs according to the prescription given in medical treatises like the *Carakasaṁhitā*.

The Srirangam inscription, dated Śaka 1415 (1493 A.D.) registers the gift of 2 *veli* of land made by Śrīnivāsa *alias* Śrīraṅgam Garuḍavāhana-bhaṭṭa who repaired and removated the *Ārogya-śālā* or hospital. This hospital was constructed by one of Śrīnivāsa's ancestors also known as Garuḍavāhana-paṇḍita, who was a contemporary and disciple of Rāmānujācārya (11th century A.D.), during the reign of Pratāpacakravartin, but had been damaged during the Muhammadan invasion (14th century A.D.). An image of Dhanvantari, the great physician of ancient India sometimes regarded as an incarnation of Viṣṇu, is stated to have been installed in the hospital.

The establishment of the same institution is mentioned in an inscription of the time of Hoysala Vīra-Rāmanātha (1255-95 A.D.).[1] It is stated that Siṅgaṇṇa-daṇḍanāyaka, the *Pradhāna* (minister) of the Hoysala king, constructed a hall for conducting a *śālā* (*ārogya-śālā*) or hospital and placed it in the charge of Garuḍavāhana-bhaṭṭa who was assisted by two physicians and two servants called *vaidya-paricāraka*. Medicines of the value of 100 *kāsu* were daily prepared for the hospital which supplied a *kaṣāya* as an offering to the god Raṅganātha of Śrīraṅgam every night. It seems that the hospital was started by Garuḍavāhana-bhaṭṭa who received munificent gifts for the institution from Siṅgaṇṇa.

1. *Ibid.*, Vol. XXIV, p. 91.

That provision of medical facilities was also made in the Brahmanical religious institutions of Northern India during the early medieval period has been recently proved by the Paschimbhag plate[1] of king Śrīcandra (*c.* 925-75 A.D.) of South-East Bengal. A very big area in the present Sylhet District of East Pakistan was made a rent-free holding and was divided into three parts. The first consisting of 180 *Pāṭakas* of land was granted in favour of a temple of the god Brahman and was allotted to a number of people working for the temple. The second plot consisting of 280 *Pāṭakas* was likewise granted in favour of two groups of temples of the four divinities, viz., Agni-Vaiśvānara, Yogeśvara, Jaimani and Mahākāla, one belonging to the Vaṅgālas and the other built by outsiders. The third plot of the land was divided in equal shares among six thousand Brāhmaṇas. As to the first plot, it is stated that a teacher of the *Cāndra-vyākaraṇa* received 10 *Pāṭakas* while another plot of 10 *Pāṭakas* was allotted for the maintenance of his 10 students (i.e. for a hostel accommodating 10 pupils). But no provision was made for any hospital in this connection, though, out of the second plot of land, provision was made for two physicians, one each belonging to a group of four temples and receiving each 3 *Pāṭakas* of land. This allotment compares favourably with that made in favour of the *Kāyasthas* (scribes) and *Gaṇakas* (accountants), the former receiving each 2½ *Pāṭakas* and the latter only 1 *Pāṭaka* each. There are no other details; but it appears that the people working in the temple of Brahman received their medical aid from these two physicians.

1. See *N. K. Bhattasali Com. Volume*, Dacca, 1966, pp. 166ff.

Chapter XI

HIRAṆYAGARBHA AND AŚVAMEDHA

I

According to Sanskrit Lexicons, the word *Hiraṇyagarbha* has two principal meanings. First, it is a well-known epithet of the god Brahman; secondly, it is the name of one of the *ṣoḍaśa-mahādāna*, i.e., the sixteen Great Gifts which are enumerated and explained in books like the *Matsya Purāṇa*, Hemādri's *Vratakhaṇḍa* and Ballālasena's *Dānasāgara*. The sixteen Mahādānas are *dāna* (offering) of the following things—

1. Tulāpuruṣa
2. Hiraṇyagarbha
3. Brahmāṇḍa
4. Kalpapādapa
5. Gosahasra
6. Hiraṇyakāmadhenu
7. Hiraṇyāśva
8. Pañcalāṅgala
9. Dharā
10. Hiraṇyāśvaratha
11. Hemahastiratha
12. Viṣṇucakra
13. Kalpalatā
14. Saptasāgara
15. Ratnadhenu
16. Mahābhūtaghaṭa.

These names are more or less of a technical character. They have been explained in full details in the *Mahādānāvarta* section of the *Dānasāgara*, Chapter V of the *Vratakhaṇḍa* and Chapter 247ff. of the *Matsya Purāṇa*.

The word *Hiraṇyagarbha* occurs several times in the inscriptions of some South Indian kings. In the Gorantla inscription,[1] king Attivarman is called *aprameya-hiraṇyagarbha-prasava*, which phrase was translated by Fleet, the editor of the Gorantla inscription, as "who is the posterity of the inscrutable [god] Hiraṇyagarbha (i.e., Brahman)". In the Mahākūṭa pillar inscription of the Cālukya king Maṅgaleśa,[2] we have the passage *hiraṇyagarbha-sambhūta*. Here also Fleet, who edited the inscription, translated the phrase as "who was descended from [the god] Hiraṇyagarbha". It must be noticed that only particular kings have been connected with Hiraṇyagarbha in the inscriptions of their respective families. If Fleet's interpreta-

1. *Ind. Ant.*, Vol. IX, pp. 102 f.
2. *Ibid.*, Vol. XIX, pp. 9ff.

tion is correct, we should have found other kings of the family—wherein one has been called *Hiraṇyagarbha-sambhūta*—with titles of the same signification. Moreover, when we notice that in the Mahākūṭa pillar inscription, this epithet is given only to Pulakeśin I, and not to Jayasiṁha the first king mentioned, nor to Maṅgaleśa the reigning monarch, there remains no doubt that Fleet's theory is unjustifiable. We therefore agree with Hultzsh that the word Hiraṇyagarbha, in these inscriptions, signifies the second of the sixteen *Mahādānas* or Great Gifts.

While editing the Mattepad plates of Dāmodarvarman,[1] Hultzsch remarked: "A similar feat is ascribed to king Attivarman in another coper-plate grant from the Guntur District, where I translate the epithet *aprameya-Hiraṇyagarbha-prasavena* by 'who is a producer of (i.e., who has performed) innumerable Hiraṇyagarbhas."[2] Hultzsch, here, evidently takes the passage *hiraṇyagarbha-prasava* as a case of the *Ṣaṣṭhī-tatpuruṣa* compound to mean "*prasava* (origin, producer) of the Hiraṇyagarbha". But he was in difficulty with the word *Hiraṇyagarbha-prasūta* which occurs in the Ipur grant (No. 1) of the Viṣṇukuṇḍin king Mādhavavarman I.[2] As *prasūta* is an adjective, it cannot make a case of the *Ṣaṣṭhī-tatpuruṣa* compound. Hultzsch, therefore, had to correct the passage as *Hiraṇyagarbha-prasūti*, i.e., *prasūti* (origin, producer) of the *Hiraṇyagarbha*.[3] But when we notice that the epithet *Hiraṇyagarbha-prasūta* also occurs in the Polamuru plates of the same Viṣṇukuṇḍin king,[4] and further that the Mahākūṭa pillar inscription has *Hiraṇyagarbha-sambhūta*, there can be no doubt that Hultzsch is wrong in taking the passage *Hiraṇyagarbha-prasava* as a case of the *Ṣaṣṭhī-tatpuruṣa* compound. The words *Hiraṇyagarbha-prasūta* and *Hiraṇyagarbha-sambhūta* are certainly examples of the *Pañcamī-tatpuruṣa* compound and mean "born of the *Hiraṇyagarbha*". The word *Hiraṇyagarbha-prasava* must also mean the same thing. We therefore take it as a case of the *Bahuvrīhi* compound to mean "one whose *prasava* (origin, producer, progenitor) is the *Hiraṇyagarbha*". But how can a king be born of the *Hiraṇyagarbha* which we have taken to signify the second of the sixteen *Mahādānas* ?

1. *Ep. Ind.*, Vol. XVII. pp. 328ff.
2. *Ibid.*, pp. 335f.
3. *Ibid.*, p. 336, note 7.
4. *Journ. Andhra Hist. Res. Soc.*, Vol. VI, pp. 17ff.

In the performance of the *Hiraṇyagarbha-mahādāna* ceremony, the thing to be given away to the Brāhmaṇas is a *Hiraṇyagarbha*, literally, "a golden womb". *Hiraṇyagarbha* here signifies a golden *kuṇḍa*, three cubits in height. Cf.

Brāhmaṇair = ānayet kuṇḍaṁ tapanīya-mayaṁ śubham |
dvāsaptaty-aṅgul-occhrayaṁ hema-paṅkaja-garbhavat ||

To discuss in details all the functions of the ceremony is not necessary for our purpose. The quotations, which are all from the 249th[1] Chapter of the *Matsya Purāṇa*, will sufficiently clear the point.

After due *arcanā*, the performer of the *Mahādāna* ceremony is to utter a *mantra* in adoration to Lord Hiraṇyagarbha (here, the god Viṣṇu), two lines of which run :

bhūr-loka-pramukhā lokās = tava garbhe vyavasthitāḥ |
Brahm-ādayas = tathā devā namas = te viśva-dhāriṇe ||

Thereafter the performer enters into the *hiraṇyagarbha*, i.e., the golden *kuṇḍa*, and the priests perform the ceremonies of *garbhādhāna*, *puṁsavana* and *sīmantonnayana* of the "golden womb", as they would do in the case of an ordinary pregnant woman. Cf.

evam = āmantrya tan-madhyam = āviśy = āmbha udaṅ-mukhaḥ |
muṣṭibhyāṁ parisaṁgṛhya dharmarāja-caturmukau ||
jānu-madhye śiraḥ kṛtvā tiṣṭheta śvāsa-pañcakam |
garbhādhānaṁ puṁsavanaṁ sīmantonnayaṁ tathā ||
kuryur = hiraṇya-garbhasya tatas = te dvija-puṅgavāḥ ||

Then the performer is taken out of the "golden womb", and the *jāta-karman* and other necessary functions are performed by the priests, as if the performer is a newly born child. After that, the performer is to utter another *mantra*, wherein occur the following significant lines :

mātr = āhaṁ janitaḥ pūrvaṁ martya-dharmā sur-ottama |
tvad-garbha-sambhavād = eṣa divya-deho bhavāmy = aham ||

"O the best of gods, previously I was given birth to by my mother [and] was *martya-dharman* (one having the qualities of an earthly creature). [But] now owing to my rebirth from your womb, I become *divya-deha* (one having a celestial body)."

That the performer of the *Hiraṇyagarbha-mahādāna* was thought to be "born of the *Hiraṇyagarbha*, i.e., golden womb", is also clear from the next *mantra* to be uttered by the priests:

1. Ch. 275 of the Vaṅgavāsī edition.

adya-jātasya te='ṅgāni abhiṣekṣyāmahe vayam.

After the ceremony is over, the priests receive the gift of that golden womb together with many other presents.

II

In a note appearing in the *Indian Culture*, Vol. I, pp. 114-15, it was suggested that, since Mādhavavarman I Viṣṇukuṇḍin and Pravarasena I Vākāṭaka have been called simply *Mahārāja* (not *Mahārājādhirāja*) in the inscriptions, they are to be taken as petty feudatory chiefs even though they performed the Aśvamedha. In support of this theory, D. R. Bhandarkar says that "even a feudatory chieftain can perform a horse-sacrifice"[1] and that the Aśvamedha "may or may not be preceded by a *dig-vijaya*."[2] These theories, however, are not only against the evidence of the Śruti literature, but also go against the evidence of the inscriptions of these kings.

In inscriptions, Pravarasena I has been described as a member of the dynasty of the Imperial Vākāṭakas.[3] That Mādhavavarman I was not incapable of *dig-vijaya* is proved by a reference to his expedition for conquering the eastern countries in the Polamuru plates.[4] *Mahārājādhirāja*, based on *Rājātirāja*, etc., of the Scytho-Kuṣāṇas, was in early times not very often used in South India. The Kadamba king Kṛṣṇavarman I, who performed the Aśvamedha sacrifice, ruled over the Kuntala country about the middle of 5th century A.D. In inscriptions, he is simply styled *Dharma-Mahārāja*—not *Dharma-Mahārājādhirāja* like Pallava Śivaskandavarman and others. The Devagiri plates,[5] however, call him *ek-ātapatra*, "possessor of the sole umbrella", which,

1. *Ibid.*, p. 115.
2. See *op. cit.*, p. 116.
3. Cf. *samrā(mrāḍ)-Vākāṭakānāṁ mahārāja-śri-Pravarasenasya*, etc., in the Balaghat plates (*Ep. Ind.*, Vol. IX, p. 270, l. 4); also the Chammak plates (*Corp. Ins. Ind.*, Vol III, p. 235). The Dudia plates (*Ep. Ind.*, Vol. III, p. 260 and note 7), it should be noted, read *samrāṭaḥ* which, according to Kielhorn, is apparently a mistake for *samrājaḥ*. Here Pravarasena has himself been called *Samrāṭ*, i.e. an emperor.
4. *Journ. Andhra Hist. Res. Soc.*, Vol. VI, p. 17; Sircar, *Suc. Sāt.*, p. 131.
5. *Ind. Ant.*, Vol. VII, p. 34.

as scholars have suggested,[1] "is indicative of universal sovereignty". A subordinate king can hardly be called *ek-ātapatra*. The Birur plates[2] moreover call him *Dakṣiṇāpatha-vasumatī-vasu-pati*, lord of the riches of the land of Dakṣiṇāpatha", which "clearly shows that Kṛṣṇavarman I claimed a sort of suzerainty over the whole of the Deccan".[3]

Keith has pointed out that the Aśvamedha "is an old and famous rite, which kings alone can bring, to increase their realms".[4] The *Baudhāyana Śrautasūtra* (XV. 1) says that a king victorious and of all the land should perform this sacrifice. According to the *Taittirīya Brāhmaṇa* (III. 8.9.4), "he is poured aside who being weak offers the Aśvamedha," and again (V. 4.12.3), "it is essentially, like the fire offering, an *utsanna-yajña*, a sacrifice of great extent and elaboration".[5] According to the *Āpastambha Śrautasūtra* (XX. 1.1), a universal (*sārvabhauma*) king can perform the Aśvamedha, but not (*n-āpi*)[6] an un-universal (*a-sārvabhauma*) king. It is clear from these statements that in ancient India, a subordinate ruler could never celebrate the Aśvamedha. A performer of the Aśvamedha may not have been a ruler of the earth from North Pole to South Pole or of India from the Himālaya to the

1. Moraes, *Kadambakula*, p. 39, note.
2. *Ep. Carn.*, Vol. VI, p. 91.
3. See Sircar, *Suc. Sāt.*, p. 222; *Journ. Ind. Hist.*, Vol. XV, p. 305; also *An. Bhand. Or. Res. Inst.*, Vol. XVI, pp. 160ff. Note also that the Malavalli inscription (*Ep. Carn.*, Vol. VII, Sk. 264) describes an Early Kadamba king as *Kadambānaṁ rājā*, but also as *Vaijayantī-dhamma-mahārājādhirāja*. The Penukonda plates (*Ep. Ind.*, Vol. XIV, p. 331) mention the Gaṅga feudatory named Mādhava-mahādhirāja and his Pallava overlord Skandavarma-mahārāja. For *Mahārāja* Varāhasiṁha, general of *Rājan* Aparājita, see the Nagda inscription (*ibid.*, Vol. IV, p. 31).
4. *Rel. Phil. Ved. Upaniṣ.*, p. 343.
5. See Keith, *Black Yajus*, pp. cxxxii-iv.
6. In place of *n=āpi* there is an alternative reading *api*, which is a later interpolation according to Keith (*Black Yajus*, p. cxxxii). The interpolation seems to show that *asārvabhauma* (not master of all the land) kings could also perform the Aśvamedha. The word *asārvabhauma*, however, never means a feudatory. The alternative reading only shows that in later times kings who were powerful but who did not claim to be ruler of the earth (i.e., wide areas of the country) did also perform the Aśvamedha. It must, however, be noticed that the alternative reading goes against all the old texts quoted above.

Kumārikā; but he must have been an independent ruler of a considerable portion of India.

An essential feature of the Aśvamedha, besides the actual slaying of the horse, is that, about the completion of the performance, at the bidding of the Adhvaryu "a lute-player, a Rājanya, sings to the lute three *Gāthās*, verses, made by himself which refer to victories in battle connected with the sacrifice".[1] Further, "As revealed in the later texts, the sacrifice is essentially one of the princely greatness. The steed for a year roams under the guardianship of a hundred princes, a hundred nobles with swords, a hundred sons of heralds and charioteers bearing quivers and arrows, and a hundred sons of attendants and charioteers bearing staves."[2] To manage these requirements does not appear to be possible for a subordinate chief.

Moreover, that the progress of the Aśvamedha was sometimes impeded when other kings challenged one's authority to perform the sacrifice, is not only proved from the early cases referred to in *Śat. Br.* (XIII. 5.3.21-22) and *Mahābhā.* (XIV. 74-84), but is also proved by a tradition recorded in such works as Kālidāsa's *Mālavikāgnimitra* (Act V). It is stated that Puṣyamitra Śuṅga's sacrificial horse was let loose to roam for a year at its own will under the guardianship of his grandson Vasumitra who was assisted by a hundred princes and brought the horse back after defeating the Yavanas as the horse per chance reached the right bank of the Sindhu (i.e., the Indus) and was captured by the Yavana horsemen. That the Aśvamedha could not be performed without some sort of *dig-vijaya* is further conclusively proved by an eighth century inscription of the Pallavas. The Udayendiram grant (No. 2)[3] records that Udayacandra, general of Nandivarma-Pallavamalla, defeated the Niṣāda king Pṛthivīvyāghra who was accompanying an *aśvamedha-turaṅgama*, i.e., horse let loose in connection with a horse-sacrifice. This instance proves beyond doubt that the essential features of the Aśvamedha hardly changed even as late as the 8th century A.D. The famous poet Bhavabhūti, who flourish-

1. Keith, *Rel. Phil. Ved. Upanis.*, p. 344.
2. *Śat. Br.*, XIII. 4.2.5; *Baudh. Śr. S.*, XV. 1. See *Black Yajus*, *loc. cit.*
3. *Ind. Ant.*, Vol. VIII, p. 273.

ed in the same century, also recognises the above characteristic when he refers to the sacrifice as *aśvamedha iti viśvajayināṁ Kṣatriyānām = urjasvalaḥ sarva-Kṣatriya-paribhāvī mahān = utkarṣa-niṣkarsaḥ.*[1] Al-Bīrūnī (first half of the eleventh century A.D.) also says, "certain of them (i.e. sacrifices) can only be performed by the greatest of their kings. So, e.g., the Aśvamedha."[2]

Bhandarkar thinks[3] that the number of performances of the Aśvamedha could be increased by simply multiplying the amount of *dakṣiṇā* payable to the Brāhmaṇas. This view is, however, based on a wrong interpretation of the following verse of the *Mahābhārata* (XIV. 88.14) :

evam = atra mahārāja dakṣiṇāṁ tri-guṇaṁ kuru |
tritvaṁ vrajatu te rājan Brāhmaṇā hy = atra kāraṇam ||

The verse obviously implies that, according to a Brāhmaṇical theory, the merit accruing from the celebration of the Aśvamedha, and not the Aśvamedha itself, could be tripled if the performer offered three-fold *dakṣiṇā* to the Brāhmaṇas.[4]

In the *Indian Culture*, Vol. II, pp. 140-141, the *Harivaṁśa* has been quoted to show that feudatory rulers could also perform the Aśvamedha. Vasudeva, father of Kṛṣṇa, lived at Gokula on Mount Govardhana in the vicinity of Mathurā; he was engaged in cattle-rearing and was a *karadāyaka* to Kaṁsa, the king of Mathurā.[5] After the fall of Kaṁsa, the family of Vasudeva removed to Dvārakā. In Kṛṣṇa's conversation with Indra, there is an incidental reference which says that, while

1. *Uttararāmacarita*, Act IV. That the Aśvamedha did not lose its original and essential significance in later times is also proved by the Vaidyanātha temple inscription which refers to Ādityasena as *Śāstā samudr-ānta-vasundharāyā yaṣṭ = āśvamedh-ādya-mahākratūnām.*

2. Sachau, *Alberuni's India*, Vol. II, p. 139.

3. *Ind. Cult.*, Vol. I, p. 116.

4. It has been said (*Ind. Cult.*, Vol. I, p. 937 n), "The Aśvamedha certainly had a great imperial significance in the old days. But in the period under review, it must have lost that importance. Otherwise it would not have been repeated so often." It may, however, be pointed out that the Aśvamedha is known to "have been repeated" many times even "in the old days". Cf., e.g., Bharata Dauṣyanti's 133 Aśvamedhas in *Sat. Br.*, XIII. 3.5. 11; also *Journ. Ind. Hist.*, Vol. XIII, p. 40, and *Suc. Sāt.*, p. 125. Many of the epic and Purāṇic heroes performed more than one Aśvamedha. Parikṣit, e.g., performed three after subduing the Bhadrāśva, Ketumāla, Bhārata, Uttarkuru and Kimpuruṣa *varṣas*. See *Bhāgavata Purāṇa*, I. 16.3.13.

5. *Harivaṁśa*, LVI. 1162-61.

in Dvārakā, Vasudeva performed an Aśvamedha.[1] The question at issue, however, is whether Vasudeva was a feudatory of the Mathurā kings at the time of celebrating the sacrifice after he was established in Dvārakā. There is absolutely no proof to show that he was. The Dvārakā region is not known to have ever submitted to the kings of Mathurā. It must also be noted that the evidence of traditions recorded in works like the *Harivaṁśa* should always be taken with a grain of salt. It was obviously written for the exaltation and glorification of the family (*vaṁśa*) of Hari (i.e., Kṛṣṇa-Vāsudeva) and like similar treatises in honour of other religious heroes is not free from extravaganzas incident to a pronounced theological bias. The probability here is that the parent of the hero of the tale has been given more than his due, just as in the *New Testament* the saviour of the Christians is described as the son not of a mortal man but of God, and in the *Saundarananda* (II. 32, 39, etc.), glories of the mightiest rulers are put on the head of a petty Śākya chief named Śuddhodana.

Moreover, while describing the Aśvamedha that was attempted by Janamejaya, the *Harivaṁśa* itself[2] makes it clear that the horse-sacrifice could not be celebrated by a petty chief. When the *Sarpa-yajña* was finished, Janamejaya collected materials for the celebration of an Aśvamedha. Then he invited the *ṛtviks*, *purohitas* and *ācāryas*, and said, "I am desirous of celebrating a horse-sacrifice. Do ye dedicate the horse" (verses 5 and 6).[3] Knowing, however, that the king's sacrifice would not be successful, the omniscient Vyāsa warned him not to begin the Aśvamedha. The sage said, "The Śruti lays down that the Kṣatriyas should celebrate the Aśvamedha, the foremost of sacrifices. On account of the greatness of it, Vāsava will violate your sacrifice" (verse 28).[4] "O slayer of enemies,"

1. Vaṅgavāsī ed., Viṣṇu-parvan, 91. 24.
2. Vaṅgavāsī ed., Bhaviṣya-parvan, 2.
3. *Yakṣye='haṁ Vājimedhena hayam=utsṛjyatām=iti.*
4. *Aśvamedhaḥ kratu-śreṣṭhaḥ Kṣatriyāṇāṁ pariśrutaḥ| tena bhāvena te yajñaṁ Vāsavo dharṣayiṣyati ||* That the Aśvamedha could be performed by great kings only is also proved by the fact that Vāsava (Indra) is always represented as jealous of its performance. The *Harivaṁśa* describes how he endeavoured to spoil the Aśvamedha of Janamejaya (Bhaviṣya-parvan, 5). Note also what Viśvāvasu says to the king: 'O king, thou hast celebrated three hundred sacri-

the sage added, "as long as the world will last, the Kṣatriyas will not be able to collect materials for your horse-sacrifice" (v. 35).[1] The king became very sad and said, "Console me by saying that the Aśvamedha will again be undertaken by kings" (v. 58).[2] To this Vyāsa replied, "As energy counteracted by another lives in it, so [the knowledge of] the Aśvamedha, although stopped, will exist among the gods and Brāhmaṇas. There will be one Senānī,[3] an Audbhijja, a Dvija and a descendant of Kaśyapa, who will revive the Aśvamedha in the Kali age" (verses 39-40).[4] Could this great sacrifice, of which the *Harivaṁśa* speaks in so high terms, be performed by a petty feudatory chief ?

It has further been pointed out[5] that Śawāi Jaysingh of Amber (1699-1744 A.D.), though he was a feudatory of the Mughul emperors Farrukhsiyar (1712-19) and Muḥammad Shāh (1719-48), performed a horse-sacrifice according to Tod,[6] and that therefore subordinate rulers could perform

fices; Vāsava therefore cannot forgive thee any longer" (*tri-yajña-śata-yajvānaṁ Vāsavas=tvāṁ na mṛṣyate, ibid.*, 5. 24). In this connection note what Bhandarkar himself says in another occasion (*Ep. Ind.*, Vol. XIX, App., p. 2, note 5), "As Indra is represented as being suspicious of Govinda Gupta's power, the latter seems to have been a supreme ruler." See the *Vāmana Purāṇa*, Ch. 78, in which the significance of the Aśvamedha and the cause of Indra's unfavourable attitude are clearly described; also *Raghuvaṁśa*, III. 38-66; *Bhāgavata Purāṇa*, IV. 16. 24; etc.

1. *Tvayā vṛttaṁ kratuñ=c=aiva Vājimedhaṁ parantapa| Kṣatriyā n=āhariṣyanti yāvad=bhūmir=dhariṣyati ||*

2. *Yady=asti punar=āvṛttir=yajñasy=āśvāsayasva mām.*

3. The reference is generally thought to be to Puṣyamitra Śuṅga. But that is doubtful, as the Śuṅgas were Bhāradvājas and not Kāśyapas. On the strength of this verse and another in the *Mālavikāgnimitra*, Raychaudhuri suggests (*Ind. Cult.*, Vol. III, pp. 739ff.; Vol. IV, pp. 363 ff.) that Puṣyamitra was possibly not a Śuṅga, but a Baimbika. The unanimous evidence of the Purāṇas, however, may be set aside only on the evidence of a more positive character. Bimbaka or Bimbika appears to have been a predecessor of Puṣyamitra. It has also been supposed that the Śuṅgas were *dvyāmuṣyāyaṇa*, i.e., both Bhāradvāja and Kāśyapa.

4. *Upātta-yajño deveṣu Brāhmaṇeṣ=ūpapatsyate | tejasā vyāhṛtaṁ tejas=tejasy=ev=āvatiṣṭhate || Audbhijjo bhavitā kaś=cit senānī Kāśyapo dvijaḥ | aśvamedhaṁ Kali-yuge punaḥ pratyāhariṣyati ||*

5. *Ind. Cult.*, Vol. III, pp. 547f.

6. *Annals and Antiquities of Rajasthan*, 2nd ed., Madras, 1873, pp. 328-32.

the Aśvamedha. It seems to us, however, that, if Sawāi Jaysingh performed any horse-sacrifice, he must have regarded himself independent about the time.[1]

It is admitted by all writers on Mughul history that, within less than twenty years after the death of Aurangzīb in 1707, the actual possessions of the so-called emperors of Delhi became limited within the district round the walls of their capital, and that, after the invasion of Nādir Shāh in 1739, no power of the emperors was left in Rajasthan. It will suffice to refer to Jadunath Sarkar who says, 'The invasion of Nādir Shāh dealt such a shattering blow to the empire of Delhi that, after it, the imperial authority was totally eliminated from Rajputana in all but the name. The Rajput princes were left entirely to themselves......"[2] It is interesting in this connection to note that Tod himself takes the celebration of the sacrifice as a 'virtual assumption of universal supremacy'.[3] He also says, '......amidst revolution, the destruction of the empire, and the meteoric rise of the Mahrattas, he (i.e., Jaysingh) not only steered through the dangers, but elevated Amber above all the principalities around......'[4]

That Sawāi Jaysingh defied imperial authority even before 1739 is proved by the following facts. In the war of succession that followed the death of Aurangzīb, he attached himself to prince Bīdar Bakht, son of Ajam Shāh, and declared him successor of Aurangzīb. For this opposition, Amber was sequestered and an imperial governor sent to take its possession; but Jaysingh entered his state sword in hand, drove out the imperial garrisons and formed a league with Ajitsingh of Marwar for their mutual preservation.[5] That he had independent political relations with neighbouring states is also proved by the fact that he did 'dispossess the Birgoojur of Deoti and Rajore

1. Tod, *op. cit.*, p. 339; see also P.K. Gode (*Journ. Ind. Hist.*, Vol. XV, pp. 364ff.; *Poona Orientalist*, Vol. II, pp. 166 ff.; *Mīmānsā Prakāsh*, Vol. II, pp. 43ff.) who points out that MSS. of Sadāśiva-Daśaputra's *Ācārasmṛticandrikā*, Kṛṣṇa-kavi's *Īśvaravilāsa*, Vrajanātha's *Padyataraṅgiṇī*, Viśveśvara's *Pratāpārka* and Hariścandra's *Dharmasaṁgraha* refer to the Aśvamedha performed by Sawāi Jaysingh.

2. *Fall of the Mughal Empire*, p. 279.

3. *Op. cit.*, p. 339.

4. *Ibid.*, p. 331.

5. *Ibid.*, p. 328.

which were added to his dominions; they embraced all the tract now called Macherri'.[1]

The only proof of Sawāi Jaysingh's vassalage to the Dehli emperors is that, according to traditions, he was successively the governor of Agra and Malwa and was made governor of Malwa a second time in 1732 under Muḥammad Shāh. We must, however, note in this connection that the great Marāṭhā leader, the Peshwā, snatched away the provinces of Gujarat and Malwa from Muḥammad Shāh who issued a *farmān* bestowing the *nāib subahdārī* on the Peshwā.[2] The Marāṭhā leader replied that 'though the *cauth* of the whole of Hindusthān was his due, he would be satisfied with the above two *subhās*'.[3] Will any student of Marāṭhā history believe that the great Peshwā, formally the *nāib subahdār* of Muḥammad Shāh, was a feudatory of the *rois faineants* of Dehli? Again, the so-called Mughul emperors occupied the throne of Dehli as late as 1858 when Bahādur Shāh II (1837-58) was deposed, and the East India Company pretended to rule in the name of the Mughul emperors. Would it justify us to suppose that the Governors-General of the East India Company were feudatory to the puppet emperors of Dehli ?

The suggestions that Sawāi Jaysingh of Amber performed a horse-sacrifice as a feudatory of the Mughul emperors and that therefore the Aśvamedha could be celebrated by a feudatory chief therefore appear to be inadmissible.

III

Inscriptions describe a number of Indian monarchs as performers of the Aśvamedha sacrifice; but, only in a few instances, they are known from any other source. In some cases, the celebration of the horse-sacrifice is mentioned in the records of the performer himself, while in others it is referred to in the inscriptions of his descendants. There is sometimes reference to the celebration of the Aśvamedha by a king in the

1. *Ibid.*, pp. 337-38.

2. It is interesting to note that the emperor of Dehli conferred (June 12, 1723) the dignified title *Rājādhirāja* on Sawāi Jaysingh (*Poona Orientalist*, Vol. II, p. 168).

3. Sarkar, *op. cit.*, p. 277.

legend on his coins, but not in any of the inscriptions of himself or his descendants. The names of some of the performers of the horse-sacrifice as known from such sources are enumerated below.

1. Puṣyamitra Śuṅga (2nd century B.C.) of Pāṭaliputra (Maghadha) is mentioned as celebrating an Aśvamedha in Kālidāsa's *Mālavikāgnimitra* ; but the epithet *dvir-aśvamedha-yājin* (performer of two horse-sacrifices) is applied to him in the Ayodhyā inscription of his descendant Dhanadeva, king of Kosala.[1]

2. Gājāyana Sarvatāta (1st century B.C.) of the Chitodgadh region of Rajasthan is mentioned as the performer of an Aśvamedha in his Ghosundi and Hathibada inscriptions.[2]

3. Śātakarṇi I (1st century B.C.) of the Śātavāhana dynasty of the Deccan performed two Aśvamedhas, the second of which is referred to in the fragmentary Nanaghat inscription probably incised after his death.[3]

4. King Devīmitra (1st century B.C.) of the Kanpur-Allahabad region of U.P. is known from his Musanagar brick inscription to have celebrated a horse-sacrifice.[4]

5. King Śīlavarman (3rd century A.D.) of the Vārṣagaṇya dynasty holding sway over the Dehradun region of U.P. is known to have performed no less than four Aśvamedhas, the fourth of them being referred to in his Jagatpur brick inscriptions.[5]

6. Śāntamūla (Cantamūla) I (3rd century A.D.) of the Ikṣvāku dynasty of Vijayapurī (in the Nagarjunikonda valley, Guntur District, Andhra Pradesh) is credited with the performance of an Aśvamedha in the records of his son and grandson.[6]

7. The Bhāraśiva Nāgas (3rd and 4th centuries A.D.) of the Eastern Malwa region are credited with the celebration of ten horse-sacrifices in the records of their Vākāṭaka relatives[7] although the names of the kings who performed the sacrifices are unknown.

1. *Select Inscriptions*, Vol. I, p. 96.
2. *Ibid.*, pp. 91-92; *Ep. Ind.*, Vol. XVI, p. 27; Vol. XXII, pp. 203f.
3. *Select Inscriptions*, p. 188.
4. *Ep. Ind.*, Vol. XXX, pp. 118ff.
5. See *Indian Archaeology*, 1953-54, p. 11.
6. *Select Inscriptions*, pp. 222, 227, 229, etc.
7. *Ibid.*, p. 420.

8. Vākāṭaka Pravarasena I (3rd and 4th centuries A.D.), holding sway over parts of the Deccan and the central regions of India, is known from the inscriptions of his descendants to have performed four Aśvamedhas.[1]

9-11. There are three performers of the Aśvamedha in the Pallava royal family of Kāñcīpura near Madras. The first of them is Śivaskandavarman (4th century A.D.) who claims to be an Aśvamedha-yājin in his Hirahadagalli plates;[2] the second is Kumāraviṣṇu (4th century) described similarly in his great-grandson's Omgodu grant,[3] and the third is Siṁhavarman, who has been tentatively identified with Narasiṁhavarman I (*circa* 630-68 A.D.), and also with the Pallava ruler who claims to have performed ten Aśvamedhas in his Sivanvayal (Chingleput District, Tamil Nadu) pillar inscription.[4]

12. Among the Śālaṅkāyanas of Veṅgī (near Ellore in the W. Godavari District, Andhra Pradesh), king Devavarman (4th century A.D.) claims to have celebrated an Aśvamedha in his Ellore plates.[5]

13-14. Amongst the mighty Guptas of Pāṭaliputra, king Samudragupta (4th century A.D.) and his grandson Kumāragupta I (5th century A.D.) are known to have celebrated the horse-sacrifice. In the records of his descendants, Samudragupta is described as *cir-otsann-āśvamedha-āhartṛ*,[6] 'performer of the Aśvamedha which was for a long time in abeyance', while some of his own coins also support the claim.[7] It has to be noticed that the reference to the horse-sacrifice having been in abeyance for a long time is true only with reference to Magadha in South Bihar (where Puṣyamitra Śuṅga performed the Aśvamedha in the 2nd century B.C.), as South Indian monarchs like Vākāṭaka Pravarasena, Śālaṅkāyana Devavarman and Pallava Śivaskandavarman appear to have celebrated their Aśvamedhas shortly before the performance of Samudragupta's horse-sacrifice. The Aśvamedha celebrated

1. *Ibid.*, pp. 407, 419.
2. *Ibid.*, p. 437.
3. *Ep. Ind.*, Vol. XV, pp. 249ff.
4. *Ibid.*, Vol. XXVII, pp. 59ff.
5. *Ibid.*, Vol. IX, pp. 56ff.
6. *Select Inscriptions*, pp. 278.
7. *Ibid.*, pp. 267-68.

by Kumāragupta I is only alluded to in the legends on his coins of the Aśvamedha type.[1]

15. Traikūṭaka Dahrasena (5th century A. D.) of the Northern Konkan region claims in his Pardi plates of 455 A.D. to have performed the Aśvamedha.[2]

16. Among the Kadambas of the Kannaḍa-speaking area, Kṛṣṇavarman I (5th century A.D.) performed an Aśvamedha according to the Birur and Devagiri plates of his sons.[3] A very late inscription from Talagunda wrongly assigns the celebration of eighteen horse-sacrifices to Mayūravarman, a name that was later fabricated for Mayūraśarman (4th century A.D.), founder of the Kadamba dynasty.[4]

17. The Viṣṇukuṇḍin king Mādhavavarman I (6th century A.D.) of the Guntur-Krishna-Godavari region is stated, in his own epigraphs as well as in those of his successors, to have performed no less than eleven Aśvamedhas.[5]

18. Cālukya Pulakeśin I (6th century A.D.) of Badami celebrated an Aśvamedha which is referred to in the records of himself and his descendants. See his own Bādāmi inscription of 543 A.D.,[6] the Mahākūṭa pillar inscription and Nerur grant of his son Maṅgaleśa[7] and the Aihole inscription of his grandson Pulakeśin II.[8]

1. *Ibid.*, p. 297.
2. *JBRAS*, Vol. XVI, p. 346.
3. *The Successors of the Sātavāhanas in the Lower Deccan*, p. 280.
4. *Ibid.*, p. 240.
5. *Ibid.*, pp. 97ff.
6. *Ep. Ind.*, Vol. XXVII, pp. 4ff.
7. *Bombay Gaz.*, Vol. II, Part I, p. 344.
8. *Ep. Ind.*, Vol. VI, p. 4. A set of copper plates was discovered at Mudhol in the Bijapur District of the Mysore State. The charter was issued sometime about the middle of the 6th century A.D. by Pūgavarman, described as the eldest son of Pṛthivīvallabha-mahārāja who is said to have performed the Agniṣṭoma, Agnicayana, Vājapeya and Aśvamedha sacrifices as well as the Hiraṇyagarbha-mahādāna. See *Progress of Kannada Research in Bombay Province from* 1941 *to* 1946, pp. 69ff.; *Ep. Ind.*, Vol. XXXII, pp. 293ff. The description of Pṛthivīvallabha-mahārāja in the said epigraph of about the middle of the 6th century A.D. reminds us of the celebrated Cālukya king of Bādāmi (Bijapur District, Mysore), Pulakeśin I (middle of the 6th century A.D.), who is often found to be mentioned as Śrī-Pṛthivī-vallabha, Śrī-vallabha or Vallabha and is credited with the performance of the Agniṣṭoma, Agnicayana, Vājapeya, Bahusuvarṇa, Pauṇ-

19-20. Among the kings of the Bhauma, Nāraka or Varman dynasty of Assam, there are three Aśvamedha-yājins. In the legend on the seals of Bhāskaravarman who flourished in the first half of the 7th century A. D., his grandfather Sthiravarman (c. 566-90 A. D.) is described as *dvir-aśvamedha-yājin* (performer of two Aśvamedhas) while the latter's great-grand-father Nārāyaṇavarman (c. 496-518 A. D.) is called *dvis-turagamedh-āhartā* (performer of two horse-sacrifices) ; but Bhūtivarman, son of Nārāyaṇavarman, is not credited with the

ḍarīka and Aśvamedha sacrifices and the Hiraṇyagarbha-mahādāna (*Bomb. Gaz.*, Vol. I, Part II, pp. 343-44; *Ep. Ind.*, Vol. XXVII, p. 8.). There seems to be a *prima facie* case in favour of the identification of Pṛthivīvallabha of the Mudhol inscription with Cālukya Pulakeśin I, although it is difficult to determine whether Pūgavarman of the Mudhol record should have to be identified with Kīrtivarman I (566-98 A.D.), son and successor of Pulakeśin I. It is difficult, in the absence of any corroborative evidence, to identify the bearers of the two distinct names, viz. Kīrtivarman and Pūgavarman. Moreover, Kīrtivarman is nowhere called the eldest son of Pulakeśin I. Under the circumstances, it appears better to think that Pūgavarman was the eldest amongst the sons of Pulakeśin I including his successor Kīrtivarman I. But, if such was the case, we have no knowledge of the circumstances that prevented this eldest son of Pulakeśin I from ascending his paternal throne after his father's death. The most probable cause of this seems to be that Pūgavarman predeceased his father. Of course in Indian history there is no dearth of instances of the supercession of the 'eldest son' in favour of the 'dear son', and Kīrtivarman I really claims to have been the 'dear son' of Pulakeśin I in the Godachi plates (*Ep. Ind.*, Vol. XXVIII, p. 62). We cannot therefore rule out such a possibility totally. It is well known that Maṅgaleśa speaks of Kīrtivarman I as his *jyeṣṭha bhrātā* (*Ind. Ant.*, Vol. III, p. 305). But Kīrtivarman may have been the eldest son of his mother who was also the mother of Maṅgaleśa, but not of Pūgavarman. We may also think that, while Kīrtivarman's mother was the chief queen of Pulakeśin I, Pūgavarman's mother was an ordinary queen of that monarch and that this fact led to Kīrtivarman's accession to the throne on his father's death. It should, however, be remembered that, if Pūgavarman predeceased Pulakeśin I, Kīrtivarman's accession to the throne on his father's death and mention as *jyeṣṭha-bhrātā* in Maṅgaleśa's record can be explained without conjectures like the above.

The next question is whether the Mudhol plates were issued during the reign of his father Pulakeśin I or during the chaotic condition in the Cālukya empire resulting from the civil war between Maṅgaleśa and his nephew Pulakeśin II, son of Kīrtivarman, about the close of the 6th and in the first decade of the 7th century. The first alternative seems to be more probable celebration of any Aśvamedha.[1] It is, however, interesting to note that, in the Barganga inscription[2] of his own reign, Bhūtivarman (c. 518-42 A. D.) is described as an *Aśvamedha-yājin*. It has therefore been suggested that the second of the two Aśvamedhas, ascribed to Nārāyaṇavarman in the legend of Bhāskaravarman's seals, was celebrated when the king was aged and the *de facto* king was his son Bhūtivarman.[3]

22. The Śailodbhava king Sainyabhīta Mādhavavarman II Śrīnivāsa (7th century A.D.) of Koṅgoda (Ganjam District, Orissa) is credited with the performance of a horse-sacrifice in his own records as well as in those of his successors.[4] But some inscriptions of his son Ayaśobhīta Madhyamarāja and grandson Mānabhīta Dharmarāja vaguely describe them as performers of the same sacrifice, although others indicate different meanings of the passages in question and suggest that they did not actually celebrate any Aśvamedha, but merely took part in the horse-sacrifice performed by Sainyabhīta Mādhavavarman II Śrīnivāsa.[5]

23. The 'Later Gupta' king Ādityasena (7th century A.D.) of Magadha is credited with the performance of three Aśvamedhas in an inscription on the right-hand side pier in the porch of the Vaidyanātha temple at Deoghar in the Santal Parganas District of Bihar.[6]

24. The Udayendiram plates[7] of the Pallava king Nandivarman II Pallavamalla (8th century A.D.) refers to the victory of his general Udayacandra over a ruler named Pṛthivīvyāghra who was engaged in guarding the horse let loose in connection with an Aśvamedha sacrifice. Although some scholars have attributed the performance of this Aśvademha to the Pallava

under the circumstances, although the other possibility cannot be altogether ruled out. It is not absolutely impossible that Pūgavarman was the governor of the Mudhol area in the latter half of the sixth century and, during the civil war referred to above, had an opportunity of ruling independently or semi-independently for sometime.

1. *IHQ*, Vol. XXI, pp. 143 ff.
2. *Ep. Ind*. Vol. XXVII, pp. 18ff.
3. Cf. Section IV below.
4. *Ep. Ind*. Vol. XXIX, pp. 32ff.
5. Cf. *ibid*., p. 39, note 4.
6. See *Corp. Ins. Ind*., Vol. III, p. 213, note.
7. *Ind. Ant*., Vol. VIII, p. 276,

king, the more reasonable interpretation of the epigraphic passage is that it was celebrated either by Pṛthivīvyāghra or by the monarch to whom he owed allegiance. This Pṛthivīvyāghra is sometimes identified with the Nala king Pṛthivīrāja of the Rajim inscription.[1]

25. The Cola king Rājādhirāja performed a horse-sacrifice about 1044 A.D.[2]

26. Sawāi Jaysingh (1699-1744 A.D.) of Amber performed an Aśvamedha as we have seen above.

IV

There are some suggestions in N.K. Bhattasali's paper entitled 'New Light on the History of Assam' in *IHQ*, March, 1945, pp. 19-28, with which we find it difficult to agree. Here we shall offer a few comments on his views regarding the legend on Bhāskaravarman's seal.

The text of the legend runs as follows :—

1. *Śrīman-Naraka-tanayo Bhagadatta-Vajradatt-ānvayo mahārājādhirāja-śrī-Prāgjyotiṣe-*
2. *ndraḥ Puṣyavarmā* (/*) *tat-putro mahārājādhirājaḥ śrī-Samudravarmā* (/*) *tasya tanayo Dattavatyāṁ samutpannaḥ*
3. *Mahārājādhirāja-śrī-Balavarmā* (/*) *tena* (*tasmāt*) *jāto devyāṁ śrī- Ratnavatyāṁ mahārājādhirā-*
4. *ja-śrī-Kalyāṇavarmā* (/*) *śrī-Gandharvavatyāṁ śrī-Gaṇapati-varmā* (/*) *śrī-Yajñavatyāṁ śrī-Mahe-*
5. *endravarmā* (/*) *dvis-turagamedh-āhārttā śrī-Suvratāyāṁ śrī-Nārāyaṇavarmā* (/*) *śrī-De-*
6. *vavatyāṁ śrī-Bhūtivarmā* (/*) *śrī-Vijñānavatyāṁ śrī-Candra-mukhavarmā* (/*) *śrī-Bho-*
7. *gavatyāṁ dvir-aśvamedha-yājī śrī-Sthiravarmā* (/*) *tena śrī-Nayanaśobhāyāṁ*
8. *śrī-Susthiravarmā* (/*) *tena śrī-Dhruvalakṣmyāṁ* (?) *śrī-Supratiṣṭhita-*
9. *varmā* (/*) *tasy=ānujo mahārājadhirāja-śrī-Bhāskaravarm =eti* //

The first point to note in the above text is the passage *śrīman-Naraka-tanayo Bhagadatta-Vajradatt-ānvayo....Puṣyavarmā.*

1. *Ep. Ind.*, Vol. XVIII, p. 15, note 3.
2. See *The Struggle for Empire*, ed. Majumdar, p. 241.

The use of the word *tanaya* in the secondary sense of a 'male descendant' in preference to its primary sense of a 'son', especially in view of the word *anvaya* used in the adjoining expression, is rather peculiar. In the second place, the relation of a king with his predecessor is indicated fully in the cases of Samudravarman, Balavarman and Kalyāṇavarman and imperfectly in those of Susthiravarman, Supratiṣṭhitavarman and also Bhāskaravarman; but the relation of Gaṇapativarman, Mahendravarman, Nārāyaṇavarman, Bhūtivarman, Candramukhavarman and Sthiravarman with their predecessors has not been indicated at all. The third point of interest is that the title *Mahārājādhirāja* is applied only to the names of the first four kings of the list and is absent in regard to those of the remaining rulers with the only exception of the latest of them. It may be suggested that the absence of the title and of words indicating the relationship of many of the kings with their predecessors is due to want of space. As, however, there could hardly have been any rigid rule about the size of the seal, it could have been made a little larger, or the size of the figure of elephant occupying the upper half of the seal's surface could have been made smaller in order to accommodate the whole of the properly worded epigraph.

Exceptionally strange seems to be the fact that while two of the kings mentioned have been referred to as performers of the Aśvamedha sacrifice, Bhūtivarman, who is known to have celebrated the horse-sacrifice according to his own Barganga inscription, is not called an *aśvamedha-yājin*. It may be pointed out in this connection that the epithet *dvir-aśvamedha-yājī* in line 7 admittedly refers to the following name of Sthiravarman, and, on the same analogy, the epithet *dvis-turagamedh-āhartā* in line 5 should refer not to the preceding name of Mahendravarman, but to the following name of Nārāyaṇavarman. The difference in the position of the queen-mothers' names in the two expressions, *śrī-Bhogavatyāṁ dvir-aśvamedha-yājī śrī -Sthiravarmā* and *dvis-turagamedh-āharttā śrī-Suvratāyāṁ śrī-Nārāyaṇavarmā*, does not make any difference in Sanskrit syntax. It therefore seems that not Mahendravarman, grandfather of Bhūtivarman, but Nārāyaṇavarman, father of Bhūtivarman, is mentioned in the epigraph on the seal as a performer of two Aśvamedhas. Is it then possible to suggest that the second of the two horse-sacrifices assigned here to Nārāyaṇavarman was celebrated when that king was too old and his son Bhūtivarman was ruling the country on his father's behalf and that this was the reason why Bhūtivarman is said to be a performer of the Aśvamedha in a record of his own reign ? Verse 12 of the Nidhanpur inscription comparing Mahendravarman with *yajña-vidhīnām = āspadam = analam* and his mother Yajñavatī with *yajñavatī araṇiḥ* need not be taken to point to Mahendravarman's performance of the Aśvamedha, as the poet apparently played on the word *yajña* in the name of the queen-mother and as Mahendravarman may have celebrated some of the numerous Vedic sacrifices other than the Aśvamedha.

Bhattasali thinks that Mahendravarman, a performer of two horse-sacrifices according to him, reigned in the period 450-90 A.D. as a contemporary of the Gupta emperors Kumāragupta I. Skandagupta and Budhagupta. It is, however, more probable that the earliest Aśvamedha was celebrated in Kāmarūpa by Nārāyaṇavarman about the beginning of the sixth century when the suzerain power of the Guptas declined. Bhūtivarman may be assigned roughly to the second quarter of the sixth century and his father Nārāyaṇavarman (performer of the Aśvamedha) and grandfather Mahendravarman respectively to the beginning of that century and the end of the fifth. Puṣyavarman who seems to have been a subordinate ally of Samudragupta and named his son after his overlord[1] should better be assigned to the third quarter of the fourth century and not to 310-30 A.D. as suggested by Bhattasali.

1. There are some cases of the naming of the son of a feudatory after his overlord (Sircar, *Suc. Sāt.*, p. 176). In all these cases, however, the overlord may have been also the father-in-law of the feudatory so that the son was named after his maternal grandfather according to an established early Indian practice. It is thus possible to think that Samudragupta gave one of his daughters in marriage to Puṣyavarman.

CHAPTER XII

DECLINE OF BUDDHISM IN BENGAL

I

The date of the first advent of Buddhism in Bengal cannot be clearly determined in the present state of our knowledge. The Buddhist canonical work *Saṁyuttanikāya* (about the 3rd-2nd century B.C.) as well as the introduction to the *Telapatta Jātaka* speaks of the Buddha's visit to a locality called Desaka or Setaka in the Sumbha or Sumha country in South-West Bengal.[1] The life story of the Buddha in early Buddhist literature, however, shows that the Buddha's activities were limited to North and South Bihar as well as the eastern parts of Uttar Pradesh, although in later times stories of his visit to many distant lands (such as Ceylon and Khotan) were fabricated.[2] There is doubt whether the Buddha, who flourished in the 6th-5th century B.C., actually visited the Sumha or Rāḍha country especially in view of the cultural backwardness attributed to the people of that country by the Jain canonical work *Āyāraṅgasutta* (I. 8.3), a work of about the same age as the *Saṁyuttanikāya*. The *Āyāraṅgasutta* speaks of the wild nature of the people of Rāḍha and the uncivil reception they offered to Mahāvīra, founder of Jainism and contemporary of the Buddha, who is said to have travelled in their country.[3] It is possible to suspect that Mahāvīra himself never visited Rāḍha, but that the treatment received from the people of that country by the Jain monks at a subsequent period was reflected in the above story regarding the founder of Jainism. Whatever that may be, there is no doubt that Buddhism gained a firm hold in most parts of Bengal during the reign of the Maurya emperor Aśoka (269-232 B.C.) who was a Buddhist and a great champion and propagator of Buddhism.[4] If the traditions recorded in the

1. Malalasekera, *Dictionary of Pali Proper Names*, s.v. *Sumbha*.
2. Cf. Oldenberg, *Buddha*, Calcutta, p. 391.
3. *History of Bengal*, Dacca University, Vol. I, pp. 9, 36.
4. Sircar, *Inscriptions of Aśoka*, 2nd ed., pp. 18ff. Cf. *Select Inscriptions*, p. 77 and also pp. 28, 30, 49, 51, 71, 73, 76.

seventh century by the celebrated Chinese pilgrim Hiuen-tsang are to be believed, Aśoka built numerous Buddhist monasteries in different parts of Bengal.[1] The pilgrim is known to have seen some of these monasteries, the construction of which was attributed to the Maurya emperor of the third century B.C. While defining the limits of Āryāvarta for the purpose of ordination, the *Vinayapiṭaka* places the eastern frontier of that land at Kajaṅgala near Rajmahal on the eastern fringe of Bihar, while, in the Sanskrit *Vinaya*, the eastern limit is given as the kingdom of Puṇḍravardhana (North Bengal).[2] This has led some scholars to believe that "Buddhism had probably obtained a footing in North Bengal even before Aśoka's time".[3] Although the tradition of the Sanskrit *Vinaya* may not refer to a pre-Aśokan date, there is little doubt, in view of the *Vinaya* evidence, that in Bengal Buddhism first made considerable headway only in the northern part of the country. But, at a subsequent period, Vaṅga (Southern and South-Eastern Bengal) became famous as one of the centres of Buddhism. This is suggested by the mention of Vaṅga (and not of any other tract of Bengal) in a list of Buddhist countries found in a Nagarjunikonda inscription of the third century A.D.[4]

Although there is some evidence regarding the existence of Buddhist monasteries in Bengal as early as the third century B.C., no undoubtedly Buddhist inscription of a pre-Christian date has so far been discovered in the country. Some scholars however believe that the Mahasthan (Bogra District, North Bengal) inscription of the third century B.C. refers to an establishment of the Ṣaḍvargīya sect of the Buddhists at Puṇḍranagara.[5] If this suggestion is to be accepted, we have another evidence in support of the early entry of Buddhism in North Bengal referred to above. The Chinese pilgrim I-tsing, who travelled in India in 671-95 A.D., saw the ruins of the 'Temple of China' said to have been built near the Mṛgaśikhāvana or Mṛgasthāpana monastery in Varendra (later name of Puṇḍra or North Bengal) for some Chinese pilgrims by a *Mahārāja*

1. Watters, *On Yuan Chwang's Travels in India*, Vol. II, pp. 184ff.
2. *History of Bengal*, *op. cit.*, p. 411.
3. *Ibid.*, p. 412.
4. *Select Inscriptions*, p. 225.
5. *Ibid.* p. 83; *History of Bengal*, *op. cit.*, p. 415.

named Śrīgupta about five hundred years before the pilgrim's time, i.e., in the second century A.D.[1] This king is sometimes identified with *Mahārāja* Gupta who was the progenitor of the celebrated Gupta emperors of Magadha and flourished about the end of the third century. The Chinese pilgrim Fa-hien, who visited Bengal about the beginning of the fifth century A.D., noticed the flourishing condition of Buddhism at Tāmralipti in South Bengal, while the Ganaighar copper-plate inscription of 507 A.D. speaks of a number of Buddhist monasteries in the Tippera District of East Bengal.[2] There is archaeological, epigraphic and literary evidence to prove the existence of numerous Buddhist establishments as well as many Buddhist ruling families in different parts of Bengal in the post-Gupta period.[3]

Inscriptions appear to show that the patrons of Jain and Buddhist religious establishments in Bengal were Brāhmaṇical Hindus and that the lay followers of Jainism and Buddhism were not socially distinct quite markedly from the ordinary Hindus. The Paharpur inscription of 479 A.D. records the benefactions of a Brāhmaṇa named Nāthaśarman and his wife Rāmī in favour of a Jain monastery in North Bengal.[4] The Gunaighar inscription, referred to above, records a grant in favour of a Buddhist monastery made by a king, who was a Śaiva, for the increase of the merit of himself and his parents. It is not stated in the inscription whether the subordinate ruler, on whose representation the grant was made, was a Brāhmaṇical Hindu or a lay follower of Buddhism. On this point, the Kailan inscription of the Vaiṣṇava king Śrīdhāraṇarāta (second half of the seventh century) throws some additional light.[5] According to this record, a minister of the Rāta king, named Jayanātha, approached his master for the grant of a piece of land which he was inclined to dedicate to the *Bhagavat* Tathāgata (Buddha) or the *Ratna-traya* (the Buddhist trinity

1. Allan, *Catalogue of the Coins of the Gupta Dynasties*, p. xv; *History of Bengal*, *op. cit.*, p. 69. A Bhaikṣukī inscription in the Malda Museum, published in the *Epigraphia Indica*, Vol. XXVIII, pp. 224ff., seems to point to the existence of a community of foreign (possibly Mongoloid) monks in Varendra.

2. *History of Bengal*, *op. cit.*, pp. 412-13; *Select Inscriptions*, pp. 331ff.
3. *History of Bengal*, *op. cit.*, pp. 413ff.
4. *Select Inscriptions*, pp. 346ff.
5. *IHQ*, Vol. XXIII, pp. 221ff.

of the Buddha, Dharma and Saṅgha symbolised in a Buddhist monastery) for the worship of the Buddha, the reading and writing of Buddhist religious texts and the provision of food, clothing and other necessaries for the Āryasaṅgha (Buddhist monks), as well as to a number of learned Brāhmaṇas for the performance of their *pañca-mahāyajña* (the five daily sacrifices to be performed by a Brāhmaṇa, viz. *adhyāpana*, *tarpaṇa*, *homa*, *bali* and *atithi-pūjana*). Whether Jayanātha was a Brāhmaṇical Hindu or a Buddhist is not stated in the inscription; but, whatever may have been his religious belief, it is clear that, in seventh century Bengal, when the Brāhmaṇical and Buddhist philosophers were busy in refuting one another's views, the life of the ordinary man was marked by absolute toleration.

Another interesting fact disclosed by inscriptions is the gradual merger of the lay Buddhists in the Hindu community. A Vajrayoginī (now in the Dacca Museum) tortoise-shell inscription[1] of about the eleventh century A.D., as we shall see below, contains the adoration: *namo bhagavate Vāsudevāya | namo Buddhāya || svasti-niśreyasāy=āstu Jino janānām ||* "Adoration to the most worshipful Vāsudeva. Adoration to the Buddha. May the Jina (Buddha) be for the prosperity and salvation of the people !" It has to be noticed that a shell seems to have been discarded by the engraver of the inscription because he was not inclined to incise *namo bhagavate Vāsudevāya* after *svasti-niśreyasāy=āstu Jino janānām*. Another interesting fact is that, while Vāsudeva has been adored before the Buddha, the former has been called a *Bhagavat* which epithet has not been used with the Buddha's name. It is apparent that Vāsudeva is given more prominence than the Buddha or Jina. At least the former is not subordinated to the latter. It is well-known from works like the *Sādhanamālā* and the *Niṣpannayogāvalī Tantra* that the Buddhists tried to incorporate Brāhmaṇical deities in their own pantheon. But orthodox Buddhists always placed Brāhmaṇical deities in a position subordinate to that of the Buddhist gods and goddesses often as carriers or attendants of the latter.[2] Thus an orthodox Buddhist is not expected to have placed Vāsudeva in a position superior to that of the

1. *JRASB*, Letters, Vol. XV, pp. 101ff.
2. Cf. B. Bhattacharya, *Indian Buddhist Iconography*, pp. 81, 143, 145, 146; A. Getty, *Gods of Northern Buddhism*, 2nd ed., p. 53.

Buddha as is done in the inscription under discussion, although the reference to the Buddha shows that the person responsible for the inscription was a Buddhist. The inscription no doubt points to a rapprochement between the worship of Vāsudeva and that of the Buddha. This is also indicated by the fact that the Buddha was regarded as an *avatāra* of Viṣṇu before Kṣemendra (11th century) and Jayadeva (12th century).[1] This further suggests that a number of Buddhists were gradually absorbed in the fold of the Vaiṣṇavas.

The Pāla emperors, who ruled in Bengal and Bihar from the eighth to the twelfth century, claimed to have been staunch followers of the Buddhist faith (*parama-saugata*). It is, however, interesting to note that, like typically zealous kings avowing the Brāhmaṇical faith, the Pālas were eager to suppress the social evil styled *varṇa-saṅkara*.[2] The Manahali plate of the *parama-saugata* Madanapāla (1144-61 A.D.) records the king's grant of some land in favour of the Brāhmaṇa, *Bhaṭṭaputra* Vaṭeśvaraśarman, as a fee for reading the *Mahābhārata* to the *paṭṭa-mahādevī* (chief queen) Citramatikā.[3] The Bhagalpur plate of the *parama-saugata* Nārāyaṇapāla (*circa* 854-908 A.D.) not only records the king's gift of a village in favour of the temple of Śiva-bhaṭṭāraka and the *Pāśupatācārya-pariṣad* in a locality called Kalasapota, but also refers to his boasts of having built one thousand-roomed temple for the said god in the same locality.[4] This inscription seems to point to a rapprochement between Śaivism and Buddhism. Although it is difficult to say definitely whether some Buddhists merged themselves in the religious group of the Śaivas as in that of the Vaiṣṇavas, this seems to be quite probable.[5]

The merger of the Buddhists in the Hindu community is also suggested by the Narayanpur inscription of the time of

1. The Buddha is mentioned in the list of the ten *Avatāras* in an inscription of about the eighth century A. D. (*MASI*, No. 26, p. 5). The verse in question seems to be quoted from an earlier Purāṇic text. See above, p. 42; below, p. 194, note 7.

2. *Gauḍalekhamālā*, p. 36 (Monghyr plate of Devapāla, verse 36).

3. *Ibid.*, pp. 147-58.

4. *Ind. Ant.*, Vol. XV, pp. 304ff.

5. It appears that sometimes the Buddha was also identified with Śiva as with Viṣṇu.

Mahīpāla I (*circa* 988-1038 A.D.).[1] This epigraph records the establishment of an image of Vināyaka by a merchant named Buddhamitra who was the son of Jambhalamitra and an inhabitant of Bilikandhaka in Samataṭa (modern Tippera-Noakhali region in South-East Bengal). The names of both Buddhamitra and his father Jambhalamitra are Buddhistic and suggest that the said persons were Buddhists. But an interesting point to be noticed in this connection is that the god Vināyaka installed by Buddhamitra, as is clearly indicated by the iconography of the image on which the inscription in question is engraved, is not the Mahāyānist (Buddhist) deity of that name, but the Brāhmaṇical god Vināyaka made according to the directions of the Brāhmaṇical Śilpaśāstras such as in the *Viṣṇudharmottara*. This fact seems to show either that Buddhamitra and Jambhalamitra were Buddhists, but were Hinduised enough to pay homage to the Brāhmaṇical deity or that their family had been Buddhist at an earlier date although they were themselves followers of the Brāhmaṇical faith. But, as suggested above, there was hardly any difference between the Brāhmaṇist and Buddhist householders in the early medieval period. The distinction between Brāhmaṇism and Buddhism seems in that period to have been exhibited mainly in the debates of the philosophers of the two schools. It may be pointed out in this connection that, from the view point of society, the lay Buddhists differed little from the Brāhmaṇist householders even in the early period,[2] although then the difference between the religions of the two sects was somewhat marked. In early-medieval Bengal, the religious distinction gradually died out so far as the ordinary people were concerned. In that age, the Buddhist mass had no growing popular literature and the attention of the Buddhists was being gradually more attracted by the recitation and representation on the stage of the stories of the *Rāmāyaṇa*, the *Mahābhārata* and the growing Purāṇic literature, often translated into the local languages, rather than by the old Jātakas and Avadānas. The ordinary Buddhist householders do not appear to have had real touch with the Buddhist

1. *Ind. Cult.*, Vol. IX, pp. 121ff. The evidence of the Mandhuk inscription, published in the *Indian Historical Quarterly*, Vol. XXVIII, pp. 51-57, supports that of the Narayanpur inscription.

2. See Oldenberg, *op. cit.*, pp. 282ff.

philosophers. These were apparently some of the causes that led to the absorption of the Buddhist masses into the Brāhmaṇical society. The Mahāyāna Buddhists worshipped deities quite similar to the Brāhmaṇical gods and goddesses. This must have gradually done away with the marked barriers that characterised the two religions at the early period. In the early medieval age, the Buddhists appear to have been joining the worship of Brāhmaṇical deities and the social and religious festivals of the Hindus and were enjoying recitations, on such occasions, of stories from Brāhmaṇical literature along with their Hindu neighbours, who on their part, it should be remembered, adopted wholly or partially some of the Buddhist deities including the Buddha himself and certain Buddhist social and religious festivals. The old Mahāyāna form of Buddhism (including the Yogācāra and Mādhyamika schools) assumed such forms as are known by the names of Vajrayāna, Sahajayāna and Kālacakrayāna. Much of the religious concepts of these sects was adopted by the Tāntrika school and various other religious communities of the Hindus.[1]

There are some traces of Buddhism in Bengal even in inscriptions later than the age of the Pālas and there is a Buddhist population in the Chittagong area on the south-eastern fringe of Bengal even today. But Buddhism does not appear to have played any important part in the religious life of Bengal after the decline of the Buddhist royal family of the Pālas in the twelfth century A.D. The antipathy of the Sena rulers of Bengal, who succeeded the Pālas, may have supplied an additional force to the elements that led to the withering of Buddhism in the country.

II

Two pieces of inscribed tortoise-shells were found in the course of reclamation of a tank at Vasupāḍā in the village of Vajrayoginī in Vikrampur within the jurisdiction of the Munshiganj Sub-Division of the Dacca District, East Pakistan. They were presented to the Dacca Museum and were published with facsimiles by N.K. Bhattasali in the *Annual Report of the Dacca Museum* for 1939-40, pp. 7-8.

1. *History of Bengal, op. cit.*, pp. 420ff.

The first of the two pieces of shells is blackish in colour and measures 5¾"×4⅛", while the second is a greyish piece measuring 6⅛"×4⅛". Both the pieces are broken, the first into two and the second into four fragments. There are two lines of writing on the first shell and six (actually, five) lines on the second. The characters belong to that class of the Northern Alphabet which is commonly styled Proto-Bengali, although a better name is Gauḍī. The inscriptions may be palaeographically assigned to the eleventh century. The single or double *daṇḍa* indicating stop is always preceded by a *visarga*-like sign in the second record. The language of the records is Sanskrit, although it is influenced by the local dialect.

The text of the inscription on the first shell was deciphered by Bhattasali as follows :—

1. [Symbol.] *Svasti śreyasāya | Sujino janānāṁ ||*
2. [Symbol.] *na*

His translation of the text runs as follows : 'Peace. For the welfare of the good Buddhists.'

Bhattasali's reading of the text of the inscription on the second shell runs as follows:—

1. [Symbol.] *Śrī*
2. [Symbol.] *namo bhagavate Vāsudevāya | namo Buddhāya |*
3. *svasti nisreyasāya | sujino janānāṁ | . Śrī-*
4. *ma namo bhagavate*
5. *Manarasarmma kārāvadhamma || Śrī*
6. *namo bhagavate Vāsudevāya*

Bhattasali did not translate this record, but appended a note in which his views as regards its interpretation are made perfectly clear. He says, "Leaving out an individual *siddhir=astu* figure and the *Śrī* following, the inscription has five lines, the last three of which appear to be incomplete. The fourth line appears to pray for the death or incarceration of one Manaraśarman (Manorathaśarman?) and helps us to understand the trend and nature of these curious inscriptions. They pray for the welfare of the good followers of Buddhism and invoke death or jail of Manaraśarman, showing thereby that they are *mantras* or charms for *Abhicāra* or *Māraṇa* (i.e. killing or injuring one's foes), and the unclean nature of the material, on which the inscriptions are incised, also bespeaks of a sinister design. It would appear from these curious tablets that, sometime between 1000 and 1100 A.D., the Buddhists were in a bad way in Vikrampur where these tablets were found, and the hands of one Manaraśarman lay specially heavily on them. This helps us to understand, to some extent, the religious history of the period following the fall of the Buddhist Candras of Vikrampur, who were supplanted by the Brāhmaṇical Varmans, when Bhavadevabhaṭṭa, minister of Harivarmadeva, is boastfully described as the Agastya of the Jaina and Buddhist seas in his Bhubaneswar inscription." The name of the village, Vajrayoginī, may have lent colour to Bhattasali's views as it shows that there was originally a temple of the Buddhist goddess Vajrayoginī in the locality. Vajrayoginī, sometimes said to be the consort of Heruka, was adopted by the Brāhmaṇical Tāntrikas as Chinnamastā.[1]

These far-reaching conclusions in regard to the religious history of ancient Bengal arrived at by Bhattasali on the basis of the two inscriptions are, however, entirely unwarranted as his reading and interpretation of the records are both full of mistakes.

Bhattasali's reading of the first inscription (line 1) contains no less than three mistakes. The word read as *śreyasāya* is actually *niśreyasāya*, *ni* being written above the line. The engraver at first omitted *ni*, but corrected himself, when he noticed the mistake, by incising it above the line. This is of course a common practice followed even today. The fact is that while *niśreyasa* is a familiar Sanskrit word meaning the same thing as *mokṣa*, the word *śreyasa* is not recognized by Sanskrit lexicons. It should be pointed out that the second inscription (line 3) uses the same word *niśreyasa* in the same context. After *niśreyasāya*, Bhattasali finds a *daṇḍa* which is, however, undoubtedly a medial *ā* sign. Nowhere in these two records is a *daṇḍa*, double or single, joined above with the top *mātrā* of the preceding *akṣara*; cf. the five cases of the use of the *daṇḍa* in the first (line 1) and the second (lines 2, 3 and 5) inscriptions. There is absolutely no doubt that the reading is *niśreyasāyā* and not *niśreyasāya* / as deciphered by Bhattasali. The next *akṣara* is read as *su*; but any one who would care to compare

1. Bhattacharya, *Indian Buddhist Iconography*, pp. 155-56.

the *akṣara su* in the expression *Vāsudevāya* in the second inscription (lines 2 and 6) would certainly be convinced that this *akṣara* is anything but *su.* Medial *u* in *Vāsudevāya* as well as in *Buddhāya* in the second inscription (line 2) is a slanting stroke joined below a consonant; but in the *akṣara* after *niśreyasāyā*, the upper part of which is represented by *s*, there is besides the *u* sign a clear subscript which is either *n* or *t*; but that it is a subscript *t* becomes absolutely certain when one compares this *akṣara* with the subscript *t* in the word *svasti* in both the inscriptions; cf. the first line of the first and the third (actually, second) line of the second inscription. The reading of the passage is therefore *svasti niśreyasāy=āstu Jino janānāṁ* and certainly not *svasti-śreyasāya | sujino janānāṁ* as Bhattasali deciphered it. In the second line, the engraver began to incise *namo bhagavate Vāsudevāya*, but gave up writing after engraving only the first *akṣara*.

Bhattasali's translation of the above passage is also equally unfortunate. The interpretation of *svasti* as 'peace' and *śreyasāya* as 'for the welfare' can hardly be regarded as ideal; but the climax is reached when *sujino janānāṁ* is translated as 'of the good Buddhists'. Of course Jina was a name of the Buddha; but how can *sujina* mean 'a good Buddhist' ? And even if *sujina* can be taken in the sense of a good Buddhist, how can one account for the *visarga* changed into *o* after that word ? Even if therefore we ignore the mistakes in Bhattasali's reading and accept his reading of the passage as correct, it has to be admitted that his translation is altogether absurd. There is absolutely no reference to good Buddhists in the first inscription. It simply says, 'Let the Jina (Buddha) be for the prosperity and salvation of men.'

In the first line of the second inscription, what Bhattasali reads as the *siddham* symbol may actually be a figure for *1* indicating that the *akṣara śrī* that follows was omitted in line 1 and has to be inserted therein. The use of *śrī* before *namo bhagavate* in two other cases below in this record may suggest that the engraver wanted to insert *śrī* before *namo bhagavate* also in line 2 which may actually be regarded as line 1 of the inscription. Otherwise, Bhattasali deciphered this line quite correctly. Line 3 (actually, line 2), however, reads : *svasti-niśreyasāy=āstu Jino janānāṁ || śrī.* The main passage is exactly the same as we find in the first inscription. As already pointed out in connection with the first inscription, it is impossible to read it as *svasti-niśreyasāya / sujino janānāṁ* after Bhattasali. Line 4 (actually, line 3) is also correctly deciphered by Bhattasali. The first *akṣara ma* is redundant. Whether the engraver was thinking of the second *akṣara* of *namo* or the first letter of the name at the beginning of the next line cannot be determined. Line 5 (actually, line 4) is read by Bhattasali as *Manarasarmma kārāvadhamma // śrī*. But there appear to be some inaccuracies. In the first place, there is a clear sign of *anusvāra* above between *na* and *ra* of *Manarasarmma*. It is also possible that we have to read *nu* instead of *na*. But even correcting *sarmma* to *śarmma*, we have a rather peculiar name *Manaṁraśarman* or *Manuṁraśarman*. Secondly, the third *akṣara* of what has been read as *kārāva* is certainly *ta* and not *va*, while the preceding *akṣara* looks more like *ri* than *rā*. The reading thus appears to me to be *kārita* (for Sanskrit *kārita*). The next word *dharma* no doubt stands for Sanskrit *dharmaḥ*. The last *akṣara* reads *śi*, the intended reading being no doubt *śrī*. There is no mistake in Bhattasali's reading of the last line.

Now we come to Bhattasali's interpretation of the second inscription. Bhattasali thinks that these lines 'pray for the welfare of the good followers of Buddhism and invoke death or jail for Manaraśarman, showing thereby that they are *mantras* or charms for *Abhicāra* or *Māraṇa*'. But it has already been shown that the passage *svasti-niśreyasāy=āstu Jino janānām*, which he wrongly deciphered, has absolutely nothing to do with a prayer typically 'for the welfare of the good followers of Buddhism'. Attention of scholars may be drawn to another fact in this connection. One of the causes of abandoning the first shell seems to be that the engraver was not inclined to incise *namo bhagavate Vāsudevāya* after *svasti-niśreyasāy= āstu Jino janānām*. This is suggested by the second inscription in which the arrangement is altered. Another fact is that Vāsudeva has been called a *Bhagavat* which epithet has not been used with the Buddha's name. The text of the second inscription clearly shows that Vāsudeva is given more prominence than the Buddha or Jina; at least the former is not subordinated to the latter. We know that attempts of the Buddhists to incorporate Brāhmaṇical deities in their own pantheon can be traced in works like the

Sādhanamālā and the *Niṣpannayogāvalī Tantra*.[1] The latter work describes twenty-seven magic circles of the Buddhist deities and mentions a host of Brāhmaṇical gods and goddesses as companions of those deities. But orthodox Buddhists always placed Brāhmaṇical deities in a position subordinate to that of the Buddhist gods and goddesses often as *vāhanas*. Their attitude is truly represented in the conception, e.g., of Vidyujjvālā Karālī, a form of Ekajaṭā (an emanation of Akṣobhya), who is said to have originated from the Buddha's sweat, as having Indra, Brahman, Viṣṇu and Śiva together as her *vāhana*.[2] The *vāhana* of Vajrahuṅkāra is Śiva,[3] that of Vajrajvālānalārka is Viṣṇu and his wife,[4] that of Trailokyavijaya is Śiva and Gaurī.[5] Mahācakra Vajrapāṇi treads on Brahman and Śiva.[6] It is therefore highly improbable that an orthodox Buddhist would have placed Vāsudeva in a superior or equal position with the Buddha. This fact shows that the inscriptions under discussion have nothing exceptionally and typically Buddhist in them. But they no doubt point to a rapprochement between the worship of Vāsudeva and that of the Buddha, which is also indicated by the fact that the Buddha was regarded as an *Avatāra* of Viṣṇu long before Kṣemendra (eleventh century) and Jayadeva (twelfth century).[7] This further suggests that a number of Buddhists were gradually absorbed in the fold of the Vaiṣṇavas. And this is probably supported by the present records which point to the joint adoration of both Vāsudeva and the Buddha. The reference to the Buddha shows beyond doubt that the person responsible for the inscriptions was a Buddhist. Had he been merely a Vaiṣṇava, there is no meaning of the adoration to the Jina or Buddha. The fact that Buddha was regarded as Viṣṇu's *Avatāra* is not material since no other incarnation is adored at the same time. But the same man also adored Vāsudeva and could hardly have been

1. Cf. *Ariana Antiqua*, 1947, pp. 36-39.
2. Bhattacharya, *op. cit.*, p. 81.
3. *Ibid.*, p. 143.
4. *Ibid.*, p. 145.
5. *Ibid.*, p. 146.
6. Getty, *Gods of Northern Buddhism*, p. 53.
7. The Purāṇic verse giving the list of 10 *Avatāras* including the Buddha is quoted in an inscription, from Mamallapuram, of about the eighth century while the Buddha is represented among the *Avatāras* in the Sirpur temple of the same age. See *Mem. ASI*, No. 26, p. 5; No. 18, pp. 5-6; above, p. 187n.

an orthodox Buddhist. There is thus little possibility of these two being communal Buddhistic records as believed by Bhattasali.

It is impossible to understand how, even if one accepts Bhattasali's reading *Manarasarmma-kārā-vadha-mma,* the passage can signify that a person's incarceration or death was prayed for. *Kārā-vadha-mma* of course cointains *kārā* and *vadha*; but the expression is no doubt as meaningless as *sujino-janānām.*[1] The actual reading of the passage is, as shown above, *Manaṁrasarma-kārita-Dharma,* i.e. *Manaṁraśarma-kārita-Dharmaḥ.* It appears to mean that a person named Manaṁraśarman caused a Dharma to be made in his behalf. Now the word *Dharma* may indicate anything, the making of which is related to the maker's religious merit. The word *kīrti,* 'fame', is known likewise to be used in the sense of any construction (e.g. a temple for a deity) leading to the fame of the person responsible for it. But the material on which the inscriptions are incised appears to preclude the possibility of the above interpretation. What pious construction was possible by means of tortoise-shells ? It thus seems possible to suggest that the tortoise-shells (or earthen images of tortoise covered by these shells) were worshipped as Dharma Ṭhākur whose worship in the shape of a tortoise is prevalent in the Burdwan and Presidency Divisions of West Bengal even at the present time.[2] As regards the tortoise form of the deity, Sukumar Sen in a paper entitled 'Is the Cult of Dharma a Living Relic of Buddhism in Bengal ?' published in the *B.C. Law Volume,* Part I, says, 'The emblem of Dharma—rather his *pāda-pīṭha* on which

1. Bhattasali's interpretation reminds us of a Kannaḍa story in which a person, who had been asked to purchase *meṇasu* (pepper) and *jīrige* (cumin seed), bought *meṇa* (wax) and *sūji* (needle) and explained that *rige* was unknown in the market. The hopeless position of *mma* in Bhattasali's transcript resembles that of *rige* in the story.

2. Vide 'Dharma Worship' by K.P. Chattopadhyay in *JRASBL.,* Vol. VIII, 1942, pp. 99-135. Most of the images examined by Chattopadhyay in the Districts of Birbhum, Midnapur and 24-Parganas were shaped like tortoises measuring about 6″ ×4″ (12″ × 12″ in one case). 'In one case, it had a tortoise back only.' Cf. *loc. cit.,* pp. 104-05. Coomaraswamy (*The Arts and Crafts of India and Ceylon,* p. 185) refers to an Allahabad 'jade tortoise' in the British Museum, 17″ long, as an ancient work. This appears to point to the prevalence of the worship of the tortoise-shaped deity outside Bengal in ancient times. Cf. the Kūrma *Avatāra* of Viṣṇu.

was placed or engraved the *pādukā* (boots or sandals) of Dharma—is a tortoise. In most cases, it is a natural bit of stone shaped like a tortoise; in other cases, it is a chiselled stone image of the same.' In the introduction (p. xi) to the *Rūp-rāmer Dharma-maṅgal*, edited by Sen jointly with Panchanan Mandal, the following two verses, one in Sanskrit and the other in Bengali, have been quoted from the ritualistic literature of the Dharma cult :

ulūka-vāhana Dharmadeva tejomay-ātmaka |
idānīṁ kūrma-pṛṣṭhe tu divya-rūpa namo=stu te ||
hāt pātiyā Dharma sṛjilen sṛṣṭi |
pādukā sthāpiba lae kūrmer pṛṣṭi ||

Sen and Mandal further point out that, although the worship of Dharma Ṭhākur is now prevalent only about the Burdwan Division, it was in former times also current in other parts of Bengal.[1] They trace it in the present day ceremony of Del or worship of Pāṭ Ṭhākur in East and North Bengal and point to the existence of 'Dharma Ṭhākur's *Gādi*' not far from the chief town of the Bogra District. They further connect the Dharma cult with the Chaṭ Parav or Ṣaṣṭhī-parva prevalent in Bihar. The present records coming from the Dacca District support their contention. We have referred above to the ancient jade tortoise from Allahabad.

Another important fact suggested by these records of a Vaiṣṇavite Buddhist is that they associate the Dharma cult with Buddhism and Vaiṣṇavism. Haraprasad Sastri[2] pointed out that Dharma Ṭhākur's *dhyāna* represents the deity as *Śūnya-mūrti* and *nirañjana*, which connect the Dharma cult with the theory of the Void, so popular with the later Buddhists, and show the latter's influence on the former. Chattopadhyay speaks of 'the wheel of Dharma' in connection with the Dharma Ṭhākur cult.[3] But Sastri's theory that the present-day Dharma cult of Bengal is a relic of Buddhism seems to be unwarranted in spite of the fact that the present records point to its popularity with the Buddhists. Sastri confused the tortoise shape of Dharma with the form of a Buddhist Caitya and ignored the fact that Buddhist literature does not represent Dharma (one

1. *Op. cit.*, p. i.
2. *Proc. ASB*, 1894, p. 135; *JASB*, 1894, pp. 55-61, 65-68.
3. Cf. *op. cit.*, pp. 112, 115; figs. 2-3.

of the celebrated Buddhist *Tri-ratna* or 'three jewels', viz., the Buddha, Dharma and Saṅgha) in the shape of a tortoise. It may be pointed out that the Kailan inscription of Śrīdhāraṇarāta (seventh century) and the Sundarban inscription of Ḍommanapāla (twelfth century) use the expression *Ratnatraya* to indicate a Buddhist establishment. This is probably because the images of the Buddha, Dharma and Saṅgha came to be worshipped later in Buddhist monasteries. But the three *Ratnas* of the Buddhists are known to have been represented in human form. When represented in art, the four-armed Dharma usually shows *añjali* against the breast by one pair of hands and carries the rosary and double-lotus in the other.[1] We know that the Mahāyānists placed Dharma instead of the Buddha in the first place amongst the *Ratnas*.[2] It is also known that the Dhyāni-Buddha is the first *kāya* or body of the Buddhist trinity called *Trikāya* and that he is the *Dharmakāya* or the inner intelligence of the body of the Buddha. This *Dharma-kāya* is identified by some Buddhist sects with Dharma of the Buddhist *Tri-ratna*.[3] Buddhist scriptures represent Ādi-Dharma as a goddess who revealed herself from the centre of a triangle and produced the Buddha, Dharma and Saṅgha from its three sides. Dharma that was produced from its second side is the wife of the Buddha, produced from the first side, and is the mother of the other Buddhas.[4] But these conceptions had apparently little to do with the tortoise form of Dharma Ṭhākur whose name, however, connects him with the Buddhist *Ratna*. In Brāhmaṇical mythology, Dharma is sometimes a separate deity (justice or virtue personified as a bull, dog or dove and identified with Viṣṇu or Prajāpati) and sometimes another name of Yama and of Yudhiṣṭhira.[5] No representation of the independent deity called Dharma is known. The figure of Yama (or Yudhiṣṭhita) as conceived by Brāh-

1. Cf. Bhattacharya, *op. cit.*, Plate III.
2. *Ibid.*, p. xv.
3. A. Getty, *op. cit.*, p. 28.
4. *Ibid.*, p. 197.
5. Yudhiṣṭhira is worshipped in the Madras Presidency as Dharmarāja. This Dharmarāja cult of South India may be related to the Dharma Ṭhākur worship of Bengal; but it does not explain the tortoise form of Dharma. For the Dharmarāja cult of South India, see Chattopadhyay, *op. cit.*, pp. 129-30.

maṇical literature and represented in art has likewise nothing to do with a tortoise. The conception of the tortoise and other non-human incarnations of Viṣṇu[1] was no doubt based partly on the ancient worship of the tortoise and other animals amongst the totemistic peoples of India and partly on local adoration of mysterious animals such as that of Dakṣiṇrāy, the tiger divinity of the Sundarbans, at the present time in Bengal. There are tales about the helpfulness of mysterious fishes (usually of the class known as Śol and Gajār in Central Bengal) living in the waters of particular *Bils* (lakes). The story is always the same. People used to get whatever they wanted from the strange inhabitant of the waters; but its favour was discontinued as a result of the dishonesty exhibited by one of the recipients of favours. It seems that an old tortoise worship in ancient Bengal was later influenced by both Buddhism and Vaiṣṇavism. Its association with Vaiṣṇavism can easily be traced through the conception of the tortoise incarnation of Viṣṇu. But its origin in Buddhism is rather difficult to trace excepting its association with one of the Buddhist *Triratna* by name. Both Sen and Chattopadhyay think that the Buddhist conception of the Void 'may indicate the influence of the Dharma cult on Tāntric Buddhism', and this view seems to be supported by the importance of the Void in the religious and philosophical beliefs of the Austric-speaking people of Polynesia. But even admitting the influence of Buddhism on the Dharma cult, there is no reason to believe that the worship of Dharma in the shape of a tortoise originated with the Buddhists.[2] The name Dharma, applied to the deity, is regarded by Suniti Kumar Chatterji as derived from some Austric word meaning 'tortoise' and sounding like *daram*.[3]

1. The tortoise incarnation was originally ascribed to Prajāpati (cf. *Śatapatha Brāhmaṇa*, VII. 5.1.5-6), but was later attributed to Viṣṇu.

2. Some writers have associated the Dharma-kām ceremony, prevalent among the Chakmas who are a Buddhist tribal people of the Chittagong region of East Bengal, with the cult of Dharma Ṭhākur. Cf. Madhav Chandra Chakma Master, *Cākmā Jātir Itihās*, p. 54; Satis Chandra Ghosh, *Cākmā Jāti*, p. 200. But Dharma-kām of the Chakma Buddhists is actually nothing but a ceremonial worship of the Buddha, the name of Dharma being conspicuous by its absence from the *mantras* employed in the ceremony. The expression *dharma-kām* is a corruption of Sanskrit *dharma-karman* meaning 'a religious rite'. The Chakma ceremony is so called because it is the religious rite *par excellence* amongst the Chakma Buddhists.

3. Cf. Sen and Mandal, *op. cit.*, p. xv.

Dharma Ṭhākur is usually identified with Viṣṇu, but in many cases also with Śiva.[1] It is interesting to note that the form of Pāṭ Ṭhākur, worshipped in the Faridpur region of Central Bengal as identical with Śiva, has actually both Śaiva and Vaiṣṇava characteristics. It is made of Nimba or Bilva wood roughly in the shape of an alligator and has the emblems of the bull and the trident, associated with Śiva, as well as the conch, discus, club and lotus symbols of Viṣṇu. The text of a work on the procedure of Pāṭ Ṭhākur's worship, copied by us, also supports this. Cf. the section called *Pāṭ-sṛṣṭi* which runs :

ācambite jaṭā nāḍilen Paśupati |
bīj paḍiyā Bel-vṛkṣa Nimer utpatti ||
goḍā kāṭiyā āgā kāṭiyā madhye dilen cheo |
mājhkhāne bānāilen Pāṭ-bāṇ bhāo ||
Viśvakarmā dilen Pāṭ nirmāṇ kariyā |
śaṅkha cakra gadā padma cāri mudrā diyā ||
gāḍilen triśūl goṭā kāṇṭā tin sāri |
śukla-vastra diyā morā Pāṭ-bāṇ ghiri ||
kahen o to satya-guru Maheśeri var |
Pāt-bāṇ śuddha karilen prabhu Bholā-Maheśvar ||

Sen and Mandal suggest that the cult of the Vedic and Iranian Sun-god, Vedic Varuṇa, the war-god of such peoples as the Ḍoms and Caṇḍālas, and several other deities, mostly Nonaryan, contributed to the growth and development of the Dharma Ṭhākur cult. As to the solar origin of Dharma Ṭhākur, Sen observes, 'Dharma is the Sun-god. The tortoise (Kūrma, Kaśyapa) as the symbol or emblem of the (rising ?) sun is probably a Nonaryan concept. But the identitity of the tortoise with the sun appears early in Indo-Aryan religion, at least as early as the *Śatapatha Brāhmaṇa* (VII.5.15). As an Aryan god, the Sun moves in a chariot. So does Dharma. As a matter of fact, the ceremony of Rathayātrā was originally concerned with Dharma.[3] Like the Sun-god, Dharma cures

1. *Ibid.*, p. xiv.
2. *Op. cit.*, pp. xiiiff.
3. Ratha-yātrā, popular in the religious life of South India, seems to have been brought to Eastern India by the South Indians. The Gaṅga kings appear to have popularised the Ratha-yātrā at the Purī temple and the practice seems to have spread to other Vaiṣṇava temples in these parts.

incurable diseases like leucoderma. The Sun-god has a bird as his *vāhana* and the god of death (Yama) as his son. Dharma's direct creation Ulūka (owl) combines the two personalities. The monkey cult was originally associated with Sun worship. In the cult of Dharma, Hanumān is his factotum.' Chattopadhyay lays greater stress on Dharma's relation with Vedic Varuṇa and the latter's association with the Sun. He also points to Dharma Pennu, the creator god of the Khonds and to Dharma regarded as a great god by the Santals. In Brāhmaṇical mythology, Dharma is the name of as on (Yama) and an attendant of the Sun-god.

The antiquity of the cult of Dharma Ṭhākur in Bengal is definitely established by the present inscriptions. The tortoise-shaped deity was no doubt called Dharma as early as the tenth or eleventh century. But when precisely this Sanskritic name came to be applied to the tortoise deity for the first time cannot be determined.

There is thus absolutely no reason to believe that the Vajrayoginī inscriptions are *mantras* or charms for *Abhicāra* or *Māraṇa*, as suggested by Bhattasali. Had they been so, it may further be pointed out, they would have certainly contained certain mystic *bīj-ākṣaras*, such as *hrīṁ*, etc., which abound in such *mantras* noticed in Tāntric works both Brāhmaṇical and Buddhistic.

III

In a paper entitled 'Aiḍuka' in the *Journal of the Oriental Institue*, Vol. I, No. 3, pp. 278ff., it has been said that the Vedic origin of *Aiḍuka*, which has been suggested by the author, would justify its inclusion in the *Viṣṇudharmottara*; because, if it were a Buddhist form, it could not have found a place in it. It is further pointed out that the word *Aiḍuka* is used in the *Mahāvastu* to indicate a Buddhist *Stūpa*. It is therefore concluded that, as it happens in the case of other words like *Caitya*, etc., "the word *Aiḍuka* also must have been used as a synonym of *Stūpa*".[1] But in the eagerness to disprove the Buddhist association of the *eḍuka* or *aiḍuka*, not only is the stamp of non-

1. *Op. cit.*, 282.

Brāhmaṇical character put on the *eḍuka* in the verses quoted from the Vana-parvan of the *Mahābhārata* been explained away, but a clear indication of the *Viṣṇudharmottara* itself has also been ignored.

In the analysis of the *Viṣṇudharmottara* description of the *eḍuka* or *aiḍuka*, it has been said, "Below the *bhūmikās* (floors) but above the *liṅga* should be placed in the four directions the *Lokapālas* carrying *śūlas* in their hands. Their names are Virūḍha, Dhṛtarāṣṭra, Virūpākṣa and Kubera. All of them should have the dress of the Sun and should wear armours. They should be adorned with ornaments. Virūḍhaka represents Śakra the lord of the Devas; Dhṛtarāṣṭra, Yama the leader of the nether-worlds; Virūpākṣa, Varuṇa the lord of waters; and Kubera is the lord of the Yakṣas."

It should be noticed that the association of the *eḍuka* in the above description with Virūḍhaka, Dhṛtarāṣṭra, Virūpākṣa and Kubera clearly demonstrates its original Buddhist character, as they are the famous *Lokapālas* of early Buddhist mythology.[1] The attempt of the *Viṣṇudharmottara* to identify the Buddhist *Loka-pālas* with the Brāhmaṇical *Loka-pālas* of the early period, viz. Indra, Yama, Varuṇa and Kubera,[2] no doubt points to the assimilation of an essentially Buddhist institution in the fold of Brāhmaṇism.

IV

The donor of the Ratnagiri (Cuttack District, Orissa) copper-plate inscription[3] was *Paramabhaṭṭāraka Mahārājādhirāja Trikaliṅgādhipati* Karṇadeva *alias* Mahāśivagupta who was the younger brother of Purañjaya (feared by the Gauḍa, Ḍāhala, Kaliṅga and Vaṅga kings), the son of Janamejaya and the grandson of Uddyotakesarin. Karṇa or Karṇakesarin, grandson of Uddyotakesarin, seems to have ended his rule over Utkala before the conquest of that country by the Gaṅga king Anantavarman Coḍagaṅga probably before 1112 A.D.[4] The issue of the present charter from Yayātinagara[5] is thus inter-

1. See Barua and Sinha, *Barhut Inscriptions*, pp. 65ff.
2. Vide *Suc. Sāt.*, p. 196.
3. See *Ep. Ind.*, Vol. XXXIII, pp. 263ff.
4. *JIH*, Vol. XXXIV, pp. 273ff.
5. The city seems to be called Abhinava-Yayātinagara in the *Mādalā Pāñji.*

esting. The city of Yayātinagara (near Binka in the former Sonepur State in ancient Kosala), built by and named after Yayāti I, was originally the capital of the Somavaṁśīs of Kosala. It appears that, after the expansion of Somavaṁśī power over Utkala, their capital in Utkala was also given the name Yayātinagara or Yayātipura, probably after Yayāti III who seems to have been the first Somavaṁśī king of Utkala. This new 'city of Yayāti' seems to be the modern Jājpur (possibly a corruption of Yayātipura) which was previously the capital of the Bhauma-Karas, the predecessors of the Somavaṁśīs in Utkala.

An interesting fact is that the lady Karpūraśrī, the donee of the grant, is described as a *Rāṇī* or queen and as the daughter of a woman and the granddaughter of another woman. The word *pautrī* in this context seems to be used in the sense of 'the daughter's daughter'. The absence of any reference to Karpūraśrī's father and grandfather and her representation as the daughter and granddaughter of females appear to suggest that she was born of a harlot. There are other instances of similar representation of a harlot in inscriptions. Thus the Mahākūṭeśvara (Bādāmi) temple inscription[1] of the time of Cālukya Vijayāditya records the donations of the harlot Vināpoṭi described as the daughter of Kuci-poṭi and granddaughter of Revamañcal and the heart's darling (*prāṇa-vallabhe*) of king Vijayāditya Satyāśraya. Similarly, an inscription[2] of the time of Rāṣṭrakūṭa Dhruva in the Virūpākṣa temple at Pattadakal records the donation of Bādi-poḍḍi described as the daughter of Goyinda-poḍḍi who was a harlot (i.e. *Devadāsī*) of the temple of the queen Loka-mahādevī. These inscriptions are in the Kannaḍa language, in which the word *poṭi*, *poḍḍi* or *boḍḍi* means 'a harlot'.[3]

If Karpūraśrī, apparently one of the secondary queens or concubines of the Somavaṁśī king Karṇa, was a harlot's daughter, there are a few points to be explained. The first of these is that whether the word *devī* suffixed to her mother's

1. *Ind.*, *Ant.*, Vol. X, p. 103.
2. *Ibid.*, Vol. XI, p. 125.
3. A Telugu inscription from Velpuru in the Sattenapalli Taluk of the Guntur District, dated Śaka 1131, mentions Kassadi Sūramadevī, concubine (*bhoga-strī*) of the Kota chief Ketarāja, and her mother Amara-sāni who was a harlot (*SII*, Vol. X, No. 249).

name should have to be taken to indicate the latter's status as a queen. We have, however, inscriptions mentioning harlots with names ending in *devī*.[1] Even if Karpūraśrī's mother was the secondary queen or concubine of some ruler, we may think that she was originally a harlot, but was later married to or associated with a king, while Karpūraśrī had been born before her mother was associated with the ruler. The name of Karpūraśrī's mother is *Mahārī* Māhūṇadevī, the epithet *mahārī* being undoubtedly the same as Oriya *māhārī* (Prakrit *mehārī*) meaning a songstress or dancing girl or a *Devadāsī* or harlot. Secondly, Karpūraśrī is stated to have belonged to the Kāśyapa-gotra. This appears to have been the *gotra* of one of her direct female ancestors, who first took to the profession of a harlot.[2]

The third point to be noticed in this connection is that Karpūraśrī is described as *Saloṇapura-mahāvihāra-vinirgatā*, i.e. hailing from Saloṇapura-mahāvihāra. Since the *Devadāsīs* are generally associated with Brāhmaṇical temples, one may doubt that the harlots in question were residents of the monastery at Saloṇapura and may suggest that Saloṇapura-mahāvihāra has been used as the name of the locality where the harlots lived, the entire area under the possession of the Saloṇapura monastery or the village or township around it being known under that name as in the case of the town of Bihar (i.e. Bihar-sharif) and the Bihar State, both names essentially derived from the word *vihāra* meaning a Buddhist monastery originally standing at the site or in the vicinity of the modern town of Bihar called Bihar-sharif by the Muhammadans.

But there is some proof to show that *Devadāsīs* were maintained in the early medieval period not only in the Brāhmaṇical temples but also in the Buddhist shrines at least in Eastern India. There was therefore no difference in this respect between the Brāhmaṇical and Buddhist temples in the area and age to which the Ranagiri plates belong. Thus Karpūraśrī and probably also her mother, if not her maternal grandmother as well, had really been *Devadāsīs* attached to the Buddhist

1. See *Ep. Ind.*, Vol. XXXIII, p. 244, text line 7.

2. According to a Bengali saying, one having no *gotra* can claim the Kāśyapa-gotra. Cf. also Brough, *Gotrapravaramañjarī*, p. 171.

temple in the *mahāvihāra* at Saloṇapura (modern Solampur near Jājpur) before she went to king Karṇa's harem. She may have been purchased by the king from the authorities of the monastery.

Bhagavanlal Indraji published an inscription embedded in the wall of a temple of the Sun-god on the western side of the tank called Dakṣiṇa-mānasa near the Viṣṇupada at Gayā in the *Indian Antiquary*, Vol. X, 1881, pp. 341ff. Dated in the Buddha-parinirvāṇa year 1883 (probably 1270 A.D.), this inscription records the construction of a *Gandhakuṭī* by Puruṣottamasiṁha, the son of Kāmadevasiṁha and grandson of king Jayatuṅgasiṁha of the Kāma country (probably Kumaun in the Himalayas or Kaman in the Bharatpur District, Rajasthan). The expression *gandhakuṭī* originally meant the Buddha's private chamber in a Buddhist establishment and later a shrine where the Buddha's image was worshipped in a Buddhist monastery. The Buddhist temple in question is said to have been built for the merit of Māṇikyasiṁha, the deceased son of Puruṣottamasiṁha's daughter Ratnaśrī, with the help of the local Chinda king and of king Aśokavalla of the Sapādalakṣa country (the Siwalik hills or the land around Śākambharī or Sāmbhar in the Jaipur District, Rajasthan), both Puruṣottamasiṁha and Aśokavalla probably being pilgrims to Gayā or leading retired lives at the holy place.

Verse 12 of the said inscription has been read and translated as follows :

pūjāḥ pūjyatamasya pañcama-gatair = vādyais = trisandhyaṁ sadā
Rambhā-sannibha-bhāvinībhir = abhitaś = ceṭībhir = atyadbhutam |
nṛtyantībhir = anaṅga-laṅgima-gatair = ggīt-ādi-raṅgair = imā
yasmāt = santi hi śāsane Bhagavataḥ satkāra-visphāritāḥ ||

"Since, in the religion of the *Bhagavat* (Buddha), worship is here [offered] to the most worshipful, always three times a day, by means of instrumental music in the highest key (*pañcama-gata*) together with Rambhā-like *Bhāvinīs* and *Ceṭīs* dancing round wonderfully with mirth in singing and so on, in a way appertaining to the unions of Anaṅga (Kāma)—[worship] increased by hospitable entertainments."

On the words *bhāvinī* and *ceṭī*, Indraji observes as follows: "*Bhāvinīs* are the dancing girls attached to temples. *Ceṭīs* are maid-servants belonging to temples, who perform certain menial services as well as join with the *Bhāvinīs* in singing...."

The word *bhāvinī* in the sense of 'a wanton woman' is interesting since this meaning may have developed from its use in expressions like *Hari-bhāvinī*, 'devoted to Hari' probably often applied to dancing girls attached to Vaiṣṇava temples.

CHAPTER XIII

RELIGIOUS SUICIDE

I

It is now admitted that the loose socio-religious organisation called Hinduism absorbed in it, in the course of its gradual development, contributions of various racial and cultural elements, one of them being Aryan. A large number of conceptions associated with Hindu religion and thought is believed to be Nonaryan in origin. A great deal of the Epic and Purāṇic myths and much of our cultural and social and other usages are supposed to be a legacy from our pre-Aryan ancestors. The attitude towards suicide, as revealed in Indian literature of the pre-British period, seems to suggest that the Aryans abhorred it while certain influential Nonaryan elements in the population approved of it, at least under special circumstances, and that the Aryan approach to the problem was gradually overshadowed by Nonaryan ideas relating to suicide.

According to the *Yajurveda*, "Those who have killed themselves repair after death to the worlds of the Asuras which are enveloped in blinding darkness."[1] There is another Vedic passage which says, "One who desires heaven should not seek to die before the appointed span of one's life is at an end."[2] The *Śatapatha Brāhmaṇa* and *Īśāvāsyopaniṣad* agree to this view when they say that suicide does not lead one to heaven.[3] The same view is expressed in the Ādi-parvan of the *Mahābhārata*.[4] Certain other authorities[5] including Gobhila compare an *āhitāgni* (i.e. one who maintains the sacred fire in his house) Brāhmaṇa committing suicide with one killed by the Caṇḍālas in a defiant fight with them and say that his corpse should be

1. *Vāj. Saṁ.*, 40.3; cf. *Bṛhad. Up.*, IV.4.11; *Uttararāmacarita*, Act IV (after verse 3).
2. See Medhātithi on Manu, VI.32; Kane, *Hist. Dharm.*, Vol. II, p. 927.
3. *Śat. Br.*, X. 2.67; *Īśā.*, 3.
4. 179.20.
5. See Kane, *op. cit.*, Vol. II, pp. 924ff.; Vol. III, pp. 939, 949; Vol. IV, pp. 603ff.

cremated by Śūdras without proper cermonies. According to the *Dharmasūtra* of Vasiṣṭha,[1] "Whoever kills himself becomes guilty of a mortal sin and his *sapiṇḍas* have to perform no death rites for him; a man becomes a self-killer by destroying himself by entering wood-fire or water, by striking self with clubs or stones or weapons, by taking poison or being hanged on ropes." The same authority quotes a verse saying that "a Brāhmaṇa who through affection performs the last rites of one that has committed suicide, must undergo the penance of Cāndrāyaṇa with Taptakṛcchra."[2] The *Vasiṣṭha Dharmasūtra* also prescribes a Prāyaśchitta for merely resolving to commit suicide even when no attempt is actually made.[3] Parāśara states that, if a man or woman commits suicide by hanging through extreme pride or rage or through affection or fear, he or she falls into hell for 60,000 years.[4] Hārita quoted by Āpastamba[5] puts suicide on the same footing as homicide and condemns it even as a Prāyaścitta for a great sin committed although, as will be seen below, some authorities allow suicide in various ways as *Prāyaścitta* for the *Mahāpātakas* committed.

Manu says that no water is to be offered and no rites, such as the *sapiṇḍikaraṇa*, are to be performed for persons who have committed suicide.[6] Gautama, Yājñavalkya and Viṣṇu are also of the same opinion.[7] According to Yama, quoted in the *Mitākṣarā*,[8] for such persons there should be no *aśauca* (ceremonial impurity) observed, no water offered, no tears shed, no cremation and last rites performed. Vṛddha-Yājñavalkya and Chāgaleya, quoted by the same authority, however, concur that, in the case of persons guilty of suicide, a rite called Nārāyaṇa-bali should be performed after a year and then their *śrāddha* may be celebrated.[9] The Nāgara-khaṇḍa section of the *Skanda Purāṇa* says that *śrāddha* may be performed for persons, who have committed suicide or met a violent death, on the fourteenth day of the dark fortnight of a month.[10]

1. 23.14-15.
2. Kane, *op. cit.*, Vol. II, p. 924.
3. 23.18.
4. IV. 1-2.
5. I.10.28. 15-17.
6. V. 89-90.
7. *Yāj.*, III. 6; *Viṣṇ. Dh. S.*, 22.56.
8. On *Yāj.*, III.6.
9. *Loc. cit.*
10. Ch. 219, verses 19-21; Kane, *op. cit.*, Vol. IV, p. 525.

Although, suicide is thus generally condemned by many ancient Indian writers of great authority, there is another side of the picture. Manu and several other *Dharmaśāstrakāras* including Yājñavalkya, Gautama, Vasiṣṭha and Āpastamba allow suicide in different forms as *Prāyaścitta*, involving death, to atone for the commission of *Mahāpātakas* or great sins, such as incest.[1] In this connection, it is interesting to note that some of the ordeals, so popular with the medieval Indian courts, involved death of the litigant.[2] According to some *Śāstrakāras* like Atri[3] and many of the Purāṇic writers, old men above 70, very weak persons who cannot observe the rules of physical purification, those who have no longer any desire for worldly pleasures and those who have no more duties or tasks to perform, may be allowed to start on the *Mahāprasthāna* (the last journey to meet their death) or to die at Prayāga (Allahabad).[4] In such cases, proper *aśauca* had to be observed and the usual water offering and *śrāddha* should have to be performed.

There is evidence to show that suicide under particular circumstances was popular in India even in very early times; but such oppositions as noticed in the works on law and usage came to be more popular, as days passed by, till ultimately a section of writers regarded the *Mahāprasthāna* and suicide on the part of old men by falling down from a precipice and in fire, as forbidden for the Kali age. But the great popularity enjoyed by various kinds of religious suicide in medieval India can be gauged by the Epic and Purāṇic injunction: "You should not pass over your wish about dying at Prayāga on account of the words of the Veda or the words of the people."[5] The Ādi-khaṇḍa of the *Padma Purāṇa*[6] even says, "A man, who suffering from no diseases, having no deficiency as to his limbs and being in full possession of five senses, burns in cowdung fire, remains honoured in heaven for as many years as there are pores on the whole of his body." Jainism, although it lays

1. *Manu.*, XI. 73, 90-91; *Yāj.*, III.248, 253; *Gaut.*, 23.1; *Vas. Dh.S.*, 20.22; cf. 13.4; *Āp. Dh.S.*, I.9.25.1-3 and 6.
2. See Sircar, *The Successors of the Sātavāhanas*, 1939, pp. 354ff.
3. Verses 218-19.
4. Cf. Kane, *op. cit.*, Vol. II, p. 926.
5. *Ibid.*, Vol. IV, p. 606.
6. Ādi-khaṇḍa, 44.3; cf. *Matsya Purāṇa*, 107. 9-10.

particular emphasis on non-injury to living beings, encourages religious suicide called *sallekhanā*.[1]

The antiquity of the practice of religious suicide in India is suggested by an instance quoted by Alexander's historians. An Indian gymnosophist from Taxila, named Kalanos, who accompanied Alexander (336-323 B.C.), is stated to have burnt himself to death on a funeral pyre at Sousa, when at the age of 70 he was afflicted with a malady that made his life a burden.[2] According to Strabo, another Indian gymnosophist of Broach, named Zarmanochegas, who accompanied an embassy to Augusts Caesar (27 B.C.-14 A.D.), at Athens consigned himself to flames.[3] The seventh century Chinese pilgrim Hiuen-tsang speaks of religious suicide committed by Indians at Prayāga or Allahābād.[4] About 1030 A.D., the celebrated Muslim savant Al-Bīrūnī says that religious suicide "was resorted to by those who are tired of life, who are distressed over some incurable disease, some irremovable bodily defect or old age or infirmity". He further observes, "This, however, no man of distinction does, but only Vaiśyas and Śūdras. Burning oneself is forbidden to Brāhmaṇas and Kṣatriyas by a special law. Therefore, these, if they want to kill themselves, do so at the time of an eclipse in some other manner or they hire somebody to drown them in the Ganges."[5] According to the '*Ain-i-Akbarī*, the Hindus committed religious suicide in the following ways—(1) starving, (2) burning oneself in cowdung-fire, (3) burying oneself in snow, (4) drowning oneself at the Gaṅgā-sāgara-saṅgama, and (5) killing oneself at Allahābād.[6]

An interesting fact can be deduced from what has been said above about the ancient Indians' attitude towards suicide. The act of suicide seems to have been mainly governed by certain social regulations and the king's court had probably little to do with it. It has to be noticed that no fines, etc., have been prescribed by the authorities quoted above for the

1. Kane, *op. cit.*, Vol. II, pp. 927-28.
2. Majumdar, *The Classical Accounts of India*, pp. 187, 200-01.
3. *Ibid.*, pp. 282, 452.
4. Beal, *Buddhist Records of the Western World*, Vol. I, pp. 232-34.
5. Sachau, *Alberuni's India*, Vol. II, p. 170.
6. See Kane, *op. cit.*, Vol. IV, p. 605, note 1373.

commission of suicide. But the fact cannot be ignored that India is a vast country. The customs relating to suicide and the degree of its popularity, especially of the particular methods of self-immolation, could not have been the same in all parts of the country. Moreover in ancient India, there was often little distinction between the functioning of law within the jurisdiction of the society and that of the court. That suicide of various kinds was usually not an offence recognisable by ancient Indian courts, seems to be suggested by the fact that, according to Kalhaṇa's *Rājataraṅgiṇī*, any Brāhmaṇa of ancient Kashmir was entitled to begin a fast to death at the gate of the royal residence in order to force the king to try his case speedily and that there was a class of royal officers called *Prāyopaveś-ādhikṛta*, i.e. superintendent of suicide by fast [in the royal palace].[1] At least one authority of antiquity, however, makes a distinction between the punishment a person, attempting to commit suicide, should receive at the king's court and that he should suffer socially. This is Yama[2] who prescribes that, when a person attempting to commit suicide, by such methods as hanging, dies, his body should be smeared with impure things, but that, if he lives, he should be fined 200 Paṇas. According to this authority, that person's friends and sons should each be fined one Paṇa and then they should undergo the penance prescribed by the *śāstras*.

P. V. Kane, author of the *History of Dharmaśāstra*, has grouped the types of suicide, allowed by various authorities, under the following heads :

(1) suicide in different ways as a *Prāyaścitta* for those who are guilty of any of the *Mahāpātakas*, viz. murder of a Brāhmaṇa, drinking wine, theft and incest ;

(2) setting out on the *Mahāprasthāna* by a hermit suffering from incurable diseases and unable to perform the duties of his order;

(3) suicide committed by old men or those who cannot observe the rules of physical purification or who are so ill that their recovery is not expected, by killing themselves by falling from a precipice or in fire or by

1. VI. 14.
2. 20-21.

drowning or fasting or starting on the *Mahāprasthāna* in the Himalayas or by jumping from a branch of the *Akṣaya-vaṭa* at Prayāga;

(4) suicide committed by householders in the ways stated in No. 3 above if their lives' work is done, if they have no desire for worldly pleasures and do not desire to live or if they are *Vedāntins* and are convinced of the ephemeral nature of life;

(5) religious suicide at the confluence of the Gaṅgā and the Yamunā at Prayāga and under the *Vaṭa* there and also at various other holy places; and

(6) *Satī* committed by wives by means of *Sahamaraṇa*, *Sahagamana* or *Anvārohaṇa* (burning oneself with the husband's dead body) and *Anugamana* (burning oneself on hearing the news of the husband's death).[1]

Among the holy places (especially the waters of particular rivers) commended for religious suicide, Prayāga or Allahābād is often mentioned in ancient Indian works including the Vanaparvan of the *Mahābhārata*. The great poet Kālidāsa, who flourished in the 4th and 5th centuries A.D., believed that people, killing themselves at Prayāga or under the *Vaṭa* tree there, became free from the cycle of births and deaths.[2] The *Kūrma Purāṇa*[3] prescribes suicide in the Ganges especially at the Gaṅgā-Yamunā-saṅgama at Prayāga and at Vārāṇasī. The *Padma Purāṇa*[4] similarly says, "One who dies in the Gaṅgā, knowingly or unknowingly, wilfully or unintentionally, secures heaven and salvation on death." The Śalya-parvan[5] commends Pṛthūdaka (modern Pehoa or Pehava on the northern bank of the Sarasvatī) and the *Matsya Purāṇa*[6] the holy *tīrtha* of Amarakaṇṭaka, the source of the Narmadā and the Mahānadī. The *Padma Purāṇa* similarly commends suicide in the waters of the Narmadā and the Kāverī.[7] The *Brahma Purāṇa*[8] calls upon Brāhmaṇas to secure salvation by suicide at Puruṣottama-

1. Vol. IV, pp. 604-05.
2. *Raghu.*, VIII. 94.
3. I.32.22; I.37.16,39.
4. Sṛṣṭi-khaṇḍa, 60.65.
5. Ch. 39, verses 33-34.
6. Ch. 186, verses 34-35.
7. Ādi-khaṇḍa, 16. 14-15.
8. 177-25; cf. 68.75, and 177.16-17.

kṣetra or Purī. The *Liṅga Purāṇa*[1] says that Śrīśaila is as efficacious for religious suicide as Avimukta or Vārāṇasī. As we shall see below, an interesting verse attributed to the *Kūrma Purāṇa* says that salvation is attained on death in the waters of any part of the Ganges, that at Vārāṇasī it is attained on death in the waters as well as on the banks of the river and that at Gaṅgā-sāgara-saṅgama it is attained on death in the waters, on the banks, and even in the air. It seems that originally religious suicide in the waters of the Ganges (at Prayāga, Vārāṇasī and Gaṅgāsāgara) was popular, but that the popularity of the custom was later extended to other rivers and holy places.

There are many instances of religious suicide quoted in early literary and epigraphic records. The story of the Ikṣvāku king Rāma drowning himself with his followers in the waters of the Sarayū is well-known.[2] We shall see below how the later Gupta king Kumāragupta (sixth century A.D.) is stated to have died at Prayāga either in the waters or in cowdung-cake fire, how Candella Dhaṅga (*circa* 950-1002 A.D.) is known to have committed suicide in the waters of the Gaṅgā-Yamunā-saṅgama and Kalacuri Gāṅgeyadeva Vikramāditya (*circa* 1015-41 A.D.) committed suicide under the *Akṣaya-vaṭa* at the same place. We shall also see how, according to Bilhaṇa's *Vikramāṅkadevacarita*, the Cālukya king Someśvara I Āhavamalla (1943-68 A.D.) committed suicide in the waters of the Tuṅgabhadrā.

There are similar instances of *Satī* in early literary and epigraphic records. Alexander's historians refer to a case of *Satī* committed in North-West India in the 4th century B.C.[3] The story of Mādrī burning herself on the funeral pyre of her husband Pāṇḍu as given in the *Mahābhārata* is well known.[4] The Nanduru (Guntur District, Andhra Pradesh) earthen pot inscription of the third century A.D. seems to record one of the earliest instances of *Satī* committed by an ordinary householder's wife.[5] The Eran (Saugor District, Madhya-Pradesh)

1. I. 92. 168-69.
2. *Rām.*, VII. 110.
3. Strabo (XV. 1.30 and 62) refers to the practice among the Kathaean people. See Majumdar, *op. cit.*, p. 259.
4. *Mahā.*, I. 95.65; cf. I. 125.31.
5. Sircar, *Stud. Soc. Adm. Anc. Med. Ind.*, Vol. I, pp. 210ff.

inscription speaks of the *Satī* committed by the queen of a Central Indian ruler named Goparāja in 510 A.D.[1]

In the late medieval period some sort of revulsion of feeling against religious suicide was gradually developing in some sections of writers in various parts of India. This is not only evident from the fact referred to above that *Mahāprasthāna* and suicide, prescribed for old men, by falling into fire or from a precipice, were regarded by many authors as *Kalivarjya*,[2] but also by the attempt of authors like Nīlakaṇṭha, commentator on the *Mahābhārata*, to explain verses prescribing religious suicide, in a different way.[3] In his *Tristhalīsetu*, Nārāyaṇa-bhaṭṭa says that no one has authority to commit suicide at Prayāga after abandoning one's old parents, young wife and children requiring support, nor should a woman, who is pregnant or who has young children or who has no permission from her husband, commit suicide at that place.[4] A section of the late *Nāradīya Purāṇa* similarly says that a woman should not burn herself on the funeral pyre of her husband, if she has young children or is pregnant or has not attained puberty or is in her monthly sickness at the time.[5] Although some medieval digests allow religious suicide for people of all communities, the *Tīrthaprakāśa* (part of Mitramiśra's *Vīramitrodaya*, first quarter of the 17th century) confines it to non-Brāhmaṇas only.[6] But in Eastern India, the customs of *Satī* and *Gaṅgāyātrā* (i.e. travel of old men to the banks of the Ganges to breathe their last in its waters) became even more popular in the late medieval period. Hook-swinging on the occasion of the *Caḍaka-pūjā* became another form of self-torture popular in the eastern part of the country during the age in question.

The British Government, established over wide regions of India about the last quarter of the 18th century, assumed in the beginning a policy of strict neutrality in the religious and social matters of the Indian people. Soon, however, this policy of benevolent neutrality came into conflict with the

1. Sircar, *Select Inscriptions*, Vol. I, 1965 ed., pp. 345-46.
2. Kane, *op. cit.*, Vol. II, p. 939; Vol IV, p. 608.
3. On Vana-parvan, 85.83.
4. Cf. Kane, *op. cit.*, Vol. IV, p. 609.
5. I. 7. 52-53.
6. Cf. Kane, *loc. cit.*

humane and pregressive ideas which animated liberal Englishmen working in the administration of the country. Consideration of humanity impelled them to co-operate with a gradually developing school of Indian reformers to remove the evils including those discussed above, which prevailed in Hindu society under the sanction of religion and usage. The famous Regulation XIII declaring the *Satī*, one of the most horrible of such practices, illegal and punishable by courts, was passed on the 4th December, 1829.

II

In the *Indian Historical Quarterly*, Vol. X, June, 1934, pp. 322-31, B.C. Sen edited the Sundarban (Rakshaskhali) copper-plate grant, dated Śaka 1118, belonging to a ruler of Southern Bengal, whose name was read as śrī-Maḍommanapāla. In the *Indian Culture*, Vol. I, April, 1935, pp. 679-82, we made an attempt to improve upon the reading and interpretation of the record as published by Sen and suggested *inter alia* that the name of the ruler was very probably śrīmaḍ-Ḍommanapāla. This suggestion and some others were later supported by R.C. Majumdar in the *History of Bengal*, Dacca University, Vol. I, p. 222, note, The inscription was re-edited by R. K. Ghoshal in the *Epigraphia Indica*, Vol. XXVII, pp. 119ff., where some of our views were commented upon, while some of them were accepted.

As regards the name of the ruler in question, Ghoshal seems to be inclined to prefer Maḍommanapāla to Ḍommanapāla suggested by us. In this, he apparently ignores the important fact that a name like Maḍommana is not known to have been borne by any Indian in any period of history, while Ḍomana (no doubt the same as Ḍommana) is a fairly popular name even now in Bengal and the neighbouring regions.[1] That the name was popular among the Vaidyas of Bengal also in early times is proved by the mention of Ḍomanadāsa in Bharatamallika's *Candraprabhā* (Śaka 1597) and of Ḍamanasena (the same as Ḍomana°) in Kavikaṇṭhahāra's *Sadvaidygkula-pañjikā* (Śaka 1575) as the ancestors respectively of the Dāsas

1. Cf. *Ind. Cult.*, Vol. II, p. 152.

and the Senas among the Vaidyas.[1] Another interesting fact is that the name Ḍommana = Ḍomana = Ḍamana may be of South Indian origin as we have the name Dommana (probably a variant of Ḍommana) in the southern records; cf. the Mangallu grant[2] of the Eastern Cālukya king Amma II (*circa* 945-70 A.D.) and the Dibbida plates[3] (Śaka 1191) of the Matsya chief Arjuna. As regards the South Indian association of the Bengal Vaidyas, among whom the name Ḍomana = Ḍamana is found to have been popular even during the medieval period, we have elsewhere[4] observed, "The present day Ambaṣṭhas of the Tamil land and Malabar (their early distribution in South India may have been wider) appear to be referred to as Vaidya in inscriptions dating from the seventh century.[5] Their entry into Bengal during the rule of the Senas, hailing from Karṇāṭa or the Kanarese country of the Deccan, is very probable, as the Senas of Bengal must have patronized South Indians in the same way as the Muslim rulers of India entertained Musalmans of other countries at their courts. It is thus very probable that the crystallization of the professional community of the Vaidyas or physicians of Bengal into a caste was a result of their amalgamation with the tribal Ambaṣṭha-Vaidyas of Southern India. This seems to have been the background on which the theory identifying the Vaidyas with the Ambaṣṭhas of early Indian literature (Manu calling them physicians) was fabricated in the late medieval

1. *Candraprabhā*, Calcutta, B. S. 1299, p. 19 : *Ḍomanaḥ Pāla-jāmātā Vaidyaḥ Pālo na vidyate | vaṁśyo Ḍomanadāsasya Vāmanaḥ kulavān katham || iti cintā na kartavyā Vāmane bahavaḥ guṇāḥ ||* This Ḍomanadāsa was one of the ancestors of the Kulīna Dāsas in the Vaidya community of Bengal. According to the *Sadvaidyakulapañjikā*, Ḍamanasena was the grandson's great-grandson of Vināyaka whom tradition assigns to the age of Ballālasena (*circa* 1158-79 A.D.). Ḍamanasena of the *Sadvaidyakulapañjikā* is called Ḍomanasena in the *Candraprabhā* (p. 69). For the great popularity of the name Ḍomana among the Vaidyas, see *Candraprabhā*, pp. 27, 69, 129, 212, 218, 233, 319, 334, 359.

2. *An. Rep. S. Ind. Ep.*, 1917, Part II, para. 24.

3. *Ep. Ind.*, Vol. V, p. 111.

4. *JRASB*, Letters, Vol. XIV, p. 106, note 2.

5. *Ep. Ind.*, Vols. IX, p. 101; VIII, pp. 317-21; XVII, pp. 291 ff.; *Ind. Ant.*, 1893, pp. 57f.

period."[1] It may be added that the Senas themselves came to be regarded as Vaidyas in the Vaidya Kula-pañjikās.[2] Since Ḍommanapāla bore a name that may have been South Indian in origin, was a subordinate apparently of the South Indian Senas and used the Śaka era which was popular in the South and seems to have been popularised in Bengal by the Senas, I suggested that his family may have originally belonged to South India; but this has been regarded by Ghoshal as "the absurdity of Dr. Sircar's persistent and curious Southern complexes".

King Ḍommanapāla made the grant in question when he was *svīya-mukti-bhūmau Dvārahaṭāke*, i.e., at Dvārahaṭāka which was his *mukti-bhūmi*.[3] Ghoshal interprets the expression *mukti-bhūmi* as 'the place of initiation', without any regard to Sanskrit lexicons, and says, "Dr. D. C. Sircar asked if this term indicated Maḍommanapāla's imminent death!" His use of the note of exclamation clearly indicates that he discovered here another of my 'absurdities'. But *mukti-bhūmi* is apparently the same as the well-known *mukti-kṣetra* which is often used as an epithet of holy places and means 'a place where salvation is attainable on death'. That the Indian kings regarded death at a *tīrtha* as especially meritorious is definitely known from numerous sources including Varāhamihira's *Bṛhatsaṁhitā*, Ch. 68, verses 19 :

bhuktvā samyag=vasudhāṁ śauryeṇ=opājitām=aśīty-abdaḥ |
tīrthe prāṇāṁs=tyaktvā bhadro dev-ālayaṁ yāti ||

In connection with the merits of religious suicide which

1. See *JRASB*, Vol. XIV, 1948, p. 106, note 2; also *JUPHS*, Vol. XVIII, pp 148-61; Sircar, *Stud. Soc. Adm. Anc. Med. Ind.*, Vol. I, pp. 104ff. The village Vaidyas in South India are barbers.

2. Cf. *Sadvaidyakulapañjikā*, Dacca, B.S. 1292, pp. 1-2 : *purā Vaidya-kul-odbhūta-Ballālena mah-aujasā*. It is interesting to note that, like Ḍomana, the typical Southern name Ballāla was extremely popular among the Vaidyas of Bengal. Cf. *Candraprabhā*, pp. 48, 126, 141, 151, 175, 176, 184, 189, 212, 225, 238, 264, 319, 331, 332, 335, 338, 362, 403, 420.

3. Dvārahaṭāka was not the capital of Ḍommanapāla as, in that case, the charter would have been probably issued from there. Similar mention of the place from where a grant (recorded in a charter issued from the capital) was made by a king is also found in other records. The Nagari plates (*Ep. Ind.*, Vol. XXVIII, pp. 235ff.) of Anaṅgabhīma III, e.g., say that the Gaṅga king made certain grants when he was at *Abhinava-Vārāṇasyāṁ bhagavataḥ Puruṣottamasya sannidhau*.

was popular with most classes of Indians in the medieval period, the importance of the holy waters of the Gaṅgā and other rivers is often specially mentioned. The *Śabdakalpadruma* (s.v. *gaṅgā*), e.g., quotes the following verses from the *Kūrma Purāṇa* :

Gaṅgāyāṁ jñānato mṛtvā muktim=āpnoti mānavaḥ |
a-jñānād=brahma-lokañ=ca yāti n=āsty=atra saṁśayaḥ ||
Gaṅgāyāṁ ca jale mokṣo Vārāṇasyāṁ jale sthale |
antarikṣe ca Gaṅgāyāṁ Gaṅgā-sāgara-saṅgame ||

The practice of *Gaṅgā-yātrā* (i.e. going to the bank of the Gaṅgā with a view to die and to go to heaven as a result of such a meritorious death) is well known in Bengal even today.[1] The prevalence of the same custom also in other parts of India is indicated by P. Thomas who observes, "........ old people, on the point of death, make long journeys to Banaras or some other sacred city on the banks of the Ganges so that they may wash their sins away in the sacred stream or die in the waters. A dying man is often carried by his relatives to the Ganges and is held immersed knee-deep in the waters of the river. The banks of the Ganges at Banaras are as sacred as the Ganges itself and people of the neighbourhood who fall sick and are not expected to survive, are made to live in huts on the banks of the river till they die."[2] The celebrated Abbé Dubois also points to the custom as well as similar others when he asks. "......how shamelessly they violate nature by placing the sick, whose recovery is despaired of, on the banks of the Ganges, or of some other so-called holy river, so that they may be drowned by the floods or devoured by crocodiles ? Have they ever attempted to restrain the frenzy of those fanatics who, in their mistaken devotion, foolishly allow themselves to be crushed under the wheels of the car of their idols, or throw themselves headlong into the stream at the junction of the Ganges and the Jumna ?"[3] Now Ḍommanapāla's plate was found on the small island of Rakshaskhali on the southern seaboard of West Bengal only about 12 miles due east of the

1. The great popularity of the practice as late as the nineteenth century is clearly demonstrated by the newspapers of those days. Cf. B. N. Banerji, *Saṁvādpatre Sekāler Kathā*, Vol. I (B. S. 1344), p. 150; Vol. II (B. S. 1348), pp. 535-36.

2. *Hindu Religion, Customs and Manners*, p. 93.

3. *Hindu Manners, Customs and Ceremonies*, trans. Beauchamp, 3rd ed., p. 606.

celebrated *tirtha* of Gaṅgā-sāgara-saṅgama at the mouth of the river Bhāgīrathī or Gaṅgā popularly called Hooghly. We have seen how salvation was regarded as the result of death in the waters of the Gaṅgā at any place, how the same was believed to be obtained from death at Vārāṇasī either in the waters of the Gaṅgā or on its banks and how death not only in the waters and on the banks of the Gaṅgā but also in the air at Gaṅgā-sāgara-saṅgama was regarded as equally meritorious. That the locality of Dvārahaṭāka lay probably in the vicinity of the Gaṅgā as well as of Gaṅgā-sāgara-saṅgama seems to be indicated by the discovery of the plate in the neighbourhood and by the fact that Dvārahaṭāka is said to have been situated in the small district of Pūrva-Khāṭikā or the Eastern Khāḍi which was bounded on the west by the lower course of the Gaṅgā.[1] The second part of the name Dvārahaṭāka is the same as Sanskrit *haṭṭaka*, modern °*hāṭā* which is the common name-ending of many localities; but whether the first word in the name of our locality indicates one of the 'doors' or mouths through which the Gaṅgā flows into the sea and actually refers to a locality within the Gaṅgā-sāgara-saṅgama area cannot be determined in the present state of our knowledge.[2] There is, however, hardly any absurdity in the suggestion that Ḍommanapāla went to Dvārahaṭāka with a view to dying in the waters of the Gaṅgā for attaining salvation and made the grant in question on that sacred occasion. In that case only is the epithet *svīya-mukti-bhūmi*, applied to the locality, easily explan-

1. *History of Bengal*, Dacca University, Vol. I, pp. 25-26.

2. There is a place called Dwarahat in the Almora District, Uttar Pradesh. The *Candraprabhā* (pp. 145, 155, 185, 192, 309, etc.) mentions Dvārahaṭṭa as a seat of the Bengal Vaidyas. J.N. Gupta identifies this place with Dwarhata near Haripal in the Hooghly District of West Bengal. It may be noted that, though the word *dvāra* in the sense of the mouth of a river is not generally found in the Sanskrit lexicons and the name Gaṅgā-dvāra is applied to Hardwar where the Gaṅgā enters into the plains from the Himalayas, the Lunsadi copper-plate inscription (*Ep. Ind.*, Vol. IV, pp. 74ff.) of 668-69 A.D. appears to use the word in the said sense. It records the gift of some land in a village situated at the Madhumatī-dvāra which has been interpreted as 'the mouth of the river Madhumatī (i.e. the modern Nikol Creek)'. The localities mentioned in the enumeration of the boundary of the gift land support the said interpretation of the word *dvāra*. In Tamil, the expression *mukta-dvāra* means the mouth of a river especially where it falls into the sea (*Ep. Ind.*, Vol. XXXV, pp. 98-99).

able. I do not see how it can be interpreted in any other equally satisfactory way.

Of kings ending their lives in the waters of the holy rivers we have the well-known instances of Candella Dhaṅga (c. 950-1002 A.D.), who committed suicide in the Triveṇī at Prayāga (Allahābād),[1] and Cālukya Someśvara I Āhavamalla (1043-68 A.D.) who drowned himself in the waters of the Tuṅgabhadrā described as 'the Gaṅgā of Dakṣiṇāpatha'.[2] According to Bilhaṇa's *Vikramāṅkadevacarita*, the Cālukya king's proposal to end his life in the Tuṅgabhadrā was hailed by his ministers as a right act, and the king made grants of a heap of gold before entering into the waters. On the authority of Hindu scriptures, Colebrooke speaks of the custom of making gifts by a dying man as he says, "When at the point of death, donation of cattle, land, gold, silver or other things, according to his ability, should be made by him, or, if he be too weak, by another person in his name."[3] There is thus no absurdity in Ḍommanapāla granting a village on a similar occasion.

Verse 12 of the Jabalpur inscription[4] of Yaśaḥkarṇa says that Kalacuri Gāṅgeyadeva Vikramāditya (*circa* 1015-41 A.D.)

1. Cf. *Ep. Ind.*, Vol. I, p. 146 (Khajuraho inscription, verse 55) : *Rakṣitvā kṣitim=ambu-rāśi-rasanām=etām=anany-āyatiṁ jīvitvā śaradāṁ śataṁ samadhikaṁ śrī-Dhaṅga-pṛthvīpatiḥ | Rudraṁ mudrita-locanaḥ sa hṛdaye dhyāyan japan Jāhnavī-Kālindyoḥ salile kalevara-parityāgād=agān=nirvṛtim.* For religious suicide at Prayāga, see *JUPHS*, Vol. X, 1937, pp. 65ff. See also Kane, *History of Dharmaśāstra*, Vol. IV, pp. 604-13, on such suicides, and above, pp. 206ff.

2. *Vikramāṅkadevacarita*, Canto IV, verses 59-68: *utsaṅge Tuṅgabhadrāyās=tad=eṣa Śiva-cintayā | vāñchāmy=ahaṁ nirākartuṁ deha-graha-viḍambanam || yāto=’yam=upakārāya kāyaḥ Śrīkaṇṭha-sevayā | kṛtaghna-vratam=etasya yatra tatra visarjjanam || tath=eti vacanaṁ rājñaḥ pratyapadyanta mantrinaḥ | ucit-ācaraṇe keṣāṁ n=otsāha-caturaṁ manaḥ || ataḥ katipayair=eva prayāṇaiḥ pranayi-priyaḥ | tāṁ kṣoṇīpatir=adrākṣid=Dakṣiṇāpatha-Jāhnavīm || Tuṅgabhadrā narendreṇa ten=āmanyata māninā | taraṅga-hastair=utkṣipya kṣipant=īv=endra-mandire || uddaṇḍā tena diṇḍire piṇḍa-paṅktir=adṛśyata | vimāna-haṁsa-māl=eva prahitā padma-sadmanā || atidūraṁ samutplutya nipatadbhiḥ saśikaraiḥ | arājata dharā-candraḥ pratyudgata iva grahaiḥ || tair=avatīrya dhaureyo dhīrāṇāṁ dharaṇī-patiḥ | snātvā Caṇḍīśa-caraṇa-dvandva-cintā-paro=’bhavat || adatta c=āparicchinnam=akhinnaḥ kāñcan-otkaram | na kṛcchre=’pi mahābhāgās=tyāga-vrata-parāṅmukhāḥ || praviśya kaṇṭha-daghne=’tha sarit-toye jagāma saḥ | kallola-tūrya-nirghoṣaiś=Candracūḍāmaṇeḥ purīm ||*

3. *Miscellaneous Essays*, Vol. I, p. 155.

4. *Ep. Ind.*, Vol. II, p. 4 : *prāpte Prayāga-vaṭa-mūla-niveśa-bandhau sārdhaṁ śatena gṛhiṇībhir=amutra muktim.*

attained *mukti*, i.e., committed religious suicide, at Prayāga together with his hundred wives. Prayāga was thus the *mukti-bhūmi* of Gāṅgeya and those of his queens who died with their husband. The *Adbhutasāgara*[1] states how king Ballālasena of Bengal gave numerous gifts at the time of committing religious suicide, together with his queens, in the waters of the Gaṅgā. King Kalaśa (1063-89 A.D.) of Kashmir, "knowing, in his helpless condition, that his life was about to escape, hurried to proceed to a *tīrtha* to die", and there he dedicated a gold image of the god worshipped at the place.[2]

Ghoshal's explanation of the expression *ratna-traya*, which not only occurs in the present record and the Manahali plate of Madanapāla, as pointed out by him, but also in such other inscriptions as the Ashrafpur plate (B)[3] of the Khaḍgas, the Kailan (or Kailain) plate of Śrīdhāraṇarāta[4] and the Tipperah plate[5] of Bhavadeva, is clearly wrong. It can neither be "right over the wealth [deposited underground]", as suggested by Ghoshal, nor "a tax levied for the maintenance and upkeep of big Buddhist establishments", as suggested by others and referred to by him. *Ratna-traya* means primarily a Buddhist religious establishment symbolising the Buddhist trinity, viz., the Buddha, Dharma, and Saṅgha, worshipped there.[6] There are instances of kings granting land in favour of the *ratna-traya*. Thus the expression *ratnatraya-bahiḥ* of Ḍommanapāla's inscription means to say that the village in question was granted with the exclusion of the area around the Buddhist establishment in it or, better, the area in the possession of a Buddhist establishment. Similarly, *ratnatraya-rājasambhoga-varjita* of the Manahali plate means "excluding lands enjoyed by the Buddhist establishment and those belonging to the king's *Khās Mahāl*".

1. Cf. Ojha, *Palaeography of India* (Hindi), 1918, p. 184, note 2: *nānā-dāna-cit-āmbu-saṁcalanataḥ Sūryātmajā-saṅgamaṁ Gaṅgāyāṁ viracayya nirjara-puraṁ bhāry-ānuyāto gataḥ*. Cf. N.G. Majumdar, *Inscriptions of Bengal*, Vol. III. p. 147. The expression *nirjara-puraṁ gataḥ* means 'gone to heaven (i.e. died)'. It is therefore strange that some scholars speak of Ballālasena's retirement 'alongwith his queens to a place called Nirjarapura on the Triveṇī' (*The Struggle for Empire*, ed. Majumdar, p. 38).

2. *Rājataraṅgiṇī*, VII. 708, 715.

3. *Memoirs of the Asiatic Society of Bengal*, Vol. I, p. 90.

4. *IHQ*, Vol. XXIII, p. 235.

5. *Journal of the Asiatic Society*, Letters, Vol. XVII, p. 88.

6. Cf. N. G. Majumdar, *A Guide to Sculptures in the Indian Museum*, Part II, pp. 74-75.

CHAPTER XIV

ARDHANĀRĪ-NĀRĀYAṆA

An interesting conception of Lakṣmī-Nārāyaṇa is noticed in the Gaya Śītalā temple inscription of the local ruler Yakṣapāla who flourished in the latter half of the eleventh century A.D.[1] Verse 12 of this epigraph runs as follows—

Maunāditya-Sahasraliṅga-Kamalārdhāṅgīna-Nārāyaṇa-
-dvā-Someśvara-Phalgunātha-Vijayādity-āhvayānāṁ kṛtī |
sa prāsādam=acīkarad=diviṣadām Kedāreśvarasya ca
khyātasy=Ottaramānasasya khananaṁ sattraṁ Vaṭe c=ākṣaye ||

The stanza says that Yakṣapāla excavated (or re-excavated) the Uttaramānasa tank and established a *sattra* (free feeding centre) near the Akṣaya-vaṭa and also raised a temple for the following gods— (1) Maunāditya (Sun-god), (2) Sahasraliṅga (Śiva), (3) Kamalārdhāṅgīna-Nārāyaṇa, (4) the two gods called Someśvara (Śiva), (5) Phalgunātha (probably Viṣṇu), (6) Vijayāditya (Sun-god) and (7) Kedāreśvara (Śiva). It appears that the gods had been installed for worship by various persons, and Yakṣapāla built a temple for accommodating all of them.

The third name in the list of deities for whom the temple was built by Yakṣapāla is interesting, because Kamalārdhāṅgīna-Nārāyaṇa means 'Nārāyaṇa, one half of whose body is Kamalā (Lakṣmī)'.[2] The conception of such a combined form of Lakṣmī and Nārāyaṇa was doubtless imitated from the well-known Ardhanārīśvara form of Śiva, in which the right half represents Śiva and the left his consort Pārvatī.[3] This combined form of Lakṣmī-Nārāyaṇa has not been clearly traced in the Purāṇas, though Yakṣapāla's inscription proves its prevalence in Eastern India in the eleventh century A.D.

Recently P. Pal has drawn our attention to the combined form of Lakṣmī and Nārāyaṇa in a bronze sculpture and in a *paṭa*, both from Nepal, as well as in a *dhyāna* quoted in

1. *Ep. Ind.*, Vol. XXXVI, pp. 92 ff.
2. *Ibid.*, p. 92.
3. Ardhanārīśvara first occurs on Kaniṣka's coin and a Mathurā miniature relief. Bardesanes (c. 154-222 A.D.) learnt about it from an Indian embassy visiting Syria. See *Prācyavidyā-taraṅgiṇī*, ed. Sircar, pp. 218 ff.; *JAS*, Vol. IX, 1967, p. 181.

the *Tantrasāra*.[1] But the sculpture and painting have been assigned to the thirteenth century A.D. and the *dhyāna* stanza may be of a still later date. The image referred to in our inscription, which is earlier than the specimens alluded to by Pal, was under worship at Gaya in Bihar, so that the conception does not appear to have originated in Nepal, but was imported from East India to that land. From this point of view, the reference to the combined deity in the Śītalā temple inscription is of considerable importance. The prevalence of the worship of the said deity in Eastern India is also suggested by the *dhyāna* in the *Tantrasāra* which was compiled by the Bengali Tāntric named Kṛṣṇānanda Āgamavāgīśa in the seventeenth century.[2] In this connection, it may be mentioned that the *Brahmavaivarta Purāṇa* seems to refer to a form of Viṣṇu's consort, the left half of which represented Mahālakṣmī and the right half Rādhā, and also to one of Viṣṇu having two arms on the right side and four arms on the left.[3] The latter may be a combined image, the left half being the wife of the right half. No specimen of such images, however, seems to be known.

The Nepalese bronze image is now preserved in the Museum für Volkerkunde at Basel in Switzerland while the Nepalese *paṭa* is at present in the collection of the Ramakrishna Mission Institute of Culture, Calcutta. In the sculpture, the eight-armed composite deity, with its right half represented as male and left half as female exactly as in the Ardhanārīśvara form of Śiva and Pārvatī, stands in the *sama-pada* posture on a double-petalled lotus pedestal. While the plain diaphanous garment clings to the right leg, the left leg is draped in cloth with a floral design. The necklace, waist-band and anklets are common to both halves of the body; but the right ear is adorned with a *kuṇḍala* and the four right arms with *aṅgada*, while the left ear has a large ring and the four left arms have ornaments of a type different from that of those on the right

1. *Journ. As. Soc.*, Vol. V, 1963, pp. 73 ff.
2. See Sircar, *The Śākta Pīṭhas*, pp. 74 ff.
3. Prakṛti-khaṇḍa, XXXV. 10-12—
tad-vām-āṁśo Mahālakṣmīr=dakṣiṇ-āṁśaś=ca Rādhikā /...
Kṛṣṇas=tad=gauraveṇ=aiva dvidhā-rūpo babhūva ha //
dakṣiṇ-āṁśaś=ca dvibhujo vām-āṁśaś=ca caturbhujaḥ /

arms. As regards the attributes, the right hands bear respectively *cakra* (discus), *gadā* (mace), *śaṅkha* (conch-shell) and lotus-mark, and the left hands, likewise, the *pustaka* (manuscript), *darpaṇa* (mirror) and *kalasa* (water-vessel), the fourth left arm being broken.

In the *paṭa*, the central eight-armed figure of the *maṇḍala* is white and stands in the *samapada-sthānaka* pose on a double-petalled lotus in a shrine. The right half of the figure is male, the left half being female and having the feminine breast indicated by a large circle. The right leg is covered to the knee only; but the left leg is covered down to the ankle. Near the right foot of the figure is Garuḍa and near the left foot is what is described as *kūrma* (tortoise). The attributes in the four right hands are respectively—(1) *cakra*, (2) *śaṅkha*, (3) *gadā* and (4) *padma*, while those respectively in the left hands are—(1) *pustaka*, (2) *utpala*, (3) *darpaṇa* and (4) *kalasa*.

An epigraph at the bottom of the *paṭa*, dated in Nepālavarṣa 383, Kārttika-śu-di 11 (4th November, 1261 A.D.), begins as follows—

Oṁ namo Bhagavate Vāsudevāya ||
Hima-kund-endu-sadṛśaṁ padma-kaumodakī-punaḥ(dharam) |
śaṅkha-cakra-dharaṁ daṇḍa(bimbaṁ) vāme ca kalasaṁ tathā |
darpaṇam=utpalaṁ vidyā Vaiṣṇavaṁ Kamal-ānvitam |
pātu daitya-nirākāra trāhi nāṁ(māṁ) Puruṣottamaḥ(ma) ||

The *dhyāna* quoted in the epigraph seems to represent the figure as a Vaiṣṇava (Viṣṇu) image united with Kamalā and describes it as Puruṣottama, also called *Bhagavat* Vāsudeva in the introductory *maṅgala*. The figure is described as white and as bearing the attributes *padma*, *kaumodakī* (Viṣṇu's mace), *śaṅkha* and *cakra* (in the right hands) and in the left—*kalasa*, *darpaṇa*, *utpala* and *vidyā* (manuscript).

The *Tantrasāra* stanza runs as follows—

Vidyuc-candra-nibhaṁ vapuḥ Kamalajā-Vaikuṇṭhayor=ekatāṁ
prāptaṁ sneha-rasena ratna-vilasad-bhūṣā-bhar-ālaṁkṛtam |
vidyā-paṅkaja-darpaṇān maṇimayaṁ kumbhaṁ sarojaṁ gadāṁ
śaṅkhaṁ cakram=amūni bibhrad=amitāṁ diśyāc=chriyaṁ vaḥ sadā ||

'Let the body of Kamalajā and Vaikuṇṭha, which resembles the lightening and the moon, bears a load of ornaments endowed with jewels, is united in love and holds *vidyā*, *paṅkaja*, *darpaṇa*, *maṇimaya-kumbha* (bejewlled jar), *saroja, gadā, śaṅkha* and *cakra*, bestow unlimited prosperity on you."

It appears, however, that the conception of the combined form of the god Viṣṇu and his consort was not confined to the eastern part of India. In a paper entitled 'Some Lakṣmī-Nārāyaṇa Images from Western India', published in the *Journal of Oriental Institute*, Vol. XIV, 1965, pp. 392-96, Sm. Kalpana S. Desai rightly points to the prevalence of the said conception on the strength of the following two stanzas in the *Śilparatna* (XXIII. 23, and XXV. 75)—

(1) *haste bibhrat sarasija-gadā-śaṅkha-cakrāṇi vidyāṁ*
padm-ādarśau kanaka-kalasaṁ megha-vidyud-vilāsam |
vām-ottuṅga-stanam=aviral-ākalpam=āśleṣa-lobhād=
ekībhūtaṁ vapur=avatu vaḥ Puṇḍarīkākṣa-Lakṣmyoḥ ||

(2) *cakraṁ vidyā-dara-ghaṭa-gadā-darpaṇān padma-yugmaṁ*
dorbhir=bibhrat suruciratarāṁ megha-vidyun-nibh-ābham |
gāḍh-otkaṇṭha-vivaśam=aniśaṁ Puṇḍarīkākṣa-Lakṣmyor=
ekībhūtaṁ vapur=avatu vaḥ pīta-kauśeya-kāntam ||

Both the stanzas speak of the *ekībhutaṁ vapuḥ* (the two bodies combined into one) of Puṇḍarīkākṣa (Viṣṇu) and Lakṣmī. The attributes in the eight hands of the two deities are given as—(1) lotus, mace, conch-shell and discus for the god, and (2) manuscript, lotus, looking glass and golden jar for the goddess. The second verse also mentions the same attributes for the combined form of the two deities.

L. K. Tripathi of Varanasi drew my attention to S. B. Deo's paper entitled 'Some Ardhanārī Forms of Viṣṇu' appearing in the *Bhāratī*, Varanasi, Vol. X-XI, 1966-68, pp. 125-33. Deo describes twelve late medieval icons representing the Ardhanārī forms of Viṣṇu in the Nārāyaṇa temple in the Svāthe area adjacent to the Sundarī Chowk at Lalit Patan (Nepal), which has been assigned to the beginning of the eighteenth century. The twelve images bear the following labels which do not appear to have any known textual support —(1) Keśava-Lakṣmī, (2) Nārāyaṇa-Sarasvatī, (3) Mādhava-Dāntī, (4) Govinda-Kānti, (5) Viṣṇu-Dāntī, (6) Madhusūdana-Vidhṛti, (7) Trivikarama-Aticchā, (8) Vāmana-Atipātī, (9) Śrīdhara-Dhṛti, (10) Hṛṣīkeśa-Mohinī, (11) Dāmodara-Matimā (?), and (12) Padmanābha-Dharmadā. The attributes in the hands of the god are the usual *śaṅkha*, *cakra*, *gadā* and *padma*, although differently arranged in the different cases. As regards the attributes in the hands of the goddess, besides the usual ones referred to above, sometimes *akṣamālā*, *puṣpamālā*, *kamaṇḍalu*, *cāmara*, *vyajana*, etc., have been mentioned. Of the four hands of Sarasvatī, two are broken, the other two holding manuscript and lotus bud.

Deo's contention that the Ardhanārī conception of Viṣṇu developed in Nepal during the medieval period, "for which no iconographical precedents can be had in India so far as the Viṣṇu forms are concerned" does not take into consideration all the evidence at our disposal and is wrong. His attempt to explain away the clear evidence of the *Śilparatna* is no doubt unfortunate.

In connection with the Nepalese *paṭa* discussed above, it may be pointed out that the tortoise as the vehicle or emblem of the goddess Lakṣmī in the *paṭa* does not appear to be known from early sources which generally represent the deity as standing or seated on the lotus.[1] In the modern mythology of Bengal and some other areas, Lakṣmī is said to have the Owl (*pecaka*, *ulūka*) as her *vāhana*.[2] In other respects also the figures do not quite conform to the prescription of old texts; cf. what Gopinatha Rao has said about the goddess : "The figure of Lakṣmī should have only two hands when she is by the side of Viṣṇu. But when she is worshipped in a separate temple, she should have four hands, and be seated upon a lotus of eight petals placed upon a *siṁhāsana*. In one of the two right hands she should hold a lotus with a long stalk and in the other a *bilva* fruit. The left hands should carry an *amṛtaghaṭa* (a pot containing ambrosia) and a *śaṅkha* respectively."[3] Of course this is what is known as the Gaja-lakṣmī,

1. Cf. *aravinda-sthitā* and *padm-āsana-sthā* in the following *dhyānas* quoted in the *Śabdakalpadruma*, s.v. *Lakṣmī*: *kāntyā Kāñcana-sannibhāṁ Himagiri-prakhyaiś=caturbhir=gajair=hast-otkṣipta-hiraṇmay-āmṛta-gaṭair=āsicyamānāṁ Śriyam / bibhrāṇāṁ varam=abja-yugmam=abhayaṁ hastaiḥ kirīṭ-ojjavalāṁ kṣaum-ābaddha-nitamba-bimba-lalitāṁ vande='ravinda-sthitām // Pāś-ākṣamālik-āmbhoja-śṛṇibhir=yāmya-saumyayoḥ / padm-āsanasthāṁ dhyāyec=ca Śriyaṁ trailokya-mātaram //*

2. The figure of Lakṣmī is now painted or made with that of an owl near her feet. Cf. *Foreigners in Ancient India and Lakṣmī and Sarasvatī in Art and Literature*, ed. Sircar, pp. 123, 192.

3. *Elements of Hindu Iconography*, Vol. I, Part II, p. 374.

i.e. Lakṣmī being bathed by two elephants from two sides holding water-jars in their trunks.

The manuscript, which seems to be unknown from early sources as an attribute of Lakṣmī, has been recognised by Pal as referring to the *jñāna* aspect of the goddess. He draws our attention to an image of Lakṣmī in the Vaṅgīya Sāhitya Praiṣad, which is known to hold a manuscript in one of the left hands,[1] to the *Viṣṇu Purāṇa* representing Lakṣmī as intellect,[2] and to the *Tantrasāra* stating that the Lakṣmī-kavaca ensures a person proficiency in all the branches of knowledge.[3] As we have seen, the *Śilparatna* (by Śrīkumāra who flourished in the sixteenth century, the work being originally written in the Malayalam script) mentions *vidyā* or manuscript apparently as one of the attributes of the goddess Lakṣmī.

This aspect of Lakṣmī takes her quite close to the goddess Sarasvatī who is usually conceived as *viṇā-pustaka-dhāriṇī*, i.e. holding the lute and the manuscript.[4] In East Indian mythology, Lakṣmī and Sarasvatī are the two wives of Viṣṇu[5] and

1. R. D. Banerji, *Eastern Indian School of Medieval Sculpture*, p. 211, plate LXII-a.

2. Wilson's trans., 1849, p. 60.

3. Cf. *vidy-ārthinā sadā sevyā viśeṣe Viṣṇu-vallabhā || asyāś=catur-akṣarī-Viṣṇu-vanitāyāḥ kavacasya śrī-Bhagavān Śiva ṛṣir=Anuṣṭup chando Vāgbhavī devatā Vāgbhavaṁ bījaṁ Lajjā Śaktiḥ Ramā kīlakaṁ kāmabīj-ātmakaṁ kavacaṁ mama sukavitva-supāṇḍitya-sarvasiddhi-samṛddhaye viniyogaḥ* || (Pal, *op. cit.*, p. 76).

4. *Devībhāgavata*, IX. 4. 46.

5. Cf. The well-known stanza—

Ekā bhāryā prakṛti-mukharā cañcalā ca dvitīyā
putro='py=eko bhuvana-vijayī Manmatho durnivāraḥ |
Śeṣaḥ śayyā śayanam=udad'.ir=vāhanaṁ Pannagāriḥ
smāraṁ smāraṁ sva-gṛha-caritaṁ dāru-bhūto Murāriḥ ||

See also *Ep. Ind.*, Vol. XII, p. 13, and note the combined Nārāyaṇa-Sarasvatī image referred to above. The *Devibhāgatata* (IX.6) and *Brahmavaivarta Purāṇa* (II.6), which are apparently East Indian products of medieval times, say how Lakṣmī, Sarasvatī and Gaṅgā were originally the wives of Hari (Viṣṇu) and how later Lakṣmī remained Hari's wife, but Gaṅgā and Sarasvatī became the wives respectively of Śiva and Brahman.

Cf. *Lakṣmīḥ Sarasvatī Gaṅgā tisro bhāryā Harer=api* |
premṇā samās=tās=tiṣṭhanti satataṁ Hari-sannidhau ||
(*Devībhāgavata*, IX.6.17)

Gaccha Gaṅge Śiva-sthānaṁ Brahma-sthānaṁ Sarasvati |
atra tiṣṭhatu mad-gehe suśilā Kamal-ālayā ||
(*ibid.*, IX.6.65)

they are now also regarded in the popular mythology of Bengal as sisters, both being the daughters of Śiva and Pārvatī,[1] even though their rivalry and quarrels are also proverbial. That there was a raprochement between the conceptions of Lakṣmī and Sarasvatī seems to be further indicated by the *Saṁvatsarapradīpa* quoted in S. M. Bhattacharya's *Purohitdarpaṇ* (Bengali):[2]

Pañcamyāṁ pūjayel=Lakṣmīṁ puṣpa-dhūp-ānna-vāribhiḥ |
masy-ādhāraṁ lekhanīñ=ca pūjayen=na likhet=tataḥ ||
Māghe māsi site pakṣe pañcamī yā Śriyaḥ priyā |
tasyāṁ pūrv-āhna ev=ca kāryaḥ Sārasvat-otsavaḥ ||

According to this, pen, ink-pot, etc., should be worshipped on the occasion of the worship of both Lakṣmī and Sarasvatī on Māgha-sudi 5 which is called Śrī-pañcamī, i.e. *pañcamī* sacred to the goddess Śrī or Lakṣmī, though Sarasvatī is worshipped on that day in many parts of the country.

If thus Lakṣmī and Sarasvatī were both sometimes conceived as the goddess of learning, we have probably an explanation of the *maṅgala* at the beginning of the Nāgpur *praśasti* (Vikrama 1161) of the Paramāras, which runs as follows—

Oṁ namo Bhāratyai |
Prasād-audāryo-mādhurya-samādhi-samat-ādayaḥ |
yuvayor=ye guṇāḥ santi Vāgdevyau te='pi santu naḥ ||[3]

Here the devotee salutes the goddess Bhāratī (Sarasvatī) and prays that the qualities of the two goddesses of learning may be bestowed on him. The qualities enumerated are *prasāda*, *audārya*, *mādhurya*, *samādhi*, *samatā*, etc., which are, in reality, some of the qualities of good compositions as indicated in Daṇḍin's *Kāvyādarśa* and other works.[4] The two goddesses of learning may be Sarasvatī and Lakṣmī.

It is also said that, in parts, Sarasvatī still remained with Viṣṇu. For Sarasvatī and Gāyatrī as the wives of the god Brahman, see, e.g., *Padma Purāṇa*, Uttara-khaṇḍa, Ch. 111.

1. This is well known from the Bengali *maṅgala-kāvyas* of the late medieval period. Charu Chandra Bandyopadhyay says that Lakṣmī and Sarasvatī are represented as the daughters of Śiva and Parvatī 'in the *Nāradīya*, *Dharma* and *Kūrma Purāṇas*' (*Caṇḍīmaṅgalabodhinī*, Vol. I, pp. 47, 89).

2. B.S. 1368 ed., p. 245.

3. See *Ep. Ind.*, Vol. II, p. 182.

4. Cf. *Kāvyādarśa*, I. 41—

Śleṣaḥ prasādaḥ samatā mādhuryaṁ sukumāratā |
arthavyaktir=udāratvam=ojaḥ-kānti-samādhayaḥ ||

In connection with the Ardhanārī form of Viṣṇu, reference may be made to a similar form of the Sun-god mentioned in works like the *Agni Purāṇa*[1] and *Sāradātilaka.*[2] This aspect of the deity is sometimes regarded as a combination of Śiva (Ardhanārīśvara) and Sūrya (Sun-god) and seems to be given the name Mārtaṇḍa-Bhairava.[3] The Ardhanārī from of the god Gaṇapati (Gaṇeśa) is likewise mentioned in the *Halāyadhastotra* inscribed in 1063 A.D. in the Amareśvara temple at Māndhātā in the Nimar District of Madhya Pardesh.[4]

Prasāda=graciousness of disposition, clarity of style; *audārya*, *udāratva*=magnanimity, depth of meaning; *mādhurya*=sweetness of behaviour or style; *samādhi*=intentness, attribution of one's characteristic to another; *samatā*=impartiality, having similar sounds throughout (*bandheṣv=aviṣamam*).

1. 301.9—*sindūr-āruṇam=iśāne vām-ārdha-dayitaṁ Ravim*. For *iśāne*, some manuscripts have *Iśānam*.

2. Cf.

hem-āmbhoja-pravāla-pratimā-nija-ruciṁ cāru khaṭṭāṅga-padmau
cakraṁ śaktiṁ ca pāśaṁ sṛṇim=atiruciram=akṣamālāṁ kapālam |
hast-āmbhojair=dadhānaṁ trinayana-vilasad=veda=vaktr-ābhirāmaṁ
Mārtaṇḍaṁ vallabh-ārdhaṁ maṇimaya-mukuṭaṁ hāra-dīptaṁ bhojāmaḥ ||

3. See *Agni Purāṇa*, 301.8; cf. *Liṅga Purāṇa*, II.19.7; *Matsya Purāṇa*, 55. 5-6.

4. See *Journ. Anc. Ind. Hist.* Vol. II, p. 112; *Ep. Ind.*, Vol. XXV, p. 175, verse 1; cf. Vol. I, p. 104. Cf. also Śakti-Gaṇapati described in the *Śilparatna* (*Journ. As. Soc.*, Vol. VIII, 1966, No. 4. pp. 265-66, and *JAIH*, Vol. IV, in the press).

CHAPTER XV

MAHIṢAMARDINĪ

The ten-armed Durgā is generally worshipped in modern Bengal in her Mahiṣamardinī aspect. She is fashioned in clay as standing with her right foot on a lion and with different weapons in her ten hands. The Asura, whom she is shown as overpowering, is represented as emerging from the neck of a headless buffalo, lying at her feet, with a *khaḍga* (scimitar) in his right hand. The head of the Devī's spear is shown as piercing the chest of the demon. The goddess has a benign smile on her face, which seems to be quite unsuitable in one engaged in fierce fighting with an enemy. She is flanked on either side by her sons (Gaṇapati and Kārttikeya) and daughters (Lakṣmī and Sarasvatī), Sarasvatī and Gaṇapati on the right and Lakṣmī and Kārttikeya on the left. There is nothing in the expression and attitude of these deities to show that they are in any way interested in the battle which their mother is fighting with the demon. This also appears to be rather strange.

What appears to be even more strange is that, according to the late mediaeval Bengali tradition, Durgā goes in this form, along with her sons and daughters, to the home of her father Himālaya on the 6th day of the bright fortnight of the month of Āśvina and returns to the abode of her husband Śiva on Mount Kailāsa on the tenth day of the same fortnight. It is difficult to reconcile this conception of the Devī with her militant Mahiṣamardinī form, because a lady is hardly expected to move towards her parents' place while fighting fiercely with an enemy, in the company of her children who are, however, indifferent to the struggle. The fact is that, in Bengal, Durgā is predominantly conceived as a village housewife just as Śiva is conceived as a poor villager, and these conceptions have greatly influenced the local mythology of the goddess.[1] In any case, the first definite reference to the above strange

1. For a Bengal story explaining why Durgā's son Kārttikeya preferred to remain a *Kumāra* or bachelor by suggesting that it was in order to allay the fear of his mother that she might be starved by her daughter-in-law, see *Journ. Anc. Ind. Hist.*, Vol. II, p. 266.

form of Durgā, as worshipped in Bengal at present, seems to be found in the well-known *Caṇḍīmaṅgala-kāvya*[1] of Mukundarāma who flourished in the sixteenth century.

Durgā is worshipped in Bengal both in spring and in autumn. Since, according to the Bengali tradition, Rāmacandra in order to kill Rāvaṇa worshipped her in autumn, the autumnal worship of Durgā is more popular. The worship of the goddess and the obscene Śavar-otsava performed on the Vijayā-daśamī day (Āśvina-sudi 10) were prevalent in Bengal during the medieval period. In the *Rāmacarita*[2] of Sandhyākaranandin (12th century A.D.), mention is made of the festivities associated with the worship of Umā, while the *Kālikā Purāṇa* and the *Kālaviveka* of Jīmūtavāhana refer to the obscene *utsava*.[3] It seems that, in the mediaeval period, Mahiṣamardinī Durgā was worshipped in Bengal singly and not along with her sons and daughters.

We have, however, evidence to show that autumnal worship of the goddess was known much earlier. Hiuen-tsang's *Life* by Shaman Hwui Li tells us that, in Ayodhyā, robbers used to sacrifice a handsome youngman before Durgā in autumn every year.[4] But Hwui Li does not indicate the particular aspect of the goddess worshipped by them though it is possible that the Mahiṣamardinī form was meant.

The legend of the Durgā-Mahiṣāsura encounter cannot be later than thefirst century B. C. We have sculptural represen-

1. See *Kavikaṅkaṇ-Caṇḍī*, ed. D. C. Sen and others, Vol. I, p. 209-10: *Mahiṣamardinī rūp dharen Caṇḍikā* |......*siṁha-pṛṣṭhe-āropilā dakṣiṇ caraṇ* | *Mahiṣer pṛṣṭhe vām pad āropaṇ* || *vām kare Mahiṣāsurer dhari cul*| *savya kare tār vuke āropilā śūl*|| *pāś-āṅkuś-ghaṇṭā-manta kheṭak śarāsan* | *vām pāṃc kare śobhe pāṃc praharaṇ* || *asi cakra śūl ār se sitaśar* | *pāṃc astre śobhaye dakṣiṇe pāṃc kar* ||......*aṅgad-kaṅkaṇ-yutā haila daśa-bhujā* |......*cāridige lambamān śobhe jaṭājuṭ* |......*vām bhāge Kārttik dakṣiṇe Lambodar* | *vṛṣe ārohaṇ Śiv mastak upar* || *dakṣiṇe Jaladhisutā vāme Sarasvatī* |

2. III. 25.

3. *Hist. Beng.*, Vol. I, ed. Majumdar, p. 606; cf. Sircar, *The Śākta Pīṭhas*, pp. 105-06. The Bengali jurist Jīmūtavāhana is assigned by some to the fifteenth century and by others to the eleventh or twelfth century.

4. See *Life of Hiuen Tsiang*, trans. Beal, p. 86. In the *Kathāsaritsāgara*, there are many references to such human sacrifices before the goddess. See *Kathāsaritsāgara* (pub. Munshiram Manoharlal, Delhi), Vol. I, pp. 133, 176, 226, 521, 548; Vol. II, pp. 170, 191, 255, 263, 381.

tations of Mahiṣamardinī of that period.[1] The earliest representation of the said form of the Devī found so far is probably a terracotta plaque from Nagar near Uniyara, Tonk District, Rajasthan. It is now preserved in the Amber Museum and has been assigned by scholars to the first century B. C. or the beginning of the first century A. D.[2] Six statues of the Kuṣāṇa age, preserved in the Mathurā Museum, appear to contain some other early representations of the Mahiṣamardinī form.[3] The Devī is shown in these as holding a buffalo raised to her waist, the demon being represented in his animal form. With one hand, she presses the hind part of the buffalo or hits it with a club, throttling or breaking the animal's neck with another. Five of the statuettes represent the goddess with six arms, and in one she is four-armed. The weapons in the Devī's hands are the spear and trident; but the animal is killed more with her hands than with the weapons. The lion is absent in the sculptures. Several interesting Mahiṣamardinī sculptures belonging to the Gupta age are known. Among them mention may be made of an image found in the Udayagiri cave near Vidisha (c. 400 A. D.) and that found in the Bhumara temple (c. 6th century A. D.).[4] Some fine miniature stone reliefs of two-armed Mahiṣamardinī belonging to the Gupta period were unearthed by Marshall at Bhita.[5] The Ellora image[6] of the goddess should also be mentioned in this connexion for it is one of the most lively sculptures of the place. A very large number of post-Gupta Mahiṣamardinī images are preserved in the different museums of India. The Māmallapuram image (7th century A.D.) and the image in the Vaitāl Deul at

1. See V.S. Srivastava, *Catalogue and Guide to the Ganga Golden Jubilee Museum*, Bikaner, 1961, p. 5; cf. A. K. Chatterjee in the *Indian Museum Bulletin*, Vol. IV, No. 1, p. 61; also *IHQ*, Vol. XXII, pp. 154 f.

2. See V. S. Srivastava, *loc. cit.*; also *Lalit Kala*, Nos. 1-2, pp. 72-74; *Adyar Library Bulletin* (N.S.), Vol. XIX, pp. 37 ff.

3. *JUPHS* (O.S.), Vol. XXII, pp. 158-59; cf. *Artibus Asiae*, Vol. XXXI, p. 180.

4. See also K. Bharatha Iyer, 'An Early Gupta Seal of the Mahiṣamardinī' in the *Artibus Asiae*, Vol. XXXI, pp. 179 ff., and Plates, Figs. 1-5.

5. *ASI,AR*, 1911-12, p. 86, Pl. XXXI, Figs. 13-14.

6. See J.N. Banerjea, *Deevelopmert of Hindu Iconography* (2nd ed.), p. 499 and Pl. XLI, Fig. 2.

Bhubaneswar are among the famous representations of the goddess belonging to the post-Gupta period.

Among the early images of Mahiṣamardinī found so far, some are two-armed, four-armed or six-armed, while the later images have often eight, ten, twelve, sixteen, eighteen, twenty or even thirty-two hands.[1] In the early images, the demon is a buffalo or a buffalo-headed human being; but the demon emerging from the neck of a headless buffalo and fighting with the goddess is also found in the medieval sculptures of Bengal, Bihar and Orissa. As we have seen, often the lion is absent.[2]

It is interesting to note that, in the *Mahābhārata*, Kārttikeya is represented as the destroyer of Mahiṣa. His fight with that demon is described in some details in the Vana-parvan.[3] Among the names of Kārttikeya given in the *Mahābhārata*, we have Mahiṣārdana.[4] Of the two *Durgāstotras* preserved in the *Mahābhārata* (IV. 6; VI. 23), only the first one endows the goddess with the epithet Mahiṣāsuranāśinī; but the said *stotra* is not found in the southern recension of the epic. It has been suggested therefore that the story of Durgā's killing of Mahiṣa was borrowed from the Kārttikeya legend at a somewhat later period.[5] We should, however, remember that the *Mahābhārata* once speaks of Śiva as the destroyer of Mahiṣa, and it therefore appears that the destruction of Mahiṣa was attributed by some to Śiva, by others to Kārttikeya and by a third group of people to Durgā, probably in different areas of our vast country. Since Mahiṣamardinī Durgā is represented in art from about the first century B.C. or the beginning of the first century A.D., while the latest sections of the *Mahābhārata* are believed to have been composed about the fourth century A.D., it is difficult to be sure that Durgā's Mahiṣamardinī aspect is later than the conception of Kārttikeya as the destroyer of Mahiṣa, even though

1. J.N. Banerjea, *Pañcopāsanā*, pp. 244-46. Durgā worshipped in Bengal is ten-armed as noted above. Reference to the eighteen-handed Devī is often met with; see *Devībhāgavata*, V. 8. 44; also *Kathāsaritsāgara*., Vol. II, p. 263.

2. Cf. above; also Banerjea, *loc. cit.*

3. Ch. 231.

4. III. 232. 3.

5. See A. K. Chatterjee in the *Indian Museum Bulletin*, *op. cit.*, pp. 60 f.

6. Soerensen, *Index to the Mahābhārata*, p. 458. Śiva is called Mahiṣaghna.

the *Mahābhārata* attributes the destruction of Mahiṣa more often to Kārttikeya than to Śiva and Durgā.

The struggle between Durgā and Mahiṣāsura is one of the principal subjects of the *Devīmāhātmya* preserved in the *Mārkaṇḍeya Purāṇa*. The episode is also indirectly mentioned in the *Matsya*,[1] *Brahmāṇḍa*[2] and other Purāṇas. It is generally supposed that the oldest parts of the *Mārkaṇḍeya Purāṇa* were compiled during the third century A.D. or earlier while the *Devīmāhātmya*, which may rightly be called the testament of Śākta philosophy, is said to have been added to the text by the sixth century A.D.[3] The story of the Devī's fight with Mahiṣa as found in the *Devībhāgavata*, *Skanda Purāṇa*, *Vāmana Purāṇa* and other texts appears to have been borrowed from the *Mārkaṇḍeya* at a later date,[4] though there are minor differences.

There are some interesting points on which the images of Mahiṣamardinī discovered so far differ from the description of that goddess found in the *Devīmāhātmya*. The story says that the goddess bound the demon by her noose and the latter then became a lion whose head the Devī cut off. Then the demon appeared in human form with scimitar and shield in hands and was pierced by the Devī's arrows. Next he became an elephant and tugged the Devī's lion with his trunk; but the goddess cut off the elephant's trunk with her sword. Then the demon assumed the buffalo shape once again. The description goes on : "....she leaped upwards and sat herself on that great Asura, and pressed him on the neck with her foot and struck him with her spear. And thereupon, he, being assailed by her foot, half issued forth from his own mouth, in sooth, being completely encompassed by the goddess' valour....The goddess struck off his head with her great sword and laid him low."[5]

1. 152. 17. 24.
2. IV. 29. 75 and 78.
3. See Winternitz, *A History of Indian Literature*, Vol. II, pp. 560, 565.
4. The *Mārkaṇḍeya Purāṇa* (XI. 55) stanza—
ittham yadā yadā vādhā dānav-otthā bhaviṣyati |
tadā tad=āvatīry=āhaṁ kariṣyāmy=ari-saṁkṣayam ||
imitated from the *Bhagavadgītā* (IV. 8), is modified in the *Devībhāgavata* (V. 18. 22) as—
yadā yadā hi sādhūnāṁ duḥkhaṁ bhavati dānava |
tadā teṣāñ=ca rakṣ-ārthaṁ dehaṁ sandhārayāmy=aham ||
5. III. 38-40 :
evam=uktvā samutpatya s=ārūḍhā taṁ mah-āsuram |
pāden=ākramya kaṇṭhe ca śūlen=ainam=atāḍayat ||

We are told that the goddess killed Mahiṣāsura with a sword (*asi*). But the images usually show her as killing that demon with a *śūla* (spear).[1] The demon in human form is again said to have come out of the mouth of the buffalo and not out of its headless trunk.

In the later adaptation of the episode as found in Book V of the *Devībhāgavata*, the Devī is stated to have struck the chest of Mahiṣ-āsura by her sharp trident (*triśūla*) so that the demon fell into a swoon;[2] but when he again attacked the goddess, she killed him neither by the spear nor by a sword, but by her thousand-poked discuss.[3] Elsewhere in the same work, the demon is said to have been killed by the goddess with her *khaḍga* (scimitar.).[4]

The *Skanda Purāṇa* refers to the Durgā-Mahiṣāsura episode at several places. In one place, it is said that the Devī killed the demon by her spear and then cut off his head by her scimitar.[4] At another place, the description of Mahiṣa's slaughter

tataḥ so='pi pad-ākrāntas=tayā nija-mukhāt=tataḥ |
ardha-niṣkrānta ev=āsīd=Devyā vīryeṇa saṁvṛtaḥ |
ardha-niṣkrānta ev=āsau yudhyamāno mah-āsuraḥ |
tayā mah-āsinā Devyā śiraś=chittvā nipātitaḥ ||

1. In the Chhoti Sadri inscription found in the Udaipur District of Rajasthan, dated in 491 A.D., Durgā is described as killing the Asura (Mahiṣāsura) with a *śūla*. This inscription represents the goddess not as riding a lion, but a chariot drawn by one or more lions. See *Ep. Ind.*, Vol. XXX, pp. 120 ff.

2. V. 20. 59 :
Caṇḍik=āpi ca taṁ pāpaṁ triśūlena balād=hṛdi |
tāḍayāmāsa tikṣṇena krodhād=aruṇa-locanā ||

3. V. 20. 62 and 64 :
tato Devī sahasr-āraṁ su-nābhaṁ cakram=uttamam |
kare kṛtvā jagād=occaiḥ saṁsthitaṁ Mahiṣ-āsuram ||...
ity=uktvā dāruṇaṁ cakraṁ mumoca Jagadambikā |
śiraś=chinnaṁ rath-āṅgena dānavasya tadā raṇe ||

4. X. 12. 33 :
pāśena baddhvā sudṛḍhaṁ chittvā khaḍgena tac-chiraḥ |
pātayāmāsa Mahiṣaṁ Devī devagaṇ-āntakam ||
The Devī is called *evaṁ Lakṣmīḥ samutpannā Mahiṣāsura-mardinī* (X. 12. 35).

5. Prabhāsa-khaṇḍa, Prabhāsakṣetra-māhātmya, Chap. 83, verses 20-21 :
padbhyām=ākramya śūlena nihato daitya-puṅgavaḥ ||
chinne śirasi khaḍgena tad-rūpo niḥsṛtaḥ pumān |
raudro='pi sa gataḥ svargaṁ daityo Devy-āstra-pātitaḥ ||

in this Purāṇa resembles the same in the *Mārkaṇḍeya Purāṇa* which we have discussed above.[1] The story of Mahiṣa's discomfiture as given in the *Vāmana Purāṇa*, not in the usual *Anuṣṭubh* but in the *Indravajrā* or *Upajāti* metre, is similar to that of the *Mārkaṇḍeya Purāṇa*.[2]

The *Agni Purāṇa* describes the ten-armed Caṇḍikā as holding various weapons, riding a lion and having Mahiṣa, struck by her spear, in her front.[3] Elsewhere the same Purāṇa[4] speaks of Caṇḍī as having twenty, ten or eighteen arms while the nine Durgās are all sixteen-armed, have different complections, are in the *ālīḍha* pose on the back of the lion and catch the hair of the armed male emerging from a buffalo.[5] The twenty- or ten-armed Caṇḍī-Durgā has a buffalo with his head cut off and lying near by and an angry male emerging out of his neck with raised hand bearing weapon. This demon is further described as bearing a spear, vomitting blood, having red garland, hair and eyes, being mauled by the lion and having the noose strongly pressing his neck.[6] The *Agni Purāṇa*,

See also *ibid.*, Arbuda-khaṇḍa, Chap. 36, verses 152-53 :
siṁha-skandhañ=ca sā Devī tatas=tam=adhyarohata /
khaḍgena tīkṣṇena śiro Devī tasya nyakṛntata //
śūlena bhedayāmāsa pṛṣṭha-deśe sureśvarī / etc.
For another delineation of the episode, see further the Nāgara-khaṇḍa section of the same Purāṇa, Chapters 117-21.

1. *Ibid.*, Brahma-khaṇḍa, Setumāhātmya-varṇana, Chap. (6 or 7). 41:
kaṇṭhaṁ śūlena tīkṣṇena pīḍayāmāsa kopitā /
tato Devy=asim=ādāya cakart=āsya śiro mahat //
2. XX. 45-48.
3. 52.16 :
Caṇḍikā daśa-hastā syāt khaḍga-śūl-āri-śakti-dhṛk /
dakṣe vāme nāgapāśaṁ carm-āṅkuśa-kuṭhārakam /
dhanuḥ siṁhe ca mahiṣaḥ śūlena prahato='grataḥ //
4. See Chap. 50.
5. 5 .10-12 :
Rudracaṇḍā Pracaṇḍā ca Caṇḍogrā Caṇḍanāyikā //
Caṇḍā Caṇḍavatī c=aiva Caṇḍarūp=Āticaṇḍikā /
Ugracaṇḍā ca madhyasthā rocanābh=āruṇ=āsitā //
nīlā śuklā dhūmrikā ca pītā ś. tā ca siṁhagāḥ /
mahiṣ-otthaḥ pumān śastrī tat-kaca-dhṛta-muṣṭikāḥ //
ālīḍhā nava Durgāḥ syuḥ sthāpyāḥ putr-ādi-vṛddhaye //
6. 50.3-6 :
tad-adho mahiṣaś=chinna-mūrdhā pātita-mastakaḥ //
śastr-odyata-karaḥ kruddhas=tad-grīvā-sambhavaḥ pumān /

which is supposed to be an early medieval East Indian work in its present form, also mentions the Lalitā form of Durgā as having her left hand on Skanda's head and holding a looking glass in the right hand.[1] Elsewhere in the same Purāṇa, Lalitā is described as standing on a lotus, having two of her four hands on Skanda and Gaṇa (Gaṇeśa) and holding a looking glass and a spear in the remaining two hands.[2] This second Lalitā image representing the Devī with Kārttikeya and Gaṇeśa seems to be close to the modern Durgā image of Bengal representing the goddess with Kārttikeya, Gaṇeśa, Lakṣmī and Sarasvatī. The modern Bengali conception of Durgā may be an extention of a combination of Lalitā of the *Agni Purāṇa* and Mahiṣamardinī.

Recently we have found the following description of a sculpture discovered at Rajshahi in the *Report on the Working of the Varendra Research Museum* (Rajshahi, East Pakistan, 1969): "Museum No. 2650—Durgā. Durgā in sandstone, 32″ × 8″. The goddess is standing on a plain pedestal in *samabhaṅga* pose with standing figures of Gaṇeśa on her right and Kārttikeya on her left. Her *vāhana*, the lion, is seen crouching on the pedestal. The goddess wears a transparent petticoat-like garment which is held at her waist by a jewelled girdle. She has also put on a necklace, *patrakuṇḍalas*, armlets, bangles and anklets. Her hair is done up in a high bun which is encircled by a jewelled fillet. The lower right hand of the goddess is shown in *varada-mudrā*. There is a sword in her upper right hand, a shield in the corresponding left, and an indistinct object (fruit ?) in her lower left hand. The upper part of the plain back slab is rounded. The sculpture, which is much corroded, is datable in the 10th century A.D." The image seems to be four-armed. It is probably not Mahiṣamardinī; but, if Gaṇeśa and Kārttikeya are correctly identified and the indication of the date is not incorrect, the Rajshahi sculpture

śūla-hasto vamad-rakto rakto sraṅ-mūrdhaj-ekṣaṇaḥ ||
siṁhen=āsvādyamānas=tu pāśa-baddho gale bhṛśam |
yāmy-āṅghry-ākrānta-siṁhā ca sa vy-āṅghrir=nicag-āsure ||
Caṇḍik=eyaṁ tri-netrā ca sa-śastrā·ripu-mardanī | etc.

1. 50.14—*Skanda-mūrdha-karā vāme dvitīye dhṛtadapraṇā.*

2. 52.15—*abjasthā Lalitā Skanda-Gaṇ-ādarśa-śalā(ḥ*) kayā(rāḥ).*

is of considerable importance, because its conception approaches the idea underlying that of Lalitā described in the *Agni Purāṇa* and also the type of the Durgā image that is worshipped in Bengal since the sixteenth century.

The *Matsya Purāṇa*[1] also speaks of the image of Umā-Maheśvara flanked by Jayā, Vijayā, Kārttikeya and Vināyaka, and it will be even closer to the Durgā image (which has Maheśvara in a small form above the head of the Devī) if Jayā and Vijayā are substituted by Lakṣmī and Sarasvatī.

1. Chapter 260, verses 11 ff.; cf. verses 19-20—
Jayā ca Vijayā c=aiva Kārttikeya-Vināyakau ||
pārśvayor=darśayet=tatra toraṇe gaṇa-guhyakān |

The goddess Mahiṣamardinī is described in this Purāṇa (260. 55 ff.) as Kātyāyanī who is called *atasī-puṣpa-varṇ-ābhā* (260.57), i.e. dark-complectioned, although the goddess as worshipped in Bengal is *gaurī*, i.e. fair-complectioned.

Chapter XVI

GUARDIANS OF THE QUARTERS

Malalasekera quotes the *Dīgha*- and *Aṅguttara-nikāyas* in giving an account of the lowest Deva-world of the Buddhists, which is known as Cātummahārājika (Cāturmahārājika), where the four Mahārājas dwelt as guardians of the four quarters; e.g., Dhataraṭṭha (Dhṛtarāṣṭra), lord of the Gandhabbas (Gandharvas), in the east; Virūḷhaka (Virūḍhaka), lord of the Kumbhaṇḍas (Kuṣmāṇḍas), in the south; Virūpakkha (Virūpākṣa), lord of the Nāgas, in the west; and Vessavaṇa (Vaiśravaṇa-Kubera), lord of the Yakṣas, in the north.[1] Childers' *Dictionary of the Pali Language* refers to the *Abhidhānappadīpikā*, etc., and assigns Dhataraṭṭha to the north, Virūḷha or Virūḷhaka to the south, Virūpakkha to the west and Vessavaṇa to the east. Thus Dataraṭṭha is assigned to the east or north and Vessavaṇa to the north or east. Of the four Mahārājas or guardians of the quarters, Kubera alone is known from Brāhmaṇical mythology and, as we shall see below, there also the quarter assigned to him is not the same in different accounts. The date of the evolution of the 'six Deva-world' conception and the idea of the lowest heaven called 'the world of the four Mahārājas' in Buddhist mythology cannot be determined with certainty, because the date of the Nikāyas is uncertain.[2] It should, however, be noted that the Mahārājas

1. *Dictionary of Pali Proper Names*, s.v. *Cātummahārājika*, *Dhataraṭṭha*, etc.

2. The canons of the Buddhists are supposed to have been summarily compiled shortly after the Buddha's death about 486 B.C., they were revised after a century in 386 B.C. and were more or less completed 236 years after the Buddha's *parinirvāṇa* (i.e. about the 19th year of Aśoka's reign, probably about 250 B.C.). Cf. Winternitz, *A History of Indian Literature*, Vol. II, p. 6. The texts of the Buddhist canonical works, at first transmitted orally, are said to have been committed to writing in the first century B.C. (*ibid.*, pp. 8, 13), though they are supposed to have suffered considerable change and modification even in later times, and in many cases 'commentaries penetrated into the texts and became mixed with them' (*ibid.*, p. 14).

are mentioned in the inscriptions[1] (really labels to the Mahārājas' images) from the Buddhist establishment at Barhut, belonging to the Śuṅga age (c. 187-75 B. C.), though they are called merely Yakṣas and not Mahārājas, probably because the Mahārāja concept was still on its way to development. Sanskrit Buddhist literature associates Kubera with Maṇibhadra, Dhṛtarāṣṭra with Sūrya, Virūḍhaka with Yama and Virūpākṣa with Varuṇa,[2] probably due to the influence of Brāhmaṇical mythology.[3]

The earliest epigraphical reference to the Brānmaṇical Dikpālas (guardians of the quarters) or Lokapālas (protectors of the worlds) is found in the Nanaghat inscription of queen Nāganikā of the Śātavāhana dynasty, who seems to have flourished about the close of the first century B. C.[4] It is interesting to note that salutations are offered in this record to the four Lokapālas, viz. Yama, Varuṇa, Kubera and Vāsava (Indra), separately from those to Dharma (Yama) and Indra (Vāsava). It seems that a distinction was made between Yama and Indra as Lokapāla and the well-known gods of the same names, so that the identification of Dharma and Yama and of Indra and Vāsava may belong to a later date.[5]

The Brāhmaṇical conception of the four Dikpālas or Lokapālas is not as elaborate and definite as the Buddhist ideas about the four Mahārājas. We have seen above how the Nanaghat inscription refers to Yama, Varuṇa, Kubera and Vāsava (Indra) as the four Lokapālas, while the *Mahāvastu* and

1. Barua and Sinha, *Barhut Inscriptions*, pp. 67 ff. Besides the *Dighanikāya*, the authors quote the *Divyāvadāna*, *Mahāvastu* and *Lalitavistara* in this connection.

2. *Loc. cit.* For a conflicting account in the *Viṣṇudharmottara*, see above, p. 201.

3. Hopkins (*Epic Mythology*, p. 152, note) says that 'the four Mahārājas of the Buddhists combine the Lokapāla gods and the elephants of the directions (Vessavaṇa and Dhaṭaraṭṭha) with other un-Brāhmaṇic features'. But Vessavaṇa and Dhataraṭṭha are not mentioned in the Disāgaja list which is borrowed from the Brāhmaṇical list of the Diggajas.

4. Sircar, *Select Inscriptions*, Vol. I, 1965 ed., p. 193. For the number 'four', note also that the *Mahābhārata* (III. 112.1, and 161.8; XII. 327.7) compares four mighty brothers as the Lokapālas. Here as well as in IX. 61.64, the Lokapālas are indirectly represented as great heroes. I. 225.3 represents Varuṇa as the fourth Lokapāla.

5. Sircar, *loc. cit.*, note 3.

Lalitavistara of the early centuries of the Christian era mention, as we have seen, the Brāhmaṇical counterparts of Kubera, Dhṛtarāṣṭra, Virūḍhaka and Virūpākṣa as Maṇibhadra, Sūrya, Yama and Varuṇa who are respectively located in the north, east, south and west. The quarters assigned to the different Brāhmaṇical Dikpālas or Lokapālas are not specifically mentioned along with the names of the divinities in many cases. The *Mahābhārata*[1] mentions Vaivasvata (Yama), Varuṇa, Śatakratu (Indra) and Dhaneśa (Kubera) as welcoming a dead hero. In the epics, the position of Yama and Varuṇa respectively in the south and west is more or less fixed, though the names of the deities are not always the same. At one place, the Vana-parvan[2] mentions Varuṇa, Kubera, Yama [of the south] and Śakra (Indra) as Lokapālas offering some gifts to Arjuna, while elsewhere[3] the group of four gods are enumerated as Indra, Agni, Varuṇa and Yama without using the designation Lokapāla. Thus Agni takes here the place of Kubera, and Hopkins thinks that 'the grouping Agni, Yama, Varuṇa and Indra seems older than when Kubera is substituted for Agni'.[4] But the Karṇa-parvan[5] represents Jātavedas (Agni), Yama, Varuṇa and *Bhagavat* Soma as leaders respectively of the gods in the east, the Pitṛs in the south, the gods in the west and the ruling priests in the north. Here Agni and Soma take the places of Indra and Kubera as guardians respectively of the east and north, so that Soma was another early claimant for the guardianship of the northern quarter. Mahendra (Indra) is also clearly separated from the four Lokapālas Kubera, Yama, Soma and Varuṇa in the Udyoga-parvan.[6]

The reference in the *Mahābhārata*[7] to the four Lokapālas living on the Himavat like the Diśāmpālas of the north seems to make a distinction between Lokapāla (world-protector) and

1. VII. 70.45. Yama, Kubera, Varuṇa and Indra or Mahendra are also mentioned in Ch. 91, verse 13 and in I. 74.85. For the epic evidence, see Hopkins, *Epic Mythology*, pp. 149 ff.
2. Ch. 41. verses 6 ff.
3. Ch. 55, verse 6.
4. *Op. cit.*, p. 149.
5. VIII. 45. 31-32.
6. V. 16. 27 ff.
7. See Śānti-parvan, Ch. 327; Hopkins, *op. cit.*, p. 150.

Diśāmpāla (quarter-protector). This may be related to the reference in the Anuśāsana-parvan[1] to the three *lokas* (worlds) and the three Lokapālas. In the same way, the *Rāmāyaṇa*[2] recognises Vajradhara (Indra), Yama, Varuṇa and Dhaneśa (Kubera) as the guardians of the east, south, west and north; but in one place,[3] it speaks of the three Lokapālas headed by Śakra (Indra). This exhibits a confusion between the conception of the guardians of the four quarters and that of the protectors of the three worlds (the earth, the heaven and the nether world).

In the Udyoga-parvan,[4] Mahendra (Indra) requests the Lokapālas Varuṇa, Yama, Soma and Kubera for helping him against Nahuṣa, makes Varuṇa the lord of waters, gives Yama and Kubera lordship (mentioned later as respectively of the Pitṛs and of the Yakṣas and wealth) like his own and offers Agni a share (meant for Indra and Agni) in the sacrifice. Hopkins notices the confused nature of the story and points out that 'here Soma comes in first, and is then displaced by Agni'.[5] Indra is sometimes excluded and Agni included in the list of Lokapālas,[6] while in some cases both Śakra (Indra) and Agni are included in the list along with Varuṇa and Yama.[7]

Hopkins refers to 'the explicit correlation of three protectors of worlds with three worlds to point to an earlier group of guardians of the three', and goes on to say, "Soma still lingers in the epic as one of these; later he rules 'above'. Yama and Varuṇa may have been the other two. What remains also, however, is the later addition of Kubera who was not a world-protector or even a god at first, so that when the four were established as guardians of directions rather than of worlds, the first grouping was probably Agni, Yama, Varuṇa and Soma, the first and last then yielding to Indra and Kubera.

1. Ch. 158, verse 31.
2. II. 16.24. They imparted greatness, restraint, beauty and weatlh (Hopkins, *op. cit.*, p. 150).
3. II. 91.13.
4. Ch. 16, verses 27 ff. Indra gave the sword to the Lokapālas (XII. 166.67).
5. Hopkins, *loc. cit.*
6. *Mbh.*, III. 54.24.
7. *Ibid.*, 55.6.

Finally, the ejected ones (Soma and Agni, cf. *Mbh.*, IV. 30.25) came back as guards of the intermediate points, north-east and south-east respectively, Indra setting into the east (*Mbh.*, VII. 184.47) after Kubera had got the north."[1] It is, however, difficult to prove the antiquity of the three Lokapāla conception which was never popular.

Chapter 37 of the Harivaṁśa-parvan of the *Harivaṁśa* says how Indra was the lord of the three worlds and how he made Viratha (a son of Kaśyapa), Yama, Amburāja (Varuṇa) and Pulasya's son who is the one-eyed Piṅgala (Kubera), lords (*rājan, adhipa*) respectively of the east, south, west and north. It will be seen from the above accounts that, while the position of Yama in the south and Varuṇa in the west is constant, Agni, Kubera, Indra and Viratha are assigned to the east, and Indra, Kubera and Soma to the north.

We have seen above how the Nanaghat inscription of the first century B. C. gives the number of the Lokapālas specifically as four and how the said number is also often specified by the epics. The same number is often indicated by the representation of the king as the fifth Lokapāla. Thus Rāvaṇa makes the said claim in the *Rāmāyaṇa* story incorporated in the *Mahābhārata*.[2] Likewise, the Pallava kings Skandavarman II [of copper-plate grants like the Uruvupalli, Oṁgoḍu No. 2 and Pikira records] and Kumāraviṣṇu I [of the Cendalūra grant], who flourished in the 6th and 5th centuries respectively, are called *Pañcama-Lokapāla*, 'the fifth Lokapāla'.[3] The idea is that, while the four Lokapāla's guarded the four directions, the king was the protector of the central region of the

1. *Op. cit.*, p. 151. He further says, "As a matter of fact, Indra belongs to the north-east, at least according to epic ideas, and epic tradition still recognises that Kubera was raised to the position of world-protector and added to the group of Yama, Indra and Varuṇa (*Rām.* , VII. 3.17 f.)." In *Mbh.*, 163. 3f., Dhaumya 'takes Yudhiṣṭhira by the right hand, looks at the east', and says, "Here is to be seen Mt. Mandara which covers the earth to the ocean. It is the district which Indra and Vaiśravaṇa (Kubera) together guard, and the seers call it the seat of Mahendra and Vaiśravaṇa; it is where the sun rises." Hopkins tries to show that Kubera and Indra are really guardians of the north and east together, meeting in the north-east.

2. III. 280.14.

3. Sircar, *The Successors of the Sātavāhanas in the Lower Deccan*, p. 196.

earth. The same idea is also sometimes expressed by the epithet *Madhyyama-Lokapāla*, 'protector of the middle region'. Kālidāsa's *Raghuvaṁśa*[1] (the 4th or 5th century A. D.) applies the said epithet to a king.

The number of the Dikpālas, identified with the Lokapālas, was later raised to eight because, besides the protectors of the east, west, north and south, those of the south-east, south-west, north-east and north-west were also conceived. The *Manusmṛti*[2] (early centuries of the Christian era) says that the king is made out of parts taken from, and is equal to, the eight gods—Indra, Anila (Vāyu), Yama, Arka (Sūrya), Agni, Varuṇa, Candra (Soma) and Vitteśa (Kubera), while the *Amarakośa*[3] (about the sixth century A.D.) recognises Indra, Vahni (Agni), Pitṛpati (Yama), Nairṛta, Varuṇa, Marut (Vāyu), Kubera and Īśa (Īśāna) as the lords of the quarters beginning with the east, i.e. east, south-east, south, south-west, west, north-west, north and north-east. It will be seen that Sūrya (Arka) and Soma of the *Manusmṛti* are replaced by Nairṛta (south-east) and Īśa or Īśāna (north-east) in the *Amarakośa*. Even, however, after the introduction of the conception of the eight Dikpālas or Lokapālas, we have references to the older idea of the four quardians of the quarters as mentioned in the *Raghuvaṁśa* and the Pallava inscriptions referred to above and also in many other epigraphic and literary records. The Allahabad pillar inscription[4] of Samudragupta (c. 335-76 A.D.) regards the king as equal to Dhanada (Kubera), Varuṇa, Indra and Antaka (Yama). Daṇḍin's *Kāvyādarśa*,[5] which may be assigned to the seventh century A.D., also has a stanza speaking of Yama, Varuṇa, Kubera and Sahasrākṣa (Indra) as the four Lokapālas with the king as the fifth.

We have seen above that the Buddhists regarded the guardians of the quarters as the four Mahārājas, although the Buddhist inscriptions of about the second century B.C. call

1. II. 16.
2. VII. 4-7.
3. II. ii.6. The *Śabdakalpadruma* (s. v. *Lokapāla*) quotes a stanza from the *Vahni Purāṇa* offering the same list with Nirṛti (for *Nairṛta*), Anila (for *Marut*), Dhanada (for *Kubera*) and Śaṅkara (for *Īśa*).
4. Sircar, *Sel. Ins.*, *op. cit.*, p. 267, text line 26.
5. II. 331.

them Yakṣas and not Mahārājas. The Lokapālas are not generally called Mahārāja in the Brāhmaṇical works, even though, as we have seen, the *Harivaṁśa* (III. 37. 22) says that Indra made Viratha *Rājan* and *Adhipa* of the eastern quarter. Of course, if they were conceived as lords of the quarters, they could have been mentioned as *Rājan* or *Mahārāja*; but that is not usually done in Brāhmaṇical mythology. Very rarely, Kubera has been called Mahārāja in Brāhmaṇical works like the late *Taittirīya Āraṇyaka* and the *Mahābhārata*[1] probably under Buddhist influence. We have seen, however, that Kubera's position in the list of Lokapālas was not at all fixed since the *Mahābhārata*[2] mentions Agni and Soma as guardians of the east and north respectively in the place of Indra and Kubera while elsewhere[3] Agni is mentioned in the place of Kubera. The *Kūrma Purāṇa*[4] also substitutes Soma for Kubera.

Pāṇini's *sūtra—Mahārājāṭ=ṭhañ*[5] speaks of *bhakti* (attachment or devotion) to Mahārāja. Another *sūtra*[6] is sometimes supposed to refer to Mahārāja as a *devatā* or divinity, though it is doubtful. Jayaswal took *bhakti* directed to Mahārāja in a political sense; but the conception of divine kingship is much later than the age of Pāṇini who flourished in the fifth century B. C., its earliest mention probably being in the *Manusmṛti*[7] of the early centuries of the Christian era. However, *bhakti* to the Mahārāja may mean here attachment to the king. Bhusari, Coomaraswamy and others take Mahārāja in the sense of the Lokapālas called Mahārāja by the Buddhists.[8] It should be admitted, however, that the said Buddhist conception is also considerably later than Pāṇini's days and that it was not popular with the Brāhmaṇical writers.

The sixth century Buddhist lexicographer Amara does

1. III. 154.9.
2. VIII. 45.31-32.
3. III. 55.4; 56.9-12.
4. I. 40.34-35.
5. IV. 3. 97.
6. IV. 2. 35.
7. VII. 7-8.
8. Bhusari in *ABORI*, Vol. VIII, 1926, p. 199; Coomaraswamy, *Origin of the Buddha Image*, Calcutta reprint, p. 18, note 21; A. C. Chakravarti in *The Bhakti Cult and Ancient Indian Geography*, ed. Sircar, p. 49.

not recognise Mahārāja as a name of Kubera though he speaks of the names Kubera, Tryambakasakha, Yakṣarāt, Guhyakeśvara, Manuṣyadharman, Dhanada, Rājarāja, Dhanādhipa, Kinnareśa, Vaiśravaṇa, Paulastya, Naravāhana, Yakṣa, Ekapiṅga, Ailavila, Śrīda and Puṇyajaneśvara as synonymous.[1] Amara, however, recognises Mahārājika as a class of divinities, and Kṣīrasvāmin's commentary says *ṣaṭtriṁśad=dve śate Mahārājikāḥ, Mahārāja-śabdo='sty=eṣām=iti,* i.e. the Mahārajikas, 236 in number, were so called because they enjoyed the designation *Mahārāja*. Kṣīrasvāmin further says, *s=āsya devatā* (Paṇini, IV.2.24) *iti Māhārājika ity=eke, Mahārāja-Proṣṭhapadāṭ=ṭhañ* (Pāṇini, IV. 2.35) which indicates that, according to some, the word is *Māhārājika* meaning one who worships the *devatā* called Mahārāja. The alternative interpretation, however, seems to be unsatisfactory because in Pāṇini's *sūtra* for the formation of the two words *Māhārājika* and *Prauṣṭhapadika*, the latter apparently means related to the Proṣṭhapada-nakṣatras, i.e. Pūrva-Bhādrapada and Uttara-Bhādrapada, which do not look like objects of special worship. In any case, Pāṇini seems to have lived much earlier than the development of the Buddhist conception of the divinities called Mahārāja, so that the word *Mahārāja* used by Pāṇini probably means 'a king' rather than 'a deity'. It may be noted here that Patañjali's *Mahābhāṣya* ignores the *sūtra*—*Mahārājāṭ=ṭhañ* as unnecessary because the formation of the word *Māhārājika* has already been suggested by the earlier *sūtra, Mahārāja-Proṣṭhapadāṭ=ṭhañ*, the word as formed by the two *sūtras* having the same sense. Modern lexicographers have taken the word *Māhārājika* in the sense of 'fit for a great king, imperial, royal', and 'attached or devoted to the ruling prince'.

A medieval Purāṇic conception of the Dikpālas regards them as ten in number, viz. Indra in the east, Vahni in the south-east, Yama in the south, Nirṛta in the south-west, Varuṇa in the west, Marut in the north-west, Kubera in the north, Īśa in the north-east, Brahman in the zenith and Ananta in the nadir.[2]

1. *Amarakośa*, I. 1.38-39.
2. *Śabdakalpadruma*, s. v. *Dikpāla*.

CHAPTER XVII

SUN TEMPLE AT MUṆḌĪRA

The *Skanda Purāṇa* in its present form is a medieval work.[1] The name of the Nāgara-khaṇḍa section of this Purāṇa is associated with the Nāgara Brāhmaṇas of Gujarat, and the section deals mainly with the holy spots in Hāṭakeśvara which is located in the present Ahmedabad District of Gujarat and contained the city of Camatkārapura identified with Ānandapura (modern Vaḍnagar), also called Nagara whence the Nāgara Brāhmaṇas are supposed to have received their name.[2]

Chapter 67 of the Nāgara-khaṇḍa mentions three famous images of the Sun-god, the first in Eastern India, the second in Mid-India and the third in Western India, though all the three were supposed to combine into one image worshipped in a temple in Hāṭakeśvara. This is indicated in the following stanzas (verses 1-6) :

tath=ānyad=api tatr=āsti Bhāskara-tritayaṁ śubham |
yais=tuṣṭais=triṣu lokeṣu mānavo muktim=āpnuyāt ||
Muṇḍīraṁ prathamaṁ tatra Kālapriyaṁ tath=āparam |
Mūlasthānaṁ tṛtīyañ=ca sarva-vyādhi-vināśanam ||
tatra saṅkramate Sūryo Muṇḍīre rajanī-kṣaye |
Kālapriye ca madhy-āhne Mūlasthāne kṣap-āgame ||
tasmin kāle naro bhaktyā paśyed=apy=ekam=eva ca |
kṛta-kṣaṇo naro mokṣaṁ satyaṁ yāti na saṁśayaḥ ||
Muṇḍīraḥ pūrva-dig-bhāge dharityāḥ śrūyate kila |
madhye Kālapriyo devo Mūlasthānaṁ tad-antare ||
tat kathaṁ te trayas=tatra sañjātāḥ sūta Bhāskarāḥ ||
Hāṭakeśvaraje kṣetre sarvaṁ no brūhi vistarāt ||

Of the three places sanctified by the presence of images of the Sun-god, Mūlasthāna is well known and the location of Kālapriya is also satisfactorily established; but the location of Muṇḍīra seems to be otherwise unknown. Mūlasthāna is modern Mūltān, headquarters of the District of the same name

1. Cf. Sircar, *The Śākta Pīṭhas*, p. 25, note 2. It mentions Rāmānuja (11th and 12th centuries A.D.) in the Viṣṇu-khaṇḍa, Chap. 21.

2. See Dey, *Geog. Dict.*, s. v. *Hāṭaka* and *Camatkārapura*.

in the Punjab region of West Pakistan. It is situated near the left bank of the Chenab in lat. 30° 12′, long. 71° 30′ 45″. Mūlasthāna is famous in the Purāṇas as the place of the Sun-god.[1] The Yādava prince Sāmba is said to have worshipped the god at this place and was cured of leprosy. The great Sun temple at Mūltān was seen by Hiuen-tsang in the seventh century and is referred to by Al-Bīrūnī in the eleventh century.[2]

The identification of Kālapriya with Kālpī in the Jalaun District of U. P., lying on the southern bank of the Jamuna, lat. 22° 4′, long. 88° 18°, is also certain.[3] It is at this place that the Rāṣṭrakūṭa emperor Indra III (915-28 A.D.) crossed the Jamuna in the course of his expedition against Kanauj, then the capital of the Gurjara-Pratihāras. The *Varāha Purāṇa* speaks of a temple of the Sun-god at Kālapriya or Kālpī, which is located to the south of the Jamuna.[4]

The location of Muṇḍīra, where the Sun-god was worshipped under the name Muṇḍīrasvāmin, is not clear from the passage quoted above from the Nāgara-khaṇḍa, which, however, places it in Eastern India (*pūrva-dig-bhāge dharitryāḥ*). This is possibly also suggested by the fact that the Sun-god was worshipped at Muṇḍīra at sunrise in the morning, at Kālapriya at noon and at Mūlasthāna at sunset in the evening. Muṇḍīra was thus situated in Eastern India, considerably to the east of Kālpī. The expression *śrūyate kila*, 'as we have heard it reported', seems to suggest that the author of the

1. See *Bhaviṣya Purāṇa*, Brāhma, Chap. 74; *Brahma Purāṇa*, I. 140; cf. Dey, *Geog. Dict.*, s. v. *Mūlasthānapura*. Dey says that the old city of Multan was situated on both banks of the Ravi, This is doubtful though the frequent changes in the courses of the rivers are well known.

2. Watters, *On Yuan Chwang's Travels in India*, Vol. II, p. 254; Sachau, *Alberuni's India*, Vol. I, pp. 116-17, etc. The mistakes in the Chinese pilgrim's account led Watters to doubt the identification of Mou-lo-san-pu-lu with Mūltān ; but the mention of the great Sun temple makes it absolutely certain. Hiuen-tsang speaks of the image at Multan as made of gold while Al-Bīrūnī mentions it as made of wood. The priests must have made the wooden image (of little value as a loot) after the golden one had been taken away by the iconoclasts. But even this could not save the image and his temple.

3. Sircar, *Stud. Geog. Anc. Med. Ind.*, 2nd ed., pp. 303 ff.

4. See below; also V.V. Mirashi, *Stud. Indol.*, Vol. I, p. 38.

stanzas heard an old tradition about the existence of Muṇḍīra in Eastern India, but had no personal knowledge about it.

The most important Sun temple in Eastern India, which is regarded as 'the most exquisite memorial of Sun worship in India', stands at Koṇārak (lat. 19° 54′, long. 86° 10′), on the shore of the Bay of Bengal, nineteen miles north-west of Purī in Orissa.[1] There is no definite evidence that any other temple of the Sun-god, of all-India celebrity, existed in Eastern India. The latitudes and longitudes of the three places show that they stand on the same line drawn from the south-east to the north-west, Kālpī standing almost exactly in the middle of the distance between Koṇārak and Mūltān. It is therefore possible that, by Muṇḍīra, the Nāgara-khaṇḍa section of the *Skanda Purāṇa* refers to Koṇārak.[2] Kaliṅga (comprising parts of Coastal Orissa and Andhra Pradesh) is mentioned as the country of Āditya or the Sun in a list relating to the nine *grahas* in the medieval *Āśvalāyana Gṛhyasūtra Pariśiṣṭa*, probably with reference to Koṇārak.[3]

In the copper-plate grants[3] of the successors of the Gaṅga king Narasiṁha I (1239-65 A.D.) of Orissa, we have a stanza referring to the construction of the temple of Uṣmaraśmi (Sun-god) by the said king at Koṇākoṇa, i.e. modern Koṇārak,

1. Cf. Hunter, *A Statistical Account of Bengal*, Vol. XIX, pp. 84 ff. The name is sometimes written 'Kanarak'.

2. R. C. Hazra (*Studies in the Upapurāṇas*, Vol. I, pp. 105 ff.) identifies Muṇḍīra with Koṇārak.

3. See T. P. Bhattacharya, *The Canons of Indian Art*, 1963, p. 489. For the late date of such lists found even in the *Āśvalāyana Gṛhyasūtra* (not to speak of its *Pariśiṣṭa*), see Winternitz, *A History of Indian Literature*, Vol. I, 1927, p. 471, note 2—"The date of the *Āśvalāyana Gṛhyasūtra* is, however, entirely unknown, and lists of this nature could easily have been enlarged at any time in *Āśvalāyana's* school. For this reason, we are not justified in drawing in chronological conclusion from this passage." The passage in question relates to the mention of *Bhārata* and *Mahābhārata* in a list of teachers and sacred books (III. 4.4.).

4. See, e.g., the Kendupatna plates (first set) of Narasiṁha II, edited by N. N. Vasu in *Journ. As. Soc. Beng.*, Vol. LXV, Part I, 1896, pp. 229 ff.; the Asankhali plates of the same king in *Ep. Ind.*, Vol. XXXI, p. 123 (text lines 134-35) :

kurvan prakāśam=aniśaṁ dvijasāc=ca kṛtvā
meruṁ tulāpuruṣa-mukha-mahārtha-dānaiḥ |
sthātuṁ suraiḥ saha mahat kalay=ātra Koṇā-
koṇe kuṭīrakam=acīkarad=Uṣmaraśmeḥ ||

which name is probably a modification of Koṇākoṇ-ārka, 'Arka (Sun-god) of Koṇākoṇa'. The worship of the Sun at Koṇārak is mentioned in some other Purāṇas. Thus the *Brahma Purāṇa*,[1] another medieval work in its present form, speaks of the great importance of the Sun-god named Koṇ-ārka or Koṇ-āditya worshipped on the sea-shore in the Oḍra or Utkala country. The mention of the locality as Koṇākoṇa in the thirteenth century epigraph seems to suggest that Koṇārak is not so called because of its position 'in the north-east corner (*koṇa*) with respect to Purī'.[2]

Since king Narasiṁha I was a devotee of the god Viṣṇu with some inclination to the original Śaivism of his ancestors,[3] it may be that the king was not a special devotee of the Sun so that he could have installed the Sun-god at Koṇākoṇa after being cured of a desease like leprosy through the god's grace; otherwise, he only constructed the temple or made arrangements or paid money for its construction at the entreaty of the devotees of the god already in worship at the place; but, in any case, it is difficult to be sure that Muṇḍīra was the older name of the place because, in that case, this celebrated name would probably have been used in the inscriptions. In case Narasiṁha I installed the god in the middle of the thirteenth century, Muṇḍīra may have been different from Koṇārak, because all the Purāṇic references to Muṇḍīra may not be later than the said date. It may be noticed that the epigraphic verse speaks of the construction of the temple and not of the installation of the god.

The *Bhaviṣya Purāṇa*[4] says that the three famous places of Sun worship in Jambu-dvīpa are Muṇḍīra, Kālapriya and Mitravana [in the Punjab] and that the god resides permanently at Sāmbapura [in Mitravana, i.e. at Mūltān]. Else-

1. See Chapter 28.

2. Cf. R. C. Hazra, *Studies in the Upapurāṇas*, Vol. I, p. 105, note 164; M. M. Ganguly, *Orissa and her Remains* , p. 437.

3. *Ep. Ind.*, Vol. XXXIII, p. 43. The king's father Anaṅgabhīma III dedicated the Gaṅga kingdom to the god Puruṣottama-Jagannātha of Purī and thenceforth the Gaṅga kings and their successors ruled the kingdom theoretically as vassals of the god. See Sircar, in *Indian Studies : Past & Present*, Vol. VIII, No. 3, April-June, 1967, pp. 269 ff.; also above, pp. 59 ff.

4. I. 72. 4-6; see Hazra, *op. cit.* p. 101, note 151.

where in the same Purāṇa,[1] the name Muṇḍīra is given as Sutīra, literally, 'the beautiful [sea]-shore'. In the place of Sutīra, Kālapriya and Mitravana, the *Bhaviṣya Purāṇa* elsewhere mentions Puṇḍīrasvāmin (sic—Muṇḍīrasvāmin), Kālapriya and Mūlasthāna[2] and also Suṇḍīrasvāmin (sic—Muṇḍīrasvāmin), Kālapriya and Mitravana.[3] This would suggest the identification of Mitravana and Mūlasthāna or the location of Mūlasthāna in Mitravana. The *Varāha Purāṇa*[4] refers to three images of the Sun-god installed by Sāmba, the first on the Uday-ācala, the second called Kālapriya to the south of the Yamunā and the third called Mūlasthāna on the Astamān-ācala. This would equate Uday-ācala and Muṇḍīra.

According to another section of the *Skanda Purāṇa*,[5] the sun resides in the morning as Muṇḍīrasvāmin at Gaṅgāsāgara-saṅgama, [at mid-day] as Kālapriya [on the bank of the Yamunā] and in the evening [at Mūlasthāna] on the bank of the Candrabhāgā. The *Sāmba Purāṇa*[6] says that Muṇḍīra was the name of the Sun-god installed in the Sun's penance forest [in Orissa] on the sea-shore. This would suggest the identification of Muṇḍīra with Koṇārak. It has, however, to be noted that the said section of the *Sāmba Purāṇa* is an interpolation in the original work according to Hazra[7] who thinks that it was inserted in the Purāṇa for the special purpose of glorifying the sanctity of the Orissan holy places. Even the name Mitravana, situated on the bank of the Candrabhāgā in the Punjab, has been applied to the Orissan holy place.[8]

1. I. 129. 16b-17a. The stanza speaks of the Sun's proximity at Sutīra in the forenoon, at Kālapriya at mid-day and 'here' (Mitravana) in the afternoon.
2. I. 189. 23-26.
3. I. 55. 27.
4. Chap. 177.
5. Prabhāsa-khaṇḍa, i. 139. 11-12 :
   Muṇḍīrasvāminaṁ prātar=Gaṅgāsāgara-saṅgame |
   Kālapriyaṁ c=āstamāne Candrabhāgā-taṭe sthitam ||

   The second half of the stanza seems to be an awkward combination of two halves.
6. Chaps. 42-43.
7. *Op. cit.*, p. 99.
8. *Sāmba Purāṇa*, 42. 2.

The name Candrabhāgā was also applied to an Orissan stream, a branch of the Prācī river.[1]

The *Skanda Purāṇa* reference to the worship of Muṇḍīrasvāmin at Gaṅgāsāgarasaṅgama may suggest that originally the god was associated with the holy confluence of the Gaṅgā and the sea, even though, like the name Candrabhāgā applied to an Orissan stream, some locality in the Purī coast may have later been called Gaṅgāsāgarasaṅgama.[2] This seems to be supported by the *Varāha Purāṇa* reference to Muṇḍīrasvāmin's worship on the Uday-ācala which was the mythical Sun-rise mountain on the eastern fringe of India. The name Udayagiri, however, was also later applied to a spur of the Assia range in Orissa. It may, however, be noticed that both the Sun-rise mountain associated with the Eastern Sea and the confluence of the Gaṅgā and the said Sea are sometimes placed on the eastern boundary of the Indian Cakravarti-kṣetra;[3] but neither Purī nor any other place in Orissa enjoys that distinction. On the other hand, Purī is often associated with the Southern Sea.[4]

We had occasion to discuss the ancient glory of the Gaṅgāsāgarasaṅgama, which was originally the greatest *tīrtha* in Eastern India situated near the eastern border of India, and to show how, on the decline of the importance of Gaṅgāsāgarasaṅgama, its glory was gradually appropriated by the medieval Purī-tīrtha.[5] The transport of the names Gaṅgāsāgarasaṅgama, Udayagiri and Muṇḍīra to Orissa may be ascribed to the above period.

It may be noted that the *Bhaviṣya Purāṇa*[6] mentions Gaṅgā-

1. Hazra, *op. cit.*, p. 106.

2. See *ibid.*, p. 107.

3. Cf. Sircar, *Studies in the Geography of Ancient and Medieval India*, 2nd ed., pp. 9 ff. (for the Sun-rise mountain) and p. 11 (Gaṅgāsamet-āmbudhi in the *Gauḍalekhamālā*, p. 36, verse 7).

4. See *Journ. As. Soc.*, Letters, Vol. XVII, p. 25 (*Śrī-Puruṣottama-kaṭake Dakṣiṇa-mahodadhi-tīre*); *Ep. Ind.*, Vol. XXVIII, p. 257 (*Śrī-Puruṣottama-kṣetre Dakṣiṇa-tīrtharāja-taṭe*); *ibid.*, Vol. XXX, p. 322 (*velāyāṁ Dakṣiṇ-ābdher=Musaladhara-Gadāpāṇi-saṁvāsa-vedyām*).

5. *Studies in the Geography of Ancient and Medieval India*, 2nd ed., pp. 220 ff.

6. I. 55. 24-30.

dvāra, Gaṅgāsāgara, Kālapriya, Mitravana and Suṇḍīrasvāmin (sic—Muṇḍīrasvāmin) in a list of *tīrthas* to be named at the bathing ceremony of the Sun's image during its annual worship. This may also refer to an age after the grafting of Muṇḍīrasvāmin to Orissa. What is interesting here is that Gaṅgasāgara is associated with the worship of the Sun-god. This is an aspect of the *tīrtha* which seems to have been later forgotten.

APPENDIX I

Repudiation of Buddhism by the Candras

The royal family of the Candras of South-East Bengal adopted Buddhism as well as the Buddhist symbol of the *Dharmacakra* as the emblem on their seal. The kings of the dynasty were called *Paramasaugata,* i.e. devout follower of the Sugata or Buddha. Of the published copper-plate records of the family, the grants of Śrīcandra (c. 925-75 A.D.) were made in the name of the Buddha-bhaṭṭāraka.[1] The recently published Mainamati plates[2] of Laḍahacandra (c. 1000-20 A.D.) and Govindacandra (c. 1020-55 A.D.), however, show that the latest members of the Candra family repudiated the Buddhist faith of their predecessors and that they made grants of land in favour of a Vaiṣṇavite or Śaivite deity in the name of Vāsudeva-bhaṭṭāraka or Śiva-bhaṭṭāraka. Although these two kings were also conventionally called *Paramasaugata,* their documents make it clear that they adopted Paurāṇic Hinduism, Laḍahacandra being specially devoted to the god Viṣṇu, and Govindacandra to Śiva.[3] Laḍahacandra's gifts were made in favour of the Vaiṣṇavite god Laḍahamādhava-bhaṭṭāraka, installed by and named after himself. 'Ladahamādhava' really means 'Mādhava installed by or named after Laḍaha', and Mādhava is a well-known name of the god Viṣṇu-Kṛṣṇa. Govindacandra made his grant in favour of the dancing form of Śiva called Naṭṭeśvara (or Narteśvara)[4] whose worship may have been popularised in Bengal by South Indian settlers. The records of both the kings abound in references to Hindu mythology; but there is not a single reference to any Buddhist legend in them. Laḍahacandra visited Vārāṇasī and Prayāga on pilgrimage, though, significantly enough, Vārāṇasī is associated in the Mainamati inscriptions with Śiva and

1. See, e.g., the Rampal plate of Śrīcandra in Majumdar's *Ins. Beng.*, Vol. III, pp. 1 ff.
2. *Pakistan Archaeology*, No. 3, 1966, Karachi, pp. 22-55.
3. It is possible to think that Laḍahacandra received initiation in the Viṣṇu-mantra and Govindacandra in the Śiva-mantra.
4. Cf. *Ep. Ind.*, Vol. XVII, p. 351.

Pārvatī, and the god Brahman, and not with the Buddha's turning of the Wheel of Law at the Mṛgadāva (Sārnāth).

An analysis of the Mainamati records in order to show the Hindu leanings of the two monarchs is made below.

The two grants of Laḍahacandra begin with the Vaiṣṇavite *maṅgala—Oṁ namo bhagavate Vāsudevāya* and introduce in verse 1 the Moon-god, the progenitor of the Candra dynasty, as springing from the eye of the sage Arti. Candra's rise from Atri's eye is not only noticed in the Purāṇas[1] and numerous epigraphical and literary works, but is even supported by such names of the Moon-god as Atrijāta, Atridṛgja, Atrinetraja, Atrinetrabhū, etc., recognised in the lexicons. In verse 2, the Hindu Trinity is introduced in the description of the dynasty as *deva-tray-ātman* by using the words *vidhātā* (Brahman), *acyuta* (Kṛṣṇa-Viṣṇu) and *maheśvara* (Śiva) each in two different senses. Verse 7 describes king Kalyāṇacandra as pure or purifying (*pāvana*) like the waters of the Trisrotas (Ganges). Verse 9 says how Kalyāṇacandra's queen Kalyāṇadevī gave birth to Laḍahacandra just as Kuntī gave birth to Satyavāc (Yudhiṣṭhira) and Rudrāṇī to the god Mahāsena (Skanda Kārttikeya). The same stanza represents king Kalyāṇacandra as Puruṣottama (Viṣṇu) and Kalyāṇadevī not only as Lakṣmī, but also as worshipping the said goddess. Verse 11 states how at Laḍahacandra's birth, the divine drum sounded, the Vidyādharas danced, flowers dropped from heaven, pleasant winds blew and the goddess of earth, together with the ocean, became highly gladdened. Laḍahacandra is described in verse 12 as having the goddesses Gir (Sarasvatī), Śrī (Lakṣmī) and Vasundharā (Earth) under his control. This verse also mentions the king's mastery of all the sciences while verse 9 of Govindacandra's grant speaks of his *kavitva* and *pāṇḍitya* as we shall see below, so that the king may be identified, as we have elsewhere suggested, with the poet named Laḍahacandra known from Sanskrit anthologies.[2] Verse 14 indirectly represents the king, through a series of puns, as the gods Puruṣottama (Viṣṇu) and 'the Victor of Kāma' (Śiva).

According to verse 16, Laḍahacandra visited Vārāṇasī,

1. *Bhāgavata Purāṇa*, IX. 14.3.
2. *Ep. Ind.*, Vol. XXVIII, p. 339, note 7.

the abode of Śambhu and Girisutā (Pārvatī), took bath in the waters of the Ganges and offered *tarpaṇa* to his ancestors and granted gold to numerous Brāhmaṇas. Verse 17 also speaks of the king's pilgrimage to Vārāṇasī, purified by the waters of the Ganges where the god Svabhū (Brahman) performed ten Aśvamedhas [at the Daśāśvamedha Ghāṭ] and the god Śrīkaṇṭha (Śiva) and the goddess Durgā resided happily. Verse 18 describes similar pious activities of the king at the junction of the Gaṅgā and the Yamunā (Prayāga near Allahabad). The next stanza refers to the gifts made by the king at the said *tīrtha* which is sanctified by the Gaṅgā and the Yamunā and is the place where the eternal banyan tree (*akṣaya-vaṭa*) stands. It is well known that there is one *akṣaya-vaṭa* at Prayāga and another at Gayā.[1]

The two charters of king Laḍahacandra record the grant of several villages and plots of land in the name of Lord Vāsudeva in favour of the deity Laḍahamādhava-bhaṭṭāraka installed at Paṭṭīkeraka by the king himself for the increase of the religious merit and fame of his own self and his parents.

Verse 2 in Govindacandra's plate introduces the Moon-god who sprang from Atri's eye and was progenitor of the royal family to which the donor belonged. Verse 4 describes Śrīcandra, the donor's great-grandfather, as more intelligent than Vāgīśa (the god Brahman) and as the master of the sciences (*vidyā*). Verse 6 introduces Śrīcandra's son and successor Kalyāṇacandra as equal to Bali in liberality, Rāma in prowess causing fear to the enemies, Yudhiṣṭhira in truthfulness and Arjuna in great prowess, though it is difficult to be sure as to which one of the three Rāmas (viz. Rāma Dāśarathi, Rāma Jāmadagnya and Rāma Haladhara) is meant. Verse 8 says that, just as the Golden Mountain (Sumeru) is accessible to the celestial beings known as Vidyādhara, Laḍahacandra could be easily approached by the learned men (*vidyādhara*). Verse 9 refers to Laḍahacandra's pilgrimage to Vārāṇasī and his bath in the waters of the Ganges as well as to this *kavitva* and *pāṇḍitya*.[2] Verse 10 in-

1. See Kane, *Hist. Dharm.*, Vol. IV, pp. 603-53; also *Ep. Ind.*, Vol. II, p. 4; Vol. XXXVI, p. 92; etc.

2. Cf. our remarks on verse 12 of his own grants, above, p. 254.

troduces his queen Saubhāgyadevī who is stated to have been like Śiva's wife Śivā and Hari's wife Śrī. Verse 13 represents young Govindacandra as equal to Śaktimān Mahāsena (Mahāsena, holder of the *śakti*, i.e., Skanda-Kārttikeya) and his parents to Śiva and Śivā who were the latter's parents. Verse 15 states that he was equal to Ākhaṇḍala (Indra) the king of the gods in splendour, the Sun in terrible vigour and Mṛkaṇḍa's son (Mārkaṇḍa or Mārkaṇḍeya) in the matter of long life.[1] Verse 16 of the inscription contains a prayer to the gods Svayambhū, Hari and Hara, i.e., the Hindu Trinity.

The grant recorded in the document was made permanently in favour of the god Naṭṭeśvara-bhaṭṭāraka in the name of Lord Śiva for the religious merit and fame of the donor and his parents.

As against the above points, the epithet *Paramasaugata* applied to the names of the kings and the *Dharmacakra-mudrā* affixed to their grants appear to be a mere legacy of the past. The Buddhist *maṅgala* in verse 1 in Govindacandra's grant which is a prayer to the Buddhist Triad, the Jina (Buddha), Dharma and Saṅgha, may also be explained in the same way. It is, however, interesting to note that the author who composed this Buddhistic stanza was also the author of the various other verses of the record, discussed above, which allude to Hindu mythology. He appears to be a Hinduised Buddhist like the author of the tortoise shell inscriptions in the Dacca Museum, in which the first foot of the Buddhist *maṅgala* stanza (*niśreyasāy=āstu Jino janānām*) occurs together with an adoration to the god Vāsudeva.[2] There is no other trace of Buddhism in the Mainamati records of Laḍahachandra and Govindacandra. It may be noted that the Vaiṣṇava king Laḍahacandra named his son Govindacandra after the god Govinda, i.e., Kṛṣṇa-Viṣṇu.

In the early medieval period, the Buddhists of Eastern India appear to have been attracted more and more by some of the Hindu gods and goddesses, the epico-Purāṇic literature, the religious festivals and the mythological shows and dramatical performances of the Hindus especially because they had

1. The story of the long-lived sage is told in the Purāṇas, e.g., *Padma*, Sṛṣṭi-khaṇḍa, Ch. XXXIII, and *Skanda*, Nāgara-khaṇḍa, Ch. XXI, and Prabhāsa-khaṇḍa, Ch. XLI.

2. See above, pp. 189 ff.

themselves not enough that was as attractive. On the other hand, some of the popular deities and festivals of the Buddhists were gradually appropriated by the Hindus or were popular among the Hinduised Buddhists. These points[1] appear to be emphasised by the evidence of the Mainamati plates of Laḍahacandra and Govindacandra discussed above. Of course in this age, the Buddha was already accepted by the Brāhmaṇical Hindus as an incarnation of Viṣṇu, and there is indirect allusion to this aspect of the problem in the tortoise-shell inscriptions referred to above, but not in the Mainamati records.

1. They have already been referred to above, pp. 185 ff.

APPENDIX II

Gems for the Propitiation of Planets

We know that the Indian students of astronomy, mathematics and some other subjects generally composed their works in verse and that the work on some of the subjects necessitated the repeated mention of numbers, e.g., in the setting and solution of the problems of arithmetical sums. There was, however, usually one numerical word in Sanskrit to indicate a particular number (e.g., *eka* for 'one'), and since the repeated use of the same word in the same sense was a bad style of composition and such a word would often not easily suit the metre of a stanza, the authors required a large number of words to indicate the same number. Therefore a conception gradually developed, according to which non-numerical words which can somehow be associated with particular numbers were used to imply those numbers. Thus all the Sanskrit words meaning 'the hand' came to be used to indicate 'two' because man has only two hands. Likewise, all the words meaning 'arrow' were employed in the sense of 'five' since the Indian god of love is represented in mythology as armed with five arrows of flowers. When there were more than one tradition regarding the number associated with a particular object, only one of them was adopted because precision was the very basis of scientific treatises. Thus, although the Vedas are traditionally three or four and the oceans (*samudra*, etc.) four or seven, the early astronomers, mathematicians and others used the said words in the sense respectively of 'four' and 'seven' only. But uncritical writers of the medieval age are often found to have violated the old convention and introduced a good deal of confusion by using often one word in several numerical senses.[1]

G. H. Ojha points out that the fashion of expressing a number by an ordinary word is old, though it became popular from the sixth and seventh centuries A. D.[2] He has traced the

1. On this subject, see Sircar, *Indian Epigraphy*, pp. 228 ff.
2. *Bhāratīya Prācīn Lipimālā*, p. 121.

use of the word *kṛta* in the sense of 'four' in the *Śatapatha* (XIII.3.2.1) and *Taittirīye* (I.5.11.1) *Brāhmaṇas*, and that of *gāyatrī* = 24 and *jagatī* = 48 in the *Kātyāyana* (Weber's ed., p. 1015) and *Lāṭyāyana* (IX. 4.31) *Śrautasūtras*. Such expressions have been often used in the *Vedāṅga-jyotiṣa* and Piṅgala's *Chandaḥsūtra* and more frequently by Varāhamihira (sixth century), Brahmagupta (seventh century) and other later writers.

How the numerical sense of the word *ratna* has suffered in the hands of medieval writers is illustrated by the fact that it is found to indicate no less than three numbers —five, nine and fourteen.[1] It may be noticed that these conceptions have not been influenced by the early Buddhist ideas about the number of *ratnas*. In Pali literature, the jewels are primarily three, viz., Buddha, Dharma and Saṅgha; but mention is often made of the seven *ratnas* as (1) gold, (2) silver, (3) pearl, (4) ruby (*maṇi*, i.e. *māṇikya*), (5) cat's-eye, (6) diamond and (7) coral, while the seven *ratnas* of the Cakravartin are (1) wheel (i.e. chariot or state), (2) elephant, (3) horse, (4) gem or ruby (*maṇi*), (5) queen, (6) the house-holder subjects and (7) crown-prince.[2]

The *pañca-ratna* are enumerated variously in Brāhmaṇical literature, one of the stanzas running as follows:—

nīlakaṁ vajrakaṁ c=eti padmarāgaś=ca mauktikam |
prabālaṁ c=eti vijñeyaṁ pañca-ratnaṁ manīṣibhiḥ ||

They are here given as the sapphire, diamond, ruby, pearl and coral. Another stanza enumerating the *pañca-ratna* runs as follows:—

suvarṇaṁ rajataṁ muktā rājāvartaṁ prabālakaṁ |
ratna-pañcakam=ākhyātam. . . . . ||

This list mentions the five *ratnas* as gold, silver, pearl, diamond and coral. The third list of the *pañca-ratna* is the following:—

kanakaṁ hīrakaṁ nīlaṁ padmarāgañ=ca mauktikam |
pañca-ratnam=idaṁ proktam=ṛṣibhiḥ pūrva-darśibhiḥ ||

Mention is here of gold, diamond, sapphire, ruby and pearl.

1. See Sircar, *op. cit.*, pp. 231-32; also Apte's *Sans.-Eng. Dict.*, s.v. *pañcan*, *navan* and *catur* for the passages quoted below.

2. See Childers' *Pali-English Dictionary*, s. v. *ratana*. *Pariṇāyaka*, the seventh of the Cakravartin's *ratnas*, may also mean 'an adviser'.

The last of the three verses has been quoted in the *Śabdakalpadruma*, under *pañca-ratnam*, from Hemādri. It also says that, according to the Gauḍa people, the list enumerates *kanaka*, *rajata*, *prabāla*, *mauktika*, and *rājapaṭṭa*, i.e. gold, silver, coral, pearl and diamond. From this well-known conception of the five *ratnas*, the five most admired episodes of the *Mahābhārata* are sometimes called *pañca-ratna*.[1]

Likewise the *nava-ratna* are enumerated as :—

muktā-māṇikya-vaidūrya-gomedā vajra-vidrumau |
padma (puṣpa) rāgo marakataṁ nīlaś = c = eti yathā-kramam ||

Mention is made in this list of—pearl, ruby, cat's eye, jacinth, diamond, coral, topaz, emerald and sapphire.

The *Śabdakalpadruma* quotes the above stanza from the *Tantrasāra* under *nava-ratnam*, but cites some other verses from the *Dīpikā* indicating the following list of jewels required for the propitiation of the nine *grahas* —(1) *vaidūrya* (cat's eye) for the Sun, (2) *nīla* (sapphire) for the Moon, (3) *māṇikya* (ruby) for Mars, (4) *padma (puṣpa) rāga* (topaz) for Mercury, (5) *muktā* (pearl) for Jupiter, (6) *vajra* (diamond) for Venus, (7) *nīla* (sapphire) for Saturn, (8) jacinth (*gomeda*) for Rāhu, and (9) *marakata* (emerald) for Ketu. It seems that the two lists are the same and that *nīla* has been twice mentioned in the second list through mistake in place of *vidruma* or *prabāla* meaning coral.[2]

In the same way, the *Caturdaśa-ratna* are enumerated in the following stanza :—

1. Apte, *op. cit.*, s. v. *paṁcan*; see also Monier-William's *Sans.-Eng. Dict.*, s.v. *pañca*. According to Bandyopadhyay's *Vaṅgīya Śabdakoṣa*, s. v., *pañca-ratna* also means a group of five didactic stanzas.

2. In the *Mṛcchakaṭika*, Act IV, there is a Prakrit passage enumerating the following jewels—*vaidūrya* (cat's eye), *mauktika* (pearl), *prabāla* (coral), *puṣparāga* (topaz), *indranīla* (*nīla*, sapphire), *padm rāga* (ruby), *marakata* (emerald) and what is called *kakketaraa* (*karketaraka*) or *kakkeraa* (*karkeraka*). The last name is found in Sanskrit lexicons as *karketana* for which see also the *Garuḍa Purāṇa*, Part I, Chapter 75. Monier-Williams recognises the forms *karkeṇata* (from Caraka) and *karketila* (from the lexicons) and explains it as a kind of quartz. In the *Mṛcchakaṭika*, the word may mean *sphaṭika* or crystal, though the *Garuḍa Purāṇa* has a separate chapter on *sphaṭika* (chap. 79). The said *Purāṇa* (Part I, Chapters 69-80) describes (1) *vajra*, (2) *muktā*, (3) *padmarāga*, (4) *marakata*, (5) *indranīla*, (6) *vaidūrya*, (7) *puṣparāga*, (8) *karketana*, (9) *bhīṣma*, (10) *pulaka*, (11) *rudhira*, (12) *sphaṭika*, and (13) *vidruma*. These are also mentioned in the list in Chap. 68, verses 9-10.

Lakṣmīḥ kaustubha-pārijātaka-surā Dhanvantariś=Candramā
gāvaḥ kāmadughāḥ sureśvara-gajo Rambh-ādi-dev-āṅganāḥ |
aśvaḥ sapta-mukho viṣaṁ Hari-dhanuḥ śaṅkho='mṛtaṁ c= āmbudhe
ratnān=iha ... pratidinaṁ kuryuḥ sadā maṅgalam ||

The fourteen *ratnas* that came out of the ocean after it had been churned are—the goddess Lakṣmī, the jewel *kaustubha*, the *pārijāta* plant, wine, Dhanvantari, the Moon, the wish-fulfilling cow, Indra's elephant (Airāvata), the celestial damsels including Rambhā, the 'seven-faced' horse (Uccaiḥśravas),[1] poison which Śiva drank, Hari's bow (rainbow), the conch-shell, and nectar.

The above conception of the nine gems was utilised by *Gaṇaka* Kālidāsa who wrote the astronomical work *Jyotirvidābharaṇa* in the thirteenth or sixteenth century[2] in enumerating, for the first time, the gems of courtiers at the court of king Vikramāditya whom tradition represents as the founder of the Vikrama era of 58 B.C. The stanza in the *Jyotirvidābharaṇa* runs as follows :—

Dhanvantariḥ Kṣapaṇak-Āmarasiṁha-Śaṅku-
Vetālabhaṭṭa-Ghaṭakarpara-Kālidāsāḥ |
khyāto Varāhamihiro nṛpateḥ sabhāyāṁ
ratnāni vai Vararucir=nava Vikramasya ||[3]

The list includes the following nine names—Dhanvantari, Kṣapaṇaka, Amarasiṁha, Śaṅku, Vetālabhaṭṭa, Ghaṭakarpara, Kālidāsa, Varāhmihira and Vararuci. Of these nine, Varāhamihira is known to have flourished in the sixth century A.D. and not in the middle of the first century B.C. whence the so-called Vikrama era started. According to Pṛthusvāmin, a commentator on Brahmagupta's works, Varāhamihira died in Śaka 509=587 A.D. Varāhamihira's own *Pañcasidhāntikā*, however, quotes the year of the Śaka-kāla counted by *sapt-āśvi-veda*, i.e. 7, 2 and 4 or Śaka 427 (505 A.D.) according to the principle *aṅkānāṁ vāmato gatiḥ*.[4] Thus the idea of

1. *Sapta-mukha* is not a usual epithet of the Uccaiḥśravas.
2. Keith, *A History of Sanskrit Literature*, p. 534; Winternitz, *A History of Indian Literature*, Vol. III, Part II, p. 659; Sircar, *Ancient Malwa and the Virkamāditya Tradition*, pp. 120 ff.
3. Apte, *op. cit.*, s.v. *navan*.
4. See Sircar, *Ancient Malwa and the Vikramāditya Tradition*, p. 126, note 42.

the *nava-ratna* at Vikramāditya's court is a late concoction. This view is supported by other evidences discussed in our *Ancient Malwa and the Vikramāditya Tradition*, pp. 106 ff. (cf. pp. 120 ff.) to which we may now add the fact that the conception of the *nava-ratna* or nine precious objects from which the idea of Vikrama's nine courtiers was borrowed is itself a late one. Its lateness is indicated by the fact that the word *ratna* is not found in the sense of 'nine' in any early work.

It will also be seen from the above discussion that the number of different lists is the largest in the case of the *pañca-ratna*, the conception of which was therefore more popular than that of the *nava-ratna* and *caturdaśa-ratna*. Probably the idea of the *nava-ratna* developed out of the requirement of nine gems for the propitiation of the nine planets. This seems also to suggest that the *pañca-ratna* conception is older than *nava-ratna* and *caturdaśa-ratna*, so that the idea of the nine learned men at Vikramāditya's court was formulated not much earlier than the medieval age.

That the idea of the propitiation of the unfavourable planets by wearing gems passed through several stages of development can be easily proved. Early works prescribing the worship and appeasement of the planets do not speak of the gems at all, while the wearing of jewels is prescribed for kings for prosperity, etc., even in some early medieval texts without any reference to the planets. On the other hand, works assignable to the age before the late medieval period prescribe the appeasement of the various planets by wearing certain objects including mostly metals (both cheap and costly) and rarely a gem and some other object. In later works, nine gems are prescribed for the propitiation of nine planets, while very late works offer separate lists of gems, metals and other objects for the appeasement of each one of the planets.

Thus the *Yājñavalkyasmṛti*[1] (c. 4th century A.D.), which

1. I. 295-308 (or 309). The *Agni Purāṇa* (Ch. 164) copies Yājñavalkya's stanzas, while the *Bṛhadyogayātrā* (Ch. 18, verses 1-24) of Varāhamihira (6th century; cf. also the *Yogayātrā*, Ch. 6) adds a few details here and there. Yājñavalkya's short and simple *graha-yajña* has become an elaborate affair in later works like the *Bhaviṣyottara Purāṇa* (141. 6-85). See Kane, *Hist.*, *Dharm.* Vol. V, pp. 749 ff. For the development of the conception of the planets, see Sircar, *Cosmography and Geography in Early Indian Literature*, p. 13.

is one of the earliest works prescribing *graha-pūjā* or *graha-yajña*, does not speak of any gem or any other object which one could wear for appeasing the planets. It is interesting to note that the *Garuḍa Purāṇa*, which is a medieval work in its present form,[1] offers valuable evidence on the subject. In one place, it enumerates thirteen varieties of jewels and prescribes the wearing of all of them for prosperity, etc., though no mention is made of the planets in this connection. Elsewhere the same Purāṇa prescribes the following objects (which cannot all be called gems) for the said purpose (1) Sun—copper, (2) Moon—bell-metal, (3) Mars—crystal, (4) Mercury—red-sandal, (5) Jupiter—gold, (6) Venus—silver, (7) Saturn—iron, (8) Rāhu—lead, and (9) Ketu—bell-metal.[2] A simliar list is found in the medieval *Āśvalāyana Gṛhyasūtra Pariśiṣṭa*; e.g., (1) Sun—copper, (2) Moon—crystal, (3) Mars—red-sandal, (4) Mercury—gold, (5) Jupiter—gold, (6) Venus—silver, (7) Saturn—iron, (8 Rāhu—lead, and (9) Ketu—bronze.[3] A later work cited by U. N. Mukhopadhyay in his *Jyotiṣaratnākara*,[4] gives the list as follows : (1) Sun—copper, (2) Moon—conch-shell, (3) Mars—coral (*vidruma*), (4) Mercury—gold, (5) Jupiter—silver, (6) Venus—..., (7) Saturn—lead (*trapu*), (8) Rāhu—diamond (*rājapaṭṭa*) and (9) Ketu—iron. It has to be noticed that the lists do not tally with one another and that they contain the names not only of jewels, but also of metals and other objects. But Mukhopadhyay also quotes the *Dīpikā* stanzas referred to above which prescribe nine real gems for the nine planets.[5] In his *Bhārate Jyotiṣ-*

1. See Sircar, *Stud. Geog. Anc. Med. Ind.*, 2nd ed., p. 29; above, p. 250, note 2.

2. Vaṅgavāsī ed., Part I, Chap. 101, verses 2-3. Cf.
tāmra-kāṁsya-sphāṭikāc=ca raktacandana-svarṇakāt /
rajatād=ayasaḥ sīsāt kāṁsyād=dṛṣṭiḥ praśāmya ti //

3. See T. P. Bhattacharya, *The Canons of Indian Art*, 1963, pp. 489-90. For the late date of such lists found even in the *Āśvalāyana Gṛhyasūtra* (not to speak of its *Pariśiṣṭa*), see Winternitz, *A History of Indian Literature*, Vol. I, 1927, p. 471, note 2. See also above, p. 248, note 3.

4. Vasumatī Sāhitya Mandir, Calcutta, p. 391.

5. *Ibid.*, p. 390 :
vaidūryaṁ dhārayet Sūrye nīlañ=ca Mṛgalāñchane /
Āvaneye='pi māṇikyaṁ padmarāgaṁ Śaśāṅkaje //
Gurau muktāṁ Bhṛgau vajram=indranīlaṁ Śanaiścare /
Rāhau gomedakaṁ dhāryaṁ Ketau marakataṁ tathā //

carcā O Koṣṭhi-vicārer Sūtrāvalī,[1] N.N. Bagal offers separate lists of (a) objects pleasing to the planets, (b) gems for wearing with a view to pleasing them and (c) to removing their disfavour and (d) metals to be worn for pleasing them, on the authority of several late works, as follows: (1) Sun —(a) copper, (b) ruby (*māṇikya*), (c) cat's-eye (*vaidūrya*) and (d) gold, copper; (2) Moon—(a) silver, conch-shell, (b) pearl (*muktā*), (c) sapphire (*nīlā*) and (d) silver, conch-shell; (3) Mars —(a) gold, copper, vermillion, red arsenic (*manaḥśilā*), red chalk (*gairika*) ; (b) coral, (c) ruby (*māṇikya*) and (d) copper, iron; (4) Mercury—(a) mercury, gold, bell-metal, (b) emerald (*marakata*), (c) topaz (*puṣparāga*) and (d) mercury; (5) Jupiter—(a) gold, zinc (*dastā*), myrobalan, (b) topaz (*puṣparāga*), (c) pearl (*muktā*) and (d) zinc; (6) Venus—(a) silver, (b) diamond, (c) diamond and (d) lead, silver; (7) Saturn—(a) lead, iron, (b) sapphire (*nīlā*), (c) sapphire (*nīlā*) and (d) lead; (8) Rāhu—(a) *durvā* grass, sandal, (b) jacinth (*gomeda*), (c) jacinth and (d) iron; and (9) Ketu—(a) *kuśa* grass, camphor (*karpūra*), (b) cat's-eye (*vaidūrya*) , (c) emerald (*marakata*) and (d) iron, diamond. Such lists are not found in early works.

Indeed the divergence among the lists proves the worthless character of astrological prescriptions. Another point to be remembered in this connection is that, even if it is believed that planets may have some influence on the destiny of man, Rāhu and Ketu are not planets at all. They are merely the ascending and descending nodes of the moon.

1. Indian Associated Publishing Co., Calcutta, B.S. 1372, pp. 254-55.

APPENDIX III

Narasimha Cult

The theory of the *Avatāra* (Descent or Incarnation) of a god, as we have seen, is based essentially on his identification with men and animals endowed, in old tales, with mysterious powers of assistance and molestation, an animal of the type being the modern tiger-god Dakṣiṇarāya of the Sundarbans in Lower Bengal. Many such divinities were identified with the god Viṣṇu at a later date.[1]

The worship of the *Avatāras* of Viṣṇu is an important feature of Bhāgavatism in the Gupta age, the germ of the *Avatāra* conception having been traced in the later Vedic literature. While, however, the conception of the Vāmana (Dwarf) form, associated with Viṣṇu, and of the Varāha (Boar), Matsya (Fish) and Kūrma (Tortoise) forms, not yet connected with the said god, have been traced in the *Śatapatha* and other Brāhmaṇas, it is only in the late *Taittirīya Āraṇyaka* that we have an allusion to the Narasiṁha (Man-lion) incarnation of Viṣṇu together with the Varāha. Of these two, Varāha has been the most popular *Avatāra* of Viṣṇu in all parts of India since the early centuries of the Christian era. But the *Mahābhārata* also points to the growing popularity of the Narasiṁha (Man-lion) form of the god[2] from about the same age.

The Nārāyaṇīya section of the *Mahābhārata* includes Narasiṁha in several lists of the *Avatāras* of Viṣṇu e.g., (1) 4 *Avatāras*—Boar, Dwarf, Man-lion and Man (Vāsudeva-Kṛṣṇa); (2) 6 *Avatāras*—the said 4 together with Rāma-Bhārgava and Rāma-Dāśarathi; and (3) 10 *Avatāras*—the above 6 together with Haṁsa, Kūrma, Matsya and Kalki or Kalkin. It is well known that the number 10 for the *Avatāras* of Viṣṇu was gradually stereotyped in the Purāṇas, the popular list of the 10 *Avatāras* consisting of (1) Matsya, (2) Kūrma, (3) Varāha, (4) Narasiṁha, (5) Vāmana, (6) Rāma-Bhargava, (7) Rāma-Dāśarathi, (8) Rāma-Saṁkarṣaṇa,

1. Cf. above, p. 42; also *The Classical Age*, ed. Majumdar, p. 415.
2. Above, pp. 42-43.

(9) Buddha and (10) Kalkin.[1] We have seen that the Purāṇic stanza giving these 10 names is quoted in a South Indian inscription of the 8th century A.D.,[2] while the Daśāvatāra panel in the Sirpur Lakṣmaṇa temple of the same age also represents the said 10 forms of the god Viṣṇu.[3]

The evidence indicated above would suggest that the Man-lion incarnation of Viṣṇu became popular in the early centuries of the Christian era. It is thus rather curious that writers on the history of Vaiṣṇavism have succeeded in tracing the mention of the Narasiṁha *Avatāra* in no inscription earlier than the Alina copper-plate record of the Maitraka dynasty of Valabhī in Kathiawar (Gujarat State), which was issued in the year 766 A.D.[4] It is, however, not generally noticed that the popularity of the cult of Narasiṁha is clearly indicated by a large number of personal names occurring in much earlier epigraphic records.

Just as we have in early inscriptions names like Varāhadāsa ('slave of the Boar form of Viṣṇu'),[5] or Varāhadinna=Varāhadatta ('given by the Boar', or 'dedicated to the Boar') and Matsyagupta ('protected by the fish incarnation of Viṣṇu'),[6] the names Sīhadatta=Siṁhadatta ('dedicated to the Lion or Man-Lion form of Viṣṇu') and Sīharakhita=Siṁharakṣita ('protected by the Siṁha or Narasiṁha incarnation') in the Prakrit inscriptions of the first and second centuries A. D. from Sanchi, Mathura and other places.[7] A few

1. *Ibid.*, pp. 43-44. It has been shown that the Purāṇic lists of the 10 *Avatāras* do not always contain the same names; e.g. the *Matsya Purāṇa* speaks of 3 divine *Avatāras* (viz. Nārāyaṇa, Narasiṁha and Vāmana) and 7 human *Avatāras* (viz. Dattātreya, Māndhātṛ, Rāma-Jāmadagnya-Bhārgava, Rāma-Dāśarathi, Vedavyāsa, the Buddha and Kalkin), while the *Harivaṁśa* omits Matsya, Kūrma, one Rāma and the Buddha, but includes in their places Padma, Datta (Dattātreya), Keśava and Vyāsa.

2. Cf. above, pp. 42, 187, 194; *MASI*, No. 26, p. 5.

3. See *MASI*, No. 18, pp. 5-6.

4. *CII*, Vol. III, p. 188 and note 1; cf. above, p. 46; *The Classical Age*, p. 417.

5. *CII*, Vol. III, pp. 124, 129, 134, 139, 156.

6. *Ep. Ind.*, Vol. XXVIII, p. xi.

7. Lüders' List of Inscriptions, Nos. 48, 186, 228, 1090, etc.

of these records may probably be assigned even to earlier dates.

Names like Siṁhavarman ('one whose protector is the Lion or Man-lion'), Siṁhaviṣṇu ('Viṣṇu in the form of the Lion or Man-lion') and Narasiṁhavarman ('one whose protector is the Man-lion') were popular in the Pallava dynasty of South India. The earliest such name in the family of the Pallava kings is that of Sīhavamma = Siṁhavarman of the Manchikallu (Guntur District, Andhra Pradesh) inscription assigned to the fourth century A.D.[1] The founder of the greatness of the Imperial Pallava dynasty was Siṁhaviṣṇu, son of Siṁhavarman, both of whom flourished about the last quarter of the sixth century. Narasiṁhavarman I, also called Narasiṁhaviṣṇu, was the greatest of the Pallava kings, who flourished in c. 630-68 A.D., while his great-grandson, Narasiṁhavarman II (c. 700-25 A.D.), was famous for his building activities. The Narasiṁha form of Viṣṇu thus seems to have been a favourite deity with the Pallava dynasty, many of its rulers being Vaiṣṇavas in faith.[2]

Sewell's *Historical Inscriptions of Southern India*[3] enumerates no less than 40 kings of the early and medieval periods, who bore the name Narasiṁha. Most of these rulers flourished in South India, one distinguished king from the North in the said list being Narasiṁhagupta Bālāditya of the Vaiṣṇavite Gupta dynasty of Magadha, who reigned in the latter half of the fifth or the first quarter of the sixth century A.D. Epigraphic evidence thus points to the popularity of the Narasiṁha cult in early times, especially in South India.

Among the medieval kings of other parts of the country, who were devoted to the Man-lion form of Viṣṇu, king Lakṣmaṇasena of Eastern India is described in the epigraphic records of the Sena dynasty generally as *Paramavaiṣṇava* and particularly as *Paramanārasiṁha*.[4] He therefore appears to have been especially devoted to the Narasiṁha *Avatāra*. It

1. *Ep. Ind.*, Vol. XXXII, p. 86.
2. Cf. *The Classical Age*, pp. 255 ff., 275 ff.
3. See *op. cit.*, pp. 233-34.
4. Cf. N. G. Majumdar, *Ins. Beng.*, Vol. III, pp. 85, 101 (for *Paramavaiṣṇava*), and pp. 95 , 111 (for *Paramanārasiṁha*).

is of course difficult to say whether this has anything to do with the South Indian origin of the Sena dynasty.

Early images of Narasiṁha together with the Boar and Dwarf forms of Viṣṇu are found in the rock-cut temples at Udayagiri, Bādāmi and Māmallapuram belonging respectively to the Gupta, Early Cālukya and Pallava periods.[1]

1. *The Classical Age*, pp. 425-26; T.A. Gopinatha Rao, *Elements of Hindu Iconography*, Vol. I, pp. 128 ff., Plates XXXVI ff. The fact that the *Avatāra* is often mentioned in early records as *Siṁha* instead of *Narasiṁha* may suggest that the deity was once conceived by some as having the form of a lion (not a combined form of man and lion).

INDEX

ADDENDA ET CORRIGENDA

Page 2, line 28.	—*Read*—fantastic
„ 4, line 32.	—*Read*—Yajñabhāvana
„ 8, line 25.	—Read—*vayunāni*
„ 17, line 7.	—*Add note*—See *Bṛhatsaṁhitā*, 58.32 ; cf. *Ep. Ind.*, Vol. X, p. 80. Early Western Gaṅga inscriptions describe Padmanābha (Viṣṇu) as *gata-ghana-gagan-ābha*, i.e. having the colour of the clear (free from clouds) sky. See *Sel. Ins.*, 1965, p. 480. For Viṣṇu's complexion like the colour of the thunder clouds, see below, p. 135, note 3.
„ 20, line 16.	—*Read*—Vidisha District
„ 41, note 5.	—*Add*—The Kūrma-avatāra reminds us of the tortoise Akūpāra of boundless dimension, in whom is found the cosmic tortoise that finds the earth in the ocean (Keith, *Rel. Phil. V. Up.*, p. 242).
„ 45, note 5, line 2.	—*Read*—Rāmagiri
„ 82, line 4.	—*Add note*—For a bronze image of Balabhadra bearing an inscription of Devapāla's reign (c. 810-50 A.D.), see *Mem. ASI*, No. 66, pp. 88-89.
„ 124, line 18.	—Read—*salilamaye*
„ 161, line 8.	—*Read*— Vikramaśilā (Vikramaśīla)
„ 168, note 3.	—*Add*—The Kadamba king Ravivarman (c. 490-538 A.D.) was also merely a *Mahārāja*; but the Davangere plates (*Ep. Ind.*, Vol. XXXIII, pp. 90ff.) refer to his *sāmrājya* and to his claim of lordship over the southern *cakravarti-kṣetra*, i.e. the whole of South India as far as the Narmadā in the north.

Page 175, line 20. —*Add*—4a. King Dāmamitra (1st century A. D.) probably belonging to Devīmitra's line, is known to have performed an Aśvamedha, from his Lucknow Museum brick inscription (*Ep. Ind.*, Vol. XXXIII, pp. 99-100).